Interpretive Social Science

Interpretive Social Science

A READER

Edited by Paul Rabinow and William M. Sullivan

University of California Press

BERKELEY · LOS ANGELES · LONDON

University of California Press
Berkeley and Los Angeles, California
University of California Press, Ltd.
London, England
Copyright © 1979 by
The Regents of the University of California
ISBN 0-520-03834-7
Library of Congress Catalog Card Number: 77-085743
Printed in the United States of America

3 4 5 6 7 8 9

TO ROBERT N. BELLAH

For the waking there is one world,
and it is common; but sleepers turn aside each one
into a world of his own.
HERACLITUS

Contents

Preface

This book grew out of many intense discussions during the course of a National Endowment for the Humanities Seminar directed by Robert N. Bellah on "Tradition and Interpretation: The Sociology of Culture" held at the University of California at Berkeley during the academic year 1976/77. The nature of the materials collected in this volume, in our opinion, would make an index of little use. Consequently, we have not included one.

Our deepest debt, and the one most happily borne, is to Robert Bellah. His Socratic enthusiasm showed us that friendship is the indispensable soil from which both wisdom and virtue spring.

Our thinking has been honed and deepened through many hours of philosophical jousting with Hubert Dreyfus, whose demon is always the truth.

To our companions in Berkeley's *agora,* Fred Ballitzer, Shigeo Kanda, Jane Rubin, Steve White, Paul Wiebe, Gwen Wright, Aram Yengoyan, we want to express our thanks for sharing their insights and friendship.

We wish to thank the secretaries at the Center for Japanese and Korean Studies, Julie Cleland, Vicky May, and Kristen Spexarth, for their selfless help and encouragement.

Grant Barnes, our editor, deserves our special acknowledgment for his unswerving support.

P.R.   W.S.

The Interpretive Turn: Emergence of an Approach

PAUL RABINOW AND WILLIAM M. SULLIVAN

As long as there has been a social science, the expectation has been that it would turn from its humanistic infancy to the maturity of hard science, thereby leaving behind its dependence on value, judgment, and individual insight. The dream of modern Western man to be freed from his passions, his unconscious, his history, and his traditions through the liberating use of reason has been the deepest theme of contemporary social science thought. Perhaps the deepest theme of the twentieth century, however, has been the shattering of the triumphalist view of history bequeathed to us by the nineteenth. What Comte saw as the inevitable achievement of man, positive reason, Weber saw as an iron cage.

The aim of this anthology is to present to a wide audience — historians, sociologists, anthropologists, psychologists, historians of religion, scientists, and philosophers — a carefully selected group of papers exemplary of the interpretive or hermeneutic approach to the study of human society.

These readings address major theoretical issues by situating the approach critically against positivist, structuralist, and neo-Marxist positions. They also provide rich and developed examples of the interpretation of symbols, cultures, and historical moments. Although our aim is not to present a school or a new dogma, we do feel that there are important unities of theme and approach present here. In this introduction the editors — an anthropologist and a philosopher — will

1

situate in a historical and theoretical context the emergence, through the readings, of an interpretive social science.

DECONSTRUCTION

Interpreting the Crisis in the Social Sciences

Many contemporary searchers in the social sciences continue to see themselves, as did their predecessors, as the heralds of the new age of an at last established science. They remain, like their predecessors, disappointed.

The strength of natural science, according to Thomas Kuhn, has lain in its ability to go beyond endless methodological discussions by developing general shared paradigms which define problems and procedures. Social scientists have seized upon Kuhn's thesis in part as a way of explaining the embarrassing failure of any of the social sciences, including linguistics and economics, to develop either the agreement on method or the generally acknowledged classic examples of explanation characteristic of the natural sciences. While not denying the persistence and theoretical fruitfulness of certain explanatory schemes in the social sciences, social investigators have never reached the extraordinary degree of basic agreement that characterizes modern natural science.[1] For Kuhn, such agreements among practicing investigators constitutes the stage of "paradigmatic" science, a time of secure development, of extending the explanatory capacity of an agreed-upon paradigm. Paradigms are the result of a chaotic stage that Kuhn calls "pre-paradigmatic," in which the insights and mode of discourse later to become universally accepted must fight it out with competing pre-paradigm explanations. Most fields, throughout their history, find themselves in this situation.[2]

This much of Kuhn's argument might be construed to buttress the defenses of social sciences waiting to "take off" into a paradigm stage of science. Behaviorism, structural-functionalism, various schools of materialism, Keynesianism, structuralism, and others have all put themselves forward at some time as paradigm candidates. If none has yet succeeded in silencing its opponents with Newtonian authority,

1. S. N. Eisenstadt has discussed the importance of these recurrent types of understanding in a recent work with M. Curelaru: *The Form of Sociology: Paradigms and Crisis* (New York: Wiley & Sons, 1976).

2. Thomas S. Kuhn, *The Structure of Scientific Revolution,* 2nd ed. (Chicago: University of Chicago Press, 1970). See esp. "Postscript – 1969."

perhaps a few more studies, or theories, or methodological battles and our paradigms will emerge, at last triumphant. However, even if we admit this as a possibility — and we shall show shortly that there are compelling reasons for *not* admitting it — Kuhn's account of scientific development concludes on a disquieting note. He shows that in the history of science even after the breakthrough into the paradigm stage occurs, the stability achieved is only a relative one. The great paradigms of natural science have all, after flourishing, finally been replaced by others. The epochal case is the revolution in twentieth-century physics in which relativity theory and quantum mechanics undermined and succeeded the Newtonian system. From that point on, in physics the nineteenth century's conception of logical, cumulative progress through a purely objective science of observation and deductive explanation has been progressively undermined.

Yet the issue for the human sciences is not simply that all scientific facts depend on a context of theory, nor that no logic of inquiry can be formulated to match the rigor of the procedures of scientific verification. The Kantian critical philosophy already emphasized the relations between the objects of observation and the subject of knowledge. For Kant and his followers the universal and objective validity of proven hypotheses is guaranteed precisely because the subject constituting the fields of objects is a universal and purely formal one. The explanatory power of science is the consequence of its basis in a logical, epistemic subject whose activities can be generalized and understood as context-free operations. However, for comprehending the human world Kant acknowledged the necessity of a "practical anthropology" focusing on a subject not reducible to the pure theoretical subject of the *Critique of Pure Reason*. This subject knows himself through reflection upon his own actions in the world as a subject not simply of experience but of intentional action as well. While the interpretive approach is not in any strict sense Kantian, it shares the postulate that practical understanding in context cannot be reduced to a system of categories defined only in terms of their relations to each other.

To put forward an approach to the human sciences as a paradigm candidate requires that one accept the analogy to natural science according to which human actions can be fixed in their meaning by being subsumed under the law like operations of the epistemic subject. Gregory Bateson's recent attempt to apply models from systems theory to the problems of the relations of mind to society, and Jean

Piaget's development of the structuralist project, represent significant advances over what Paiget terms the atomistic empiricism of causal explanation in social science. For both the key focus is upon holism, for which Bateson uses the metaphor of ecology.

Holistic explanation in these new forms seeks to organize a wide variety of human phenomena that cannot be comprehended through models based on linear relations among elements. The emphasis on mutually determining relationships is the powerful central insight of cybernetic and structuralist thinking. However, it is crucial that these relations are conceived as reducible to specific operations that can be defined without reference to the particular context of human action. Although this position is an advance in sophistication, it remains an effort to integrate the sciences of man within a natural scientific paradigm. Action in the historical, cultural context is again reduced to the operations of a purely epistemic subject. The Kantian criticism of this effort remains unsurpassed or at least unrefuted in that the problem of the concrete, practical subject remains unresolved.[3]

Now the time seems ripe, even overdue, to announce that there is not going to be an age of paradigm in the social sciences. We contend that the failure to achieve paradigm takeoff is not merely the result of methodological immaturity, but reflects something fundamental about the human world. If we are correct, the crisis of social science concerns the nature of social investigation itself. The conception of the human sciences as somehow necessarily destined to follow the path of the modern investigation of nature is at the root of this crisis. Preoccupation with that ruling expectation is chronic in social science; that *idée fixe* has often driven investigators away from a serious concern with the human world into the sterility of purely formal argument and debate. As in development theory, one can only wait so long for the takeoff. The cargo-cult view of the "about to arrive science" just won't do.

The interpretive turn refocuses attention on the concrete varieties of cultural meaning, in their particularity and complex texture, but without falling into the traps of historicism or cultural relativism in their classical forms. For the human sciences both the object of investigation — the web of language, symbol, and institutions that constitutes signification — and the tools by which investigation is car-

3. Gregory Bateson, *Steps to an Ecology of Mind* (San Francisco: Chandler Pub., 1972.) Jean Piaget, *Structuralism* (New York: Harper and Row, 1970).

ried out share inescapably the same pervasive context that is the human world. All this is by no means to exalt "subjective" awareness over a presumed detached scientific objectivity, in the manner of nineteenth-century Romanticism. Quite the contrary, the interpretive approach denies and overcomes the almost de rigueur opposition of subjectivity and objectivity. The current emergence of interpretive approaches in philosophy and the social sciences is moving in a very different direction. The interpretive approach emphatically refutes the claim that one can somehow reduce the complex world of signification to the products of a self-consciousness in the traditional philosophical sense. Rather, interpretation begins from the postulate that the web of meaning constitutes human existence to such an extent that it cannot ever be meaningfully reduced to constitutively prior speech acts, dyadic relations, or any predefined elements.[4] Intentionality and empathy are rather seen as dependent on the prior existence of the shared world of meaning within which the subjects of human discourse constitute themselves.[5] It is in this literal sense that interpretive social science can be called a return to the objective world, seeing that world as in the first instance the circle of meaning within which we find ourselves and which we can never fully surpass.

Charles Taylor offers us a "strong reading" of the interpretive position in his article "Interpretation and the Sciences of Man" reprinted in this volume. The baseline realities for both the observer and the observed in the human sciences are practices, socially constituted

4. Cultural meaning as intersubjective and irreducibly fundamental to understanding is the base-point of the whole interpretive project. This idea is set out powerfully by philosophers such as Paul Ricoeur and Hans-Georg Gadamer. See Hans-Georg Gadamer, "On the Scope and Function of Hermeneutical Reflection" in *Philosophical Hermeneutics* (Berkeley and Los Angeles: University of California Press, 1976), pp. 18–43. There Gadamer criticizes what he sees as Jürgen Habermas's grounding of meaning in a pure logic of language. Paul Ricoeur contrasts these positions lucidly in "Ethics and Culture: Habermas and Gadamer in Dialogue," *Philosophy Today* 17, no. 3 (Summer 1972): 153–165.

5. Intentionality, resident in a knowing subject, has been thought of by the Phenomenological tradition stemming from Edmund Husserl as the defining human characteristic. Empathy, as intuitive access to the mind of another, is a term often associated with the interpretive tradition, especially with the early thinkers Wilhelm Dilthey and Max Weber. In fact, neither Weber nor the later Dilthey held the kind of "mystical" conception of cultural understanding often associated with the term "empathy." For a clarification of Weber's usage of "understanding" (*Verstehen*), see Max Weber, *Economy and Society: An Outline of Interpretive Sociology*, Guenther Roth and Claus Wittrik, eds. (New York: Bedminster Press, 1968), vol. 1. Relatively little of Dilthey's work is currently available in translation. Cf. esp. Wilhelm Dilthey, "The Development of Hermeneutics," in H. P. Rickman, ed., *W. Dilthey: Selected Writings* (Cambridge: Cambridge University Press, 1976), pp. 247–263.

actions "and these cannot be identified in abstraction from the languages we use to describe them."[6] These baseline practices are intersubjective and form the most general level of shared meaning. They are the basis of community, argument, and discourse. They are not subjective opinions. These meanings or norms "are not just in the minds of the actors but are out there in the practices themselves, practices which cannot be conceived as a set of individual actions, but which are essentially modes of social relations, of mutual action."[7] These meanings are intersubjective; they are not reducible to individual subjective psychological states, beliefs, or propositions. They are neither subjective nor objective but what lies behind both.

A view of meaning flows from this position, and Taylor spells it out. Meaning is for a subject, in a situation; it is about something; and it exists as a part of a field; there are no simple elements of meaning. This view, in turn, rests on a set of assumptions about the situation of man. For Taylor, human life is characterized by being in an open system. It cannot be shielded from external interference and studied in a vacuum or a scientifically controlled environment. From this it follows that the exactitude that is open to the human sciences is quite different from that available to the natural sciences. Our capacity to understand is rooted in our own self-definitions, hence in what we are. What we are is a self-interpreting and self-defining animal. We are always in a cultural world, amidst a "web of signification we ourselves have spun." There is no outside, detached standpoint from which to gather and present brute data. When we try to understand the cultural world, we are dealing with interpretations and interpretations of interpretations.

Culture, the shared meanings, practices, and symbols that constitute the human world, does not present itself neutrally or with one voice. It is always multivocal and overdetermined, and both the observer and the observed are always enmeshed in it; that is our situation. There is no privileged position, no absolute perspective, no final recounting.[8]

If we accept these points we soon realize that when we begin to conduct an inquiry we are caught in a circle. "Ultimately a good

6. See Chapter 1, p. 45.　　　　7. p. 48.
8. See "Conclusion" to Paul Rabinow, *Reflections on Fieldwork in Morocco*. (Berkeley and Los Angeles: University of California Press, 1977).

explanation is one which makes sense of the behavior. But to agree on what makes sense necessitates consensus; what makes sense is a function of one's readings; and these in turn are based on the kind of sense one understands."[9] The only way out of this circle would be (1) through simple, brute data which we could hold on to, or (2) through a neutral language to describe the data, or both. For Taylor neither of these exists, precisely because of the primacy of context just described.[10]

Taylor draws the most radical conclusions from these arguments, conclusions not fully shared by all the other practitioners of the art. He says there is "no verification procedure we can fall back on. We can only continue to offer interpretations."[11] Therefore, insight and judgment are an essential part of any inquiry. If this is the case, then some form of the claim " 'if you don't understand, then your intuitions are at fault, are blind or inadequate,' will be justified; some differences will be nonarbitrable by further evidence, but each side can only make an appeal to deeper insight than the other."[12] A superior position would be one that could encompass its opponent and make its claims stick.[13]

Most of the other partisans of the interpretive approach are somewhat more hesitant about this last point. Geertz and Bellah, for instance, although not explicitly confronting these issues, clearly hold to a modified notion of social science in which there is advance, contribution, and refutation of one sort or another which a community of researchers could agree on, if they agreed on starting points. Ricoeur, more explicitly, directs his attention to this important point. He offers us a sketch of what he calls a "dialectic of guessing and validation." He holds out a hope for a new form of confirmation and refutation which

9. Ibid., p. 14.

10. The primacy of context is another statement of the irreducibility of cultural meaning discussed above. (See note 5 above.) This theme has extremely important implications for the understanding of the validity and use of formal models in the natural sciences, especially the field of cybernetics. Hubert Dreyfus has lucidly explored this area in *What Computers Can't Do: A Critique of Artificial Intelligence* (New York: Harper and Row, 1972).

11. See chapter 1, p. 66.   12. Ibid.

13. Such an approach to the question of how interpretations are validated and judged is quite close to the rhetorical tradition in philosophy, one which has often stood opposed to claims for strictly deductive "demonstrations" in practical matters. Philosopher Richard McKeon has ably developed the considerable resources of that tradition. See Gerard A. Hauser and Donald P. Cushman, "McKeon's Philosophy of Communication: The Architectonic and Interdisciplinary Arts," *Philosophy and Rhetoric* 6, no. 4: 211–234.

would not be either based on a propositional model or one of falsifiability. For Ricoeur a method of mediating and judging between conflicting interpretations would look rather more like a transformed
version of textual criticism in the humanities. But even he acknowledges that at present we have only the barest beginning of such a
dialectic.

A formulation farther from the current positivist orthodoxy would
be hard to find. We propose a return to this human world in all its lack
of clarity, its alienation, and its depth, as an alternative to the continuing search for a formal deductive paradigm in the social sciences. The
common theme joining both Romanticist subjectivism and Positivist
objectivism is the search for a reality before and behind the cultural
world to which it can be reduced. For Romanticism this reality is the
self or subject as present to itself as a self-evident source of meaning,
while positivists have stressed the epistemological and ontological
priority of models of deductive inference (and sometimes causal explanations) over the often tacit meanings guiding discourse. The ideal
remains to find a truth *behind* these elusive lived-in symbols, practices,
and customs. But this has always been proposed in the face of the
dependence of the constructs of both "self" and "law" upon the very
context they were intended to replace. Thus the enormous attention
given to strategies for demonstrating some context in which concepts
would be free from cultural variation: stable, self-evident, unequivocally clear in their meanings, like the well-defined concepts of mathematics and physics.[14] For most paradigm-expectant social scientists
this has meant fascination with the development of reductionistic
models and quantification techniques whose foundational concepts
could be thought of as securely based in logical self-evidence of one
form or another.

The Deconstruction of the Positivist Idea of Science

The dominant direction in twentieth-century science and philosophy has been the thorough undermining of the Comptean ideal of

14. The literature discussing the relations of Logical Empiricism to mathematics
and physics, on the one hand, and concern with language and culture on the other, is
vast. The work of Richard Rorty provides a useful summary and interpretation. See
Richard Rorty, ed., *The Linguistic Turn: Recent Essays in Philosophical Method* (Chicago:
University of Chicago Press, 1967). The single best overall discussion of the career of
this ideal in social investigation is probably Gerald Radnitsky, *Contemporary Schools of
Metascience* (Göteborg: Scandinavian University Books, 1970), vol. 1.

science. The philosophers of interpretation have been important figures in this undermining, and it is internally consistent with their positions that they have articulated their insights through a direct concern with their society and culture in its historical context. In this they have continued the Aristotelian notion of reason as a vital aspect of human existence, a means toward awareness and self-reflection, yet thoroughly embedded in the practices of everyday life. It is important to note the impoverishment of the term that results from the equation of reason with a strictly formal scientific methodology. The aim of this innovation was not to illuminate the world of common meanings, but to explain and finally replace the contextual understandings of every-day life with context-free categories. This reductionistic ideal has come under increasing attack.

The logical empiricist ideal of a unified science embracing both the natural and the human sciences was promulgated and widely accepted in the first decades of the twentieth century. Its leading exponents, the Vienna circle centered around Rudolph Carnap, put forward the idea of an ideal logical language to stand in contrast to the "confusion" of natural languages. Russell's logical empiricism in Britain and the early Wittgenstein might be looked upon as "fellow travelers," as in a very different way could Husserl. Logical Positivists attempted to erect a norm for paradigmatic science. The then new discipline of meta-mathematics was looked to, to provide this norm. It offered an ideal of intelligibility according to which the meaning of any term or element in a system is unequivocally determined in a rigorous manner according to its relation to the other elements within the system. The system itself was conceived as those elements related by rules of inference whose consistency can be determined according to formalizable rules. It is important to note that while this conception of meaning is holistic in that the parts are defined in relation to the whole, the meaning derives from the self-referential and formalizable character of the sys-tem. Physics was the positivists' approximation to the formal paradigm of mathematical logic, and they issued the dictum that ap-proximation to that approximation was the criterion of science and so of truth.[15]

The ideal of a Unified Science acted among social scientists to focus attention on formal models of explanation. Since it was evident

15. See Radnitsky, *Metascience*, pp. 56–75.

from the outset that the cultural world could not meet the norm, the problem of investigation was posed as the explanation of the *ex-hypothesi* confused world of "vague" meaning by means of a logically consistent system of concepts that could account for the confusion without incoherence. Since by definition only these explanatory systems could be true, strictly speaking, the role of the investigator's own prescientific understanding of these multivocal symbols was not emphasized, often ignored. At best this was conceived as a step that, once taken, could be safely forgotten until one came to replace the everyday terms with the new, formally defined concepts. So a society's world became an interlocking group of "belief systems," "institutional" systems, "personality" systems, conceptual entities the investigator put forward as the truth behind the appearance of everyday, lived experience.

Jean Piaget's synthetic conception of structuralism is one of the latest, most sophisticated restatements of this project to reduce meaning to explicit rules operationally defined. For Piaget the novelty of structuralism lies in the more general conception of logic inherent in the concept of structure. Structuralism's premise is "an ideal (perhaps a hope) of intrinsic intelligibility supported by the postulate that structures are self-sufficient and that, to grasp them, we do not have to make reference to all sorts of extraneous elements."[16] The importance of "operational structuralism," according to Piaget, is that, thanks to the logical priority of the rules of transformation over the elements that they govern, it promises to provide mathematical models of the linguistic, personality, and symbolic systems that have resisted the older, atomistic approach of logical empiricism.[17]

From the interpretive point of view what is most striking about structuralism is not its difference from but its continuity with the older reductionism. That massive continuous theme is the priority and independence of logical structures and rules of inference from the contexts of ordinary understanding. As Lévi-Strauss puts it, one must avoid the "shop-girl's web of subjectivity" or the "swamps of experi-

16. Jean Piaget, *Structuralism*.
17. Ibid., pp. 9–10 and 141–142. The field of Systems Theory has developed a formal methodology very like Structuralism, and subject to the same accusations and critique. A clear explication of Systems Theory has recently been advanced by Irvin Laszlo, *The Systems View of the World: The Natural Philosophy of the New Developments in the Sciences* (New York: G. Braziller, 1972).

ence" to arrive at structure and science. The ideal or "hope" of the intrinsic intelligibility of structures apart from "all sorts of extraneous elements," is the same animus that propelled the Vienna circle. Ricoeur, in several of his essays, has drawn the clearest implications of this position. For him, the goals of structuralism can be accomplished, in fact already have been, but at a price the structuralists ignore. The conditions which make the enterprise possible—the establishment of operations and elements, and an algebra of their combinations—assure from the beginning and by definition that one is working on a body of material which is preconstituted, stopped, closed, and in a certain sense, dead.[18] The very success of structuralism leaves behind the "understanding of action, operations and process, all of which are constitutive of meaningful discourse. Structuralism seals its formalized language off from discourse, and therefore from the human world.[19] A high price indeed for the sciences of man, although one the structuralists are explicitly willing to pay in the name of science.[20]

For Ricoeur, discourse is about something other than itself in an absolute sense.[21] It performs the function of bringing what is said out of the immediate situation to a World which is opened up by the references in the text. Discourse being about something, one must understand the World in order to interpret it. Discourse being public and fixed, in one form or another, is therefore freed from the motivations and subjectivity of its author; it is in public, it is intersubjective and therefore open to interpretation. The concept of *Verstehen* is brought out of private minds into the cultural world.

This notion is brought to clarity by the notion of the text.[22] The text must be treated as a whole; only then can the parts make sense. Of course, one must begin by guessing or approximating what that

18. See Paul Ricoeur, "Structure, Word, Event," in *Conflict of Interpretations: Essays in Hermeneutics* (Evanston: Northwestern University Press, 1974), p. 79.
19. Ibid.
20. An enterprise such as that of Jacques Derrida might be termed a "Poststructuralism" which conceives an "absolute text" which refers only to itself and which is the endless play of signifiers in a closed and again ultimately dead and meaningless system. See Jacques Derrida, "Structure, Sign and Play in the Discourse of the Human Sciences," in Richard Macksey and Eugenio Donato, *The Structuralist Controversy: The Languages of Criticism and the Sciences of Man* (Baltimore: Johns Hopkins Press, 1970), pp. 247–264.
21. Paul Ricoeur, "The Model of the Text: Meaningful Action Considered as a Text," which is reprinted in this volume. See p. 78.
22. Chap. 2, p. 86.

whole might be. This initial guess is highly fallible and is open to error
and recasting, to reinterpretation. There is a dialectic of guessing and
validation which Ricoeur discusses in his article.

The text is plurivocal, open to several readings and to several
constructions. But it is not infinite. Human action and interpretation
are subject to many but not indefinitely many constructions. Any
closure of the process through an external means is violence and often
occurs. But just as interpretive social science is not subjectivism,
neither is it simply intuitionism.

Let us be clear. What we want to understand is not something
behind the cultural object, the text, but rather something in front of it.
We approach the text as a human pro-ject. To understand a text is to
follow its movements from sense to reference, from what it says to
what it talks about.[23] To understand an author better than he could
understand himself is to display the power of disclosure implied in his
discourse beyond the limited horizon of his own existential situation.
Social structures, cultural objects, can be read also as attempts to cope
with existential perplexities, human predicaments, and deep-rooted
conflict. In this sense, these structures too have a referential dimension. They point toward the *aporias* of social existence.[24]

The thrust of this position is not to deny the role of human commitment, subjectivity, and intention in understanding human
phenomena, but only to clarify it and make it accessible to public
discourse.[25] As a model of text interpretation, understanding has nothing to do with an immediate grasping of a foreign psychic life or
with an emotional identification with a mental intention. Understanding is entirely mediated by the procedures that precede it and
accompany it. The counterpart of this personal appropriation is not
something which can be felt. It is the dynamic meaning identified
earlier with the reference to the text, that is, the power of disclosing a
world.[26]

In this approach understanding any action is analogous to textual
interpretation. This means that the intelligibility of any action requires

23. Chap. 2, p. 98.   24. Chap. 2, p. 100.   25. Ibid.
26. Ibid. "World" is the most general term for the holistic totality of cultural
meaning pointed at by the notion of "context." (See notes 5 and 10 above.) The classic
discussion of this meaning of "world" is that of Martin Heidegger in *Being and Time*, 1,
3, "The Worldhood of the World," pp. 91–148.

reference to its larger context, a cultural world. So, to take a power-fully developed example, when Clifford Geertz describes the Balinese cockfight, a text analogue, he progressively incorporates other essential Balinese symbols, institutions, and practices that are necessary to an understanding of the seemingly localized cockfight. The Balinese cultural and social world is not incorporated into the cockfight, but must be brought into the anaylsis in order to understand the event. This is the art of interpretation. The aim is not to uncover universals or laws but rather to explicate context and world.[27]

Interpretive social science has developed as the alternative to earlier logical empiricism as well as the later systems approaches, including structuralism, within the human sciences. It must continue to develop in opposition to and as a criticism of these tendencies. Here interpretive social science reveals itself as a response to the crisis of the human sciences that is constructive in the profound sense of establishing a connection between what is studied, the means of investigation, and the ends informing the investigators. But at the same time it initiates a process of recovery and reappropriation of the richness of meaning found in the symbolic contexts of all areas of culture. But it can no longer do so naively. The incisive and convincing negative dialectic and ideology-critique as developed in the Frankfurt School has demonstrated the immense difficulty of reappropriation in the modern world. Therefore we must deal with their arguments and the directions they suggest to us.

RECONSTRUCTION

Reason as Action: Criticism for Recovery

The great strength of the Frankfurt tradition of critical theory has been continually to urge that the issue of understanding in the human sciences cannot be detached from the greater problems of living in an age of technology in which traditional understandings appear problematic, at best.[28] Beginning in the 1920s Adorno and Horkheimer elaborated a dialectical hermeneutic, a contextual reason, aimed at

27. See Clifford Geertz, "Deep Play: Notes on the Balinese Cockfight," which is reprinted in this volume.

28. For a general history of the Frankfurt School, its members, and their varied developments, see Martin Jay, *The Dialectical Imagination: A History of the Frankfurt School and the Institute of Social Research, 1923–1950* (Boston: Little, Brown, 1973).

recuperating the cultural and political energies currently blocked by social forms of exploitation and domination.[29]

They insist that scientism, as the absorption in context-free method, is itself a distortion or "repression" of the contextual dialectic of tacit whole and articulated parts on which scientific rationality must stand. Their dialectic of criticism and recovery is based on two important presuppositions that constitute a general interpretive approach to contemporary conditions. The first presupposition is the superiority of dialectical reason over all forms of purely analytic reason.

The second presupposition of Frankfurt School interpretation situates the internal logic of cultural discourse within the field of social practices and social relationships. When the problem of scientism is seen in this expanded context, the clarity of analytic reason is situated in the larger opacity of social relations and practices which found it in the current age. As industrial technology and funtional organization have displaced traditional routines in modern life, the content of political discussion has also shifted. Instead of the older concern with the justice of certain kinds of social relationships — for example, the allocation of access to services on the basis of wealth — we have seen a tendency to speak of technical goals such as "economic growth." In fact, governmental and corporate spokesmen cannot relate their functional conception of rationality to the questions of proportional justice. Rather, justice in the sense of the good order of community life is reduced to a mere calculus of interests. The context that could make this calculus meaningful, the concrete understandings and concerns of citizens, is deemed a matter of subjective "preference" and so ruled out of any "rational" discussion of policy. Politicians, and our academic experts, find it easier to talk about the standard of living than about what a society might be living for. In social technocracy as in scientism, analytic reason has cut itself off from the human whole that could give some intrinsic sense to its formal operations.

The Frankfurt thinkers trace the connection between the intellectual and social forms of fragmentation and mechanical regimentation by using the Marxist theme of the dependence of consciousness on social being. Social being describes the concrete situation of think-

29. The idea of a "dialectical hermeneutic" is well set out by Frederick Jameson in *Marxism and Form: Twentieth Century Dialectical Theories of Literature* (Princeton: Princeton University Press, 1971).

ing persons as related to their habits, practices, traditions, and social relations with other groups similarly located. This powerful facticity of the social situation is the appropriation by the Frankfurt thinkers, under the influence of their teachers Max Weber and Martin Heidegger, of Marx's materialism. For critical theory the materialist premise operates as a limiting horizon with which any interpretive formulation must come to grips if it is to avoid mystification. It is not a dogmatic assertion that culture "reflects" social relations in any simple sense, nor that culture is an epiphenomenon of technology, economics, or any other "motive forces of history." The importance of the materialist presupposition is rather its insistence on the inerradicable tension between the human urges for coherent life and thought and the limitation forced on us by our involvement in bodily, social, historical existence.

From the Frankfurt School's beginning the critical theorists have concentrated on exploring the specific kinds of fragmentation and mystification that are the consequences of the increasing rationalization (in the Weberian sense) of the relations of social life. The Frankfurt thinkers have persistently made explicit the connections between the spread of ideologies of private despair or salvation and the construction of a technically managed society, bearing out Weber's doleful prophecy of systematic rationalization. The public, common world of shared symbols of morality and discourse has correspondingly shrunk and weakened. Recovery of a more fully human existence has seemed, especially to Adorno and Marcuse, to recede further from our grasp.[30] Hence their emphasis on "negative dialectic," the claim that today wholeness can be experienced only negatively as an implicit norm against which the fragmentation of late capitalist society at least appears as what it is.

This is to say that the present cultural situation is one in which the loss of community is so advanced that the unmasking of pretended totality, the "ideology critique" of Marxism, is all that remains for intellectuals. Their task is to undermine the legitimacy of all that exists, but no longer to present a new image of integration. For Adorno and Horkheimer, if one cannot confidently identify a "subject of

---

30. See Theodor Adorno, *Negative Dialectics,* translated by E. B. Ashtow (New York: Seabury, 1973); Herbert Marcuse, *One-Dimensional Man: Studies in the Ideology of Advanced Industrial Society* (Boston: Beacon Press, 1964).

history," a social group whose interests can lead to a new moral community, there can be ground only for negative dialectic. In their view the failure of Marxism's identification of the proletariat with this subject of history leaves us with only a deep historical pessimism. This failure seems to question the whole conception of the *Bildungsideal,* which is the Frankfurt School's greatest legacy from German idealism. Marcuse's cultural pessimism reflects this same sense.

Without denying the gloomy prognosis for our age, later Frankfurt thinkers, especially Jürgen Habermas, have attempted to continue the tradition of "ideology-critique" without succumbing to a total pessimism. In part Habermas's ability to move beyond the position of Adorno is a result of his encounter with the interpretive tradition, particularly with the work of Hans-Georg Gadamer. Habermas's discussion of the interpretive tradition has brought it into the mainstream of debate about the social sciences. As Habermas has pointed out, cultural knowledge is possible only because, and not in spite of, the "pre-understanding, which is derived from the interpreter's initial situation. The work of traditional meaning discloses itself to the interpreter only to the extent that his own work becomes clarified at the same time. . . . The understanding of meaning is diverted in its very structure toward the attainment of possible consensus among actors in the framework of a self-understanding derived from tradition."[31]

This emphasis on discourse as the basis for the human sciences is a position common to the later Frankfurt School and the interpretive approach. It represents a reworking of and a move beyond the earlier Frankfurt search for a historical subject to reveal the final truth of history.

Behind the search for the subject of history lay the whole course of Western metaphysics, but particularly the unquestioned Enlightenment dogma that reality is a rational whole to which reason approximates. How reason approximated reality has of course been described in many ways. The tradition that brings us to Adorno runs through Hegel and Marx. For them, the cunning of reason is the unfolding of the real through history. This is the whole which makes all the parts coherent; not to see this can only lead to mystification. There are no

31. Jürgen Habermas, *Knowledge and Human Interests* (Boston: Beacon Press, 1971), pp. 309–310.

partial truths.[32] Because of the impasse to which this tradition has come, Habermas has moved away from the Hegelian notion that the meaning of all human activity can be found in relation to the maturation of the historical subject. He attempts to reground the idealist unity of theoretical understanding, ethical norms, and social practices by returning to a position resembling a Kantian transcendentalism. Greatly simplified, this position amounts to a return to a notion of human nature in which there are universals of social life founded on explicit formal properties of the communication process. By doing this, while abandoning Hegel, Habermas continues the rationalist claim that the aim and basis of understanding lie in making concepts explicit, clear, and totally available to consciousness.[33]

Gadamer's appropriation of the *Bildungsideal* as the effort to "keep oneself open to what is other, to other, more universal points of view" breaks with the rationalist effort to achieve a purely theoretical understanding of human nature. For Gadamer the search for "hidden constants" of the human situation can never be fully detached from the working out of those self-formative practices which constitute culture.

This is therefore not to leave the understanding of human community in a state of opaque mystery or untranslatable "houses of being." Rather, Gadamer shows that the weaving of wider understanding, the expansion of horizons, remains particular, in a context, part of a cultural, historical world, as is the object of study. Gadamer's project reappropriates the Aristotelian dialectic of the one and the many for the human sciences. By the late twentieth century our cultural project requires such an understanding, one which neither abandons itself uncritically to romanticized particularity nor mistakes the spread of technological structures for a shortcut to a new universal culture.

The model for Gadamer is practical reason, not theoretical reason. Taylor, Ricoeur, and Gadamer all point out that cultural life is embedded in and is a reflection upon practical activity. The very possibility of coming to understand cultural life flows from that life. Theory can never replace social existence itself. "Thus it is essential that ethical sciences — while they may contribute to the clarification of the prob-

32. The theme of "totality" in Frankfurt dialectics is perceptively discussed by both Martin Jay and Frederick Jameson. (See notes 28 and 29 above.)
33. See Jürgen Habermas, *Legitimation Crisis* (Boston: Beacon Press, 1975).

lems of ethical consciousness—never occupy the place properly belonging to concrete ethical consciousness.... A listener must be sufficiently mature so that he does not demand of the instruction he
receives more than it can give him."[34]

Gadamer summarizes what is for us the center of the interpretive
position, when he says that "it is indispensable that through practice
and education the listener may have already formed a *habitudo* which
he takes into the concrete situations of his life, a *habitudo* which will be
confirmed and solidified by each new action."[35] What the Frankfurt
School rightly saw as the threat to or repression of the formation of
such habits remains a pervasive obstacle both to understanding and to
action. This is to tie such habits intimately to the need for criticism,
both theoretical *and* political, of received values, practices, and institutions. Tradition is always problematical. The only way to proceed to
the future is through the appropriation, the continual reappropriation,
of tradition. The goal of the interpretive approach to the human world
is to cultivate such habits, to recognize that we are condemned to
remain open, both to the past and to the future.

The final import of the *Bildungsideal* is that it points to the necessity
for standards by which to judge the world. The immense complexity
of the task should now be clearer. The necessity for it, however,
remains. Meaning is *for* something: that is what meaning is. This is no
utilitarian reduction but a return to an older tradition in which the
end of reason, its telos, was the good. The aim of interpretation is not
merely more interpretation; it points beyond itself to the fundamental
problems—theoretical, practical, and aesthetic—of human existence.

Interpretations

The readings in this volume were chosen to embody the main
themes which we see as exemplifying the interpretive approach.

Albert Hirschman elegantly shows us the interplay between model
and case. He opposes two poles, one successful and the other not. On
the one hand, the model, paradigm, or theory totally overshadows
both the material to be understood and the process of understanding
itself. He plays off against this abuse a case where the theory is "in" the

34. Hans-Georg Gadamer, "The Problem of Historical Consciousness," which is
reprinted in this volume. See p. 137.
35. Ibid. This is a paraphrase of Aristotle, *Ethics,* Book I.

narrative itself, where the paradigm and the author's stance are kept at a low profile so that the story itself can speak. But this ironically increases the power of the theory and the voice of the author. In no way is this a plea for lack of theory—quite the contrary. Hirschman emphasizes that connections must come from the material itself; that lessons and generalizations are more likely to emerge when the cognitive style which Hirschman calls "open" is present.

Clifford Geertz shows that an interpretive approach does not reduce the number and diversity of means of understanding that are available, but rather increases them. If theory per se is no longer separate from the enterprise, then insights, methods, and techniques from a variety of disciplines become available to us. Theory here is seen as itself an interpretation. It is seen as being in a situation with a particular problem to work on. Therefore, it can use what is appropriate to the case. Being itself situated, both theoretically and practically, it no longer can autonomously set the terms for discussion. But a discussion of a problem is impossible without it.

Geertz shows that cultural understanding by no means entails any form of special intuition or mysterious powers of empathy. He outlines and then demonstrates how cultural understanding starts with a picture of the whole, which leads the investigator to look for symbolic forms through which and in which the conceptions of the person, the social order, and the cosmology are articulated and displayed. This is an undertaking that requires skill—and Geertz is a deft practitioner of the art—but one which is repeatable, open to correction, and comparable to other cases.

But ambiguity is an inherent aspect of all interpretation, as much at home within our own language and culture as in the more obvious problems of interpretation which the encounter with the other reveals. Stanley Fish provocatively illustrates the inescapability of ambiguity in even our most concerted efforts at univocal clarity. Our apparently fixed, inescapably obvious, everyday meanings harbor essential complexity, which becomes manifest as soon as we try to pin them down. Fish's argument opens us to the necessarily contestable nature of all cultural material, whether it be highly stylized literary productions or the common utterances of everyday life.

Thomas Kuhn discusses the differences between an approach to the history of science that attempts to legislate what was or must have been and one that takes the opposite approach of trying to elucidate the particularity and comprehensibility of past eras of science. His aim is not to fit the "law-like sciences" under laws but rather to understand how earlier visions of nature were themselves credible. Through the opening up of the validity of the past, our own hubris is tempered; the past is no mere chronicling of error, even in physics, but an ongoing attempt to understand nature and man. Our current paradigm, too, will pass on, but that does not make it radically false, any more than its current success makes it radically true.

An important consequence of the interconnections of the theoretical and the practical, the process of understanding and the understanding achieved, is that interpretation is never a mere standing before the world, a passive contemplation of existence. The given is put in question in a wide variety of ways, and how this is done influences and shapes the whole undertaking.

The uncovering and demonstration of the powerful forces of desire, passion, and interest, which Paul Ricoeur brilliantly demonstrates in his book on Freud, is juxtaposed within the work of Freud himself to the counter-dialectic of signification and hope. Just as twentieth-century man has uncovered the deeper archaeology of his being, so must the teleology, or value-oriented recovery, of these forces through symbol and reason be taken into account. This is the genius of Freud, for Ricoeur. He presents a convincing argument for the necessity of such a twin dialectic if we are to comprehend the fullness of human existence and not fall into idealism or cease our investigation with an image of fashionable doom.

Robert Bellah draws on the recent revolts and changes, both political and religious, that have spread across America and shows that the symbols and traditions which these incidents call forth must be identified and located within a previous American history so as to reveal their continuities and discontinuities. He points out the frightening dangers which the future could hold, but he also makes a powerful case for the necessity of utopian thinking. The utopianism is not a simple one, it is rather what Ricoeur has referred to as a "second naivety," an opening of possibilities, which, although it by no means assures a successful outcome, does not preclude all hope either, even in such dark times. Bellah cites Ignazio Silone: "On a group of theories one can found a school; but on a group of values one can found a culture, a civilization, a new way of living together among men." Without such a possibility, without some openness to the future, as Bellah shows, value, judgment, and ultimately, reason are impossible.

PART ONE

The Primacy of Meaning:
Culture as Context

Chapter One

Interpretation and the Sciences of Man

CHARLES TAYLOR

I

i

Is there a sense in which interpretation is essential to explanation in the sciences of man? The view that it is, that there is an unavoidably "hermeneutical" component in the sciences of man, goes back to Dilthey. But recently the question has come again to the fore, for instance, in the work of Gadamer,[1] in Ricoeur's interpretation of Freud,[2] and in the writings of Habermas.[3]

Interpretation, in the sense relevant to hermeneutics, is an attempt to make clear, to make sense of an object of study. This object must, therefore, be a text, or a text-analogue, which in some way is confused, incomplete, cloudy, seemingly contradictory — in one way or another, unclear. The interpretation aims to bring to light an underlying coherence or sense.

This means that any science which can be called "hermeneutical," even in an extended sense, must be dealing with one or another of the confusingly interrelated forms of meaning. Let us try to see a little more clearly what this involves.

We need, first, an object or a field of objects, about which we can

Originally published in *The Review of Metaphysics* 25, no. 1 (September 1971). Reprinted with permission.
    1. See, e.g., H. G. Gadamer, *Wahrheit und Methode* (Tübingen, 1960).
    2. See Paul Ricoeur, *De l'interprétation* (Paris, 1965).
    3. See, e.g., J. Habermas, *Erkenntnis und Interesse* (Frankfurt, 1968).

speak in terms of coherence or its absence, of making sense or non-sense.

Second, we need to be able to make a distinction, even if only a relative one, between the sense of coherence made, and its embodiment in a particular field of carriers or signifiers. For otherwise, the task of making clear what is fragmentary or confused would be radically impossible. No sense could be given to this idea. We have to be able to make for our interpretations claims of the order: the meaning confusedly present in this text or text-analogue is clearly expressed here. The meaning, in other words, is one which admits of more than one expression, and, in this sense, a distinction must be possible between meaning and expression.

The point of the above qualification, that this distinction may be only relative, is that there are cases where no clear, unambiguous, nonarbitrary line can be drawn between what is said and its expression. It can be plausibly argued (I think convincingly, although there is no space to go into it here) that this is the normal and fundamental condition of meaningful expression, that exact synonymy, or equivalence of meaning, is a rare and localized achievement of specialized languages or uses of civilization. But this, if true (and I think it is), does not do away with the distinction between meaning and expression. Even if there is an important sense in which a meaning reexpressed in a new medium cannot be declared identical, this by no means entails that we can give no sense to the project of expressing a meaning in a new way. It does of course raise an interesting and difficult question about what can be meant by expressing it in a clearer way: what is the "it" which is clarified if equivalence is denied? I hope to return to this in examining interpretation in the sciences of man.

Hence the object of a science of interpretation must be describable in terms of sense and nonsense, coherence and its absence; and must admit of a distinction between meaning and its expression.

There is also a third condition it must meet. We can speak of sense or coherence, and of their different embodiments, in connection with such phenomena as gestalts, or patterns in rock formations, or snow crystals, where the notion of expression has no real warrant. What is lacking here is the notion of a subject for whom these meanings are. Without such a subject, the choice of criteria of sameness and difference, the choice among the different forms of coherence which can be identified in a given pattern, among the different conceptual fields in which it can be seen, is arbitrary.

In a text or text-analogue, on the other hand, we are trying to make explicit the meaning expressed, and this means expressed by or for a subject or subjects. The notion of expression refers us to that of a subject. The identification of the subject is by no means necessarily unproblematical, as we shall see further on; it may be one of the most difficult problems, an area in which prevailing epistemological prejudice may blind us to the nature of our object of study. I think this has been the case, as I will show below. And moreover, the identification of a subject does not assure us of a clear and absolute distinction between meaning and expression as we saw above. But any such distinction, even a relative one, is without any anchor at all, is totally arbitrary, without appeal to a subject.

The object of a science of interpretation must thus have sense, distinguishable from its expression, which is for or by a subject.

ii

Before going on to see in what way, if any, these conditions are realized in the sciences of man, I think it would be useful to set out more clearly what rides on this question, why it matters whether or not we think of the sciences of man as hermeneutical, what the issue is at stake here.

The issue here is at root an epistemological one. But it is inextricable from an ontological one, and hence, cannot but be relevant to our notions of science and of the proper conduct of inquiry. We might say that it is an ontological issue which has been argued ever since the seventeenth century in terms of epistemological considerations which have appeared to some to be unanswerable.

The case could be put in these terms: what are the criteria of judgment in a hermeneutical science? A successful interpretation is one which makes clear the meaning originally present in a confused, fragmentary, cloudy form. But how does one know that this interpretation is correct? Presumably because it makes sense of the original text: what is strange, mystifying, puzzling, contradictory is no longer so, is accounted for. The interpretation appeals throughout to our understanding of the "language" of expression, which understanding allows us to see that this expression is puzzling, that it is in contradiction to that other, etc., and that these difficulties are cleared up when the meaning is expressed in a new way.

But this appeal to our understanding seems to be crucially inadequate. What if someone does not "see" the adequacy of our interpretation, does not accept our reading? We try to show him how it makes sense of the original non- or partial sense. But for him to follow us he must read the original language as we do, he must recognize these expressions as puzzling in a certain way, and hence be looking for a solution to our problem. If he does not, what can we do? The answer, it would seem, can only be more of the same. We have to show him through the reading of other expressions why this expression must be read in the way we propose. But success here requires that he follow us in these other readings, and so on, it would seem, potentially forever. We cannot escape an ultimate appeal to a common understanding of the expressions, of the "language" involved. This is one way of trying to express what has been called the "hermeneutical circle." What we are trying to establish is a certain reading of text or expressions, and what we appeal to as our grounds for this reading can only be other readings. The circle can also be put in terms of part-whole relations: we are trying to establish a reading for the whole text, and for this we appeal to readings of its partial expressions; and yet because we are dealing with meaning, with making sense, where expressions only make sense or not in relation to others, the readings of partial expressions depend on those of others, and ultimately of the whole.

Put in forensic terms, as we started to do above, we can only convince an interlocutor if at some point he shares our understanding of the language concerned. If he does not, there is no further step to take in rational argument; we can try to awaken these intuitions in him or we can simply give up; argument will advance us no further. But of course the forensic predicament can be transferred into my own judging: if I am this ill-equipped to convince a stubborn interlocutor, how can I convince myself? how can I be sure? Maybe my intuitions are wrong or distorted, maybe I am locked into a circle of illusion.

Now one, and perhaps the only sane response to this would be to say that such uncertainty is an ineradicable part of our epistemological predicament. That even to characterize it as "uncertainty" is to adopt an absurdly severe criterion of "certainty," which deprives the concept of any sensible use. But this has not been the only or even the main response of our philosophical tradition. And it is another response which has had an important and far-reaching effect on the sciences of man. The demand has been for a level of certainty which can only be attained by breaking beyond the circle.

There are two ways in which this break-out has been envisaged. The first might be called the "rationalist" one and could be thought to reach a culmination in Hegel. It does not involve a negation of intuition, or of our understanding of meaning, but rather aspires to attainment of an understanding of such clarity that it would carry with it the certainty of the undeniable. In Hegel's case, for instance, our full understanding of the whole in "thought" carries with it a grasp of its inner necessity, such that we see how it could not be otherwise. No higher grade of certainty is conceivable. For this aspiration the word "break-out" is badly chosen; the aim is rather to bring understanding to an inner clarity which is absolute.

The other way, which we can call "empiricist," is a genuine attempt to go beyond the circle of our own interpretations, to get beyond subjectivity. The attempt is to reconstruct knowledge in such a way that there is no need to make final appeal to readings or judgments which cannot be checked further. That is why the basic building block of knowledge on this view is the impression, or sense-datum, a unit of information which is not the deliverance of a judgment, which has by definition no element in it of reading or interpretation, which is a brute datum. The highest ambition would be to build our knowledge from such building blocks by judgments which could be anchored in a certainty beyond subjective intuition. This is what underlies the attraction of the notion of the association of ideas, or if the same procedure is viewed as a method, induction. If the original acquisition of the units of information is not the fruit of judgment or interpretation, then the constatation that two such elements occur together need not either be the fruit of interpretation, of a reading or intuition which cannot be checked. For if the occurence of a single element is a brute datum, then so is the co-occurence of two such elements. The path to true knowledge would then repose crucially on the correct recording of such co-occurrences.

This is what lies behind an ideal of verification which is central to an important tradition in the philosophy of science, whose main contemporary protagonists are the logical empiricists. Verification must be grounded ultimately in the acquisition of brute data. By "brute data," I mean here and throughout data whose validity cannot be questioned by offering another interpretation or reading, data whose credibility cannot be founded or undermined by further reasoning.[4] If such a difference of interpretation can arise over given data, then it must be possible to structure the argument so as to distinguish the basic, brute data from the inferences made on the basis of them.

The inferences themselves, of course, to be valid must similarly be beyond the challenge of a rival interpretation. Here the logical empiricists added to the armory of traditional empiricism which set great store by the method of induction, the whole domain of logical and mathematical inference which had been central to the rationalist position (with Leibniz at least, although not with Hegel), and which offered another brand of unquestionable certainty.

Of course, mathematical inference and empirical verification were combined in such a way that two theories or more could be verified of the same domain of facts. But this was a consequence to which logical empiricism was willing to accommodate itself. As for the surplus meaning in a theory which could not be rigorously coordinated with brute data, it was considered to be quite outside the logic of verification.

As a theory of perception, this epistemology gave rise to all sorts of problems, not least of which was the perpetual threat of skepticism and solipsism inseparable from a conception of the basic data of knowledge as brute data, beyond investigation. As a theory of perception, however, it seems largely a thing of the past, in spite of a surprising recrudescence in the Anglo-Saxon world in the thirties and forties. But there is no doubt that it goes marching on, among other places, as a theory of how the human mind and human knowledge actually function.

In a sense, the contemporary period has seen a better, more rigorous statement of what this epistemology is about in the form of computer-influenced theories of intelligence. These try to model intel-

4. The notion of brute data here has some relation to, but is not at all the same as, the "brute facts" discussed by Elizabeth Anscombe, "On Brute Facts," *Analysis* 18 (1957–1958): 69–72, and John Searle, *Speech Acts* (Cambridge, 1969), pp. 50–53. For Anscombe and Searle, brute facts are contrasted to what may be called "institutional facts," to use Searle's term, i.e., facts which presuppose the existence of certain institutions. Voting would be an example. But, as we shall see below, some institutional facts, such as X's having voted Liberal, can be verified as brute data in the sense used here, and

ligence as consisting of operations on machine-recognizable input which could themselves be matched by programs which could be run on machines. The machine criterion provides us with our assurance against an appeal to intuition or interpretations which cannot be understood by fully explicit procedures operating on brute data — the input.[5]

The progress of natural science has lent great credibility to this epistemology, since it can be plausibly reconstructed on this model, as has been done, for instance, by the logical empiricists. And, of course, the temptation has been overwhelming to reconstruct the sciences of man on the same model; or rather to launch them in lines of inquiry that fit this paradigm, since they are constantly said to be in their "infancy." Psychology, where an earlier vogue of behaviorism is being replaced by a boom of computer-based models, is far from the only case.

The form this epistemological bias — one might say obsession — takes is different for different sciences. Later I should like to look at a particular case, the study of politics, where the issue can be followed out. But in general, the empiricist orientation must be hostile to a conduct of inquiry which is based on interpretation, and which encounters the hermeneutical circle as this was characterized above. This cannot meet the requirements of intersubjective, non-arbitrary verification which it considers essential to science. And along with the epistemological stance goes the ontological belief that reality must be susceptible to understanding and explanation by science so understood. From this follows a certain set of notions of what the sciences of man must be.

On the other hand, many, including myself, would like to argue that these notions about the sciences of man are sterile, that we cannot come to understand important dimensions of human life within the bounds set by this epistemological orientation. This dispute is of course familiar to all in at least some of its ramifications. What I want to claim is that the issue can be fruitfully posed in terms of the notion of interpretation as I began to outline it above.

---

thus find a place in the category of political behavior. What cannot as easily be described in terms of brute data are the institutions themselves.

5. See the discussion in M. Minsky, *Computation* (Englewood Cliffs, N.J., 1967), pp. 104–107, where Minsky explicitly argues that an effective procedure, which no longer requires intuition or interpretation, is one which can be realized by a machine.

I think this way of putting the question is useful because it allows us at once to bring to the surface the powerful epistemological beliefs which underlie the orthodox view of the sciences of man in our academy, and to make explicit the notion of our epistemological predicament implicit in the opposing thesis. This is in fact rather more way-out and shocking to the tradition of scientific thought than is often admitted or realized by the opponents of narrow scientism. It may not strengthen the case of the opposition to bring out fully what is involved in a hermeneutical science as far as convincing waverers is concerned, but a gain in clarity is surely worth a thinning of the ranks—at least in philosophy.

iii

Before going on to look at the case of political science, it might be worth asking another question: why should we even pose the question whether the sciences of man are hermeneutical? What gives us the idea in the first place that men and their actions constitute an object or a series of objects which meet the conditions outlined above?

The answer is that on the phenomenological level or that of ordinary speech (and the two converge for the purposes of this argument) a certain notion of meaning has an essential place in the characterization of human behavior. This is the sense in which we speak of a situation, an action, a demand, a prospect having a certain meaning for a person.

Now it is frequently thought that "meaning" is used here in a sense which is a kind of illegitimate extension from the notion of linguistic meaning. Whether it can be considered an extension or not is another matter; it certainly differs from linguistic meaning. But it would be very hard to argue that it is an illegitimate use of the term.

When we speak of the "meaning" of a given predicament, we are using a concept which has the following articulation. (1) Meaning is for a subject: it is not the meaning of the situation *in vacuo,* but its meaning for a subject, a specific subject, a group of subjects, or perhaps what its meaning is for the human subject as such (even though particular humans might be reproached with not admitting or realizing this). (2) Meaning is of something; that is, we can distinguish between a given element—situation, action, or whatever—and its meaning. But this is not to say that they are physically separable. Rather we are dealing with two descriptions of the element, in one of which it is characterized in terms of its meaning for the subject. But the relations between the two descriptions are not symmetrical. For, on the one hand, the description in terms of meaning cannot be unless descriptions of the other kind apply as well; or put differently, there can be no meaning without a substrate. But on the other hand, it may be that the same meaning may be borne by another substrate — e.g., a situation with the same meaning may be realized in different physical conditions. There is a necessary role for a potentially substitutable substrate; or all meanings are of something.

And (3) things only have meaning in a field, that is, in relation to the meanings of other things. This means that there is no such thing as a single, unrelated meaningful element; and it means that changes in the other meanings in the field can involve changes in the given element. Meanings cannot be identified except in relation to others, and in this way resemble words. The meaning of a word depends, for instance, on those words with which it contrasts, on those which define its place in the language (e.g., those defining "determinable" dimensions, like color, shape), on those which define the activity or "language game" it figures in (describing, invoking, establishing communion), and so on. The relations between meanings in this sense are like those between concepts in a semantic field.

Just as our color concepts are given their meaning by the field of contrast they set up together, so that the introduction of new concepts will alter the boundaries of others, so the various meanings that a subordinate's demeanor can have for us, as deferential, respectful, cringing, mildly mocking, ironical, insolent, provoking, downright rude, are established by a field of contrast; and as with finer discrimination on our part, or a more sophisticated culture, new possibilities are born, so other terms of this range are altered. And as the meaning of our terms "red," "blue," "green" is fixed by the definition of a field of contrast through the determinable term "color," so all these alternative demeanors are only available in a society which has, among other types, hierarchical relations of power and command. And corresponding to the underlying language game of designating colored objects is the set of social practices which sustain these hierarchical structures and are fulfilled in them.

Meaning in this sense — let us call it experiential meaning — thus is for a subject, of something, in a field. This distinguishes it from linguistic meaning which has a four- and not a three-dimensional structure. Linguistic meaning is for subjects and in a field, but it is the meaning of signifiers and it is about a world of referents. Once we are clear about the likenesses and differences there should be little doubt that the term "meaning" is not a misnomer, the product of an illegitimate extension into this context of experience and behavior.

There is thus a quite legitimate notion of meaning which we use when we speak of the meaning of a situation for an agent. And that this concept has a place is integral to our ordinary consciousness and hence speech about our actions. Our actions are ordinarily characterized by the purpose sought and explained by desires, feelings, emotions. But the language by which we describe our goals, feelings, desires is also a definition of the meaning things have for us. The vocabulary defining meaning — words like "terrifying," "attractive" — is linked with that describing feeling — "fear," "desire" — and that describing goals — "safety," "possession."

Moreover, our understanding of these terms moves inescapably in a hermeneutical circle. An emotion term like "shame," for instance, essentially refers us to a certain kind of situation, the "shameful," or "humiliating," and a certain mode of response, that of hiding oneself, of covering up, or else "wiping out" the blot. That is, it is essential to this feeling's being identified as shame that it be related to this situation and give rise to this type of disposition. But this situation in its turn can only be identified in relation to the feelings which it provokes; and the disposition is to a goal which can similarly not be understood without reference to the feelings experienced: the "hiding" in question is one which will cover up my shame; it is not the same as hiding from an armed pursuer; we can only understand what is meant by "hiding" here if we understand what kind of feeling and situation is being talked about. We have to be within the circle.

An emotion term like "shame" can only be explained by reference to other concepts which in turn cannot be understood without reference to shame. To understand these concepts we have to be in on a certain experience, we have to understand a certain language, not just of words, but also a certain language of mutual action and communication, by which we blame, exhort, admire, esteem each other. In the end we are in on this because we grow up in the ambit of certain common meanings. But we can often experience what it is like to be on the outside when we encounter the feeling, action, and experiential meaning language of another civilization. Here there is no translation, no way of explaining in other, more accessible concepts. We can only catch on by getting somehow into their way of life, if only in imagination. Thus if we look at human behavior as action done out of a background of desire, feeling, emotion, then we are looking at a reality which must be characterized in terms of meaning. But does this mean that it can be the object of a hermeneutical science as this was outlined above?

There are, to remind ourselves, three characteristics that the object of a science of interpretation has: it must have sense or coherence; this must be distinguishable from its expression, and this sense must be for a subject.

Now insofar as we are talking about behavior as action, hence in terms of meaning, the category of sense or coherence must apply to it. This is not to say that all behavior must "make sense," if we mean by this be rational, avoid contradiction, confusion of purpose, and the like. Plainly a great deal of our action falls short of this goal. But in another sense, even contradictory, irrational action is "made sense of," when we understand why it was engaged in. We make sense of action when there is a coherence between the actions of the agent and the meaning of his situation for him. We find his action puzzling until we find such a coherence. It may not be bad to repeat that this coherence in no way implies that the action is rational: the meaning of a situation for an agent may be full of confusion and contradiction; but the adequate depiction of this contradiction makes sense of it.

Making sense in this way through coherence of meaning and action, the meanings of action and situation, cannot but move in a hermeneutical circle. Our conviction that the account makes sense is contingent on our reading of action and situation. But these readings cannot be explained or justified except by reference to other such readings, and their relation to the whole. If an interlocutor does not understand this kind of reading, or will not accept it as valid, there is nowhere else the argument can go. Ultimately, a good explanation is one which makes sense of the behavior; but then to appreciate a good explanation, one has to agree on what makes good sense; what makes good sense is a function of one's readings; and these in turn are based on the kind of sense one understands.

But how about the second characteristic, that sense should be distinguishable from its embodiment? This is necessary for a science of interpretation because interpretation lays a claim to make a confused meaning clearer; hence there must be some sense in which the "same" meaning is expressed, but differently.

This immediately raises a difficulty. In talking of experiential meaning above, I mentioned that we can distinguish between a given element and its meaning, between meaning and substrate. This carried the claim that a given meaning *may* be realized in another substrate. But does this mean that we can *always* embody the same meaning in another situation? Perhaps there are some situations, standing before death, for instance, which have a meaning which cannot be embodied otherwise.

But fortunately this difficult question is irrelevant for our purposes. For here we have a case in which the analogy between text and behavior implicit in the notion of a hermeneutical science of man only applies with important modifications. The text is replaced in the interpretation by another text, one which is clearer. The text-analogue of behavior is not replaced by another such text-analogue. When this happens we have revolutionary theatre, or terroristic acts designed to make propaganda of the deed, in which the hidden relations of a society are supposedly shown up in a dramatic confrontation. But this is not scientific understanding, even though it may perhaps be based on such understanding, or claim to be.

But in science the text-analogue is replaced by a text, an account. Which might prompt the question, how we can even begin to talk of interpretation here, of expressing the same meaning more clearly, when we have two such utterly different terms of comparison, a text and a tract of behavior? Is the whole thing not just a bad pun?

This question leads us to open up another aspect of experiential meaning which we abstracted from earlier. Experiential meanings are defined in fields of contrast, as words are in semantic fields.

But what was not mentioned above is that these two kinds of definition are not independent of each other. The range of human desires, feelings, emotions, and hence meanings is bound up with the level and type of culture, which in turn is inseparable from the distinctions and categories marked by the language people speak. The field of meanings in which a given situation can find its place is bound up with the semantic field of the terms characterizing these meanings and the related feelings, desires, predicaments.

But the relationship involved here is not a simple one. There are two simple types of models of relation which could be offered here, but both are inadequate. We could think of the feeling vocabulary as simply describing pre-existing feelings, as marking distinctions which would be there without them. But this is not adequate, because we often experience in ourselves or others how achieving, say, a more sophisticated vocabulary of the emotions makes our emotional life more sophisticated and not just our descriptions of it. Reading a good, powerful novel may give me the picture of an emotion which I had not previously been aware of. But we cannot draw a neat line between an increased ability to identify and an altered ability to feel emotions which this enables.

The other simple inadequate model of the relationship is to jump from the above to the conclusion that thinking makes it so. But this clearly won't do either, since not just any new definition can be forced on us, nor can we force it on ourselves; and some which we do gladly take up can be judged inauthentic, an or in bad faith, or just wrong-headed by others. These judgments may be wrong, but they are not in principle illicit. Rather we make an effort to be lucid about ourselves and our feelings, and admire a man who achieves this.

Thus, neither the simple correspondence view is correct, nor the view that thinking makes it so. But both have prima facie warrant. There is such a thing as self-lucidity, which points us to a correspondence view; but the achievement of such lucidity means moral change, that is, it changes the object known. At the same time, error about oneself is not just an absence of correspondence; it is also in some form inauthenticity, bad faith, self-delusion, repression of one's human feelings, or something of the kind; it is a matter of the quality of what is felt just as much as what is known about this, just as self-knowledge is.

If this is so, then we have to think of man as a self-interpreting animal. He is necessarily so, for there is no such thing as the structure of meanings for him independently of his interpretation of them; for one is woven into the other. But then the text of our interpretation is not that heterogeneous from what is interpreted; for what is interpreted is itself an interpretation: a self-interpretation which is embedded in a stream of action. It is an interpretation of experiential meaning which contributes to the constitution of this meaning. Or to put it in another way: that of which we are trying to find the coherence is itself partly constituted by self-interpretation.

Our aim is to replace this confused, incomplete, partly erroneous self-interpretation by a correct one. And in doing this we look not only to the self-interpretation but to the stream of behavior in which it is set; just as in interpreting a historical document we have to place it in the stream of events which it relates to. But of course the analogy is not exact, for here we are interpreting the interpretation and the stream of behavior in which it is set together, and not just one or the other.

There is thus no utter heterogeneity of interpretation to what it is about; rather there is a slide in the notion of interpretation. Already to be a living agent is to experience one's situation in terms of certain meanings; and this in a sense can be thought of as a sort of proto-"interpretation." This is in turn interpreted and shaped by the language in which the agent lives these meanings. This whole is then at a third level interpreted by the explanation we proffer of his actions.

In this way the second condition of a hermeneutical science is met. But this account poses in a new light the question mentioned at the beginning whether the interpretation can ever express the same meaning as the interpreted. And in this case, there is clearly a way in which the two will not be congruent. For if the explanation is really clearer than the lived interpretation, then it will be such that it would alter in some way the behavior if it came to be internalized by the agent as his self-interpretation. In this way a hermeneutical science which achieves its goal, that is, attains greater clarity than the immediate understanding of agent or observer, must offer us an interpretation which is in this way crucially out of phase with the explicandum.

Thus, human behavior seen as action of agents who desire and are moved, who have goals and aspirations, necessarily offers a purchase for descriptions in terms of meaning — what I have called "experiential meaning." The norm of explanation which it posits is one which "makes sense" of the behavior, which shows a coherence of meaning. This "making sense of" is the proferring of an interpretation; and we have seen that what is interpreted meets the conditions of a science of interpretation: first, that we can speak of its sense or coherence; and second, that this sense can be expressed in another form, so that we can speak of the interpretation as giving clearer expression to what is only implicit in the explicandum. The third condition, that this sense be for a subject, is obviously met in this case, although who this subject is, is by no means an unproblematical question as we shall see later on.

This should be enough to show that there is a good prima facie case to the effect that men and their actions are amenable to explanation of a hermeneutical kind. There is, therefore, some reason to raise the issue and challenge the epistemological orientation which would rule interpretation out of the sciences of man. A great deal more must be said to bring out what is involved in the hermeneutical sciences of man. But before getting on to this, it might help to clarify the issue with a couple of examples drawn from a specific field, that of politics

II

i

In politics, too, the goal of a verifiable science has led to the concentration on features which can supposedly be identified in abstraction from our understanding or not understanding experiential meaning. These —let us call them brute data identifications —are what supposedly enable us to break out from the hermeneutical circle and found our science foursquare on a verification procedure which meets the requirements of the empiricist tradition.

But in politics the search for such brute data has not gone to the lengths which it has in psychology, where the object of science has been thought of by many as behavior qua "colorless movement," or as machine-recognizable properties. The tendency in politics has been to stop with something less basic, but —so it is thought —the identification of which cannot be challenged by the offering of another interpretation or reading of the data concerned (pp. 29-31 above). This is what is referred to as "behavior" in the rhetoric of political scientists, but it has not the rock-bottom quality of its psychological homonym.

Political behavior includes what we would ordinarily call actions, but ones that are supposedly brute data identifiable. How can this be so? Well, actions are usually described by the purpose or end-state realized. But the purposes of some actions can be specified in what might be thought to be brute data terms; some actions, for instance, have physical end-states, like getting the car in the garage or climbing the mountain. Others have end-states which are closely tied by institutional rules to some unmistakable physical movement; thus, when I raise my hand in the meeting at the appropriate time, I am voting for the motion. The only questions we can raise about the corresponding actions, given such movements or the realization of such end-states, are whether the agent was aware of what he was doing, was acting as against simply emitting reflex behavior, knew the institutional significance of his movement, and so forth. Any worries on this score generally turn out to be pretty artificial in the contexts political scientists are concerned with; and where they do arise they can be checked by relatively simple devices, for example, asking the subject: did you mean to vote for the motion?

Hence, it would appear that there are actions which can be identified beyond fear of interpretative dispute; and this is what gives the foundation for the category of "political behavior." Thus, there are some acts of obvious political relevance which can be specified thus in physical terms, such as killing, sending tanks into the streets, seizing people and confining them to cells; and there is an immense range of others which can be specified from physical acts by institutional rules, such as voting, for instance. These can be the object of a science of politics which can hope to meet the stringent requirements of verification. The latter class particularly has provided matter for study in recent decades — most notably in the case of voting studies.

But of course a science of politics confined to such acts would be much too narrow. For on another level these actions also have meaning for the agents which is not exhausted in the brute data descriptions, and which is often crucial to understanding why they were done. Thus, in voting for the motion I am also saving the honor of my party, or defending the value of free speech, or vindicating public morality, or saving civilization from breakdown. It is in such terms that the agents talk about the motivation of much of their political action, and it is difficult to conceive a science of politics which does not come to grips with it.

Behavioral political science comes to grips with it by taking the meanings involved in action as facts about the agent, his beliefs, his affective reactions, his "values," as the term is frequently used. For it can be thought verifiable in the brute data sense that men will agree to subscribe or not to a certain form of words (expressing a belief, say); or express a positive or negative reaction to certain events, or symbols; or agree or not with the proposition that some act is right or wrong. We can thus get at meanings as just another form of brute data by the techniques of the opinion survey and content analysis.

An immediate objection springs to mind. If we are trying to deal with the meanings which inform political action, then surely interpretive acumen is unavoidable. Let us say we are trying to understand the goals and values of a certain group, or grasp their vision of the polity; we might try to probe this by a questionnaire asking them whether they assent or not to a number of propositions, which are meant to express different goals, evaluations, beliefs. But how did we design the questionnaire? How did we pick these propositions? Here we relied on our understanding of the goals, values, vision involved. But then this understanding can be challenged, and hence the significance of our results questioned. Perhaps the finding of our study, the compiling of proportions of assent and dissent to these propositions is irrelevant, is without significance for understanding the agents or the polity concerned. This kind of attack is frequently made by critics of mainstream political science, or for that matter social science in general.

To this the proponents of this mainstream reply with a standard move of logical empiricism: distinguishing the process of discovery from the logic of verification. Of course, it is our understanding of these meanings which enables us to draw up the questionnaire which will test people's attitudes in respect to them. And, of course, interpretive dispute about these meanings is potentially endless; there are no brute data at this level, every affirmation can be challenged by a rival interpretation. But this has nothing to do with verifiable science. What is firmly verified is the set of correlations between, say, the assent to certain propositions and certain behavior. We discover, for instance, that people who are active politically (defined by participation in a certain set of institutions) are more likely to consent to certain sets of propositions supposedly expressing the values underlying the system.[6] This finding is a firmly verified correlation no matter what one thinks of the reasoning, or simple hunches, that went into designing the

6. Cf. H. McClosky, "Consensus and Ideology in American Politics," *American Political Science Review* 58 (1964): 361–382.

research which established it. Political science as a body of knowledge is made up of such correlations; it does not give a truth value to the background reasoning or hunch. A good interpretive nose may be useful in hitting on the right correlations to test, but science is never called on to arbitrate the disputes between interpretations.

Thus, in addition to those overt acts which can be defined physically or institutionally, the category of political behavior can include assent or dissent to verbal formulae, or the occurrence or not of verbal formulae in speech, or expressions of approval or rejection of certain events or measures as observed in institutionally defined behavior (for instance, turning out for a demonstration).

Now there are a number of objections which can be made to this notion of political behavior; one might question in all sorts of ways how interpretation-free it is in fact. But I should like to question it from another angle. One of the basic characteristics of this kind of social science is that it reconstructs reality in line with certain categorical principles. These allow for an intersubjective social reality which is made up of brute data, identifiable acts and structures, certain institutions, procedures, actions. It allows for beliefs, affective reactions, evaluations as the psychological properties of individuals. And it allows for correlations for example, between these two orders or reality: that certain beliefs go along with certain acts, certain values with certain institutions, and so forth.

To put it another way, what is objectively (intersubjectively) real is brute data identifiable. This is what social reality *is*. Social reality described in terms of its meaning for the actors, such that disputes could arise about interpretation which could not be settled by brute data (e.g., are people rioting to get a hearing, or are they rioting to redress humiliation, out of blind anger, because they recover a sense of dignity in insurrection?), this is given subjective reality, that is, there are certain beliefs, affective reactions, evaluations which individuals make or have about or in relation to social reality. These beliefs or reactions can have an effect on this reality; and the fact that such a belief is held is a fact of objective social reality. But the social reality which is the object of these attitudes, beliefs, reactions can only be made up of brute data. Thus any description of reality in terms of meanings which is open to interpretive question is only allowed into this scientific discourse if it is placed, as it were, in quotes and attributed to individuals as their opinion, belief, attitude. That this opinion, belief, and so forth is held is thought of as a brute datum, since it is redefined as the respondent's giving a certain answer to the question- naire.

This aspect of social reality which concerns its meanings for the agents has been taken up in a number of ways, but recently it has been spoken of in terms of political culture. Now the way this is defined and studied illustrates clearly the categorical principles above. For instance, political culture is referred to by Almond and Powell[7] as the "psychological dimension of the political system" (p.23). Further on they state: "Political culture is the pattern of individual attitudes and orientations towards politics among the members of a political sys- tem. It is the subjective realm which underlies and gives meaning to political actions" (p. 50). The authors then go on to distinguish three different kinds of orientations, cognitive (knowledge and beliefs), af- fective (feelings), and evaluative (judgments and opinions).

From the point of view of empiricist epistemology, this set of categorical principles leaves nothing out. Both reality and the mean- ings it has for actors are coped with. But what it in fact cannot allow for are intersubjective meanings, that is, it cannot allow for the va- lidity of descriptions of social reality in terms of meanings, hence not as brute data, which are not in quotation marks and attributed as opinion, attitude, and so forth to individual(s). Now it is this exclu- sion that I should like to challenge in the name of another set of categorical principles, inspired by a quite other epistemology.

ii

We spoke earlier about the brute data identification of acts by means of institutional rules. Thus, putting a cross beside someones's name on a slip of paper and putting this in a box counts in the right context as voting for that person; leaving the room, saying or writing a certain form of words, counts as breaking off the negotiations; writ- ing one's name on a piece of paper counts as signing the petition, and so forth. But what is worth looking at is what underlies this set of identifications. These identifications are the application of a language of social life, a language which marks distinctions among different

7. Gabriel A. Almond and G. Bingham Powell, *Comparative Politics: A Devel- opmental Approach* (Boston and Toronto, 1966). Page references in my text here and below are to this work.

possible social acts, relations, structures. But what underlies this language?

Let us take the example of breaking off negotiations above. The language of our society recognizes states or actions like the following: entering into negotiation, breaking off negotiations, offering to negotiate, negotiating in good (bad) faith, concluding negotiations, making a new offer. In other more jargon-infested language, the semantic "space" of this range of social activity is carved up in a certain way, by a certain set of distinctions which our vocabulary marks; and the shape and nature of these distinctions is the nature of our language in this area. These distinctions are applied in our society with more or less formalism in different contexts.

But of course this is not true of every society. Our whole notion of negotiation is bound up, for instance, with the distinct identity and autonomy of the parties, with the willed nature of their relations; it is a very contractual notion. But other societies have no such conception. It is reported about the traditional Japanese village that the foundation of its social life was a powerful form of consensus, which put a high premium on unanimous decision.[8] Such a consenus would be considered shattered if two clearly articulated parties were to separate out, pursuing opposed aims and attempting either to vote down the opposition or push it into a settlement on the most favorable possible terms for themselves. Discussion there must be, and some kind of adjustment of differences. But our idea of bargaining, with the assumption of distinct autonomous parties in willed relationship, has no place there; nor does a series of distinctions, like entering into and leaving negotiation, or bargaining in good faith (sc. with the genuine intention of seeking agreement).

Now the difference between our society and one of the kind just described could not be well expressed if we said we have a vocabulary to describe negotiation which they lack. We might say, for instance, that we have a vocabulary to describe the heavens that they lack, namely, that of Newtonian mechanics; for here we assume that they live under the same heavens as we do, only understand it differently. But it is not true that they have the same kind of bargaining as we do.

8. Cf. Thomas C. Smith, *The Agrarian Origins of Modern Japan* (Stanford, 1959), chap. 5. This type of consensus is also found in other traditional societies. Cf. for instance, the *desa* system of the Indonesian village.

The word, or whatever word of their language we translate as "bargaining," must have an entirely different gloss, which is marked by the distinctions their vocabulary allows in contrast to those marked by ours. But this different gloss is not just a difference of vocabulary, but also one of social reality.

But this still may be misleading as a way of putting the difference. For it might imply that there is a social reality which can be discovered in each society and which might exist quite independently of the vocabulary of that society, or indeed of any vocabulary, as the heavens would exist whether men theorized about them or not. And this is not the case; the realities here are practices; and these cannot be identified in abstraction from the language we use to describe them, or invoke them, or carry them out. That the practice of negotiation allows us to distinguish bargaining in good or bad faith, or entering into or breaking off negotiations, presupposes that our acts and situation have a certain description for us, for example, that we are distinct parties entering into willed relations. But they cannot have these descriptions for us unless this is somehow expressed in our vocabulary of this practice; if not in our descriptions of the practices (for we may as yet be unconscious of some of the important distinctions) in the appropriate language for carrying them on. (Thus, the language marking a distinction between public and private acts or contexts may exist even where these terms or their equivalents are not part of this language; for the distinction will be marked by the different language which is appropriate in one context and the other, be it perhaps a difference of style, or dialect, even though the distinction is not designated by specific descriptive expressions.)

The situation we have here is one in which the vocabulary of a given social dimension is grounded in the shape of social practice in this dimension; that is, the vocabulary would not make sense, could not be applied sensibly, where this range of practices did not prevail. And yet this range of practices could not exist without the prevalence of this or some related vocabulary. There is no simple one-way dependence here. We can speak of mutual dependence if we like, but really what this points up is the artificiality of the distinction between social reality and the language of description of that social reality. The language is constitutive of the reality, is essential to its being the kind of reality it is. To separate the two and distinguish them as we quite rightly distinguish the heavens from our theories about them is forever to miss the point.

This type of relation has been recently explored, for example, by John Searle, with his concept of a constitutive rule. As Searle points out,[9] we are normally induced to think of rules as applying to behavior which could be available to us whether or not the rule existed. Some rules are like this, they are regulative like commandments: don't take the goods of another. But there are other rules, for example, that governing the Queen's move in chess, which are not so separable. If one suspends these rules, or imagines a state in which they have not yet been introduced, then the whole range of behavior in question, in this case, chess playing, would not be. There would still, of course, be the activity of pushing a wood piece around on an eight-by-eight-inch board made of squares; but this is not chess any longer. Rules of this kind are constitutive rules. By contrast again, there are other rules of chess, such as that one say "j'adoube" when one touches a piece without intending to play it, which are clearly regulative.[10]

I am suggesting that this notion of the constitutive be extended beyond the domain of rule-governed behavior. That is why I suggest the vaguer word "practice." Even in an area where there are no clearly defined rules, there are distinctions between different sorts of behavior such that one sort is considered the appropriate form for one action or context, the other for another action or context; for example, doing or saying certain things amounts to breaking off negotiations, doing or saying other things amounts to making a new offer. But just as there are constitutive rules, that is, rules such that the behavior they govern could not exist without them, and which are in this sense inseparable from that behavior, so I am suggesting that there are constitutive distinctions, constitutive ranges of language which are similarly inseparable, in that certain practices are not without them.

We can reverse this relationship and say that all the institutions and practices by which we live are constituted by certain distinctions and hence a certain language which is thus essential to them. We can take voting, a practice which is central to large numbers of institutions in a democratic society. What is essential to the practice of voting is that

9. J. Searle, *Speech Acts: An Essay in the Philosophy of Language* (Cambridge, 1969), pp. 33–42.
10. Cf. the discussion in Stanley Cavell, *Must We Mean What We Say?* (New York, 1969), pp. 21–31.

some decision or verdict be delivered (a man elected, a measure passed), through some criterion of preponderance (simple majority, two-thirds majority, or whatever) out of a set of micro-choices (the votes of the citizens, MPs, delegates). If there is not some such significance attached to our behavior, no amount of marking and counting pieces of paper, raising hands, walking out into lobbies amounts to voting. From this it follows that the institution of voting must be such that certain distinctions have application: for example, that between someone being elected, or a measure passed, and their failing of election, or passage; that between a valid vote and an invalid one which in turn requires a distinction between a real choice and one which is forced or counterfeited. For no matter how far we move from the Rousseauian notion that each man decide in full autonomy, the very institution of the vote requires that in some sense the enfranchised choose. For there to be voting in a sense recognizably like ours, there must be a distinction in men's self-interpretations between autonomy and forced choice.

This is to say that an activity of marking and counting papers has to bear intentional descriptions which fall within a certain range before we can agree to call it voting, just as the intercourse of two men or teams has to bear descriptions of a certain range before we will call it negotiation. Or in other words, that some practice is voting or negotiation has to do in part with the vocabulary established in a society as appropriate for engaging in it or describing it.

Hence implicit in these practices is a certain vision of the agent and his relation to others and to society. We saw in connection with negotiation in our society that it requires a picture of the parties as in some sense autonomous, and as entering into willed relations. And this picture carries with it certain implicit norms, such as that of good faith mentioned above, or a norm of rationality, that agreement correspond to one's goals as far as attainable, or the norm of continued freedom of action as far as attainable. These practices require that one's actions and relations be seen in the light of this picture and the accompanying norms, good faith, autonomy, and rationality. But men do not see themselves in this way in all societies, nor do they understand these norms in all societies. The experience of autonomy as we know it, the sense of rational action and the satisfactions thereof, are unavailable to them. The meaning of these terms is opaque to them because they have a different structure of experiential meaning open to them.

We can think of the difference between our society and the simplified version of the traditional Japanese village as consisting in this, that the range of meaning open to the members of the two societies is very different. But what we are dealing with here is not subjective meaning which can fit into the categorical grid of behavioral political science, but rather intersubjective meanings. It is not just that the people in our society all or most have a given set of ideas in their heads and subscribe to a given set of goals. The meanings and norms implicit in these practices are not just in the minds of the actors but are out there in the practices themselves, practices which cannot be conceived as a set of individual actions, but which are essentially modes of social relation, of mutual action.

The actors may have all sorts of beliefs and attitudes which may be rightly thought of as their individual beliefs and attitudes, even if others share them; they may subscribe to certain policy goals or certain forms of theory about the polity, or feel resentment at certain things, and so on. They bring these with them into their negotiations, and strive to satisfy them. But what they do not bring into the negotiations is the set of ideas and norms constitutive of negotiation themselves. These must be the common property of the society before there can be any question of anyone entering into negotiation or not. Hence they are not subjective meanings, the property of one or some individuals, but rather intersubjective meanings, which are constitutive of the social matrix in which individuals find themselves and act.

The intersubjective meanings which are the background to social action are often treated by political scientists under the heading "consensus." By this is meant convergence of beliefs on certain basic matters, or of attitude. But the two are not the same. Whether there is consensus or not, the condition of there being either one or the other is a certain set of common terms of reference. A society in which this was lacking would not be a society in the normal sense of the term, but several. Perhaps some multi-racial or multi-tribal states approach this limit. Some multi-national states are bedevilled by consistent cross-purposes, for example, Canada. But consensus as a convergence of beliefs or values is not the opposite of this kind of fundamental diversity. Rather the opposite of diversity is a high degree of intersubjective meanings. And this can go along with profound cleavage. Indeed, intersubjective meanings are a condition of a certain kind of very profound cleavage, such as was visible in the Reformation, or the American Civil War, or splits in left-wing parties, where the dispute is at fever pitch just because both sides can fully understand the other.

In other words, convergence of belief or attitude or its absence presupposes a common language in which these beliefs can be formulated, and in which these formulations can be opposed. Much of this common language in any society is rooted in its institutions and practices; it is constitutive of these institutions and practices. It is part of the intersubjective meanings. To put the point another way, apart from the question of how much people's beliefs converge is the question of how much they have a common language of social and political reality in which these beliefs are expressed. This second question cannot be reduced to the first; intersubjective meaning is not a matter of converging beliefs or values. When we speak of consensus we speak of beliefs and values which could be the property of a single person, or many, or all; but intersubjective meanings could not be the property of a single person because they are rooted in social practice.

We can perhaps see this if we envisage the situation in which the ideas and norms underlying a practice are the property of single individuals. This is what happens when single individuals from one society interiorize the notions and values of another, for example, children in missionary schools. Here we have a totally different situation. We *are* really talking now about subjective beliefs and attitudes. The ideas are abstract, they are mere social "ideals." Whereas in the original society, these ideas and norms are rooted in their social relations, and are that on the basis of which they can formulate opinions and ideals.

We can see this in connection with the example we have been using all along, that of negotiations. The vision of a society based on negotiation is coming in for heavy attack by a growing segment of modern youth, as are the attendant norms of rationality and the definition of autonomy. This is a dramatic failure of "consensus." But this cleavage takes place in the ambit of this intersubjective meaning, the social practice of negotiation as it is lived in our society. The rejection would not have the bitter quality it has if what is rejected were not understood in common, because it is part of a social practice which we find hard to avoid, so pervasive is it in our society. At the same time there is a reaching out for other forms which have still the "abstract" quality of ideals which are subjective in this sense, that is, not rooted in practice; which is what makes the rebellion look so "unreal" to outsiders, and so irrational.

Intersubjective meanings, ways of experiencing action in society which are expressed in the language and descriptions constitutive of institutions and practices, do not fit into the categorical grid of mainstream political science. This allows only for an intersubjective reality which is brute data identifiable. But social practices and institutions which are partly constituted by certain ways of talking about them are not so identifiable. We have to understand the language, the underlying meanings, which constitute them.

We can allow, once we accept a certain set of institutions or practices as our starting point and not as objects of further questioning, that we can easily take as brute data that certain acts are judged to take place or certain states judged to hold within the semantic field of these practices. For instance, that someone has voted Liberal or signed the petition. We can then go on to correlate certain subjective meanings — beliefs, attitudes, and so forth — with this behavior or its lack. But this means that we give up trying to define further just what these practices and institutions are, what the meanings are which they require and hence sustain. For these meanings do not fit into the grid; they are not subjective beliefs or values, but are constitutive of social reality. In order to get at them we have to drop the basic premise that social reality is made up of brute data alone. For any characterization of the meanings underlying these practices is open to question by someone offering an alternative interpretation. The negation of this is what was meant as brute data. We have to admit that intersubjective social reality has to be partly defined in terms of meanings; that meanings as subjective are not just in causal interaction with a social reality made up of brute data, but that as intersubjective they are constitutive of this reality.

We have been talking here of intersubjective meanings. And earlier I was contrasting the question of intersubjective meaning with that of consensus as convergence of opinions. But there is another kind of nonsubjective meaning which is also often inadequately discussed under the head of "consensus." In a society with a strong web of

intersubjective meanings, there can be a more or less powerful set of
common meanings. By these I mean notions of what is significant
which are not just shared in the sense that everyone has them, but are
also common in the sense of being in the common reference world.
Thus, almost everyone in our society may share a susceptibility to a
certain kind of feminine beauty, but this may not be a common meaning. It may be known to no one, except perhaps market researchers,
who play on it in their advertisements. But the survival of a national
identity as francophones is a common meaning of *Québecois*; for it is
not just shared, and not just known to be shared, but its being a
common aspiration is one of the common reference points of all debate, communication, and all public life in the society.

We can speak of a shared belief, aspiration, and so forth when there
is convergence between the subjective beliefs, aspirations, of many
individuals. But it is part of the meaning of a common aspiration,
belief, celebration, that it be not just shared but part of the common
reference world. Or to put it another way, its being shared is a collective act, it is a consciousness which is communally sustained, whereas
sharing is something we do each on his own, as it were, even if each of
us is influenced by the others.

Common meanings are the basis of community. Intersubjective
meaning gives a people a common language to talk about social reality
and a common understanding of certain norms, but only with common meanings does this common reference world contain significant
common actions, celebrations, and feelings. These are objects in the
world that everybody shares. This is what makes community.

Once again, we cannot really understand this phenomenon
through the usual definition of consensus as convergence of opinion
and value. For what is meant here is something more than convergence. Convergence is what happens when our values are shared.
But what is required for common meanings is that this shared value be
part of the common world, that this sharing be shared. But we could
also say that common meanings are quite other than consensus, for
they can subsist with a high degree of cleavage; this is what happens
when a common meaning comes to be lived and understood differently by different groups in a society. It remains a common meaning,
because there is the reference point which is the common purpose,
aspiration, celebration. Such is, for example, the American Way, or

freedom as understood in the U.S.A. But this common meaning is differently articulated by different groups. This is the basis of the bitterest fights in a society, and this we are also seeing in the U.S. today. Perhaps one might say that a common meaning is very often the cause of the most bitter lack of consensus. It thus must not be confused with convergence of opinion, value, attitude.

Of course, common meanings and intersubjective meanings are closely interwoven. There must be a powerful net of intersubjective meanings for there to be common meanings; and the result of powerful common meanings is the development of a greater web of intersubjective meanings as people live in community.

On the other hand, when common meanings wither, which they can do through the kind of deep dissensus we described earlier, the groups tend to grow apart and develop different languages of social reality, hence to share less intersubjective meanings.

Hence, to take our above example again, there has been a powerful common meaning in our civilization around a certain vision of the free society in which bargaining has a central place. This has helped to entrench the social practice of negotiation which makes us participate in this intersubjective meaning. But there is a severe challenge to this common meaning today, as we have seen. Should those who object to it really succeed in building up an alternative society, there would develop a gap between those who remain in the present type of society and those who had founded the new one.

Common meanings, as well as intersubjective ones, fall through the net of mainstream social science. They can find no place in its categories. For they are not simply a converging set of subjective reactions, but part of the common world. What the ontology of mainstream social science lacks is the notion of meaning as not simply for an individual subject; of a subject who can be a "we" as well as an "I." The exclusion of this possibility, of the communal, comes once again from the baleful influence of the epistemological tradition for which all knowledge has to be reconstructed from the impressions imprinted on the individual subject. But if we free ourselves from the hold of these prejudices, this seems a wildly implausible view about the development of human consciousness; we are aware of the world through a "we" before we are through an "I." Hence we need the distinction between what is just shared in the sense that each of us has it in our individual worlds, and that which is in the common world. But the very idea of something which is in the common world in contradistinction to what is in all the individual worlds is totally opaque to empiricist epistemology. Hence it finds no place in mainstream social science. What this results in must now be seen.

III

i

Thus, to sum up the last pages: a social science which wishes to fulfill the requirements of the empiricist tradition naturally tries to reconstruct social reality as consisting of brute data alone. These data are the acts of people (behavior) as identified supposedly beyond interpretation either by physical descriptions or by descriptions clearly defined by institutions and practices; and secondly, they include the subjective reality of individuals' beliefs, attitudes, values, as attested by their responses to certain forms of words, or in some cases their overt non-verbal behavior.

What this excludes is a consideration of social reality as characterized by intersubjective and common meanings. It excludes, for instance, an attempt to understand our civilization, in which negotiation plays such a central part both in fact and in justificatory theory, by probing the self-definitions of agent, other and social relatedness which it embodies. Such definitions which deal with the meaning for agents of their own and others' action, and of the social relations in which they stand, do not in any sense record brute data, in the sense that this term is being used in this argument; that is, they are in no sense beyond challenge by those who would quarrel with our interpretations of these meanings.

Thus, I tried to adumbrate above the vision implicit in the practice of negotiation by reference to certain notions of autonomy and rationality. But this reading will undoubtedly be challenged by those who have different fundamental conceptions of man, human motivation, the human condition; or even by those who judge other features of our present predicament to have greater importance. If we wish to avoid these disputes, and have a science grounded in verification as this is understood by the logical empiricists, then we have to avoid this level of study altogether and hope to make do with a correlation of behavior which is brute data identifiable.

A similar point goes for the distinction between common meanings and shared subjective meanings. We can hope to identify the subjective meanings of individuals if we take these in the sense in which there are adequate criteria for them in people's dissent or assent to verbal formulae or their brute data indentifiable behavior. But once we allow the distinction between such subjective meanings which are widely shared and genuine common meanings, then we can no longer make do with brute data identification. We are in a domain where our definitions can be challenged by those with another reading.

The profound option of mainstream social scientists for the empiricist conception of knowledge and science makes it inevitable that they should accept the verification model of political science and the categorical principles that this entails. This means in turn that a study of our civilization in terms of its intersubjective and common meanings is ruled out. Rather this whole level of study is made invisible.

On the mainstream view, therefore, the different practices and institutions of different societies are not seen as related to different clusters of intersubjective or common meanings, rather, we should be able to differentiate them by different clusters of "behavior" and/or subjective meaning. The comparison between societies requires on this view that we elaborate a universal vocabulary of behavior which will allow us to present the different forms and practices of different societies in the same conceptual web.

Now present-day political science is contemptuous of the older attempt at comparative politics through a comparison of institutions. An influential school of our day has therefore shifted comparison to certain practices, or very general classes of practices, and proposes to compare societies according to the different ways in which these practices are carried on. Such are the "functions" of the influential "developmental approach."[11] But it is epistemologically crucial that such functions be identified independently of those intersubjective meanings which are different in different societies; for otherwise, they will not be genuinely universal; or will be universal only in the loose and unilluminating sense that the function-name can be given application in every society but with varying, and often widely varying meaning — the same term being "glossed" very differently by different sets of practices and intersubjective meanings. The danger that such

11. Cf. Almond and Powell, *Comparative Politics.*

universality might not hold is not even suspected by mainstream political scientists since they are unaware that there is such a level of description as that which defines intersubjective meanings and are convinced that functions and the various structures which perform them
can be identified in terms of brute data behavior.

But the result of ignoring the difference in intersubjective meanings can be disastrous to a science of comparative politics, namely, that
we interpret all other societies in the categories of our own. Ironically,
this is what seems to have happened to American political science.
Having strongly criticized the old institution-focussed comparative
politics for its ethnocentricity (or Western bias), it proposes to understand the politics of all society in terms of such functions, for instance,
as "interest articulation" and "interest aggregation" whose definition
is strongly influenced by the bargaining culture of our civilization, but
which is far from being guaranteed appropriateness elsewhere. The
not surprising result is a theory of political development which places
the Atlantic-type polity at the summit of human political achievement.

Much can be said in this area of comparative politics (interestingly
explored by Alasdair MacIntyre in a recently published paper).[12] But I
should like to illustrate the significance of these two rival approaches
in connection with another common problem area of politics. This is
the question of what is called "legitimacy."[13]

ii

It is an obvious fact, with which politics has been concerned since
at least Plato, that some societies enjoy an easier, more spontaneous
cohesion which relies less on the use of force than others. It has been
an important question of political theory to understand what underlies
this difference. Among others, Aristotle, Machiavelli, Montesquieu,
de Tocqueville have dealt with it.

Contemporary mainstream political scientists approach this question with the concept "legitimacy." The use of the word here can be
easily understood. Those societies which are more spontaneously
cohesive can be thought to enjoy a greater sense of legitimacy among

12. "How Is a Comparative Science of Politics Possible?" in Alasdair MacIntyre,
Against the Self-Images of the Age (London, 1971).
13. MacIntyre's article also contains an interesting discussion of "legitimacy" from
a different, although I think related, angle.

their members. But the application of the term has been shifted. "Legitimacy" is a term in which we discuss the authority of the state or polity, its right to our allegiance. However we conceive of this legitimacy, it can only be attributed to a polity in the light of a number of surrounding conceptions — for example, that it provides men freedom, that it emanates from their will, that it secures them order, the rule of law, or that it is founded on tradition, or commands obedience by its superior qualities. These conceptions are all such that they rely on definitions of what is significant for men in general or in some particular society or circumstances, definitions of paradigmatic meaning which cannot be identifiable as brute data. Even where some of these terms might be given an "operational definition" in terms of brute data — a term like "freedom," for instance, can be defined in terms of the absence of legal restriction, à la Hobbes — this definition would not carry the full force of the term, and in particular that whereby it could be considered significant for men.

According to the empiricist paradigm, this latter aspect of the meaning of such a term is labelled "evaluative" and is thought to be utterly heterogeneous from the "descriptive" aspect. But this analysis is far from firmly established; no more so in fact than the empiricist paradigm of knowledge itself with which it is closely bound up. A challenge to this paradigm in the name of a hermeneutical science is also a challenge to the distinction between "descriptive" and "evaluative" and the entire conception of *"Wertfreiheit"* which goes with it.

In any case, whether because it is "evaluative" or can only be applied in connection with definitions of meaning, "legitimate" is not a word which can be used in the description of social reality according to the conceptions of mainstream social science. It can only be used as a description of subjective meaning. What enters into scientific consideration is thus not the legitimacy of a polity but the opinions or feelings of its member individuals concerning its legitimacy. The differences between different societies in their manner of spontaneous cohesion and sense of community are to be understood by correlations between the beliefs and feelings of their members towards them on one hand and the prevalence of certain brute data identifiable indices of stability in them on the other.

Thus Robert Dahl in *Modern Political Analysis*[14] (pp. 31–32) speaks of

14. Englewood Cliffs N.J., 1963. Foundation of Modern Political Science Series.

the different ways in which leaders gain "compliance" for their policies. The more citizens comply because of "internal rewards and deprivations," the less leaders need to use "external rewards and deprivations." But if citizens believe a government is legitimate, then their conscience will bind them to obey it; they will be internally punished if they disobey; hence government will have to use less external resources, including force.

Less crude is the discussion of Seymour Lipset in *Political Man*[15] (chap. 3). But it is founded on the same basic ideas, namely, that legitimacy defined as subjective meaning is correlated with stability. "Legitimacy involves the capacity of the system to engender and maintain the belief that the existing political institutions are the most appropriate ones for the society" (p. 64).

Lipset is engaged in a discussion of the determinants of stability in modern polities. He singles out two important ones in this chapter, effectiveness and legitimacy. "Effectiveness means actual performance, the extent to which the system satisfies the basic functions of government as most of the population and such powerful groups within it as big business or the armed forces see them" (p. 64). Thus we have one factor which has to do with objective reality, what the government has actually done; and the other which has to do with subjective beliefs and "values." "While effectiveness is primarily instrumental, legitimacy is evaluative" (p. 64). Hence from the beginning the stage is set by a distinction between social reality and what men think and feel about it.

Lipset sees two types of crisis of legitimacy that modern societies have affronted more or less well. One concerns the status of major conservative institutions which may be under threat from the development of modern industrial democracies. The second concerns the degree to which all political groups have access to the political process. Thus, under the first head, some traditional groups, such as landed aristocracy or clericals, have been roughly handled in a society like France, and have remained alienated from the democratic system for decades afterwards; whereas in England the traditional classes were more gently handled, themselves were willing to compromise and have been slowly integrated and transformed into the new order. Under the second head, some societies managed to integrate the work-

15. New York, 1963. Page references are to this edition.

ing class or bourgeoisie into the political process at an early stage, whereas in others they have been kept out till quite recently, and consequently, have developed a deep sense of alienation from the system, have tended to adopt extremist ideologies, and have generally contributed to instability. One of the determinants of a society's performance on these two heads is whether or not it is forced to affront the different conflicts of democratic development all at once or one at a time. Another important determinant of legitimacy is effectiveness.

This approach which sees stability as partly the result of legitimacy beliefs, and these in turn as resulting partly from the way the status, welfare, access to political life of different groups fare, seems at first blush eminently sensible and well designed to help us understand the history of the last century or two. But this approach has no place for a study of the intersubjective and common meanings which are constitutive of modern civilization. And we may doubt whether we can understand the cohesion of modern societies or their present crisis if we leave these out of account.

Let us take the winning of the allegiance of the working class to the new industrial regimes in the nineteenth and the early twentieth century. This is far from being a matter simply or even perhaps most significantly of the speed with which this class was integrated into the political process and the effectiveness of the regime. Rather the consideration of the granting of access to the political process as an independent variable may be misleading.

It is not just that we often find ourselves invited by historians to account for class cohesion in particular countries in terms of other factors, such as the impact of Methodism in early nineteenth century England (Elie Halévy)[16] or the draw of Germany's newly successful nationalism. These factors could be assimilated to the social scientist's grid by being classed as "ideologies" or widely held "value-systems" or some other such concatenations of subjective meaning.

But perhaps the most important such "ideology" in accounting for the cohesion of industrial democratic societies has been that of the society of work, the vision of society as a large-scale enterprise of production in which widely different functions are integrated into interdependence; a vision of society in which economic relations are considered as primary, as it is not only in Marxism (and in a sense not

16. *Histoire du Peuple anglais au XIXᵉ siècle* (Paris, 1913).

really with Marxism) but above all with the tradition of Classical Utilitarianism. In line with this vision there is a fundamental solidarity between all members of society that labor (to use Arendt's language),[17] for they are all engaged in producing what is indispensable to life and happiness in far-reaching interdependence.

This is the "ideology" which has frequently presided over the integration of the working class into industrial democracies, at first directed polemically against the "unproductive" classes, for example, in England with the anti-Corn Law League, and later with the campaigns of Joseph Chamberlain ("when Adam delved and Eve span/ who was then the gentleman"), but later as a support for social cohesion and solidarity.

But, of course, the reason for putting "ideology" in quotes above is that this definition of things, which has been well integrated with the conception of social life as based on negotiation, cannot be understood in the terms of mainstream social science, as beliefs and "values" held by a large number of individuals. For the great interdependent matrix of labor is not just a set of ideas in people's heads but is an important aspect of the reality which we live in modern society. And at the same time, these ideas are embedded in this matrix in that they are constitutive of it; that is, we would not be able to live in this type of society unless we were imbued with these ideas or some others which could call forth the discipline and voluntary coordination needed to operate this kind of economy. All industrial civilizations have required a huge wrench from the traditional peasant populations on which they have been imposed; for they require an entirely unprecedented level of disciplined sustained, monotonous effort, long hours unpunctuated by any meaningful rhythm, such as that of seasons or festivals. In the end this way of life can only be accepted when the idea of making a living is endowed with more significance than that of just avoiding starvation; and this it is in the civilization of labor.

Now this civilization of work is only one aspect of modern societies, along with the society based on negotiation and willed relations (in Anglo-Saxon countries), and other common and intersubjective meanings which have different importance in different countries. My point is that it is certainly not implausible to say that it has some importance in explaining the integration of the working class in

17. *The Human Condition* (New York, 1959).

modern industrial democratic society. But it can only be called a clus-
ter of intersubjective meaning. As such it cannot come into the pur-
view of mainstream political science; and an author like Lipset cannot
take it into consideration when discussing this very problem.

But, of course, such a massive fact does not escape notice. What
happens rather is that it is reinterpreted. And what has generally happened is that the interdependent productive and negotiating society
has been recognized by political science, but not as one structure of
intersubjective meaning among others, rather as the inescapable background of social action as such. In this guise it no longer need be an
object of study. Rather it retreats to the middle distance, where its
general outline takes the role of universal framework, within which (it
is hoped) actions and structures will be brute data identifiable, and this
for any society at any time. The view is then that the political actions
of men in all societies can be understood as variants of the processing
of "demands" which is an important part of our political life. The
inability to recognize the specificity of our intersubjective meanings is
thus inseparably linked with the belief in the universality of North
Atlantic behavior types or "functions" which vitiates so much of contemporary comparative politics.

The notion is that what politics is about perennially is the adjustment of differences, or the production of symbolic and effective "out-
puts" on the basis of demand and support "inputs." The rise of the
intersubjective meaning of the civilization of work is seen as the increase of correct perception of the political process at the expense of
"ideology." Thus Almond and Powell introduce the concept of "political secularization" to describe "the emergence of a pragmatic, empirical orientation" to politics (p. 58).[18] A secular political culture is
opposed not only to a traditional one, but also to an "ideological"
culture, which is characterized by "an inflexible image of political life,
closed to conflicting information" and "fails to develop the open,
bargaining attitudes associated with full secularization" (p. 61). The
clear understanding here is that a secularized culture is one which
essentially depends less on illusion, which sees things as they are,
which is not infected with the "false consciousness" of traditional or
ideological culture (to use a term which is not in the mainstream
vocabulary).

18. *Comparative Politics.*

iii

This way of looking at the civilization of work, as resulting from the retreat of illusion before the correct perception of what politics perennially and really is, is thus closely bound up with the epistemological premises of mainstream political science and its resultant inability to recognize the historical specificity of this civilization's intersubjective meanings. But the weakness of this approach, already visible in the attempts to explain the rise of this civilization and its relation to others, becomes even more painful when we try to account for its present malaise, even crisis.

The strains in contemporary society, the breakdown of civility, the rise of deep alienation, which is translated into even more destructive action, tend to shake the basic categories of our social science. It is not just that such a development was quite unpredicted by this science, which saw in the rise of affluence the cause rather of a further entrenching of the bargaining culture, a reduction of irrational cleavage, an increase of tolerance, in short "the end of ideology." For prediction, as we shall see below, cannot be a goal of social science as it is of natural science. It is rather that this mainstream science does not have the categories to explain this breakdown. It is forced to look on extremism either as a bargaining gambit of the desperate, deliberately raising the ante in order to force a hearing. Or, alternatively, it can recognize the novelty of the rebellion by accepting the hypothesis that heightened demands are being made on the system owing to a revolution of "expectations," or else to the eruption of new desires or aspirations which hitherto had no place in the bargaining process. But these new desires or aspirations must be in the domain of individual psychology, that is, they must be such that their arousal and satisfaction is to be understood in terms of states of individuals rather than in terms of the intersubjective meanings in which they live. For these latter have no place in the categories of the mainstream, which thus cannot accommodate a genuine historical psychology.

But some of the more extreme protests and acts of rebellion in our society cannot be interpreted as bargaining gambits in the name of any demands, old or new. These can only be interpreted within the accepted framework of our social science as a return to ideology, and hence as irrational. Now in the case of some of the more bizarre and bloody forms of protest, there will be little disagreement; they will be judged irrational by all but their protagonists. But within the accepted categories this irrationality can only be understood in terms of individual psychology; it is the public eruption of private pathology; it cannot be understood as a malady of society itself, a malaise which afflicts its constitutive meanings.[19]

No one can claim to begin to have an adequate explanation for these major changes which our civilization is undergoing. But in contrast to the incapacity of a science which remains within the accepted categories, a hermeneutical science of man which has a place for a study of intersubjective meaning can at least begin to explore fruitful avenues. Plainly the discipline which was integral to the civilization of work and bargaining is beginning to fail. The structures of this civilization, interdependent work, bargaining, mutual adjustment of individual ends, are beginning to change their meaning for many, and are beginning to be felt not as normal and best suited to man, but as hateful or empty. And yet we are all caught in these intersubjective meanings insofar as we live in this society, and in a sense more and more all-pervasively as it progresses. Hence the virulence and tension of the critique of our society which is always in some real sense a self-rejection (in a way that the old socialist opposition never was).

Why has this set of meanings gone sour? Plainly, we have to accept that they are not to be understood at their face value. The free, productive, bargaining culture claimed to be sufficient for man. If it was not, then we have to assume that while it did hold our allegiance, it also had other meanings for us which commanded this allegiance and which have now gone.

This is the starting point of a set of hypotheses which attempt to redefine our past in order to make our present and future intelligible. We might think that the productive, bargaining culture offered in the past common meanings (even though there was no place for them in its philosophy), and hence a basis for community, which were essen-

19. Thus Lewis Feuer in *The Conflict of Generations* (New York, 1969), attempts to account for the "misperception of social reality" in the Berkeley student uprising in terms of a generational conflict (pp. 466–470), which in turn is rooted in the psychology of adolescence and attaining adulthood. Yet Feuer himself in his first chapter notes the comparative recency of self-defining political generations, a phenomenon which dates from the post-Napoleonic era (p. 33). But an adequate attempt to explain this historical shift, which after all underlies the Berkeley rising and many others, would, I believe,

tially linked with its being in the process of building. It linked men who could see themselves as breaking with the past to build a new happiness in America, for instance. But in all essentials that future is built; the notion of a horizon to be attained by future greater production (as against social transformation) verges on the absurd in contemporary America. Suddenly the horizon which was essential to the sense of meaningful purpose has collapsed, which would show that like so many other Enlightenment-based dreams the free, productive, bargaining society can only sustain man as a goal, not as a reality.

Or we can look at this development in terms of identity. A sense of building their future through the civilization of work can sustain men as long as they see themselves as having broken with a millennial past of injustice and hardship in order to create qualitatively different conditions for their children. All the requirements of a humanly acceptable identity can be met by this predicament, a relation to the past (one soars above it but preserves it in folkloric memory), to the social world (the interdependent world of free, productive men), to the earth (the raw material which awaits shaping), to the future and one's own death (the everlasting monument in the lives of prosperous children), to the absolute (the absolute values of freedom, integrity, dignity).

But at some point the children will be unable to sustain this forward thrust into the future. This effort has placed them in a private haven of security, within which they are unable to reach and recover touch with the great realities: their parents have only a negated past, lives which have been oriented wholly to the future; the social world is distant and without shape; rather one can only insert oneself into it by taking one's place in the future-oriented productive juggernaught. But this now seems without any sense; the relation to the earth as raw material is therefore experienced as empty and alienating, but the recovery of a valid relation to the earth is the hardest thing once lost; and there is no relation to the absolute where we are caught in the web of meanings which have gone dead for us. Hence past, future, earth, world, and absolute are in some way or another occluded; and what must arise is an identity crisis of frightening proportions.

---

have to take us beyond the ambit of individual psychology to psycho-history, to a study of the intrication of psychological conflict and intersubjective meanings. A variant of this form of study has been adumbrated in the work of Erik Erikson.

These two hypotheses are mainly focussed on the crisis in U.S. civilization, and they would perhaps help account for the fact that the United States is in some sense going first through this crisis of all Atlantic nations; not, that is, only because it is the most affluent, but more because it is has been more fully based on the civilization of work than European countries who retained something of more traditional common meanings.

But they might also help us to understand why alienation is most severe among groups which have been but marginal in affluent bargaining societies. These have had the greatest strain in living in this civilization while their identity was in some ways antithetical to it. Such are blacks in the United States, and the community of French-speaking Canadians, each in different ways. For many immigrant groups the strain was also great, but they forced themselves to surmount the obstacles, and the new identity is sealed in the blood of the old, as it were.

But for those who would not or could not succeed in thus transforming themselves, but always lived a life of strain on the defensive, the breakdown of the central, powerful identity is the trigger to a deep turn-over. It can be thought of as a liberation, but at the same time it is deeply unsettling, because the basic parameters of former life are being changed, and there are not yet the new images and definitions to live a new fully acceptable identity. In a sense we are in a condition where a new social compact (rather the first social compact) has to be made between these groups and those they live with, and no one knows where to start.

In the last pages, I have presented some hypotheses which may appear very speculative; and they may indeed turn out to be without foundation, even without much interest. But their aim was mainly illustrative. My principal claim is that we can only come to grips with this phenomenon of breakdown by trying to understand more clearly and profoundly the common and intersubjective meanings of the society in which we have been living. For it is these which no longer hold us, and to understand this change we have to have an adequate grasp of these meanings. But this we cannot do as long as we remain within the ambit of mainstream social science, for it will not recognize intersubjective meaning, and is forced to look at the central ones of our society as though they were the inescapable background of all political

action. Breakdown is thus inexplicable in political terms; it is an outbreak of irrationality which must ultimately be explained by some
form of psychological illness.

Mainstream science may thus venture into the area explored by the
above hypotheses, but after its own fashion, by forcing the psycho-
historical facts of identity into the grid of an individual psychology, in
short, by reinterpreting all meanings as subjective. The result might
be a psychological theory of emotional maladjustment, perhaps traced
to certain features of family background, analogous to the theories of
the authoritarian personality and the California F-scale. But this
would no longer be a political or a social theory. We would be giving
up the attempt to understand the change in social reality at the level of
its constitutive intersubjective meanings.

                                    IV

It can be argued, then, that mainstream social science is kept within
certain limits by its categorical principles which are rooted in the
traditional epistemology of empiricism; and secondly, that these re-
strictions are a severe handicap and prevent us from coming to grips
with important problems of our day, which should be the object of
political science. We need to go beyond the bounds of a science based
on verification to one which would study the intersubjective and
common meanings embedded in social reality.

But this science would be hermeneutical in the sense that has been
developed in this paper. It would not be founded on brute data; its
most primitive data would be readings of meanings, and its object
would have the three properties mentioned above: the meanings are
for a subject in a field or fields; they are, moreover, meanings which
are partially constituted by self-definitions, which are in this sense
already interpretations, and which can thus be re-expressed or made
explicit by a science of politics. In our case, the subject may be a
society or community; but the intersubjective meanings, as we saw,
embody a certain self-definition, a vision of the agent and his society,
which is that of the society or community.

But then the difficulties which the proponents of the verification
model foresee will arise. If we have a science which has no brute data,
which relies on readings, then it cannot but move in a hermeneutical

circle. A given reading of the intersubjective meanings of a society, or of given institutions or practices, may seem well founded, because it makes sense of these practices or the development of that society. But the conviction that it does make sense of this history itself is founded on further related readings. Thus, what I said above on the identity-crisis which is generated by our society makes sense and holds together only if one accepts this reading of the intersubjective meanings of our society, and if one accepts this reading of the rebellion against our society by many young people (sc. the reading in terms of identity-crisis). These two readings make sense together, so that in a sense the explanation as a whole reposes on the readings, and the readings in their turn are strengthened by the explanation as a whole.

But if these readings seem implausible, or even more, if they are not understood by our interlocutor, there is no verification procedure which we can fall back on. We can only continue to offer interpretations; we are in an interpretative circle.

But the ideal of a science of verification is to find an appeal beyond differences of interpretation. Insight will always be useful in discovery, but should not have to play any part in establishing the truth of its findings. This ideal can be said to have been met by our natural sciences. But a hermeneutic science cannot but rely on insight. It requires that one have the sensibility and understanding necessary to be able to make and comprehend the readings by which we can explain the reality concerned. In physics we might argue that if someone does not accept a true theory, then either he has not been shown enough (brute data) evidence (perhaps not enough is yet available), or he cannot understand and apply some formalized language. But in the sciences of man conceived as hermeneutical, the nonacceptance of a true or il-luminating theory may come from neither of these, indeed is unlikely to be due to either of these, but rather from a failure to grasp the meaning field in question, an inability to make and understand readings of this field.

In other words, in a hermeneutical science, a certain measure of insight is indispensable, and this insight cannot be communicated by the gathering of brute data, or initiation in modes of formal reasoning or some combination of these. It is unformalizable. But this is a scandalous result according to the authoritative conception of science in our tradition, which is shared even by many of those who are highly critical of the approach of mainstream psychology, or sociology, or political science. For it means that this is not a study in which anyone can engage, regardless of their level of insight; that some claims of the form "If you don't understand, then your intuitions are at fault, are blind or inadequate," some claims of this form will be justified; that some differences will be nonarbitrable by further evidence, but that each side can only make appeal to deeper insight on the part of the other. The superiority of one position over another will thus consist in this, that from the more adequate position one can understand one's own stand and that of one's opponent, but not the other way around. It goes without saying that this argument can only have weight for those in the superior position.

Thus, a hermeneutical science encounters a gap in intuitions, which is the other side, as it were, of the hermeneutical circle. But the situation is graver than this; for this gap is bound up with our divergent options in politics and life.

We speak of a gap when some cannot understand the kind of self-definition which others are proposing as underlying a certain society or set of institutions. Thus some positivistically-minded thinkers will find the language of identity-theory quite opaque: and some thinkers will not recognize any theory which does not fit with the categorical presuppositions of empiricism. But self-definitions are not only important to us as scientists who are trying to understand some, perhaps distant, social reality. As men we are self-defining beings, and we are partly what we are in virtue of the self-definitions which we have accepted, however we have come by them. What self-definitions we understand and what ones we do not understand, is closely linked with the self-definitions which help to constitute what we are. If it is too simple to say that one only understands an "ideology" which one subscribes to, it is nevertheless hard to deny that we have great difficulty grasping definitions whose terms structure the world in ways which are utterly different from, incompatible with, our own.

Hence the gap in intuitions does not just divide different theoretical positions, it also tends to divide different fundamental options in life. The practical and the theoretical are inextricably joined here. It may not just be that to understand a certain explanation one has to sharpen one's intuitions, it may be that one has to change one's orientation — if not in adopting another orientation, at least in living one's own in a way which allows for greater comprehension of others. Thus, in the sciences of man insofar as they are hermeneutical there can be a valid response to "I don't understand" which takes the form, not only "develop your intuitions," but more radically "change yourself." This puts an end to any aspiration to a value-free or "ideology-free" science of man. A study of the science of man is inseparable from an examination of the options between which men must choose.

This means that we can speak here not only of error, but of illusion. We speak of "illusion" when we are dealing with something of greater substance than error, error which in a sense builds a counterfeit reality of its own. But errors of interpretation of meaning, which are also self-definitions of those who interpret and hence inform their lives, are more than errors in this sense: they are sustained by certain practices of which they are constitutive. It is not implausible to single out as examples two rampant illusions in our present society. One is that of the proponents of the bargaining society who can recognize nothing but either bargaining gambits or madness in those who rebel against this society. Here the error is sustained by the practices of the bargaining culture, and given a semblance of reality by the refusal to treat any protests on other terms; it hence acquires the more substantive reality of illusion. The second example is provided by much "revolutionary" activity in our society which in desperate search for an alternative mode of life purports to see its situation in that of an Andean guerilla or Chinese peasants. Lived out, this passes from the stage of laughable error to tragic illusion. One illusion cannot recognize the possibility of human variation, the other cannot see any limits to mankind's ability to transform itself. Both make a valid science of man impossible.

In face of all this, we might be so scandalized by the prospect of such a hermeneutical science, that we will want to go back to the verification model. Why can we not take our understanding of meaning as part of the logic of discovery, as the logical empiricists suggest for our unformalizable insights, and still found our science on the exactness of our predictions? Our insightful understanding of the intersubjective meanings of our society will then serve to elaborate fruitful hypotheses, but the proof of these puddings will remain in the degree to which they enable us to predict.

The answer is that if the epistemological views underlying the science of interpretation are right, such exact prediction is radically impossible. This, for three reasons of ascending order of fundamentalness.

The first is the well-known "open system" predicament, one shared by human life and meteorology, that we cannot shield a certain domain of human events, the psychological, economic, political, from external interference; it is impossible to delineate a closed system.

The second, more fundamental, is that if we are to understand men by a science of interpretation, we cannot achieve the degree of fine exactitude of a science based on brute data. The data of natural science admit of measurement to virtually any degree of exactitude. But different interpretations cannot be judged in this way. At the same time different nuances of interpretation may lead to different predictions in some circumstances, and these different outcomes may eventually create widely varying futures. Hence it is more than easy to be wide of the mark.

But the third and most fundamental reason for the impossibility of hard prediction is that man is a self-defining animal. With changes in his self-definition go changes in what man is, such that he has to be understood in different terms. But the conceptual mutations in human history can and frequently do produce conceptual webs which are incommensurable, that is, where the terms cannot be defined in relation to a common stratum of expressions. The entirely different notions of bargaining in our society and in some primitive ones provide an example. Each will be glossed in terms of practices, institutions, ideas in each society which have nothing corresponding to them in the other.

The success of prediction in the natural sciences is bound up with the fact that all states of the system, past and future, can be described in the same range of concepts, as values, say, of the same variables. Hence all future states of the solar system can be characterized, as past ones are, in the language of Newtonian mechanics. This is far from being a sufficient condition of exact prediction, but it is a necessary one in this sense, that only if past and future are brought under the same conceptual net can one understand the states of the latter as some function of the states of the former, and hence predict.

This conceptual unity is vitiated in the sciences of man by the fact of conceptual innovation, which in turn alters human reality. The very terms in which the future will have to be characterized if we are to understand it properly are not all available to us at present. Hence we have such radically unpredictable events as the culture of youth today, the Puritan rebellion of the sixteenth and seventeenth centuries, the development of Soviet society, and so forth.

And thus, it is much easier to understand after the fact than it is to predict. Human science is largely *ex post* understanding. Or often one has the sense of impending change, of some big reorganization, but is powerless to make clear what it will consist in: one lacks the vocabulary. But there is a clear asymmetry here, which there is not (or not supposed to be) in natural science, where events are said to be predicted from the theory with exactly the same ease with which one explains past events and by exactly the same process. In human science this will never be the case.

Of course, we strive *ex post* to understand the changes, and to do this we try to develop a language in which we can situate the incommensurable webs of concepts. We see the rise of Puritanism, for instance, as a shift in man's stance to the sacred; and thus, we have a language in which we can express both stances — the earlier mediaeval Catholic one and the Puritan rebellion — as "glosses" on this fundamental term. We thus have a language in which to talk of the transition. But think how we acquired it. This general category of the sacred is acquired not only from our experience of the shift which came in the Reformation, but from the study of human religion in general, including primitive religion, and with the detachment which came with secularization. It would be conceivable, but unthinkable, that a mediaeval Catholic could have this conception — or for that matter a Puritan. These two protagonists only had a language of condemnation for each other: "heretic," "idolator." The place for such a concept was preempted by a certain way of living the sacred. After a big change has happened, and the trauma has been resorbed, it is possible to try to understand it, because one now has available the new language, the transformed meaning world. But hard prediction before just makes one a laughingstock. Really to be able to predict the future would be to have explicited so clearly the human condition that one would already have preempted all cultural innovation and transformation. This is hardly in the bounds of the possible.

Sometimes men show amazing prescience: the myth of Faust, for instance, which is treated several times at the beginning of the modern era. There is a kind of prophesy here, a premonition. But what characterizes these bursts of foresight is that they see through a glass darkly, for they see in terms of the old language: Faust sells his soul to the devil. They are in no sense hard predictions. Human science looks backward. It is inescapably historical.

There are thus good grounds both in epistemological arguments and in their greater fruitfulness for opting for hermeneutical sciences of man. But we cannot hide from ourselves how greatly this option breaks with certain commonly held notions about our scientific tradition. We cannot measure such sciences against the requirements of a science of verification: we cannot judge them by their predictive capacity. We have to accept that they are founded on intuitions which all do not share, and what is worse, that these intuitions are closely bound up with our fundamental options. These sciences cannot be "*wertfrei*"; they are moral sciences in a more radical sense than the eighteenth century understood. Finally, their successful prosecution requires a high degree of self-knowledge, a freedom from illusion, in the sense of error which is rooted and expressed in one's way of life; for our incapacity to understand is rooted in our own self-definitions, hence in what we are. To say this is not to say anything new: Aristotle makes a similar point in Book I of the *Ethics*. But it is still radically shocking and unassimilable to the mainstream of modern science.

Chapter Two

The Model of the Text: Meaningful Action Considered as a Text

PAUL RICOEUR

My aim in this paper is to test an hypothesis which I will expound briefly.

I assume that the primary sense of the word "hermeneutics" concerns the rules required for the interpretation of the written documents of our culture. In assuming this starting point I am remaining faithful to the concept of *Auslegung* as it was stated by Wilhelm Dilthey; whereas *Verstehen* (understanding, comprehension) relies on the recognition of what a foreign subject means or intends on the basis of all kinds of signs in which psychic life expresses itself (*Lebensäusserungen*), *Auslegung* (interpretation, exegesis) implies something more specific: it covers only a limited category of signs, those which are fixed by writing, including all the sorts of documents and monuments which entail a fixation similar to writing.

Now my hypothesis is this: if there are specific problems which are raised by the interpretation of texts because they are texts and not spoken language, and if these problems are the ones which constitute hermeneutics as such, then the human sciences may be said to be hermeneutical (1) inasmuch as their *object* displays some of the features constitutive of a text as text, and (2) inasmuch as their *methodology* develops the same kind of procedures as those of *Auslegung* or text-interpretation.

Originally published in *Social Research* 38, no. 3 (Autumn 1971). Reprinted with permission.

73

Hence the two questions to which my paper will be devoted are: (1) To what extent may we consider the notion of text as a good paradigm for the so-called object of the social sciences? (2) To what extent may we use the methodology of-text-interpretation as a paradigm for interpretation in general in the field of the human sciences?

THE PARADIGM OF TEXT

In order to justify the distinction between spoken and written language, I want to introduce a preliminary concept, that of *discourse*. It is as discourse that language is either spoken or written.

Now what is discourse?

We shall seek the answer not from the logicians, not even from the exponents of linguistic analysis, but from the linguists themselves. Discourse is the counterpart of what linguists call language-systems or linguistic codes. Discourse is language-event or linguistic usage. This pair of correlative terms — system/event, code/message — has played a basic role in linguistics since it was introduced by Ferdinand de Saussure and Louis Hjelmslev. The first spoke of language (*langue*) — speech (*parole*), the second of schema — usage. We can also add competence — "performance," in Chomsky's language. It is necessary to draw all the epistemological consequences of such a duality, namely, that the linguistics of discourse has different rules than does the linguistics of language. It is the French linguist Emile Benveniste who has gone the furthest in distinguishing two linguistics. For him, these two linguistics are not constructed upon the same units. If the sign (phonological or lexical) is the basic unit of language, the sentence is the basic unit of discourse. Therefore it is the linguistics of the sentence which supports the theory of speech as an event. I will retain four traits from this linguistics of the sentence which will help me to elaborate the hermeneutic of the event and of discourse.

First trait: Discourse is always realized temporally and in a present, whereas the language system is virtual and outside of time. Emile Benveniste calls this the "instance of discourse."

Second trait: Whereas language lacks a subject — in the sense that the question "Who is speaking?" does not apply at its level — discourse refers back to its speaker by means of a complex set of indicators such as the personal pronouns. We will say that the "instance of discourse" is self-referential.

Third trait: Whereas the signs in language only refer to other signs within the same system, and whereas language therefore lacks a world just as it lacks temporality and subjectivity, discourse is always about something. It refers to a world which it claims to describe, to express, or to represent. It is in discourse that the symbolic function of language is actualized.

Fourth trait: Whereas language is only the condition for communication for which it provides the codes, it is in discourse that all messages are exchanged. In this sense, discourse alone has not only a world, but an other, another person, an interlocutor to whom it is addressed.

These four traits taken together constitute speech as an event.

It is remarkable that these four traits only appear in the movement of effectuation from language to discourse. Every apology for speech as an event therefore is significant if, and only if, it makes visible the process of effectuation through which our linguistic competence actualizes itself in performance. But the same apology becomes abusive as soon as this event character is extended from the problematic of effectuation, where it is valid, to another problematic, that of understanding.

In effect, what is it to understand a discourse?

Let us see how differently these four traits are actualized in spoken and written language.

1. Discourse, as we said, only exists as a temporal and present instance of discourse. This first trait is realized differently in living speech and in writing. In living speech, the instance of discourse has the character of a fleeting event. The event appears and disappears. This is why there is a problem of fixation, of inscription. What we want to fix is what disappears. If, by extension, we can say that one fixes language — inscription of the alphabet, lexical inscription, syntactical inscription — it is for the sake of that which alone has to be fixed, discourse. Only discourse is to be fixed, because discourse disappears. The atemporal system neither appears nor disappears; it does not happen. Here is the place to recall the myth in Plato's *Phaedrus*. Writing was given to men to "come to the rescue" of the "weakness of discourse," a weakness which was that of the event. The gift of the *grammata* — of that "external" thing, of those "external marks," of that materializing alienation — was just that of a "remedy" brought to our

memory. The Egyptian king of Thebes could well respond to the god
Theuth that writing was a false remedy in that it replaced true reminis-
cence by material conservation, and real wisdom by the semblance of
knowing. This inscription, in spite of its perils, is discourse's destination. What in effect does writing fix? Not the event of speaking, but
the "said" of speaking, where we understand by the "said" of speaking
that intentional exteriorization constitutive of the aim of discourse
thanks to which the *sagen* — the saying — wants to become *Aus-sage* —
the enunciation, the enunciated. In short, what we write, what we
inscribe, is the *noema* of the speaking. It is the meaning of the speech
event, not the event as event.

What, in effect, does writing fix? If it is not the speech *event,* it is
speech itself in so far as it is *said.* But what is said?

Here I would like to propose that hermeneutics has to appeal not
only to linguistics (linguistics of discourse versus linguistics of language) as it does above, but also to the theory of the speech act such as
we find it in John Austin and John Searle. The act of speaking, according to these authors, is constituted by a hierarchy of subordinate acts
which are distributed on three levels: (1) the level of the locutionary or
propositional act, the act *of* saying; (2) the level of the illocutionary act
or force, that which we do *in* saying; and (3) the level of the perlocutionary act, that which we do *by* saying. In the case of an order,
when I tell you to close the door, for example, "Close the door!" is the
act of speaking. But when I tell you this with the force of an order and
not of a request, this is the illocutionary act. Finally, I can stir up
certain effects like fear by the fact that I give you an order. These
effects make my discourse act like a stimulus producing certain results.
This is the perlocutionary act.

What is the implication of these distinctions for our problem of the
intentional exteriorization by which the event surpasses itself in the
meaning and lends itself to material fixation? The locutionary act ex-
teriorizes itself in the sentence. The sentence can in effect be identified
and re-identified as being the same sentence. A sentence becomes an
e-nunciation (*Aus-sage*) and thus is transferred to others as being
such-and-such a sentence with such-and-such a meaning. But the illocutionary act can also be exteriorized through grammatical
paradigms (indicative, imperative, and subjunctive modes, and other
procedures expressive of the illocutionary force) which permit its

identification and re-identification. Certainly, in spoken discourse, the illocutionary force leans upon mimicry and gestural elements and upon the non-articulated aspects of discourse, what we call prosody. In this sense, the illocutionary force is less completely inscribed in grammar than is the propositional meaning. In every case, its inscription in a syntactic articulation is itself gathered up in specific paradigms which in principle make possible fixation by writing. Without a doubt we must concede that the perlocutionary act is the least inscribable aspect of discourse and that by preference it characterizes spoken language. But the perlocutionary action is precisely what is the least discourse in discourse. It is the discourse as stimulus. It acts, not by my interlocutor's recognition of my intention, but sort of energetically, by direct influence upon the emotions and the affective dispositions. Thus the propositional act, the illocutionary force, and the perlocutionary action are apt, in a decreasing order, for the intentional exteriorization which makes inscription in writing possible.

Therefore it is necessary to understand by the meaning of the speech-act, or by the *noema* of the saying, not only the sentence, in the narrow sense of the propositional act, but also the illocutionary force and even the perlocutionary action in the measure that these three aspects of the speech-act are codified, gathered into paradigms, and where, consequently, they can be identified and re-identified as having the same meaning. Therefore I am here giving the word "meaning" a very large acceptation which covers all the aspects and levels of the intentional exteriorization that makes the inscription of discourse possible.

The destiny of the other three traits of discourse in passing from discourse to writing will permit us to make more precise the meaning of this elevation of saying to what is said.

2. In discourse, we said — and this was the second differential trait of discourse in relation to language — the sentence designates its speaker by diverse indicators of subjectivity and personality. In spoken discourse, this reference by discourse to the speaking subject presents a character of immediacy that we can explain in the following way. The subjective intention of the speaking subject and the meaning of the discourse overlap each other in such a way that it is the same thing to understand what the speaker means and what his discourse means. The ambiguity of the French expression *vouloir-dire,* the German

meinen, and the English "to mean," attests to this overlapping. It is almost the same thing to ask "What do you mean?" and "What does that mean?" With written discourse, the author's intention and the meaning of the text cease to coincide. This dissociation of the verbal meaning of the text and the mental intention is what is really at stake in the inscription of discourse. Not that we can conceive of a text without an author; the tie between the speaker and the discourse is not abolished, but distended and complicated. The dissociation of the meaning and the intention is still an adventure of the reference of discourse to the speaking subject. But the text's career escapes the finite horizon lived by its author. What the text says now matters more than what the author meant to say, and every exegesis unfolds its procedures within the circumference of a meaning that has broken its moorings to the psychology of its author. Using Plato's expression again, written discourse cannot be "rescued" by all the processes by which spoken discourse supports itself in order to be understood—intonation, delivery, mimicry, gestures. In this sense, the inscription in "external marks," which first appeared to alienate discourse, marks the actual spirituality of discourse. Henceforth, only the meaning "rescues" the meaning, without the contribution of the physical and psychological presence of the author. But to say that the meaning rescues the meaning is to say that only interpretation is the "remedy" for the weakness of discourse which its author can no longer "save."

3. The event is surpassed by the meaning a third time. Discourse, we said, is what refers to the world, to *a* world. In spoken discourse this means that what the dialogue ultimately refers to is the *situation* common to the interlocutors. This situation in a way surrounds the dialogue, and its landmarks can all be shown by a gesture, or by pointing a finger, or designated in an ostensive manner by the discourse itself through the oblique reference of those other indicators which are the demonstratives, the adverbs of time and place, and the tense of the verb. In oral discourse, we are saying, reference is *ostensive*. What happens to it in written discourse? Are we saying that the text no longer has a reference? This would be confound reference and monstration, world and situation. Discourse cannot fail to be about something. In saying this, I am separating myself from any ideology of an absolute text. Only a few sophisticated texts satisfy this ideal of a text without reference. They are texts where the play of the signifier

breaks away from the signified. But this new form is only valuable as an exception and cannot give the key to all other texts which in one manner or another speak about the world. But what then is the subject of texts when nothing can be shown? Far from saying that the text is then without a world, I will now say without paradox that only man *has a world* and not just a situation. In the same manner that the text frees its meaning from the tutelage of the mental intention, it frees its reference from the limits of ostensive reference. For us, the world is the ensemble of references opened up by the texts. Thus we speak about the "world" of Greece, not to designate any more what were the situations for those who lived them, but to designate the non-situational references which outlive the effacement of the first and which henceforth are offered as possible modes of being, as symbolic dimensions of our being-in-the-world. For me, this is the referent of all literature; no longer the *Umwelt* of the ostensive references of dialogue, but the *Welt* projected by the non-ostensive references of every text that we have read, understood, and loved. To understand a text is at the same time to light up our own situation, or, if you will, to interpolate among the predicates of our situation all the significations which make a *Welt* of our *Umwelt*. It is this enlarging of the *Umwelt* into the *World* which permits us to speak of the references *opened up* by the text—it would be better to say that the references *open up* the world. Here again the spirituality of discourse manifests itself through writing, which frees us from the visibility and limitation of situations by opening up a world for us, that is, new dimensions of our being-in-the-world.

In this sense, Heidegger rightly says—in his analysis of *verstehen* in *Being and Time*—that what we understand first in a discourse is not another person, but a project, that is, the outline of a new being-in-the-world. Only writing, in freeing itself, not only from its author, but from the narrowness of the dialogical situation, reveals this destination of discourse as projecting a world.

In thus tieing reference to the projection of a world, it is not only Heidegger whom we rediscover, but Wilhelm von Humboldt for whom the great justification of language is to establish the relation of man to the world. If you suppress this referential function, only an absurd game of errant signifiers remains.

4. But it is perhaps with the fourth trait that the accomplishment of

discourse in writing is most exemplary. Only discourse, not language, is addressed to someone. This is the foundation of communication. But it is one thing for discourse to be addressed to an interlocutor equally present to the discourse situation, and another to be addressed, as is the case in virtually every piece of writing, to whoever knows how to read. The narrowness of the dialogical relation explodes. Instead of being addressed just to you, the second person, what is written is addressed to the audience that it creates itself. This, again, marks the spirituality of writing, the counterpart of its materiality and of the alienation which it imposes upon discourse. This *vis-à-vis* of the written is just whoever knows how to read. The co-presence of dialoguing subjects ceases to be the model for every "understanding." The relation writing/reading ceases to be a particular case of the relation speaking/hearing. But at the same time, discourse is revealed as discourse in the universality of its address. In escaping the momentary character of the event, the bounds lived by the author, and the narrowness of ostensive reference, discourse escapes the limits of being face to face. It no longer has a visible auditor. An unknown, invisible reader has become the unprivileged addressee of the discourse.

To what extent may we say that the object of the human sciences conforms to the paradigm of the text? Max Weber defines this object as *sinnhaft orientiertes Verhalten,* as meaningfully oriented behavior. To what extent may we replace the predicate "meaningfully oriented" by what I should like to call readability-characters derived from the preceding theory of the text?

Let us try to apply our four criteria of what a text is to the concept of meaningful action.

The Fixation of Action

Meaningful action is an object for science only under the condition of a kind of objectification which is equivalent to the fixation of a discourse by writing. This trait presupposes a simple way to help us at this stage of our analysis. In the same way that interlocution is overcome in writing, interaction is overcome in numerous situations in which we treat action as a fixed text. These situations are overlooked in a theory of action for which the discourse of action is itself a part of the situation of transaction which flows from one agent to another, exactly as spoken language is caught in the process of interlocution, or, if we may use the term, of translocution. This is why the understanding of action at the prescientific level is only "knowledge without observation," or as E. Anscombe says, "practical knowledge" in the sense of "knowing how" as opposed to "knowing that." But this understanding is not yet an *interpretation* in the strong sense which deserves to be called scientific interpretation.

My claim is that action itself, action as meaningful, may become an object of science, without losing its character of meaningfulness, through a kind of objectification similar to the fixation which occurs in writing. By this objectification, action is no longer a transaction to which the discourse of action would still belong. It constitutes a delineated pattern which has to be interpreted according to its inner connections.

This objectification is made *possible* by some inner traits of the action which are similar to the structure of the speech-act and which make doing a kind of utterance. In the same way as the fixation by writing is made possible by a dialectic of intentional exteriorization immanent to the speech-act itself, a similar dialectic within the process of transaction prepares the detachment of the *meaning* of the action from the *event* of the action.

First an action has the structure of a locutionary act. It has a *propositional* content which can be identified and re-identified as the same. This "propositional" structure of the action has been clearly and demonstratively expounded by Antony Kenny in *Action, Emotion and Will*.[1] The verbs of action constitute a specific class of predicates which are similar to relations and which, like relations, are irreducible to all the kinds of predicates which may follow the copula "is." The class of action predicates, in its turn, is irreducible to the relations and constitutes a specific set of predicates. Among other traits, the verbs of action allow a plurality of "arguments" capable of complementing the verb, ranging from no argument (Plato taught) to an indeterminate number of arguments (Brutus killed Caesar in the Curia, on the Ides of March, with a . . . , with the help of . . .). This variable polydicity of the predicative structure of the action-sentences is typical of the propositional structure of action. Another trait which is important for the

1. Antony Kenny, *Action, Emotion and Will* (London: Routledge, 1963).

transposition of the concept of fixation from the sphere of discourse to the sphere of action concerns the ontological status of the "complements" of the verbs of action. Whereas relations hold between terms equally existing (or non-existing), certain verbs of action have a topical subject which is identified as existing and to which the sentence refers, and complements which do not exist. Such is the case with the "mental acts" (to believe, to think, to will, to imagine, etc.).

Antony Kenny describes some other traits of the propositional structure of actions derived from the description of the functioning of the verbs of action. For example, the distinction between states, activities, and performances can be stated according to the behavior of the tenses of the verbs of action which fix some specific temporal traits of the action itself. The distinction between the formal and the material object of an action (let us say the difference between the notion of all inflammable things and this letter which I am now burning) belongs to the logic of action as mirrored in the grammar of the verbs of action. Such, roughly described, is the propositional content of action which gives a basis to a dialectic of *event* and *meaning* similar to that of the speech-act. I should like to speak here of the noematic structure of action. It is this noematic structure which may be fixed and detached from the process of interaction and become an object to interpret.

Moreover, this *noema* not only has a propositional content, but also presents "illocutionary" traits very similar to those of the complete speech-act. The different classes of performative acts of discourse described by Austin at the end of *How to Do Things with Words* may be taken as paradigms not only for the speech-acts themselves, but for the actions which fulfill the corresponding speech-acts.[2] A typology of action, following the model of illocutionary acts, is therefore possible. Not only a typology, but a criteriology, inasmuch as each type implies *rules,* more precisely "constitutive rules" which, according to Searle in *Speech Acts,* allow the construction of "ideal models" similar to the *Idealtypes* of Max Weber.[3] For example, to understand what a promise is, we have to understand what the "essential condition" is according to which a given action "counts as" a promise. Searle's "essential condition" is not far from what Husserl called *Sinngehalt,* which cov-

2. John Austin, *How to Do Things with Words* (Cambridge, Mass.: Harvard University Press, 1962).

3. John Searle, *Speech Acts* (London: Cambridge University Press, 1969), p. 56.

ers both the "matter" (propositional content) and the "quality" (the illocutionary force).

We may now say that an action, like a speech-act, may be identified not only according to its propositional content, but also according to its illocutionary force. Both constitute its "sense-content." Like the speech-act, the action-event (if we may coin this analogical expression) develops a similar dialectic between its temporal status as an appearing and disappearing event, and its logical status as having such-and-such identifiable meaning or "sense-content." But if the "sense-content" is what makes possible the "inscription" of the action-event, what makes it real? In other words, what corresponds to writing in the field of action?

Let us return to the paradigm of the speech-act. What is fixed by writing, we said, is the *noema* of the speaking, the saying as *said*. To what extent may we say that what is *done* is inscribed? Certain metaphors may be helpful at this point. We say that such-and-such event *left its mark* on its time. We speak of marking events. Are not there "marks" on time, the kind of thing which calls for a reading, rather than for a hearing? But what is meant by this metaphor of the printed mark?

The three other criteria of the text will help us to make the nature of this fixation more precise.

The Autonomization of Action

In the same way that a text is detached from its author, an action is detached from its agent and develops consequences of its own. This autonomization of human action constitutes the *social* dimension of action. An action is a social phenomenon not only because it is done by several agents in such a way that the role of each of them cannot be distinguished from the role of the others, but also because our deeds escape us and have effects which we did not intend. One of the meanings of the notion of "inscription" appears here. The kind of distance which we found between the intention of the speaker and the verbal meaning of a text occurs also between the agent and its action. It is this distance which makes the ascription of responsibility a specific problem. We do not ask, who smiled? who raised his hand? The doer is present to his doing in the same way as the speaker is present to his speech. With simple actions like those which require no previous action in order to be done, the meaning (*noema*) and the intention (*noesis*) coincide or overlap. With complex actions some segments are so remote from the initial simple segments, which can be said to express the intention of the doer, that the ascription of these actions or action-segments constitutes a problem as difficult to solve as that of authorship in some cases of literary criticism. The assignation of an author becomes a mediate inference well known to the historian who tries to isolate the role of an historical character in the course of events.

We just used the expression "the course of events." Could we not say that what we call the course of events plays the role of the material thing which "rescues" the vanishing discourse when it is written? As we said in a metaphorical way, some actions are events which imprint their mark on their time. But on what did they imprint their mark? Is it not in something spatial that discourse is inscribed? How could an event be printed on something temporal? Social time, however, is not only something which flees; it is also the place of durable effects, of persisting patterns. An action leaves a "trace," it makes its "mark" when it contributes to the emergence of such patterns which become the *documents* of human action.

Another metaphor may help us to delineate this phenomenon of the social "imprint": the metaphor of the "record" or of the "registration." Joel Feinberg, in *Reason and Responsibility,* introduces this metaphor in another context, that of responsibility, in order to show how an action may be submitted to blame. Only actions, he says, which can be "registered" for further notice, placed as an entry on somebody's "record," can be blamed.[4] And when there are no formal records (such as those which are kept by institutions like employment offices, schools, banks, and the police), there is still an informal analogue of these formal records which we call reputation and which constitutes a basis for blaming. I should like to apply this interesting metaphor of a record and reputation to something other than the quasi-judicial situations of blaming, charging, crediting, or punishing. Could we not say that history is itself the record of human action? History is this quasi-"thing" *on* which human action leaves a "trace," puts its mark. Hence the possibility of "archives." Before the archives which are intentionally written down by the memorialists, there is this

4. J. Feinberg, *Reason and Responsibility* (Belmont, Calif.: Dickenson Pub. Co., 1965).

continuous process of "recording" human action which is history itself as the sum of "marks," the fate of which escapes the control of
individual actors. Henceforth history may appear as an autonomous
entity, as a play with players who do not know the plot. This hypos-
tasis of history may be denounced as a fallacy, but this fallacy is well
entrenched in the process by which human action becomes social action when written down in the archives of history. Thanks to this
sedimentation in social time, human deeds become "institutions," in
the sense that their meaning no longer coincides with the logical intentions of the actors. The meaning may be "depsychologized" to the
point where the *meaning* resides in the work itself. In the words of
Peter Winch, in *The Idea of Social Science,* the object of the social
sciences is a "rule-governed behavior."[5] But this rule is not
superimposed; it is the meaning as articulated from within these
sedimented or instituted works.

Such is the kind of "objectivity" which proceeds from the "social
fixation" of meaningful behavior.

Relevance and Importance

According to our third criterion of what a text is, we could say that
a meaningful action is an action the *importance* of which goes "beyond"
its *relevance* to its initial situation. This new trait is very similar to the
way in which a text breaks the ties of discourse to all the ostensive
references. As a result of this emancipation from the situational context, discourse can develop non–ostensive references which we called a
"world," in the sense in which we speak of the Greek "world," not in
the cosmological sense of the word, but as an ontological dimension.

What would correspond in the field of action to the non–ostensive
references of a text?

We opposed, in introducing the present analysis, the *importance* of
an action to its *relevance* as regards the situation to which it wanted to
respond. An important action, we could say, develops meanings
which can be actualized or fulfilled in situations other than the one in
which this action occurred. To say the same thing in different words,
the meaning of an important event exceeds, overcomes, transcends,
the social conditions of its production and may be reenacted in new

5. Peter Winch, *The Idea of Social Science* (London: Routledge, 1958).

social contexts. Its importance is its durable relevance and, in some cases, its omnitemporal relevance.

This third trait has important implications as regards the relation between cultural phenomena and their social conditions. Is it not a fundamental trait of the great works of culture to overcome the conditions of their social production, in the same way as a text develops new references and constitutes new "worlds"? It is in this sense that Hegel spoke, in *The Philosophy of Right,* of the institutions (in the largest sense of the word) which "actualize" freedom as a *second nature* in accordance with freedom. This "realm of actual freedom" is constituted by the deeds and words capable of receiving relevance in new historical situations. If this is true, this way of overcoming one's own conditions of production is the key to the puzzling problem raised by Marxism concerning the status of the "superstructures." The autonomy of superstructures as regards their relation to their own infra-structures has its paradigm in the non-ostensive references of a text. A work does not only mirror its time, but it opens up a world which it bears within itself.

Human Action as an "Open Work"

Finally, according to our fourth criterion of the text as text, the meaning of human action is also something which is *addressed* to an indefinite range of possible "readers." The judges are not the contemporaries, but, as Hegel said, history itself. *Weltgeschichte ist Weltgericht.* That means that, like a text, human action is an open work, the meaning of which is "in suspense." It is because it "opens up" new references and receives fresh relevance from them, that human deeds are also waiting for fresh interpretations which decide their meaning. All significant events and deeds are, in this way, opened to this kind of practical interpretation through present *praxis.* Human action, too, is opened to anybody who *can read.* In the same way that the meaning of an event is the sense of its forthcoming interpretations, the interpretation by the contemporaries has no particular privilege in this process.

This dialectic between the work and its interpretations will be the topic of the *methodology* of interpretation that we shall now consider.

THE PARADIGM OF TEXT-INTERPRETATION

I want now to show the fruitfulness of this analogy of the text at the level of methodology.

The main implication of our paradigm, as concerns the methods of the social sciences, is that it offers a fresh approach to the question of the relation between *Erklären* (explanation) and *Verstehen* (understanding, comprehension) in the human sciences. As is well known, Dilthey gave this relation the meaning of a dichotomy. For him, any model of explanation is borrowed from a different region of knowledge, that of the natural sciences with their inductive logic. Thereafter, the autonomy of the so-called *Geisteswissenschaften* is preserved only by recognizing the irreducible factor of understanding a foreign psychic life on the basis of the signs in which this life is immediately exteriorized. But, if *Verstehen* is separated from *Erklären* by this logical gap, how can the human sciences be scientific at all? Dilthey kept wrestling with this paradox. He discovered more and more clearly, mainly after having read Husserl's *Logical Investigations,* that the *Geisteswissenschaften* are sciences inasmuch as the expressions of life undergo a kind of objectification which makes possible a scientific approach somewhat similar to that of the natural sciences, in spite of the logical gap between *Natur* and *Geist,* factual knowledge and knowledge by signs. In this way the mediation offered by these objectifications appeared to be more important, for a scientific purpose, than the immediate meaningfulness of the expressions of life for everyday transactions.

My own interrogation starts from this last perplexity in Dilthey's thought. And my hypothesis is that the kind of objectification implied in the status of discourse as text provides a better answer to the problem raised by Dilthey. This answer relies on the dialectical character of the relation between *Erklären* and *Verstehen* as it is displayed in reading.

Our task therefore will be to show to what extent the paradigm of reading, which is the counterpart of the paradigm of writing, provides a solution for the methodological paradox of the human sciences.

The dialectic involved in reading expresses the originality of the relation between writing and reading and its irreducibility to the dialogical situation based on the immediate reciprocity between speaking and hearing. There is a dialectic between explaining and comprehending *because* the writing/reading situation develops a problematic of its own which is not merely an extension of the speaking/hearing situation constitutive of dialogue.

It is here, therefore, that our hermeneutic is most critical as regards the Romanticist tradition in hermeneutics which took the dialogical situation as the standard for the hermeneutical operation applied to the text. My contention is that it is this operation, on the contrary, which reveals the meaning of what is already hermeneutical in dialogical understanding. Then, if the dialogical relation does not provide us with the paradigm of reading, we have to build it as an original paradigm, as a paradigm of its own.

This paradigm draws its main features from the status of the text itself as characterized by (1) the fixation of the meaning, (2) its dissociation from the mental intention of the author, (3) the display of non-ostensive references, and (4) the universal range of its addresses. These four traits taken together constitute the "objectivity" of the text. From this "objectivity" derives a possibility of *explaining* which is not derived in any way from another field, that of natural events, but which is congenial to this kind of objectivity. Therefore there is no transfer from one region of reality to another—let us say, from the sphere of facts to the sphere of signs. It is within the same sphere of signs that the process of objectification takes place and gives rise to explanatory procedures. And it is within the same sphere of signs that explanation and comprehension are confronted.

I propose that we consider this dialectic in two different ways: (1) as proceeding from comprehension to explanation, and (2) as proceeding from explanation to comprehension. The exchange and the reciprocity between both procedures will provide us with a good approximation of the dialectical character of the relation.

At the end of each half of this demonstration I shall try to indicate briefly the possible extension of the paradigm of reading to the whole sphere of the human sciences.

From Understanding to Explanation

This first dialectic—or rather this first figure of a unique dialectic—may be conveniently introduced by our contention that to understand a text is not to rejoin the author. The disjunction of the meaning and the intention creates an absolutely original situation which engenders the dialectic of *Erklären* and *Verstehen*. If the objective meaning is something other than the subjective intention of the author, it may be construed in various ways. The problem of the right understanding can no longer be solved by a simple return to the alleged intention of the author.

This construction necessarily takes the form of a process. As Eric Hirsch says in his book *Validity in Interpretation,* there are no rules for making good guesses. But there are methods for validating guesses.[6] This dialectic between guessing and validating constitutes one figure of our dialectic between comprehension and explanation.

In this dialectic both terms are decisive. Guessing corresponds to what Schleiermacher called the "divinatory," validation to what he called the "grammatical." My contribution to the theory of this dialectic will be to link it more tightly to the theory of the text and text-reading.

Why do we need an art of guessing? Why do we have to "construe" the meaning?

Not only — as I tried to say a few years ago — because language is metaphorical and because the double meaning of metaphorical language requires an art of deciphering which tends to unfold the several layers of meaning. The case of the metaphor is only a particular case for a general theory of hermeneutics. In more general terms, a text has to be construed because it is not a mere sequence of sentences, all on an equal footing and separately understandable. A text is a whole, a totality. The relation between whole and parts — as in a work of art or in an animal — requires a specific kind of "judgment" for which Kant gave the theory in the Third Critique. Correctly, the whole appears as a hierarchy of topics, or primary and subordinate topics. The reconstruction of the text as a whole necessarily has a circular character, in the sense that the presupposition of a certain kind of whole is implied in the recognition of the parts. And reciprocally, it is in construing the details that we construe the whole. There is no necessity and no evidence concerning what is important and what is unimportant, what is essential and what is unessential. The judgment of importance is a guess.

To put the difficulty in other terms, if a text is a whole, it is once more an individual like an animal or a work of art. As an individual it can only be reached by a process of narrowing the scope of generic concepts concerning the literary genre, the class of text to which this

---

6. Eric D. Hirsch. Jr., *Validity in Interpretation* (New Haven, Conn.: Yale University Press, 1967), p. 25. "The act of understanding is at first a genial (or a mistaken) guess and there are no methods for making guesses, no rules for generating insights; the methodological activity of interpretation commences when we begin to test and criticize our guesses." And further: "A mute symbolism may be construed in several ways."

text belongs, the structures of different kinds which intersect in this text. The localization and the individualization of this unique text is still a guess.

Still another way of expressing the same enigma is that as an individual the text may be reached from different sides. Like a cube, or a volume in space, the text presents a "relief." Its different topics are not at the same altitude. Therefore the reconstruction of the whole has a perspectivist aspect similar to that of perception. It is always possible to relate the same sentence in different ways to this or that sentence considered as the cornerstone of the text. A specific kind of onesidedness is implied in the act of reading. This onesidedness confirms the guess character of interpretation.

For all these reasons there is a problem of interpretation not so much because of the incommunicability of the psychic experience of the author, but because of the very nature of the verbal intention of the text. This intention is something other than the sum of the individual meanings of the individual sentences. A text is more than a linear succession of sentences. It is a cumulative, holistic process. This specific structure of the text cannot be derived from that of the sentence. Therefore the kind of plurivocity which belongs to texts as texts is something other than the polysemy of individual words in ordinary language and the ambiguity of individual sentences. This plurivocity is typical of the text considered as a whole, open to several readings and to several constructions.

As concerns the procedures of validation by which we test our guesses, I agree with Hirsch that they are closer to a logic of probability than to a logic of empirical verification. To show that an interpretation is more probable in the light of what is known is something other than showing that a conclusion is true. In this sense, validation is not verification. Validation is an argumentative discipline comparable to the juridical procedures of legal interpretation. It is a logic of uncertainty and of qualitative probability. In this sense we may give an acceptable sense to the opposition between *Geisteswissenschaften* and *Naturwissenschaften* without conceding anything to the alleged dogma of the ineffability of the individual. The method of conveyance of indices, typical of the logic of subjective probability, gives a firm basis for a science of the individual deserving the name of science.

A text is a quasi-individual, and the validation of an interpretation applied to it may be said, with complete legitimacy, to give a scientific knowledge of the text.

Such is the balance between the genius of guessing and the scientific character of validation which constitutes the modern complement of the dialectic between *Verstehen* and *Erklären*.

At the same time, we are prepared to give an acceptable meaning to the famous concept of a *hermeneutical circle*. Guess and validation are in a sense circularly related as subjective and objective approaches to the text. But this circle is not a vicious circularity. It would be a cage if we were unable to escape the kind of "self-confirmability" which, according to Hirsch (pp. 164ff.), threatens this relation between guess and validation. To the procedures of validation also belong procedures of invalidation similar to the criteria of falsifiability emphasized by Karl Popper in his *Logic of Scientific Discovery*.[7] The role of falsification is played here by the conflict between competing interpretations. An interpretation must not only be probable, but more probable than another. There are criteria of relative superiority which may easily be derived from the logic of subjective probability.

In conclusion, if it is true that there is always more than one way of construing a text, it is not true that all interpretations are equal and may be assimilated to so-called "rules of thumb." The text is a limited field of possible constructions. The logic of validation allows us to move between the two limits of dogmatism and skepticism. It is always possible to argue for or against an interpretation, to confront interpretations, to arbitrate between them, and to seek for an agreement, even if this agreement remains beyond our reach.

To what extent is this dialectic between guessing and validating paradigmatic for the whole field of the human sciences?

That the meaning of human actions, of historical events, and of social phenomena may be *construed* in several different ways is well known by all experts in the human sciences. What is less known and understood is that this methodological perplexity is founded in the nature of the object itself and, moreover, that it does not condemn the scientist to oscillate between dogmatism and skepticism. As the logic

7. Karl Popper, *The Logic of Scientific Discovery* (New York: Basic Books, 1959).

of text-interpretation suggests, there is a *specific plurivocity* belonging
to the meaning of human action. Human action, too, is a limited field
of possible constructions.

A trait of human action which has not yet been emphasized in the
preceding analysis may provide an interesting link between the
specific plurivocity of the text and the analogical plurivocity of human
action. This trait concerns the relation between the purposive and the
motivational dimensions of action. As many philosophers in the new
field of Action Theory have shown, the purposive character of an
action is fully recognized when the answer to the question "what" is
explained in terms of an answer to the question "why." I *understand*
what you intended to do, if you are able to *explain* to me why you did
such-and-such an action. Now, what kinds of answer to the question
"why" make sense? Only those answers which afford a motive understood as a reason for _ _ _ and not as a cause. And what is a reason
for _ _ _ which is not a cause? It is, in the terms of E. Anscombe and
A. I. Meldon, an expression, or a phrase, which allows us to consider
the action *as* this or that. If you tell me that you did this or that because
of jealousy or in a spirit of revenge, you are asking me to put your
action in the light of this category of feelings or dispositions. By the
same token, you claim to make sense with your action. You claim to
make it understandable for others and for yourself. This attempt is
particularly helpful when applied to what E. Anscombe calls the
"desirability-character" of wanting. Wants and beliefs have the character not only of being *forces* which make people act in such-and-such
ways, but of making sense as a result of the apparent good which is the
correlate of their desirability-character. I may have to answer the question, *as* what do you want this? On the basis of these desirability-
characters and the apparent good which corresponds to them, it is
possible to *argue* about the meaning of an action, to argue for or
against this or that interpretation. In this way the account of motives
already foreshadows a logic of argumentation procedures. Could we
not say that what can be (and must be) *construed* in human action is the
motivational basis of this action, that is, the set of desirability-
characters which may explain it? And could we not say that the process of *arguing* linked to the explanation of action by its motives unfolds a kind of plurivocity which makes action similar to a text?

What seems to legitimate this extension from guessing the meaning of a text to guessing the meaning of an action is that in arguing about the meaning of an action I put my wants and my beliefs at a distance and submit them to a concrete dialectic of confrontation with opposite points of view. This way of putting my action at a distance in order to make sense of my own motives paves the way for the kind of distanciation which occurs with what we called the social *inscription* of human action and to which we applied the metaphor of the "record." The same actions which may be put into "records" and henceforth "recorded" may also be *explained* in different ways according to the multivocity of the arguments applied to their motivational background.

If we are correct in extending to action the concept of "guess" which we took as a synonym for *Verstehen,* we may also extend to the field of action the concept of "validation" in which we saw an equivalent of *Erklären.*

Here, too, the modern theory of action provides us with an intermediary link between the procedures of literary criticism and those of the social sciences. Some thinkers have tried to elucidate the way in which we *impute* actions to agents in the light of the juridical procedures by which a judge or a tribunal validates a decision concerning a contract or a crime. In a famous article, "The Ascription of Responsibility and Rights," H. L. A. Hart shows in a very convincing way that juridical reasoning does not at all consist in applying general laws to particular cases, but each time in construing uniquely referring decisions.[8] These decisions terminate a careful refutation of the excuses and defenses which could "defeat" the claim or the accusation. In saying that human actions are fundamentally "defeatible" and that juridical reasoning is an argumentative process which comes to grips with the different ways of "defeating" a claim or an accusation, Hart has paved the way for a general theory of validation in literary criticism and validation in the social sciences. The intermediary function of juridical reasoning clearly shows that the procedures of validation have a polemical character. In front of the court, the plurivocity common to texts and to actions is exhibited in the form of a conflict of interpretations, and the final interpretation appears as a verdict to which it is possible to make appeal. Like legal utterances, all interpre-

8. H. L. A. Hart, "The Ascription of Responsibility and Rights," *Proceedings of the Aristotelian Society* 49 (1948): 171–194.

tations in the field of literary criticism and in the social sciences may be challenged, and the question "what can defeat a claim" is common to all argumentative situations. Only in the tribunal is there a moment when the procedures of appeal are exhausted. But it is because the decision of the judge is implemented by the force of public power. Neither in literary criticism, nor in the social sciences, is there such a last word. Or, if there is any, we call that violence.

From Explanation to Understanding

The same dialectic between comprehension and understanding may receive a new meaning if taken in the reverse way, from explanation to understanding. This new *Gestalt* of the dialectic proceeds from the nature of the referential function of the text. This referential function, as we said, exceeds the mere ostensive designation of the situation common to both speaker and hearer in the dialogical situation. This abstraction from the surrounding world gives rise to two opposite attitudes. As readers, we may either remain in a kind of state of suspense as regards any kind of referred-to world, or we may actualize the potential non-ostensive references of the text in a new situation, that of the reader. In the first case, we treat the text as a worldless entity; in the second, we create a new ostensive reference through the kind of "execution" which the act of reading implies. These two possibilities are equally entailed by the act of reading, conceived as their dialectical interplay.

The first way of reading is exemplified today by the different *structural* schools of literary criticism. Their approach is not only possible, but legitimate. It proceeds from the suspension, the *epoché,* of the ostensive reference. To read, in this way, means to prolong this suspension of the ostensive reference to the world and to transfer oneself into the "place" where the text stands, within the "enclosure" of this worldless place. According to this choice, the text no longer has an outside, it has only an inside. Once more, the very constitution of the text as text and of the system of texts as literature justifies this conversion of the literary thing into a closed system of signs, analogous to the kind of closed system which phonology discovered at the root of all discourse, and which de Saussure called "*la langue.*" Literature, according to this working hypothesis, becomes an *analogon* of "*la langue.*"

On the basis of this abstraction, a new kind of explanatory attitude may be extended to the literary object, which, contrary to the expectation of Dilthey, is no longer borrowed from the natural sciences, that is, from an area of knowledge alien to language itself. The opposition between *Natur* and *Geist* is no longer operative here. If some model is borrowed, it comes from the same field, from the semiological field. It is henceforth possible to treat texts according to the elementary rules which linguistics successfully applied to the elementary systems of signs that underlie the use of language. We have leaned from the Geneva school, the Prague school, and the Danish school, that it is always possible to abstract *systems* from *processes* and to relate these systems — whether phonological, lexical, or syntactical — to units which are merely defined by their opposition to other units of the same system. This interplay of merely distinctive entities within finite sets of such units defines the notion of structure in linguistics.

It is this structural model which is now applied to *texts,* that is, to sequences of signs longer than the sentence, which is the last kind of unit that linguistics takes into account.

In his *Anthropologie Structurale,* Claude Lévi-Strauss formulates this working hypothesis in the following way in regard to one category of texts, that of myths:

> Like every linguistic entity, the myth is made up of constitutive units. These constitutive units imply the presence of those which generally occur in the structures of language, namely phonemes, morphemes, and semantemes. Each form differs from the one which precedes it by a higher degree of complexity. For this reason we will call the elements which properly belong to the myth (and which are the most complex of all): large constitutive units.[9]

By means of this working hypothesis, the large units which are at least the same size as the sentence and which, put together, form the narrative proper of the myth, will be able to be treated according to the same rules as the smallest units known to linguistics. It is in order to insist on this likeness that Claude Lévi-Strauss speaks of mythemes, just as we speak of phonemes, morphemes, and semantemes. But in order to remain within the limits of the analogy between mythemes and the lower-level units, the analyzer of texts will have to perform

9. Claude Lévi-Strauss, *Anthropologie Structurale* (Paris: Plon, 1958), p. 233.

the same sort of abstraction as that practiced by the phonologist. For the latter, the phoneme is not a concrete sound, in an absolute sense, with its acoustic quality. It is not, to speak like de Saussure, a "substance" but a "form," that is to say, an interplay of relations. Similarly, a mytheme is not one of the sentences of a myth, but an oppositive value attached to several individual sentences forming, in Lévi-Strauss's phrase, a "bundle of relations." "It is only in the form of a combination of such bundles that the constitutive units acquire a meaning-function" (p. 234). What is here called a meaning-function is not at all what the myth means, its philosophical or existential content or intuition, but the arrangement, the disposition of mythemes, in short, the structure of the myth.

We can indeed say that we have explained a myth, but not that we have interpreted it. We can, by means of structural analysis, bring out the logic of it, the operations which relate the bundles of relations among themselves. This logic constitutes "the structural law of the myth under consideration" (p. 241). This law is preeminently an object of reading and not at all of speaking, in the sense of a recitation where the power of the myth would be reenacted in a particular situation. Here the text is only a text, thanks to the suspension of its meaning for us, to the postponement of all actualization by present speech.

I want now to show in what way "explanation" (*Erklären*) requires "understanding" (*Verstehen*) and brings forth in a new way the inner dialectic which constitutes "interpretation" as a whole.

As a matter of fact, nobody stops with a conception of myths and of narratives as formal as this algebra of constitutive units. This can be shown in different ways. First, even in the most formalized presentation of myths by Lévi-Strauss, the units which he calls "mythemes" are still expressed as sentences which bear meaning and reference. Can anyone say that their meaning as such is neutralized when they enter into the "bundle of relations" which alone is taken into account by the "logic" of the myth? Even this bundle of relations, in its turn, must be written in the form of a sentence. Finally, the kind of language game which the whole system of oppositions and combinations embodies would lack any kind of significance if the oppositions themselves, which, according to Lévi-Strauss, the myth tends to mediate, were not meaningful oppositions concerning birth and death, blindness and lucidity, sexuality and truth. Besides these existential conflicts there would be no contradictions to overcome, no logical function of the myth as an attempt to solve these contradictions. Structural analysis does not exclude, but presupposes, the opposite hypothesis concerning the myth, i.e., that it has a meaning as a narrative of the origins. Structural analysis merely represses this function. But it cannot suppress it. The myth would not even function as a logical operator if the propositions which it combines did not point toward boundary situations. Structural analysis, far from getting rid of this radical questioning, restores it at a level of higher radicality.

If this is true, could we not say that the function of structural analysis is to lead from a surface-semantics, that of the narrated myth, to a depth-semantics, that of the boundary situations which constitute the ultimate "referent" of the myth?

I really believe that if such were not the function of structural analysis, it would be reduced to a sterile game, a divisive algebra, and even the myth would be bereaved of the function which Lévi-Strauss himself assigns to it, that of making men aware of certain oppositions and of tending toward their progressive mediation. To eliminate this reference to the *aporias* of existence around which mythic thought gravitates would be to reduce the theory of myth to the necrology of the meaningless discourses of mankind. If, on the contrary, we consider structural analysis as a stage — and a necessary one — between a naive interpretation and a critical interpretation, between a surface-interpretation and a depth-interpretation, then it would be possible to locate explanation and understanding at two different stages of a unique *hermeneutical arc*. It is this depth-semantics which constitutes the genuine object of understanding and which requires a specific affinity between the reader and the kind of things the text is *about*.

But we must not be misled by this notion of personal affinity. The depth-semantics of the text is not what the author intended to say, but what the text is about, that is, the non-ostensive reference of the text. And the non-ostensive reference of the text is the kind of world opened up by the depth-semantics of the text.

Therefore what we want to understand is not something hidden behind the text, but something disclosed in front of it. What has to be understood is not the initial situation of discourse, but what points toward a possible world. Understanding has less than ever to do with the author and his situation. It wants to grasp the world-propositions opened up by the references of the text. To understand a text is to follow its movement from sense to reference, from what it says, to what it talks about. In this process the *mediating* role played by structural analysis constitutes both the justification of this objective approach and the rectification of the subjective approach. We are definitely prevented from identifying understanding with some kind of intuitive grasping of the intention underlying the text. What we have said about the depth-semantics which structural analysis yields invites us rather to think of the sense of the text as an injunction starting from the text, as a new way of looking at things, as an injunction to think in a certain manner.

Such is the reference born of depth-semantics. The text speaks of a possible world and of a possible way of orienting oneself within it. The dimensions of this world are properly opened up by, disclosed by, the text. Disclosure is the equivalent for written language of ostensive reference for spoken language.

If, therefore, we preserve the language of Romanticist hermeneutics when it speaks of overcoming the distance, of making "one's own," of appropriating what was distant, other, foreign, it will be at the price of an important corrective. That which we make our own — *Aneignung* in German — that which we appropriate, is not a foreign experience, but the power of disclosing a world which constitutes the reference of the text.

This link between disclosure and appropriation is, to my mind, the cornerstone of a hermeneutic which would claim both to overcome the shortcomings of historicism and to remain faithful to the original intention of Schleiermacher's hermeneutics. To understand an author better than he could understand himself is to display the power of disclosure implied in his discourse beyond the limited horizon of his own existential situation. The process of distanciation, of atemporalization, to which we connected the phrase of *Erklärung,* is the fundamental presupposition for this enlarging of the horizon of the text.

This second figure or *Gestalt* of the dialectic between explanation and comprehension has a strong paradigmatic character which holds for the whole field of the human sciences. I want to emphasize three points.

First, the structural model, taken as a paradigm for explanation, may be extended beyond textual entities to all social phenomena because it is not limited in its application to linguistic signs, but applies to all kinds of signs which are analogous to linguistic signs. The intermediary link between the model of the text and social phenomena is constituted by the notion of semiological systems. A linguistic system, from the point of view of semiology, is only a species within the semiotic genre, although this species has the privilege of being a paradigm for the other species of the genre. We can say therefore that a structural model of explanation can be generalized as far as all social phenomena which may be said to have a semiological character, that is, as far as it is possible to define the typical relations of a semiological system at their level: the general relation between code and message, relations among the specific units of the code, the relation between signifier and signified, the typical relation within and among social messages, the structure of communication as an exchange of messages, and so forth. Inasmuch as the semiological model holds, the semiotic or symbolic function, that is, the function of substituting signs for things and of representing things by the means of signs, appears to be more than a mere effect in social life. It is its very foundation. We should have to say, according to this generalized function of the semiotic, not only that the symbolic function is social, but that social reality is fundamentally symbolic.

If we follow this suggestion, the the kind of explanation which is implied by the structural model appears to be quite different from the classical causal model, especially if causation is interpreted in Humean terms as a regular sequence of antecedents and consequents with no inner logical connection between them. Structural systems imply relations of a quite different kind, correlative rather than sequential or consecutive. If this is true, the classical debate about motives and causes which has plagued the theory of action these last decades loses its importance. If the search for correlations within semiotic systems is the main task of explanation, then we have to reformulate the problem of motivation in social groups in new terms. But it is not the aim of this paper to develop this implication.

Secondly, the second paradigmatic factor in our previous concept of text-interpretation proceeds from the role which we assigned to depth-semantics *between* structural analysis and appropriation. This mediating function of depth-semantics must not be overlooked, since the appropriation's losing its psychological and subjective character and receiving a genuine epistemological function depends on it.

Is there something similar to the depth-semantics of a text in social phenomena?

I should tend to say that the search for correlations within and between social phenomena treated as semiotic entities would lose importance and interest if it would not yield *something like* a depth-semantics. In the same way as linguistic games are forms of life, according to the famous aphorism of Wittgenstein, social structures are also attempts to cope with existential perplexities, human predicaments, and deep-rooted conflicts. In this sense, these structures, too, have a referential dimension. They point toward the *aporias* of social existence, the same *aporias* around which mythical thought gravitates. And this analogical function of reference develops traits very similar to what we called the non-ostensive reference of a text, that is, the display of a *Welt* which is no longer an *Umwelt,* the projection of a world which is more than a situation. May we not say that in social science, too, we proceed from naive interpretations to critical interpretations, from surface-interpretations to depth-interpretations *through* structural analysis? But it is depth-interpretation which gives meaning to the whole process.

This last remark leads us to our third and last point.

If we follow the paradigm of the dialectic between explanation and understanding to its end, we must say that the meaningful patterns which a depth-interpretation wants to grasp cannot be understood without a kind of personal commitment similar to that of the reader who grasps the depth-semantics of the text and makes it his "own." Everybody knows the objection which an extension of the concept of appropriation to the social sciences is exposed to. Does it not legitimate the intrusion of personal prejudices, of subjective bias into the field of scientific inquiry? Does it not introduce all the paradoxes of the hermeneutical circle into the human sciences? In other words, does not the paradigm of disclosure *plus* appropriation destroy the very concept of a human science? The way in which we introduced this pair of terms within the framework of text-interpretation provides us not only with a paradigmatic problem, but with a paradigmatic solution. This solution is not to deny the role of personal commitment in understanding human phenomena, but to qualify it.

As the model of text-interpretation shows, understanding has nothing to do with an *immediate* grasping of a foreign psychic life or with an *emotional* identification with a mental intention. Understanding is entirely *mediated* by the whole of explanatory procedures which precede it and accompany it. The counterpart of this personal appropriation is not something which can be *felt,* it is the dynamic meaning released by the explanation which we identified earlier with the reference of the text, that is, its power of disclosing a world.

The paradigmatic character of text-interpretation must be applied down to this ultimate implication. This means that the conditions of an authentic appropriation, as they were displayed in relation to texts, are themselves paradigmatic. Therefore we are not allowed to exclude the final act of personal commitment from the whole of objective and explanatory procedures which mediate it.

This qualification of the notion of personal commitment does not eliminate the "hermeneutical circle." This circle remains an insuperable structure of knowledge when it is applied to human things, but this qualification prevents it from becoming a vicious circle.

Ultimately, the correlation between explanation and understanding, between understanding and explanation, is the "hermeneutical circle."

Chapter Three

The Problem of Historical Consciousness

HANS–GEORG GADAMER

INTRODUCTION

When in 1957 I received the invitation to teach half a semester at the Cardinal Mercier Chair at the University of Louvain, I found myself in the middle of my interpretation of hermeneutic philosophy as I had conceived it from hermeneutic praxis during a quarter century of academic activity. To be called to this chair as a German and as a Protestant imposed obligations and I owe to this institution the first premature formulation of several central ideas in my work then in progress. When the French version of these lectures appeared in 1963 — no German text exists — my larger book [*Wahrheit und Methode*] had already been published and hence the publication of the lectures seemed to me almost superfluous and at best a preliminary substitute in French for the larger work which is still only available in German.[1] I have distanced myself from the ideas as I had developed them at the time, and it is now, on the occasion of their present English transla-

Translated by Jeff L. Close from *Le Problème de la conscience historique* (Louvain: Institut Superieur de Philosophie, Université Catholique de Louvain, 1963). English translation published in the *Graduate Faculty Philosophy Journal* 5, no. 1 (1975). Introduction (1975) translated by Hans Fantel. Reprinted by permission. The numbers that appear within slashes in the body of the text refer to the pagination of the original. The translator gratefully acknowledges Mr. Daniel Cerezuelle's careful reading of the entire manuscript, and thanks especially Professor Gadamer for his many helpful suggestions on the translation. The translator enjoyed the tireless assistance of Mrs. Norma Newberg in the final preparation of the manuscript.

1. [Now see H. G. Gadamer, *Truth and Method,* edited by Garrett Barden and John Cumming (New York: Seabury Press, 1975).]

tion, that I re-read these lectures for the first time—after a span of nearly twenty years. An Italian translation of the French original text was published in 1969, but this translation already took account of the larger book and presented the text within the problematic which had been developed since.

The present reencounter with myself does not imply the rediscovery of early stages of my later thought because *Wahrheit und Methode* had already been completed at the time I wrote my French lectures. Yet this preliminary formulation of later work does imply a new emphasis because the ideational themes confronted in the manuscript had to establish their validity independently of the larger context which later surrounded them. These lectures, like any other, contain elements marked by the occasion. The role imposed by the specific location, the Institute Supérieur de Philosophie of a university which was then still Flemish-French, is particularly evident in the attempt to introduce the hermeneutic problem from the perspective of Husserl and Heidegger, whose work then stood at the center of the Institute's concerns. Neither was the choice of the topic, the problem of historical consciousness, without a particular motivation. For although the genesis of a "historical consciousness" is a process involving all of Europe, it was only in Germany that historical consciousness played a central philosophic role, especially through Wilhelm Dilthey and his so-called *Lebensphilosophie*. The Romantic tradition of the *Geisteswissenschaften* therefore had to be especially invoked outside the German cultural sphere.

This determined the choice of the topic and posed the task to accomplishing the transition from a hermeneutic methodology, in the sense of Schleiermacher and Dilthey, to a hermeneutic philosophy in the context of the special position of the *Geisteswissenschaften* relative to the natural sciences.

It is a self-contained pattern of argument which also constitutes the central position of the latter book. It is presented here with its own stringency as proof. In *Wahrheit und Methode* I have deliberately cited another instance at first, namely the experience of art and the hermeneutic dimension which certainly plays a part in the scientific approach to art, but above all, in the experience of art itself. That is generally evident in the reproductive arts in as much as reproduction is an interpretation which implies a certain *understanding* of the original text. In view of the hermeneutic experiences in the reproductive arts one is more likely to admit that there is no unequivocal objectivity and that every interpreter submits "his own" interpretation, which is nevertheless by no means arbitrary but may attain, or fail to attain, a definable degree of appropriateness. Similarly, nobody in this sphere will claim the concept of objectivity for this ideal of appropriateness. Too much of the specifically individual of the interpreter enters into the reproduction.

This reference to the reproductive arts stands in total contradiction to the theoretical orientation [*wissenschaftstheoretischen Orientierung*] under which the *Geisteswissenschaften,* particularly in Dilthey's conception, seek parity with the natural sciences. Interpretation in these two areas is certainly not similar. To be sure, the "appropriate" understanding of a text introduces into the *Geisteswissenschaften* something of the interpreter's location in time, place, and world view, but in contrast to artistic interpretation the understanding of the text as linguistically mediated in its interpretation is not independent from the original as an autonomous creation. It is not the case as in artistic interpretation that the original is "realized" only in the concrete substance of word, gesture, or tone. Reading, as distinguished from restorative "recital," does not posit itself for its own sake; it is not an autonomous realization of a thought pattern but remains subordinate to the text regenerated by the reading process. The reading is sublated in the reading of the text.

But ultimately this is also the intent guiding the interpretive process of the *Geisteswissenschaften.* Despite all the differences which separate (by circumspective linguistic expression and conceptual mediation) the interpretation from the substance of reading, there is no intention to place the realization of the text aside from the text itself. On the contrary, the ultimate ideal of appropriateness seems to be total self-effacement because the meaning [*Verständnis*] of the text has become self-evident.

All these phenomena comprise both understanding and interpretation. If Dilthey saw his task in providing an epistemic basic [*erkenntnistheoretische Grundlegung*] for the *Geisteswissenschaften,* he regarded himself not so much as a philologist understanding a text, but as a methodologist of a historical school which did not regard the "understanding of texts or other remnants of the past as its ultimate aim."

These are regarded as means to the recognition of this historical reality which they make accessible. For Dilthey, as the successor of Schleiermacher, philology also remains the guiding model. His ideal is to decode the Book of History. This is the method by which Dilthey hopes to justify the self-understanding of the *"verstehenden Wissenschaften"* (interpretive sciences) and their scientific objectivity. Just as one understands a text because it contains "pure meaning," so history is ultimately to be understood. Hermeneutics is the universal method of the historical sciences.

My analysis of Dilthey's position attempts to show that Dilthey's theoretical self-understanding in regard to the sciences is not truly consistent with his basic position in terms of *Lebensphilosophie*. What Misch and Dilthey have termed the "free distance toward oneself" [*freie Ferne zu sich selbst*] — that is, the human possibility of reflexive thought — does not in truth coincide with the objectivation of knowledge through scientific method. The latter requires its own explication. This lies in the connection between "life," which always implies consciousness and reflexivity [*Besinnung*], and "science," which develops from life as one of its possibilities. If this is the true problem, it places the foundation of the *Geisteswissenschaften* at the center of philosophy.

This is clearly evident in Heideggers's philosophical premise. Although I bypass Heidegger's philosophic intent, the revival of the "problem of Being," it becomes nevertheless clear that only the vivid thematization of human existence as "being-in-the-world" discloses the full implications of *"Verstehens"* as an existential possibility and structure. The human sciences thereby attain an "ontological" valence which could not remain without consequences for their methodological self-understanding. If *Verstehen* is the basic moment of human *in-der-Welt-sein,* then the human sciences are nearer to human self-understanding than are the natural sciences. The objectivity of the latter is no longer an unequivocal and obligatory ideal of knowledge.

Because the human sciences contribute to human self-understanding even though they do not approach the natural sciences in exactness and objectivity, they do contribute to human self-understanding because they in turn are based in human self-understanding.

Here something essentially new becomes apparent. It lies in the positive role of the determination by tradition [*Traditionsbestimtheit*] which historical knowledge and the epistemology of the human sciences share with the basic nature of human existence. It is true that the prejudices which dominate us often impare true recognition of the historical past. But without prior self-understanding, which is prejudice in this sense, and without readiness for self-criticism — which is also grounded in our self-understanding — historical understanding would be neither possible nor meaningful. Only through others do we gain true knowledge of ourselves. Yet this implies that historical knowledge does not necessarily lead to the dissolution of the tradition in which we live; it can also enrich this tradition, confirm or alter it — in short, contribute to the discovery of our own identity. The historiography of different nations is ample proof of this.

This state of affairs necessarily leads to a gain in clarity if one dared to analyze the formation of science in modern times. In fact, this was one of the first recognitions I gained from Aristotle — to apprehend the peculiar interlacing of being and knowledge, determination through one's own becoming, *Hexis,* recognition of the situational Good, and *Logos.* When Aristotle, in the sixth book of the *Nicomachean Ethics,* distinguishes the manner of "practical" knowledge, determined in this manner, from theoretical and technical knowledge, he expresses, in my opinion, one of the greatest truths by which the Greeks throw light upon "scientific" mystification of modern society of specialization. In addition, the scientific character of practical philosophy is, as far as I can see, the only methodological model for self-understanding of the human sciences if they are to be liberated from the spurious narrowing imposed by the model of the natural sciences. It imparts a scientific justification to the practical reason which sustains all human society and which is linked through millennia to the tradition of rhetoric. Here the hermeneutic problem becomes central; only the concretization of the general imparts to it its specific content.

In a final lecture I develop the theoretical consequence resulting from these thoughts concerning a philosophic grounding of hermeneutics. In particular, the traditional theory of the "hermeneutic circle" gains a new aspect and fundamental significance. It is not only the formal relation between the anticipation of the whole and the construction of the particulars, as we may remember it from our Latin lesson in the admonition to "construe," and which actually constitutes the circular structure of textual understanding. The hermeneutic circle is in fact a contentually fulfilled [*inhaltlich erfüllter*] circle, which joins the interpreter and his text into a unity within a processual whole. Understanding always implies a pre-understanding which is in turn pre-figured by the determinate tradition in which the interpreter lives and which shapes his prejudices. Every encounter with others therefore means the "suspension" of one's own prejudices, whether this involves another person through whom one learns one's own nature and limits, or an encounter with a work of art, ("There is no place which does not see you. You must alter your life."), or a text: always something more is demanded than to "understand the other," that is to seek and acknowledge the immanent coherence contained within the meaning-claim of the other. A further invitation is always implied. Like an infinite idea, what is also implied is a transcendental demand for coherence in which the ideal of truth is located. But this requires a readiness to recognize the other as potentially right and to let him or it prevail against me.

It is a grave misunderstanding to assume that emphasis on the essential factor of tradition which enters into all understanding implies an uncritical acceptance of tradition and sociopolitical conservatism. Whoever reads the present sketch of my hermeneutic theory will recognize that such an assumption reduces hermeneutics to an idealistic and historical self-conception. In truth the confrontation of our historic tradition is always a critical challenge of this tradition. Such confrontation does not occur in the workshops of the philologist or historian or in the eagerness of bourgeois cultural institutions to impart historical education. Every experience is such a confrontation.

In *Wahrheit und Methode* I have tried to describe more accurately and in a larger context how this process of challenge mediates the new by the old and thus constitutes a communicative process built on the model of dialogue. From this I derive hermeneutic's claim to universality. It signifies nothing less than that language forms the base of everything constituting man and society. In the present lectures only the very last sentence refers to language and relatedness to language [*Sprachlichkeit Sprachbezogenheit Sprachfähigkeit*] as the basis of all understanding.

Every experience is a confrontation. Because every experience sets something new against something old and in every case it remains open in principle whether the new will prevail—that is, will truly become experience— or whether the old, accustomed, predictable will be confirmed in the end. We know that even in the empirical sciences, as particularly Thomas Kuhn has shown in the meantime, not every new recognition is accepted without resistance. Rather, it is set aside as long as possible by the prevailing "paradigm." So it is basically with all experience. It must either overcome tradition or fail because of tradition. The new would be nothing new if it did not have to assert itself anew against something.

In a civilization social consciousness is determined by progress in science, perfection of technology, increase in affluence and the ideal of profit—and perhaps also by intimations of the end of this dream— newness and novelty fare badly just because the old no longer offers real resistance and no longer finds an advocate. This is probably the most important aspect in the historical consciousness which today is characterized as bourgeois: not that everything old is relativized, but that the relativized new lends a possible justification to the old.

It is not true that the question concerning that which is must always be resolved in favor of the quickly obsolete new, nor in favor of that which has been. Admittedly, historical relativism has cut the ground from under the intellectual absolution [*Repristinationen*] of earlier modes of thought and all naive systemization. But the question of philosophy cannot rest. It cannot be reduced to its social function nor can it be encompassed by rejection or legitimation based in the critique of ideology. Historical consciousness has already transcended all this in order to catch up—however belatedly—with the questioning which we call philosophy.

EPISTEMOLOGICAL PROBLEMS OF THE HUMAN SCIENCES

The subject of these lectures derives from the epistemological problem currently raised by the modern *Geisteswissenschaften.*

The appearance of historical self-consciousness is very likely the most important revolution among those we have undergone since the beginning of the modern epoch. Its spiritual magnitude probably surpasses what we recognize in the applications of natural science, applications which have so visibly transformed the surface of our planet. The historical consciousness which characterizes contemporary man is a privilege, perhaps even a burden, the like of which has never been imposed on any previous generation.

Our present-day consciousness of history is fundamentally different from the manner in which the past appeared to any foregoing people or epoch. We understand historical consciousness to be the privilege of modern man to have a full awareness of the historicity of everything present and the relativity of all opinions. Inescapably, we must acknowledge the effect of historical self-consciousness on the spiritual activity of our contemporaries: we have only to think of the immense spiritual upheavals of our times. For /8/ example, the invasion of philosophical and political thought by ideas designated in German by the words *"Weltanschauung"* and *"Kampf der Weltanschauungen"* is undoubtedly at once a consequence and a symptom of historical consciousness. It is manifest again in the way various *Weltanschauungen* currently express their differences. As a matter of fact, if, as has happened more than once, disputing parties come to a reciprocal agreement that their opposing positions form a comprehensible and coherent whole (a concession which clearly presupposes that both sides no longer refuse to reflect on the relativity of their own positions), then each party must have been fully conscious of the *particular* character of its own perspective. Today no one can shield himself from this reflexivity characteristic of the modern spirit. Henceforth it would be absurd to confine oneself to the naiveté and reassuring limits of a jealous tradition while modern consciousness is ready to understand the possibility of a multiplicity of relative viewpoints. Thus we are accustomed to respond to opposing arguments by a reflection which deliberately places us in the perspective of the other.

The modern historical sciences or *"Geisteswissenschaften"* —let us translate the term by "human sciences," realizing that it is only a convention—are distinguished by this mode of reflection and make methodic use of it. Is not this mode of reflection what we commonly mean by "having an historical sense"? We can define "historical sense" /9/ by the historian's openness to and talent for understanding the past, sometimes even the "exotic" past, from within its own genetic context. Having an historical sense is to conquer in a consistent manner the natural naiveté which makes us judge the past by the so-called obvious scales of our current life, in the perspective of our institutions, and from our acquired values and truths. Having an historical sense signifies thinking explicitly about the historical horizon which is coextensive with the life we live and have lived.

In its spiritual motifs, the method of the human sciences dates back to Herder and German romanticism, but it has diffused nearly everywhere and exerted its influence on the scientific progress of other countries. In obedience to this method modern life begins refusing to naively follow a tradition or complex of traditionally assumed truths. Modern consciousness — precisely as "historical consciousness" — takes a reflexive position concerning all that is handed down by tradition. Historical consciousness no longer listens sanctimoniously to the voice that reaches out from the past but, in reflecting on it, replaces it within the context where it took root in order to see the significance and relative value proper to it. This reflexive posture towards tradition is called *interpretation*. And if something is able to characterize the truly universal dimension of this event it is surely the role that the word *interpretation* has begun to play in the modern human sciences. This word has achieved a recognition as only happens to words which betoken the attitude of an entire epoch.

We speak of interpretation when the mean/10/ing of a text is not understood at first sight; then an interpretation is necessary. In other words, an explicit reflection is required on the conditions which enable the text to have one or another meaning. The first presupposition which implies the concept of interpretation is the "foreign" character of what is yet to be understood. Indeed, whatever is immediately evident, whatever persuades us by its simple presence, does not call for any interpretation. If we consider for a moment the art of our predecessors in textual interpretation, as applied in philology and theology, we immediately notice that it was always an occasional feature, used only when the transmitted text involved obscurities. Today, by contrast, the notion of interpretation has become a *universal concept* determined to encompass tradition as a whole.

Interpretation, as we understand it today, is applied not only to texts and verbal tradition, but to everything bequeathed to us by history; thus, for example, we will speak not only of the interpretation of an historical incident, but also the interpretation of spiritual and mimed expressions, the interpretation of behavior, and so forth. We always intend by this that the meaning of what is given over for our interpretation is not revealed without mediation, and that we must look beyond the immediate sense in order to discover the "true" hidden meaning. This generalized notion of interpretation dates back to a

Nietzschian conception. According to Nietzsche all statements dependent upon reason are open to interpretation, since their true or real
meaning only reaches us as masked and deformed by ideologies./11/

As a matter of fact, the modern methodology of our philosophical
and historical sciences corresponds exactly to this Nietzschian conception. Indeed, it presupposes that the material upon which these sciences work (i.e., sources, vestiges of a bygone era) is such that it
requires a critical interpretation. This assumption plays a decisive and
fundamental role for the modern sciences of historical and, in general,
social life. The dialogue we enter into with the past confronts us with a
fundamentally different situation from our own — we will say a
"foreign" situation — and consequently it demands an interpretative
approach. The human sciences, too, use an interpretative method,
thus placing them within our circle of interest. We ask ourselves: what
is the meaning and import of historical consciousness in the scheme of
scientific knowledge? Here again we are going to raise the same problem by examining the idea of a theory of the human sciences. Note,
however, that the theory of the human sciences is not simply the
methodology of a certain well-defined group of sciences, but is, as we
will see, philosophy properly so called in a much more radical sense
than, for instance, is the case with the methodology of natural sciences.

If we make a decided relation between the human sciences and
philosophy, it is not just for a purely epistemological elucidation. The
human sciences are not only a problem *for* philosophy, on the contrary,
they represent a problem *of* philosophy. Indeed, anything we could say
about their logical or epistemological independence vis-à-vis the natural sciences, is /12/ a very poor measure of the essence of the human
sciences and their truly philosophical significance. The philosophical
role played by the human sciences follows the law of all or nothing.
They would no longer have any role at all if we took them to be
imperfect realizations of the idea of a "rigorous science." For it would
immediately follow that so-called "scientific" philosophy would
necessarily take the idea of mathematicized natural science for the
scientific norm; as we know this would mean that philosophy would
no longer be a sort of "organon" of the sciences. On the other hand, if
we recognize an autonomous mode of knowing in the human sci-

ences, if we accord them the impossibility of being reduced to the natural scientific idea of knowledge (implying that one backs off from the absurdity of facing them with the ideal of a perfected facsimile of the methods and degree of certainty available in the natural sciences), then philosophy itself is called into question with all of its ambitions. And so, given these parameters, it is useless to restrict the elucidation of the nature of the human sciences to a purely methodological question; it is a question not simply of defining a specific method, but rather, of recognizing an entirely different notion of knowledge and truth. Consequently, the philosophy which bears these conditions in mind will have many other ambitions than those motivated by the natural scientific concept of truth. By an intrinsic necessity of things, to guarantee a genuine foundation for the human sciences, as Wilhelm Dilthey proposed not so long ago, is to guarantee a foundation in philosophy, that is to say, to consider the ground of nature and history, and the truth possible in each./13/

Let us immediately notice that, confirmed or not by the philosophic inclinations of Dilthey, the frames elaborated by the idealism of a Hegel are most readily suited to this philosophic enterprise. A logic of the *Geisteswissenschaften,* we would say, is already and always a philosophy of the Spirit.

Nevertheless, what we have just suggested in alluding to Hegel seems to contradict the intimate connections which the human sciences do have with the natural sciences, precisely those connections which distinguish the human sciences from an idealistic philosophy: the human sciences, too, would be verifiable empirical sciences, free from any metaphysical intrusion, and reject all philosophical constructions of universal history. However, is it not more true to say that the filiation of the human sciences with the natural sciences, and the anti-idealistic and anti-speculative controversy which they inherit at the same time, have up to now hindered the human sciences from moving towards a radical self-understanding? Although the constant desire of the human sciences may be to bolster themselves with contemporary philosophy, it remains no less true that in order to achieve a scientific good conscience, they continue to be attracted to the models of the natural sciences in developing their historical-critical methods. But we must raise the question whether it is meaningful, or valid, to look, by analogy with the mathematicized natural sciences, for an autonomous and specific method for the human sciences which remains constant throughout the domains of its application? Why /14/ is not the Cartesian notion of method proclaimed inadequate in the domain of the human sciences: why would it not be instead the ancient Greek concept of method which is privileged in this domain?

Let us explain. According to Aristotle, for example, the idea of a single method, a method which could be determined before even having penetrated the thing, is a dangerous abstraction; *the object itself* must determine the method of its own access. Now, curiously, if we take a look at the positive research in the human sciences during the last century, it seems that concerning the effective procedures of the human sciences (I am speaking just of those procedures which acquire evidence and knowledge of new truths, and not of the reflections on those procedures), it is much more valid to characterize them by the Aristotelian concept of method than by the pseudo-Cartesian concept of the historical-critical method. We must ask if a method which justifies detaching itself from the domain in question (and we know how fruitful this method was in the case of the mathematization of the natural sciences) does not, in the human sciences, lead to a misapprehension of the natural mode of being specific to this domain? This question leads us again into the vicinity of Hegel, for whom, as we know, every method is "a method linked to the object itself."[2] Can we learn something from the Hegelian dialectic about a "logic" of the human sciences?

I dare say, /15/ this second allusion to Hegel can appear absurd in the light of the methodological conclusions drawn by the human sciences in the period of their real efflorescence during the nineteenth century; obviously, only the natural sciences served as a model for these conclusions. This is even betrayed by the history of the word *Geisteswissenschaften*: although admitting that the intellectual survival of idealism spurred the German translator of Mill's inductive logic to render "moral sciences" by "*Geisteswissenschaften,*"[3] we must, how-

2. G. W. F. Hegel, *Wissenschaft der Logik,* edited by G. Lasson (Leipzig: Felix Meiner, 1923), vol. II, p. 486. [*Science of Logic,* tr. A. V. Miller (New York: Humanities Press, 1969) — Tr.]

3. J. S. Mill, *System der deduktiven und induktiven Logik,* translated by Schiel (1863); 6th Book: "Von der Logik der Geisteswissenschaften oder moralischen Wissenschaften."

ever, deny Mill the intention of having wished to attribute to the "moral sciences" a logic *of their own*. On the contrary, Mill's aim was to show that the inductive method found at the base of all empirical science is also the only valid method for the domain of the moral sciences. In this his doctrine is but the confirmation of an English secular tradition whose most powerful formulation we find in the introduction to Hume's *Treatise of Human Nature*. The moral sciences constitute no exception, Mill says, when we look for uniformities, regularities, and laws in the interest of predicting particular facts and events. Besides, the extension and applicability of the laws arrived at in the natural sciences is not always the same, but that does not impede meteorology, for example, from working on precisely the same basic principles as physics; the only difference which separates them is that in meteorology the system of data includes /16/ relatively more gaps than in physics. But this only affects the relative certainty of their respective predictions and in no way constitutes any methodological difference. Now, one will say, it is the same in the domain of moral and social phenomena, no less than in the natural sciences: in both cases the inductive method is independent of all metaphysical presuppositions. It is of no concern whatsoever to know, for example, what one thinks of the possibility of a phenomenon like human freedom; the inductive method has nothing to do with the search for any occult causes, it merely observes regularities. Thus it is possible to believe in free will and, at the same time, in the validity of predictions in the domain of social life. Drawing consequences on the basis of regularities does not imply any hypothesis about the metaphysical structure of the relations in question: one is concerned with them solely for the prediction of regularities. The actuality of free decisions is one of the moments of the universal derived by induction. That is the way in which the natural scientific ideal is adopted at the level of social phenomena.

Undoubtedly, certain researches conducted in this style, as for example in mass psychology, have been crowned with incontestable success. However, with the elementary acknowledgment that the discovery of regularities realizes actual progress in the human sciences, in the end we only conceal the genuine problem that these sciences raise. The adoption of this Humean model does not allow us to circumscribe the experience of a social-historical world; quite the contrary, we totally misunderstand the essence of this experience so long as we approach it merely by means of inductive procedures. For whatever is /17/ meant by *science,* neither by procuring regularities nor by their application to actual historical phenomenon will one ever grasp the peculiar component of historical knowledge.

Surely we can admit that all historical knowledge involves the application of general empirical regularities to the concrete problems it faces; yet, the true intention of historical knowledge is not to explain a concrete phenomenon as a particular case of a general rule, even if this had to be subordinated to the purely practical aim of an eventual prediction. In actuality, its true goal—even in utilizing general knowledge—is to understand an historical phenomenon in its singularity, in its uniqueness. Historical consciousness is interested in knowing, not how men, people, or states develop *in general,* but, quite on the contrary, how *this* man, *this* people, or *this* state became what it is; how each of these *particulars* could come to pass and end up specifically *there.*

But what sort of knowledge do we speak of now, and what is meant by "science" in this case? We have just presented a type of science manifesting a character and goal radically different from the natural sciences. But doesn't this characterization come back to a purely privative definition? Must we then speak of an "inexact science"? From the perspective of this question it is desirable to examine the reflections of Hermann Helmholtz who, in /18/ 1862, was already looking for a solution to the problems engaging us here.[4] Although he insisted on the importance and human significance of the *Geisteswissenschaften,* he was still inspired by the methodological ideal of the natural sciences when he attempted to define their logical character. Helmholtz distinguished between two species of induction: on the one side, logical induction, and on the other, instinctive induction, artistic induction, as it were. Note well that this is a psychological and not a logical distinction. For Helmholtz both sciences make use of inductive reasoning; in the human sciences, however, inductive reasoning is practiced implicitly, unconsciously, and happens as a tributary consequent of what we call in German *Taktgefühl,* a sort of tact or sym-

4. H. Helmholtz, *Vorträge und Reden,* 4th ed., vol. I, "Über das Verhaltnis der Naturwissenschaften zur Gesamtheit der Wissenschaften," pp. 167ff.

pathetic sensibility. In turn, this sensitivity is supported by other mental faculties, as for example the richness of memory, acceptance of authorities, and so forth. In contrast, the explicit reasoning of the naturalist rests entirely on the use of a single function: understanding [*l'entendement*].

Although we readily admit that the great scholar has, perhaps, resisted the temptation to take his own scientific activity as the measure, nevertheless, in characterizing the procedures of the human sciences, in the end he resorted to the single logical category which he took from Mill: induction. For him as well, the model that mechanics gave to the whole of eighteenth-century science remained valid. But, that this mechanics might itself be an historical phenomenon, /19/ that consequently it might be subject to historical investigation (as Pierre Duhem did so profitably much later[5]), was totally foreign to him.

Yet, in the same period, the problem appeared to many with a certain acuity; we have only to think of the prodigious research of the "historical school."

Would it not have been necessary to raise these investigations to the level of logical self-consciousness? As early as 1843, J. G. Droysen, the author who first drew attention to the history of Hellenism, wrote: "There is certainly no scientific discipline which is—theoretically speaking—so little justified, so little circumscribed and articulated as is history." And he appealed to a new Kant in order to disclose the living source of history in a categorical imperative, "from where springs," to use his words, "the historical life of humanity." That Droysen called upon Kant tells us that he did not conceive of the epistemology of history to be a logical "organon," but a truly philosophical task. He expected that "a deepened conception of history could make possible new progress in the human sciences and become the center of gravity stabilizing their oscillations."[6]

That it is still the natural scientific model that matters here finds no

5. P. H. Duhem, *Études sur Léonard de Vinci,* 3 vol. (1907–1913); and his posthumous *Le Système du monde,* 10 vols. (Paris: A. Hermann, 1913–1959).

6. J. G. Droysen, *Grudriss der Historik* (Halle: Max Niemeyer, republ. 1925), p. 97. [See *Outline of the Principles of History,* translated by E. B. Andrews (New York: Howard Fertig, 1967 reprint of 1893 ed.). This translation is from an 1867 edition of the *Historik* which does not include the final section, "Theologie der Geschichte," cited by Gadamer and which originally appeared in 1843 as an introduction to the second part of Droysen's *History of Hellenism.* For related comments on scientific and historical methods, see pp. 16, 62ff., and 107 of the Andrews translation—Tr.]

better proof than the plural used in saying *"Geisteswissenschaften"* or "human sciences." However, this "model" does not necessarily signify an epistemological unity: /20/ on the contrary, the natural sciences constitute a model for the human sciences only insofar as the latter submit to the ideal of an autonomous and grounded scientific value. Droysen's logic of history —which he called an *Historik* —was the first sketch of an epistemology of this species.

THE IMPORTANCE AND LIMITS OF WILHELM DILTHEY'S WORK

Dilthey's philosophical work is dedicated to this same task of constructing, parallel to the critique of pure reason, a "critique of historical reason." But the difference between Droysen and Dilthey is notable. Whereas Droysen remains a successor —albeit a critical one —to Hegel's philosophy (we need only recall that in his logic of history the fundamental concept of history is defined as a generic concept of man), we find in Dilthey, however, that the romantic and idealistic heritage is tangled with the influence which Mill's logic had exerted since the middle of the century. It is true that Dilthey thought himself quite superior to English empiricism on account of his vivid intuition of the superiority of the "historical school" compared to all naturalistic or dogmatic thought. Indeed, he said: "Only in Germany could the practice of an authentic experience be substituted for an empiricism which was dogmatic and burgeoning with prejudices; Mill is dogmatic for lack of historical erudition."[7] These lines are found noted in Dilthey's copy of Mill's *Logic*. As a matter of fact, the difficult work accomplished by Dilthey over several /22/ decades to ground the human sciences and distinguish them from the natural sciences is a continual debate with the naturalistic methodological ideal that Mill assigned to the human sciences in his famous last chapter.[8] To a so-called "explanatory" psychology —in the naturalistic sense of the word —Dilthey opposed the idea of a *"geisteswissenschaftliche"* psychology. It is to *geisteswissenschaftliche* psychology, disencumbered from all dogmatism and every hypothetical construction, that belongs the knowledge and description of the laws of spiritual life which are to serve as the common ground for the various human sciences. Indeed, all propositions in the human sciences concern, in the end, the facts of

7. W. Dilthey, *Gesammelte Schriften* (Stuttgart: Teubner), vol. V, p. lxxiv.
8. See Ibid., vol. V, pp. 56ff.

"internal experience": a domain of being which is put into relief not by the category of "explanation," but by that of *understanding*.

Dilthey's effort to philosophically ground the human sciences depends upon the epistemological consequences which he drew from everything the "historical school" (Ranke and Droysen) had already tried to emphasize in opposition to German Idealism. According to Dilthey, the greatest weakness in the reflections of the disciples of the "historical school" is their inconsistency: "instead of, on the one hand, exposing the epistemological presuppositions of the historical school and, on the other, examining those of idealism which made their way from Kant to Hegel, in order to discover their incompatibilities, they have uncritically confused the two, /23/ one with the other."[9] Dilthey's own intent is clear: discover on the boundary between historical experience and the idealistic heritage of the historical school a new and epistemologically solid foundation; it is this which explains his idea of completing Kant's critique of pure reason by a "critique of historical reason."

Even by posing the problem in this way Dilthey already abandons speculative idealism; the analogy which conjoins the problem of historical reason with the problem of pure reason must be taken literally. Historical reason is in search of justification no less than was pure reason not so long before. The critique of pure reason aimed at not only the destruction of metaphysics as a purely rational science of the world, of the soul, and of God, but also the simultaneous unveiling of a new domain within which rational science had a justifiable application. In this connection we witness, then, a double philosophical consequence: On the one side, if the critique of pure reason denounced "the dreams of visionaries," it did not, however, fail to furnish a response to the question: How is a pure science of nature possible? On the other side, by introducing the historical world into the autonomous development of reason, speculative idealism integrated historical consciousness into the domain of purely rational knowledge. History became a chapter in the Encyclopedia of the Spirit.

In this way philosophy came in effect to the following problem: how to produce for the world of historical consiousness something

9. Ibid., vol. VII, p. 281.

similar to what /24/ Kant succeeded in producing for the scientific knowledge of nature. Is there a way to justify empirical knowledge in history while totally renouncing all dogmatic constructions?

At this point Dilthey asks himself how to fit historical consciousness to the place previously held by Hegel's Absolute Knowledge of Spirit. But that raises more problems than it solves. Dilthey stressed that we can only know from within an historical perspective since, as it happens, we are *ourselves* historical beings. But does not the very historical mode of being of our consciousness constitute an impermeable boundary? Now Hegel solves the problem by the *Aufhebung* of history into Absolute Knowledge; but for Dilthey, who admits the possibility of unceasing variation in the interpretation of historical relations, is not the attainment of objective knowledge excluded in advance? Dilthey pondered over these problems untiringly; his reflections had precisely the goal of legitimating the scientific knowledge of the historically-conditioned as *objective science*. A great aid was provided him by the idea of a structure which was constituted as a unity emanating from its own center. It was a very flexible schema: the knowledge of infinitely complex historical relations became conceivable, even extending so far as to include universal historical knowledge. The notion that a structural relation could become intelligible through its own center corresponded to the old hermeneutic principle and, at the same time, met the /25/ exigencies of historical thought. According to these conditions every historical moment must be understood in itself and cannot be submitted to the measures of a present which may be extrinsic to it. But the application of this schema presupposes that the historian can disengage himself from his own historical situation. And, indeed, is not having an "historical sense" in fact claiming to be disencumbered from the hold exercised by the prejudices of the epoch in which one lives? Dilthey was convinced he had achieved a truly historical view of the world; but at bottom, what his historical reflections were able to justify was nothing other than the grandiose and epical self-effacement practiced by Ranke.

This explains in what specific sense the perspective of finitude and historicity did not cause, in Dilthey's opinion, any detriment in principle to the validity of knowledge in the human sciences. For Dilthey the task of historical consciousness is a victory gained over its own relativity, thus justifying objective knowledge in this domain. But how can one legitimate this claim to objectivity on the part of historical consciousness in spite of its conditioned and bounded mode of being — and even in opposition to all other cognitive forms known through history, forms always relative to a determinate perspective?

According to Dilthey, this legitimation can no longer be lodged in Hegel's Absolute Knowledge. This Hegelian Absolute Knowledge is an actual self-consciousness which re-totalizes the phases of the progress of Spirit. What is this if not the pretension of philosophical consciousness to contain in itself the total truth of the history of Spirit — exactly the thesis rejected by an historical vision on the world? We need, then, an historical *experience* /26/ since human consciousness is not an infinite intelligence to which everything can be simultaneously present. On principle, for a finite and historical consciousness, the absolute identity of consciousness and object is unattainable: it is always immersed in historical influences. But in what, then, consists its privileged capacity to transcend itself and be entitled to an objective historical knowledge?

Here is Dilthey's reply: as impenetrable as the ground of historical life may be, this life is able to historically understand its possibility of having an historical attitude. Ever since the rise and victory of historical consciousness we confront a new situation. *Hereafter,* this consciousness is no longer simply an unreflective expression of real life. It ceases to judge everything transmitted to it by the measures of the understanding it has of its own life and, in this way, to establish the continuity of tradition. This historical consciousness now knows how to situate itself in a reflexive relation with itself and with tradition; it understands itself by and through its own history. *Historical consciousness is a mode of self-consciousness.*

Dilthey proposes, then, that we understand the appearance and genesis of a scientific consciousness through an analysis of the essence of self-knowledge. But immediately his philosophical impasse, regarding the problem he chose for himself, becomes apparent.

Dilthey's point of departure is that life carries in itself reflection. /27/ We must credit Georg Misch with exposing Dilthey's orientation towards a *Lebensphilosophie.* Now this orientation has as its foundation the idea that all life as such carries within it knowledge. Even the intimate familiarity which characterizes "lived experience" contains a sort of reflection, bound up with life,"[10] says Dilthey. It is this same immanent reflexivity in life which, according to Dilthey, is at the base of our lived experience of meaning. The experience of meaning in the cohesiveness of life is possible only if one is disengaged from the "pursuit of (vital) objectives"; this reflection is possible only if we take a certain retreat by placing ourselves above the connections which secure our different activities. Likewise Dilthey emphasized — and undoubtedly he had reason —that what we call the "meaning of life" takes shape, well before any scientific objectivation, in the natural view of life on itself. This natural view of life on itself is found objectified in the wisdom of proverbs and myths, but especially in the great works of art. Art, in fact, constitutes the privileged medium through which life is understood, because, situated "in the confines between knowledge and action it allows life to be disclosed at a depth no longer accessible to observation, reflection and theory."[11]

Yet, we must not limit the reflective meaning of life to the pure expression we find in works of art. We must say that every expression of life implies a knowledge which shapes it from within. /28/ Is not expression this plastic milieu of the spirit —Hegel's Objective Spirit —whose realm encompasses every form of human life? In his language, in his moral values and juridical forms, the individual —the isolated being —is even then and always beyond his particularity. The ethical milieu, where he lives and in which he partakes, constitutes something "solid" that allows him to orient himself despite the somewhat vague contingencies of his subjective impulses. Dedication to communal purposes, to action for the community, this is what frees man, says Dilthey, from his particularity and from his ephemeral existence.

This would still have been acceptable to Droysen, but with Dilthey it takes on a quite unique profile. "Searching for solid forms"[12]: there, according to Dilthey, is the vital tendency of our life, a tendency present in contemplation and science no less than in the reflection which practical experience always involves. Thus, we understand that

10. Ibid., vol. VII, p. 18.
11. Ibid., vol. VII, p. 207. [See *Pattern and Meaning in History,* edited by H. P. Rickman (New York: Harper Torchbooks, 1961), p. 119; and "The Understanding of Others and Their Life Expressions," in Patrick Gardner, ed., *Theories of History* (Glencoe: Free Press, 1959) — Tr.]
12. Ibid., vol. VII, p. 347.

for Dilthey the objectivity of scientific knowledge, no less than the inquiring reflection of philosophy, is like an unfolding of the natural tendencies of life. What guides Dilthey's reflections is not at all a pure, simple, and superficial adaptation of the method of the human sciences to the procedures of the natural sciences, rather it is the discovery of something genuinely common to both methods. It is indeed essential to the experimental method to go beyond the contingencies of subjective observation, and in this way it succeeds in discovering the laws of nature. Likewise, the underlying aspiration of the human sciences is to go beyond the contin/29/gencies of a purely subjective perspective by methodical critique and thus achieve an historical and objective knowledge. Finally, we recognize in philosophical reflection an analogous intention and sense as well, even when it gives up the pretension of pure knowledge through merely conceptual analysis: it "objectifies itself as a human and historical fact."[13]

Dilthey's position, centered entirely on the relation between life and knowledge, thoroughly withstands the idealistic objection which accuses if of "historical relativism." To root philosophy in the primordial fact of life amounts to abandoning the search for a simple, non-contradictory system of statements and concepts. The role occupied throughout life by *Besinnung* — self-consciousness, reflection — must also be valid, according to Dilthey, for philosophical reflection. This is a *Selbstbesinnung* which brings the reflexivity of life to its highest point; consequently, philosophy must be considered as an objectification of life itself. Thus philosophy becomes a "philosophy of philosophy," but assuredly not in the sense nor with the claims that idealism earlier attributed to itself. The program of this reflection does not start from a self-sufficient speculative principle and aim at the construction of the one and only possible philosophy, instead it intends to follow solely the path of the historical *Selbstbesinnung*. And in this sense Dilthey's philosophy is quite unscathed by the accusation of relativism.

It is true that Dilthey was not untroubled by the problem of relativism. He pondered a great deal on the question of how to assure objectivity in the midst of all these relativities, how to con/30/ceive of the relationship of the finite to the absolute. "Our task consists," he said, "in explaining how the relative values of an age can have widened out

13. Ibid., vol. V, pp. 339ff; see vol. VII.

into something in some manner absolute."[14] Nevertheless, we ask Dilthey in vain for an effective answer to this problem of relativism. And this state of affairs is less because he did not find an authentic answer, than because, in the last analysis, this problem did not touch the true center of his thought at all. In fact, throughout the unfolding of the historical *Selbstbesinnung* which carried Dilthey from relativity to relativity, he always felt sure to be on the road to the absolute. In this sense Ernst Tröltsch summarizes very well Dilthey's work by the formula "from relativity to totality." This expression corresponds perfectly to Dilthey's own formula: "To be consciously a conditioned being."[15] Obviously, this formula epigrammatizes an explicit critique of idealism for which the truth or the achievement of consciousness is real only as infinite and unconditioned consciousness, that is to say, Absolute Spirit.

But considering his assiduous and unremitting meditations on the objection of relativism, one quickly realizes that Dilthey himself did not clearly countenance the full anti-idealistic implications of his philosophy inspired by the problem of "life." Indeed, how else are we to explain the fact that Dilthey did not notice and refute the intellectualist motive in the objection of relativism, intellectualism incompatable not only with the ultimate import of his philosophy of life, but even with his chosen point of departure: the immanence of knowledge in the very heart of life.

/31/ The underlying reason for this inconsistency at the heart of Dilthey's thought undoubtedly lies in his latent *Cartesianism*. His historico-philosophical reflections towards grounding the human sciences cannot really be reconciled with the starting point of his *Lebensphilosophie*. He demands that his philosophy be extended to all the domains where "consciousness, by a reflexive and dubitative attitude, will be liberated from the hold of authoritarian dogmas and aspire to genuine knowledge."[16] It seems clear to us that this statement adequately reflects the spirit of modern science and philosophy in general. Also, we cannot ignore the Cartesian resonances which it conveys. And yet, curiously, Dilthey applied it in a very different sense: "Always and everywhere, life leads to reflection on that which confronts it, reflection leads to doubt, and life can only resist doubt in

14. Ibid., vol. VII, p. 290. [See Rickman, op. cit., p. 166 — Tr.]
15. Ibid., vol. V, p. 364.   16. Ibid., vol. VII, p. 6.

the pursuit of valid knowledge."[17] This citation clearly shows that in reality Dilthey, unlike the epistemologies of the Cartesian persuasion, is not aiming towards a shattering of philosophical prejudices, but rather he contends that it is real life as a whole — the moral, religious, juridical, and other traditions — which must arouse reflection and call out for a new rational order. Nevertheless, in this passage, then, Dilthey means by "knowledge" and "reflection" something more than the simple immanence of knowing in life, a universal immanence of which we have spoken above. In fact, living traditions, like the moral, religious, and juridical traditions, are always derivatives — and without reflection — of /32/ life's spontaneous self-knowledge. We have already noted that in dedicating himself to tradition the individual is raised to the level of Objective Spirit. Thus we will agree with Dilthey in saying that the influence exercised by thought over life "springs from an intrinsic necessity to find, within the inconsistent variations in sense perceptions, desires and affections, something solid which makes possible a stable and harmonious behavior."[18] But this is carried out specifically through the objectifications of the spirit, such as morality, positive law, and religion, binding the particular being to the objectivity of society. Here now is something incompatible in the Diltheian *Lebensphilosophie*: at the same time he demands a "reflexive and dubitative" stance towards all these objectifications of the spirit in order to raise a work to the stature of "science." Here Dilthey continues to adhere to the scientific ideal of Enlightment philosophy. Now this Enlightment philosophy agrees but little with the *Besinnung* immanent in life; specifically, Dilthey's *Lebensphilosophie* is, in principle, most radically opposed to its intellectualism and dogmatism.

Actually, the sort of certitude we acquire through doubt is fundamentally different from that other — immediate — sort which is possessed by the ends and values in life which are themselves presented to consciousness with the pretension of being absolute. There is a decisive difference between this certitude grasped in the heart of life and /33/ scientific certitude. The certitudes obtained in the sciences always possess a Cartesian resonance; they are the result of a critical method. The latter puts in doubt the accepted opinions in order to achieve, through new examination, their confirmation or rectification. Rightly

17. Ibid.   18. Ibid.

we speak of methodic doubt. By the artifice of a hyperbolic doubt, through an experiment analogous to those of the laboratory, Descartes proposes to show us in his celebrated meditations the *fundamentum inconcussum*: self/consciousness. Likewise, a methodical science doubts on principle all that can be doubted in order to arrive at the certitude of its knowledge. Now it is characteristic of Dilthey's thought that he does not distinguish between this methodic doubt and the sort of doubt which assails us, so to say, without reason, without purpose, spontaneously. Dilthey treats scientific certitude as the fulfillment of this certitude which reigns at the heart of life. On the other side, we cannot say that Dilthey, with all the weight that ˈconcrete historicity burdened him, was insensible to the uncertainty of life. Quite on the contrary, the more he was devoted to the modern sciences, the more he struggled with the tension between the tradition of his origins and the historical forces which modern life had unleashed. His search for something, as he said, "solid" is explained precisely by the sort of defensive instinct that he develops in view of the tumultuous reality of life. But it is remarkable that to conquer the uncertainty of life, he hopes to find this something "solid" in science, and not in the assurances that the experience of life itself can offer.

The personal process of secularization which made Dilthey — a theological student — a philosopher, can /34/ be paralleled to the historical process of the birth of the modern sciences. Just as the natural sciences bring to bear a limited yet sure light on the secrets of nature, now we face a scientifically developed power of "understanding" focused on the mysteries of life. Enlightenment philosophy is carried out in historical consciousness.

Consequently, we will understand how Dilthey is dependent on romantic hermeneutics. In fact, romantic hermeneutics masks the essential difference between historical experience and scientific knowledge, that is, it allows one to neglect the essential historicity of the mode of knowledge of the human sciences and to coordinate them to the methodology of the natural sciences. Thus Dilthey maintained, for example, an ideal of "objectivity" for the human sciences which could only serve to assure them of a "rank" equal to that of the natural sciences. From there also stems the frequent use Dilthey liked to make of the word "results" and his preference for methodological descriptions, a usage and preference which served the same aim. In this respect romantic hermeneutics is useful to him, for it too misconceives the historical nature of the experience which is at the base of the human sciences. It starts off from the assumption that the proper object of understanding is the text to be deciphered and understood, but that every encounter with a text is an encounter of the spirit with itself. Every text is foreign enough to pose a problem, and yet familiar enough that, in principle, the possiblity of /35/ deciphering some sense out of it is assured, even when all that one knows is the fact that it is a text, that is to say, written spirit.

As we can see with Schleiermacher, the model of hermeneutics is the reciprocal understanding attained in the relation between the I and the thou. Understanding a text carries with it the same possibility of perfect adequation as the comprehension of the thou. What the author has in view is immediately evident in his text; text and interpreter are absolutely contemporaneous. Here is the triumph of the philological method: grasp the past spirit as the present, welcome the foreign as the familiar. It is evident, then, that in spite of the diversity of methods, the "differences" with the natural sciences no longer exist — since, in both cases, we address our questions to an object already fully present, to an object which contains every answer.

From this point of view Dilthey fulfilled perfectly the task he had set for himself: he justified epistemologically the human sciences by conceiving the historical world in the manner of a text to be deciphered. This proposition epitomizes the position of the "historical school." Ranke had already assigned the historian the sacred task of deciphering the hieroglyphs of history, but Dilthey goes even further. If historical reality has a sense transparent enough to be deciphered like a text, then all that is wanting is an interpreter who would reduce history to the history of Spirit. Dilthey himself draws this conclusion and recognizes in fact his kinship with Hegel's philosophy of Spirit. And while Schleiermacher's romantic hermeneutics had ambitions of being a universal instrument of the spirit (but confined itself to /36/ aiding the expression of the force of salvation in the Christian faith), for Dilthey's *Grundlegung* of the human sciences, however, hermeneutics is the *telos* of historical consciousness. For it, there exists but one species of knowledge of the truth: that which *understands expression,* and in expression, life. In history, nothing is incomprehensible. Everything is understood since everything resembles a text. "Life and history have meaning, as letters have in a word,"[19] said Dilthey. Consequently, the study of the historical past is conceived not as an historical experience, but as *deciphering*. This constitutes an important difference between Dilthey's conceptions and the views of romantic hermeneutics; despite his obvious attachments to these views we cannot be led astray and overlook this very real difference.

Now historical experience is defined by the historical acquirements from which it originates and by the impossibility of detaching it from this origin; never, then, will it be a pure method. There will always be certain means of deducing general rules from this experience, but the methodological meaning of this step forbids that one draw a law, properly so called, from it and for ever afterwards subsume the complex of given concrete cases in an unequivocal manner. The idea of experiential rules always demands — the rules being what they are only through use — that they be *tested* in use. This is what remains valid, in a general and universal way, for our knowledge in the human sciences. They never attain an "objectivity" other than that which all experience carries with it.

/37/ Dilthey's effort to understand the human sciences through life, beginning from lived experience, is never really reconciled with the Cartesian concept of science which he did not know how to throw off. Emphasize as he might the contemplative tendencies of life itself, the attractions of something "solid" that life involves, his concept of "objectivity," as he reduced it to the objectivity of "results," remains attached to an origin very different from lived experience. This is why he was unable to resolve the problem he had chosen: to justify the human sciences with the express purpose of making them equal to the natural sciences.

MARTIN HEIDEGGER AND THE SIGNIFICANCE OF HIS
"HERMENEUTICS OF FACTICITY" FOR THE HUMAN SCIENCES

In the meantime, however, phenomenological research, as inaugurated by Edmund Husserl, decisively broke the bonds of neo-Kantian methodologism. Husserl gave back an absolutely universal theme of research to the dimension of living experience and thus overcame the point of view limited to the purely methodological

19. Ibid., vol. VII, p. 281. [See Rickman, op. cit., p. 168 — Tr.]

problematic of the human sciences. His analyses of the "life-world" (*Lebenswelt*) and of this anonymous constitution of all meaning and significance which forms the ground and texture of experience, showed definitively that the concept of objectivity represented by the sciences exemplifies but a special case. The opposition between nature and spirit is reexamined; the human sciences *and* the natural sciences must be understood in terms of life's universal intentionality. This understanding alone satisfies the requirements of a philosophical *Selbstbesinnung*.

To these discoveries of Husserl, and in the light of the question of being which he revived, Heidegger ascribed an even more radical meaning. He follows Husserl in that, for him as well, it is unnecessary to separate, as Dilthey had done, historical being from the being of nature in order to legitimate on the level of the theory of knowledge /40/ the methodological uniqueness of the historical sciences. On the contrary, the natural scientific mode of knowledge is a subspecies of understanding which, as Heidegger says in *Being and Time,* "has strayed into the legitimate task of grasping the present-at-hand (the *Vorhandene,* 'substantial' being) in its essential unintelligibility."[20] For Heidegger understanding [*le comprendre*], comprehension [*la comprehension*], is no longer the ideal of knowledge to which Spirit, now grown old, must be resigned — as it was for Dilthey — but neither is it simply the methodological ideal of philosophy — as with Husserl. Contrary to both, understanding is the primordial accomplishment of human *Dasein* as being-in-the-world. And prior to any differentiation of understanding into the two directions of pragmatic interest and theoretical interest, understanding is *Dasein's* mode of being which constitutes it as "potentiality-for-Being" [*Seinkönnen*] and "possibility."

On the basis of Heidegger's existential analysis of *Dasein,* with the many new perspectives that it implies for metaphysics, the function of hermeneutics in the human sciences also appears in a totally new light. While Heidegger resurrects the problem of Being in a form which goes far beyond all traditional metaphysics — he secures at the same time a radically new possibility in the face of the classical a prioris of historicism: his concept of understanding carries an *ontological* weight. Moreover, understanding is no longer an *operation* antithetic and sub-

20. M. Heidegger, *Sein und Zeit* (1927), p. 153. [All quotations are from *Being and Time,* translated by Macquarrie and Robinson (New York: Harper and Row, 1962) — Tr.]

sequent to the operations of the constitutive life, but a primordial mode of being /41/ of human life itself. Although Misch, in departing from Dilthey, discovers in the liberating distanciation from oneself [*la distance libre à soi*] one of the fundamental possibilities of life, the possibility upon which the phenomenon of understanding must be grounded, Heidegger — also taking his departure from Dilthey — goes further to initiate a radical ontological reflection about understanding as existential and disclose all understanding as pro-ject (*Entwurf*). Understanding is the very movement of "transcendence."

For traditional hermeneutics, of course, the Heideggerian theses sound a truly provocative note. Certainly the German verb *verstehen* (to understand) has two meanings. First of all, it has the same meaning as when we say, for example: "I understand the meaning of something"; then it also signifies: "to know about or be an expert in something." Let us give an example of this last case: "er versteht *nicht* auf *das Lesen*" — translated into English: "he is incompetent when it comes to reading," that is, "he doesn't *know how* to read." In other words, the verb *verstehen* signifies, beyond its theoretical sense, a "knowing how," an "ability," a "capacity" to carry out a task at the practical level. But according to this last sense, it is essentially distinguished or so it seems — from the understanding obtained by scientific knowledge. And yet, on closer examination, even there we find something in common. In both cases there is an act of knowing, a "*knowing about* something," a "*knowing how* to go about something." Those who "understand" a text — to say nothing of a law — not only project themselves in an effort of understanding towards a significance, but acquire through understanding a new liberty of the mind. /42/ This involves numerous and new possibilities, like interpreting a text, seeing the hidden relations that it conceals, drawing conclusions, and so on — precisely those things which define what we mean when we speak of the understanding or knowledge of a text. Similarly, those with mechanical "know-how," or even those with a practical mastery in whatever craft, as for example the savant with hermeneutical "know-how," really know "how to go about it." In sum, even if it seems perfectly evident that a simply practical understanding of a rational goal has other norms than, for instance, the understanding of a text or other expression of life, nevertheless, it is still that in the end all understandings are reducible to a common level of an "I know how to go about it," that is, a self-understanding in relation to something other.

In the same way, understanding a gesture or a pantomimed expression is more than grasping directly its immediate meaning; it is to discover what is hidden in the soul and apprehend how we ought "to go about it." In this case one rightly says that accomplishing an understanding is to form a project from one's own possibilities.

The lexicological history of the German word *verstehen* confirms this result. In fact, the primitive meaning of the word seems to be what it had in the ancient juridic language which used the expression "*eine causa verstehen*" ("understanding" a cause) in the sense of "defending the cause of a party before a tribunal." That the use of the word developed later into its current and familiar sense, may be clearly explained /43/ by the fact that the defense of a "cause" necessarily means that one has assumed it completely — that one has understood it — to the point of not losing any ground in the face of any possible arguments advanced by one's adversaries.

In taking account of this it is easy to see that traditional hermeneutics greatly over-restricted the horizon of problems attached to the idea of understanding. In this respect the initiative taken by Heidegger on a great deal more vast plane than that of Dilthey, was particularly fruitful concerning our hermeneutical problem. Certainly Dilthey also rejected entirely the naturalistic methods in the human sciences, and Husserl, as we know, even deemed "absurd" the application of the naturalistic concept of objectivity to the human sciences, in showing the fundamental relativity that every type of world, every type of historical knowledge, implies. But with Heidegger we witness an ontological evaluation of the problem of the structure of historical understanding, grounded on human existence which is essentially oriented towards the future.

Although having recognized the tribute that historical knowledge pays to the projective structure of *Dasein,* no one, however, will dream of putting in doubt the immanent criteria of what we call scientific knowledge. Historical knowledge is neither a species of project, in the sense of a forecaset or program, nor is it the extrapolation of deliberate ends, nor again the disposition of things according to good will, vulgar prejudices, or suggestions of a tyrant, but is a *mensuratio ad rem*. Except that the *res* is not meant in the sense of a *factum brutum*: /44/ it is no simply "substantial entity" (*bloss vorhanden,* in the Heideggerian sense), neither is it anything instrumentally determina-

ble or measurable. To be "historical" is, on the contrary, itself a mode
of being for human *Dasein*. But now we need to fully understand the
importance of this often repeated statement. Neither does it signify
that the understandable and the understood may be simply
homogeneous modes of being, and that the "method" of the human
sciences is founded on this homogeneity. That would make the "historical" into a psychology. The common relationship which the
understandable and the understood share, this sort of "affinity" which
ties them together, is not founded on the equivalence of their modes of
being, but on what that mode of being *is*. This means that neither the
knowable nor the known are "ontic" and simply "subsistant," but that
they are "historical"; that is to say, their mode of being is historicality.
As Count Yorck said, "everything depends upon the generic difference between the ontic and the historical."[21] When Yorck shows us the
opposition which separates the homogeneity of being from the "affinity" — which distinguishes the *Gleichartigkeit* from the *Zugehörigkeit* — then appears the problem that Heidegger will develop in all of
its radicality. For Heidegger, the fact that we can only speak of history
insofar as we are ourselves historical, signifies that it is the historicity
of human *Dasein,* in its incessant movement of anticipation and forgetfulness, which is the pre-condition for our ability to revive the past.
What before appeared as prejudicial to the concept of science and
method, as only a /45/ "subjective" approach to historical knowledge,
today is placed in the foreground of fundamental inquiry. "Affinity"
(*Zugehörigkeit*) "conditions" historical interest not only in the sense of
the nonscientific and subjective factors which motivate the choices of a
theme or question. In accepting such a hypothesis we would interpret
the concept of "affinity" as a particular case of emotional servitude:
sympathy. On the contrary, "affinity" with a tradition is no less
primordially and essentially constitutive of the historical finitude of
Dasein than is the fact that *Dasein* always projects itself towards its
future possibilities. On this point Heidegger rightly emphasized the
two moments of "thrownness" (*Geworfenheit*) and "pro-ject"
(*Entwurf*) must always be thought of together. Thus there is no
understanding or interpretation whatsoever which does not bring into
play the entirety of this existential structure — even if the intention

21. P. Yorck in *Briefwechsel zwischen W. Dilthey und dem Grafen Paul Yorck von
Wartenburg, 1877–1897* (Halle-an-der-Saale: 1923), p. 191.

does not exceed a purely "literal" reading of a text of stating some specific event.

These remarks still do not constitute a sufficient response to the problem raised by hermeneutics. Nevertheless, the Heideggerian interpretation of understanding as "existential" represents neither more nor less than its most fundamental element. If "understanding" is a transcendental determination of all existence, then hermeneutic "understanding," too, receives a new dimension and universal importance. The phenomenon and problematic of /46/ "affinity" which the historical school" knew not how to justify, will henceforth have a concrete significance, and the task of hermeneutics properly so-called will be precisely to grasp this significance which is its own.

The existential structure of "thrownness," fundamental to understanding as the meaningful operation of *Dasein,* is a structure also found at the basis of daily life understanding as performed in the human sciences. The concrete links which represent an ethics or a tradition, more generally the concrete historical conditions, as well as the future possibilities which they imply, there links define what is active at the heart of the understanding proper to the human sciences. The importance of an existential doctrine such as "thrownness" — *Geworfenheit* — is precisely to show that the *Dasein* which is projected towards its future "potentiality-for-Being" is a being which here and now *has been,* so that all of its unrestrained posturing comes up against and is halted in the face of facticity of its own being. Here, then, in opposition to the quest for a transcendental constitution in Husserlian phenomenology, is the crucial point of Heidegger's "hermeneutics of facticity." It is fully aware of the insurmountable precedence of what gives it the possibility of even having a pro-ject, a pro-ject, in fact, which by the same token can only be a finite pro-ject.

The understanding of an historical tradition will also, and necessarily, carry with it the imprint of this existential structure of *Dasein*. The problem, when, is how to recognize this imprint in the hermeneutics of the human sciences. For in the human sciences there can be no question of /47/ being "opposed" to the process of tradition which is itself historical and to which these sciences owe their access to history. Detachment or being "liberated" from tradition cannot be our first worry in our attitude towards the past in which we — who are ourselves historical beings — incessantly participate. Quite the contrary, the authentic attitude is that of looking at an inherited "culture" — in the literal sense of both inherited and culture, that is, as a development [a cultivation,] and a continuation of what we recognize as being the concrete link among us all. Obviously, what is handed down by our forebears is not appreciated when it is looked at in the objectivist spirit, that is, as the object of a scientific method, as if it were something fundamentally alien or completely foreign. What we prepare to welcome is never without some resonance in ourselves; it is the mirror in which each of recognizes himself. In fact, the reality of tradition scarcely constitutes a problem of knowledge, but a phenomenon of spontaneous and productive appropriation of the transmitted content.

This said, it is time to ask if the appearance of historical consciousness has really rent an unbridgeable abyss between our scientific attitude and our natural and spontaneous approach to history. In other words, does so-called historical consciousness not deceive itself in designating the totality of its historicity as a simple prejudice which must be overcome? The "presuppositionless science" — the *vorurteilslose Wissenschaft* — does it not itself partake, and more than it realizes, in the naive receptive and reflective attitude, through which the past is presented to us as living tradition? Without /48/ other attitudes — scientific or quotidian — that it lives *only* through the solicitations which arrive to it from a tradition? Must we not admit that the meaning of the objects of investigation which it borrows from tradition is formed exclusively by a tradition? Even if a given historical object does not answer at all a current historical interest — even in this truly extreme case of historical investigation — it is still the case that there is no historical object which does not always motivate us to question it primordially as an historical phenomenon, that is to say, to grasp it as something meaningful which has nothing immutable about it except that it can never be defined once and for all.

Consequently, in order to proceed to an historical hermeneutics it is necessary to begin by clearing away the abstract opposition which lies between tradition and historical research, between history and historical knowledge. Everything that the living tradition, on the one hand, and historical research, on the other, carry with them, in the end form an effective unity which can only be analyzed as a network of reciprocal actions. Thus it would be more correct to take historical consciousness, not as a radically new phenomenon, but as a relative transformation, although a revolutionary one, within which man has always constituted his attitude towards his own past. In other words, we have to recognize the role that tradition plays within the historical attitude, and inquire into its hermeneutic productivity.

THE HERMENEUTICAL PROBLEM AND ARISTOTLE'S *ETHICS*

At this point in our exposition, it would appear that the problem with which we have been occupied manifests an intimate connection to a problematic that Aristotle developed in his ethical investigations.[22] In fact, the problem which hermeneutics poses can be defined by the question "What can we make of the fact that one and the same message transmitted by tradition will, however, be grasped differently on every occasion, that it is only understood relative to the concrete historical situation of its recipient?" On the logical level, this problem of understanding is presented as the application of something general (the self-same message) to a concrete and particular situation. Now certainly Aristotelian ethics is not interested in the hermeneutical problem, much less its historical dimensions; instead its concern is precisely what role reason plays in all ethical behavior. It is the role of reason and knowledge in Aristotle's *Ethics* which manifests such striking analogies to the role of historical knowledge.

By criticizing the Socratic-Platonic intellectualism involved in the question of the Good, Aristotle became the founder of ethics as a discipline independent from /50/ metaphysics. He demonstrated that the Platonic idea of the Good is a vacuous generality and contrasts to it a *human good*, that is to say, good in relation to human activity. The target of the Aristotelian critique is the identity of virtue and knowledge, of *arete* and *logos*, as it was promulgated in Socratic-Platonic ethics. In defining the fundamental element of human ethical knowledge as *orexis*, as *desire*, and by the organization of this desire into an habitual disposition — into a *hexis* — Aristotle reduces the doctrine of his teachers to its proper scale. Remember that according to Aristotle's theory, practice and habit [*ethos*] are at the basis of *arete*. We see this significance in the very name "ethics".

22. In the following we shall refer to especially the *Nichomachean Ethics* and in particular Book VI.

Ethical being, as a specifically human undertaking, is distinguished from natural being because it is not simply a collection of capacities or innervating forces. Man, on the contrary, is a being who only becomes what he is and acquires his "bearing" by what he does, by the "how" of his actions. It is in this sense that Aristotle differentiates between the domain of *ethos* and that of *physics*. Although it is not devoid of all natural regularities, the ethical domain is, however, distinguished by the inconstancy of human precepts and thus stands in contrast to the natural domain where stable laws prevail.

The question raised by Aristotle at this point concerns the possibility of a philosophical knowledge of man *qua* ethical being; in this regard he must ask what function knowledge should fulfill in the constitution of ethical behavior. If, in fact, man does acquire the good — his own *particular* good — within an altogether concrete and practical situation, the /51/ task which befalls ethical knowledge can only be to ferret out just exactly what demands this situation places on him. We would say the same thing by affirming that the proper task of ethical consciousness is to gauge a concrete situation by the light of the most general ethical requirements. The other side of the coin is that *general* knowledge, by virtue of its very generality, is unmindful of concrete situations and their exigencies; in itself, general knowledge knows not how to be applied to a concrete situation and even threatens to obscure the meaning of the concrete exigencies which a factual situation could pose to it. We mean here not only that the methodological aspect of philosophical ethics is far from a simple matter, but above all that in a sense every philosophical method necessarily involves a certain ethical problem. In opposition to the Platonic doctrine of the *idea* of the Good, Aristotle vigorously emphasizes that in the domain of ethics there is no question of aspiring to the rarefied exactitude of mathematics; in the concrete human situations in which we find ourselves such misguided aspirations would obscure our real goal, [which is always ethical being]. Such a calculus could only organize the elements of an ethical problem according to their major vectors and then, through plotting their contours, furnish a sort of templet [*d'appui*] to ethical consciousness. On closer examination, this immediately implies a moral problem. In fact, it is essential to the phenomenon of ethics not only that the agent knows in general how to decide and what to prefer, but also, he must know and understand how he ought to act in the given occasion, a responsibility that he can never evade. Thus it is essential that ethical sciences — while they may contribute to the clarification of the problems of ethical consciousness — never usurp the place properly belonging to concrete ethical consciousness. /52/ Indeed, for those who listen to one of Aristotle's lessons, for this audience who would find therein a templet for their ethical consciousness, all of this presupposes a whole series of things. To begin with, a listener must be sufficiently mature so that he does not demand of the instruction he receives more than it can give him. In more positive terms we might say: it is indispensible that through practice and education the listener may have already formed a *habitudo* which he takes into the concrete situations of his life, a *habitudo* which will be confirmed and solidified by each new action.

As we see, conforming to his general principle, the method which Aristotle follows is defined in terms of the particular object. According to the exposition presented in Aristotle's *Ethics,* this object is determined by the relation between ethical being and ethical know-how and we must elucidate this special relation. Aristotle remains within the Socratic-Platonic mold in the sense that for him knowledge is still an essential moment in ethical behavior. It is the *balance* that he strikes between the Socratic-Platonic heritage and his own conception of *ethos* which will constitute the subject of our following analysis.

It is obvious from our foregoing examination that hermeneutical knowledge, too, must reject an objectivist style of knowing. Moreover, in speaking of the "affinity" which characterizes the relation between the interpreter and the tradition he interprets, we saw that understanding is itself a constitutive moment in the progress of history. Now neither does Aristotle's description of ethical knowledge put it in the "objectivist" camp. Nor is the ethical subject or knower found simply confronting an entity which it must verify. From the first, the subject of ethical knowledge finds itself /53/ concerned with and invested by its "object," that is, what it will have to do.

The distinction drawn by Aristotle between ethical know-how (*phronesis*) and theoretical or "scientific" knowledge (*episteme*) is particularly evident when we remember that in the eyes of the Greeks, mathematics represented the ideal of "science." Science, that is, knowledge of the immutable, is grounded on demonstration, and consequently everyone is in a position to "learn." It is easy to contrast ethical knowledge to this theoretical knowledge. Obviously, in terms of this distinction, what we call the human sciences are to be considered as "moral sciences." Their object is man and what he has to know about himself. This human self-apprehension concerns him from the very first as an acting being; it does not in any way aim at verifying what is always the case. Quite the opposite, it relates to what is not necessarily what it is and what could be otherwise at some particular moment. Only in things of this sort [i.e., in that which is not immutable] can human action intervene.

Because it is a matter of knowledge guiding activity, we could call to mind what the Greeks called *techne,* the know-how or skill of an artisan who knows how to produce something. Is ethical knowledge similar to that of *techne,* as in the statement "I know perfectly well how I ought to go about it"? Is there a similarity between the man who makes himself what he ought to be and the artisan who /54/ acts of his own choice in terms of a preconceived intention and plan? Is there a similarity between the man who, as we said above, is a project of his own possibilities — let us now say of his *eidos* — and the artisan who prepares a deliberate plan, an *eidos,* for himself and knows how to execute it in some medium? Undeniably Socrates and Plato uncovered something very true in applying the concept of *techne* on the level of ethical activity. In fact, it is obvious that ethical know-how and technical know-how have this in common: neither of them is an abstract of knowledge; instead, in the definition and direction of activity, both of them imply a practical knowledge fashioned to the measure of the concrete tasks before them.

This last characterization leads us to a distinction that is very important in our perspective. It concerns the nuance which delineates the acquisitions due to a "teachable" technique from those acquisitions made by virtue of a thoroughly concrete experience in everyday practice. The knowledge transmitted by instruction — in a handicraft, for example — is not necessarily of a real practical value nor necessarily superior to the knowledge acquired through practice. In no way do we mean that knowledge which guides its practice (the "art") is in its turn purely theoretical; as a matter of fact, precisely in making use of this "book knowledge" in practice do we acquire the indispensable experience that is *techne*. Thus, Aristotle rightly cites the adage that "*techne* loves *tyche* and *tyche* loves *techne*," that is to say, the "chance" for success is offered first to those who "know" their craft.

What we have said is just as applicable to ethical knowledge. It is obvious that experience by itself, /55/ rich though it may be, is an insufficient foundation for ethical know-how or a morally consistent decision; the guidance of moral consciousness by prior knowledge is always indispensable. Thus there is an obvious correspondence between ethical know-how and technical know-how. This allows us to raise the difficult and urgent problem of their difference.

No one can ignore the fact that there are radical differences between ethical know-how and technical know-how. It is evident that man does not deal with himself in the same way that an artisan deals with his material. The question, then, is to learn to distinguish the knowledge one has of oneself *qua* ethical being from the knowledge required to produce something. For Aristotle, this ethical know-how is distinguished just as much from technical knowledge as it is from theoretical knowledge. In fact, he says in a bold and original formula that ethical knowledge is a "knowledge-for-the-sake-of-oneself." In this way ethical knowledge is clearly distinguished from the theoretical attitude of *episteme*. But how are we to distinguish knowledge-for-the-sake-of-oneself from technical know-how?

He who knows how to make something has learned thereby a good, and he understands this good—he knows it for "its own sake"—in such a way that he can effectively proceed from the possibility of a task to its execution. He chooses the right materials and the appropriate means. He knows how to apply what he has learned in general to a concrete situation. The man who makes an ethical decision has learned something, too. Through the education and training he has received, he possesses a general knowledge /56/ of what we call right and just behavior. The function, then, of an ethical decision is to find what is just within the bounds of a concrete situation. In other words, the ethical decision for the just is there in order to "see" all that the concrete situation demands and to put the matter in some order. In this sense, then, just like the artisan who is ready to initiate his work, the putting into effect of an ethical decision deals with a "material"—

the situation—and a choice of means. But this said, does not the anticipated distinction between the two types of knowledge vanish before our eyes?

We find a whole series of answering elements in Aristotle's analysis of *phronesis*. As Hegel once remarked, what guarantees the genius of Aristotle is the comprehensiveness of the perspectives taken into consideration in his descriptions. Let us call attention to just three:

1. A technique is learned and can be forgotten; we can "lose" a skill. But ethical "reason" can neither be learned nor forgotten. Nor is it like the professional knowledge that one can choose; one cannot put it down, like a profession, in order to take up another one. By contrast, the subject of ethical reason, of *phronesis,* man always finds himself in an "acting situation" and he is always obliged to use ethical knowledge and apply it according to the exigencies of his concrete situation.

But for this very reason, it is problematic to speak of "application," since we can only apply what we already possess. Now ethical knowledge is not our property in the same way that we have something at our disposal and choose to utilize it or not. Thus if it is true that the image that man forms of himself, that is, what he wishes and ought to be, is constituted by governing ideas such as right /57/ and injustice, courage, fellowship, and so forth, then we readily acknowledge a difference between these ideas and those that the artisan conceives of when he prepares plans for his work. To confirm this distinction it is sufficient to think of the way we are aware of what is "just." "Justice" is totally relative to the ethical situation in which we find ourselves. We cannot say in a general and abstract way which actions are just and which are not; there are no just actions "in themselves," independent of what the situation requires.

One might perhaps object that, nevertheless, a perfect analogy between *techne* and *phronesis* is actually confirmed by what is indexed by the phenomenon of right. Because, one might say, my "rights" are defined by laws, very often, moreover, by uncodified rules of behavior which are nonetheless valid for everyone. What I regard as my right, what is "just," is it not simply the result of the correct application of a law to a concrete case?

However, upon reflection we will see that the idea of application used by this objection is not unequivocal. For as soon as we consider application in its negative aspect, in the form of a non-application, it becomes evident that it means something quite different on the level of an artisan's knowledge than what it does on the level of ethical knowledge. It is quite possible, in fact, that under certain conditions the artisan may be obligated to forego the exact execution of his work plans; he is subject to external conditions, he lacks a tool or material, and so forth. But the fact that he gives up and is content with an imperfect work does not imply that his knowledge of things is augmented or has become more nearly perfect through the experience of failure. On the other hand, when we "apply" a law the situation is entirely different. /58/ It can happen that, owing to the characteristics of a concrete situation, we may be obligated to mitigate the severity of the law — but "mitigation" is not exclusive of "application." Mitigation does not ignore the right expressed in the law, no more than it condones an unjustifiable carelessness in its application. When we mitigate the law we do not abandon it; on the contrary, without this mitigation there would really be no justice.

Aristotle speaks very explicitly of *epieikeia* [or "equity"] as a "rectification" or an "accommodation" of the law. He grounds his conception on the fact that every law admits of a certain internal tension with respect to the concrete possibilities of action: a law is always general and can never address itself to all the concrete complexities of a particular case. (Let us note in passing that this is the original problem of juridical hermeneutics.) A law is always insufficient, not by reason of any intrinsic fault, but because the practical world as the field of our actions is always imperfect in comparison to the ideal order envisioned by laws.

For the same reason Aristotle adopts a subtle position on the question of natural right: for him codified law does not, in itself, fulfill the conditions for finding justice. Consequently, Aristotle sees in the deliberations about the function of equity an important juridic task, namely, perfecting codified law. In marked opposition to the strict conventionalism of a juridic positivism, he distinguishes between positive law and natural law. But it would be erroneous to apply this distinction by recourse to the single critierion of the eternity and immutability of nature — by denying these characteristics to positive law while granting them to natural law. For according to Aristotle, the idea of an immutable natural law applies only to the divine world, and he declares that with /59/ us humans natural law is in the last analysis just as inconstant as positive law. This theory is confirmed by the examples we read in Aristotle. He reminds us — borrowing the idea from Plato — that, though the right hand is by nature stronger than the left, anyone can train it to become as strong as the other. Another example: measures of wine are everywhere identical; by all appearances, however, they are smaller where purchased than where sold. Aristotle, of course, does not mean that the seller always cheats the buyer, but that each concrete application of the law carries with it the implication that it is not unjust to tolerate a certain elasticity in legal exactitude.

It follows, then, according to Aristotle that the idea of natural law serves only a critical function. Nothing in the idea authorizes us to use it dogmatically by attributing the inviolability of natural law to particular and concrete juridical contents. It is legitimately useful only when the strict application of a law appears incompatible with justice. Thus, the task of a natural law is to lead us to an equitable solution more consonant with justice.

What we have just demonstrated regarding the concept of right is, in principle, valid for all the concepts man has at his disposal in order to determine what he ought to be. These concepts are not fixed in the firmament like the stars; they are what they are only in the concrete situations in which we find ourselves. Therefore, in order to define these concepts we must refer to the use and application which ethical consciousness makes of them.

2. What we have just said also entails a /60/ different conceptual relation between the end and the means in ethical knowledge on the one hand, and in technical knowledge on the other.

To begin with, let us note that contrary to what happens on the level of technique the end of ethical knowledge is not a "particular thing," but that it determines the *complete* ethical rectitude of a lifetime. Moreover, and even more important, technical activity does not demand that the means which allow it to arrive at an end be weighed anew on each occasion and personally by the subject who is their practitioner: "He is already an expert; he already knows how to go about it." And since a similar possibility is excluded in advance from ethical knowledge, it follows that we must characterize the ethical domain as one where technical know-how gives way to deliberation and reflection. But it is better to show its positive side: in all

situations ethical consciousness — without prior avail to the knowledge of all the facts — is personally responsible for its own decisions.
Ethical consciousness does not keep counsel with anyone but itself.
Thus the whole problem is summarized in the fact that in moral
actions there is no "prior" knowledge of the right means which realize
the end, and this is so because, above all else, the ends themselves are
at stake and not perfectly fixed beforehand. This also explains why in
his discussion of *phronesis* Aristotle constantly oscillates between defining it as the knowledge of the ends and the knowledge of means.

Just as there can be no dogmatic use made of natural right, still less
can we make dogmatic use of ethics. When Aristotle describes the
concrete forms of a balanced attitude as to the choice of valid means,
he above all relies upon the /61/ ethical consciousness which is molded
within the exigencies of a concrete situation. Ethical know-how
oriented by these ideas is the same knowledge which must respond to
the momentary contingencies of a factual situation. Thus, when it is a
question of ethical ends we can never speak only of the "opportunity"
of means; the ethical rectitude of the means is an essential component
of the ethical validity of ends. To reflect on the means in moral decisions is *eo ipso* an ethical undertaking.

Now, the *"knowledge-for-the-sake-of-oneself"* of which Aristotle
speaks is precisely this "perfect application" which unfolds as personal
"knowledge" [savoir] within the intimacy of a given situation. Only in
the "knowledge" of the immediately given is ethical knowledge attained: it is, however, a "knowledge" which is not of the same order as
sensible perceptions. For even if we must pay attention to the demands
of the situation, our perception is not a brute perception of facts without meaning. Only within "ethical perception" does the situation appear to us as a situation-for-our-action and in the light of what is
"just." Our awareness of the situation is a consciousness of an act
which cuts through the situation.

Thus, "justice" is the opposite not of moral error or illusion but of
blindness. In other words, when overwhelmed by his passions man no
longer sees what is just or unjust. He is not in error but loses control of
himself and, dominated by the play of his passions, is no longer
oriented towards the good at all.

Thus, we call ethical knowledge that which encompasses in an
entirely unique way our knowledge of ends and means; and precisely
from this perspective it is opposed to a purely technical know-how.

Consequently, in this field it no longer makes any sense to distinguish between knowledge and ex/62/perience, since ethical knowledge is also in itself a subspecies of experience. On this score it is even an absolutely primordial form of experience, and perhaps all others constitute but secondary, nonprimordial forms by comparison.

3. The "knowledge-for-the-sake-of-oneself" of ethical reflection actually implies an absolutely remarkable relation to oneself. This is what the Aristotelian analyses teach us respecting the varieties of *phronesis*.

Alongside *phronesis* there is the phenomenon of "understanding" in the sense of *synesis*. This is an intentional modification of ethical knowledge when it is a moral question, not for the sake of myself, but for the sake of another. This intentional modification carries with it an ethical appreciation in the sense of being placed by it in the situation of another where the other must act. Here again it is a matter not of a generalized knowledge, but of its concretion motivated by the reality of the moment. However, to "live on good terms" with someone is presupposed and only manifests all of its ethical importance in the phenomenon of "understanding." Understanding another as a unique phenomenon is not simply the technical knowledge of the psychologist, nor the equivalent everyday experience possessed by the "wily" [*malin*] or "resourceful" [*débrouillard*] man. It supposes that one is committed to a just cause and through this commitment one discovers a link with another. This bond is concretized in the phenomenon of "moral counsel." One gives and receives, as they say, "good counsel" only among friends.

This emphasizes that the relationship established between two people is not that of two entities who have nothing to do with one another; instead, understanding is a question /63/ of—to employ an idea to which we are by now accustomed—"affinity." According to Aristotle understanding gives rise to the following two correlative phenomena: to a spirit of discernment of another's moral situation and to the resulting tolerance or indulgence. Now what is this discernment if not the virtue of knowing how to equitably judge the situation of another?

Clearly it is not a question here either of a technical know-how. In fact, Aristotle emphasizes the purely virtuous character of ethical know-how. And to put it in even greater relief, he gives a description of the degenerative form of *phronesis* which characterizes the *deinos*: the man who, by means of his shrewd intelligence, turns every situation to his own advantage. Its opposition to real *phronesis* is obvious: the *deinos* uses and abuses his capabilities without any reference to ethical considerations. It is not by chance that the term denoting this man, for whom every situation is an opportunity for self-aggrandizment, is faithfully translated by the word "redoubtable." Nothing is more terrifying than a genius so constituted that he takes not account of good or evil.

SKETCH OF THE FOUNDATIONS OF A HERMENEUTIC

Let us return to the subject, properly so called, of the present lectures. If we recall the Aristotelian approach to the problem of ethics and its inherent mode of "knowledge," it is evident that we have an excellent model at our disposal to guide us in the elucidation of the hermeneutical task. In hermeneutics, no less than with Aristotle, "application" is a constituitive moment. It can never signify a subsidiary operation appended as an afterthought to understanding: the object of our "application" determines from the beginning and in its totality the real and concrete content of hermeneutical understanding. "Application" is not a calibration of some generality given in advance in order to unravel afterwards a particular situation. In attending to a text, for example, the interpreter does not try to apply a general criterion to a particular case; on the contrary, he is interested in the fundamentally original significance of the writing under his consideration.

In order to elucidate the meaning of an authentically historical hermeneutics we started from the failure of historicism we found in Dilthey and then recalled the new ontological dimensions that we owe to the phenomenological analyses of Husserl and Heidegger. Historical knowledge cannot be described according to the model of an objectivist knowledge because it is itself a process which has all the characteristics of an /66/ historical event. Understanding must be comprehended in the sense of an existential act, and is therefore a *"thrown pro-ject."* Objectivism is an illusion. Even as historians, that is, as representatives of a modern and methodic science, we are members of an unbroken chain through which the past addresses us. We have seen that ethical consciousness is at the same time ethical know-how and ethical being. It is this integration of practical knowledge into the substance of morality, the "belongingness" of "education" or "culture" (in the etymological sense) to ethical consciousness and the concrete knowledge of obligations and ends, that will provide us with the model to analyze the ontological implications of historical consciousness. Just like Aristotle, though on a very different level, we will see that historical knowledge is at the same time historical know-how and historical being.

It is now a question of determining more concretely the structure of understanding found at the basis of hermeneutics; it is, we have seen, something like an essential "affinity" with tradition. At this point a traditional hermeneutical rule comes to our aid. It was formulated for the first time by romantic hermeneutics, but its origin dates back to ancient rhetoric. It concerns the circular relation between the whole and its parts: the anticipated meaning of a whole is understood through the parts, but it is in light of the whole that the parts take on their illuminating function.

The study of a text in a foreign language will serve as our example. In a general way, before we understand anything in a sentence, we /67/ proceed by a certain preliminary structuration which thus constitutes the groundwork for later understanding. This process is dominated by a global meaning we have in view, and is based on the relations which an earlier context affords us. But, of course, this purely anticipatory global meaning awaits confirmation or amendment pending its ability to form a unified and consistent vision. Let us think of this structure in a dynamic way; the effective unity of the anticipated meaning comes out as the comprehension is enlarged and renovated by concentric circles. The perfect coherence of the global and final meaning is the criterion for *the* understanding. When coherence is wanting, we say that understanding is deficient.

The hermeneutical circle of the whole and its parts, especially in its objective and subjective aspects, was examined by Schleiermacher. On the one hand, every text belongs to the whole of the author's works and then to the literary genre from which it originates. On the other hand, if we wish to grasp the text in the authenticity of its unique meaning, then we must see it as a manifestation of a creative moment and replace it within the whole spiritual context of the author. Only from the totality formed, not only by objective facts, but in the first place by the subjectivity of the author, can understanding arise. In the extrapolation of Schleiermacher's theory we encounter Dilthey who tells us about an "orientation towards the center" to describe the understanding of the whole. In this way Dilthey applied to the complex of historical research the traditional hermeneutical principle that a text must be understood through itself. It remains to be seen, however, if the idea /68/ of the circle of understanding is grounded upon an accurate description.

On the one hand, to relate, as Schleiermacher and romanticism tell us, to the subjective factors of understanding does not seem at all convincing. When we understand a text we do not put ourselves in the place of the other, and it is not a matter of penetrating the spiritual activities of the author; it is simply a question of grasping the meaning, significance, and aim of what is transmitted to us. In other words, it is a question of grasping the intrinsic worth of the arguments put forward and doing so as completely as possible. In one move we find ourselves within the dimension of the aim [*la visée*], already comprehensible in itself, and without so much as a second look at the subjectivity of the partner. The meaning of hermeneutical inquiry is to disclose the miracle of understanding texts or utterances and not the mysterious communication of souls. Understanding is a participation in the common aim.

On the other hand, the objective aspect of the hermeneutical circle will also be described in a different way than what we read in Schleiermacher. For it is really what we have *in common* with tradition that we relate to and which determines our anticipations and guides our understanding. Consequently, this "circle" is not at all of a purely formal nature, from neither a subjective nor an objective viewpoint. On the contrary, it comes into play solely within the space established between the text and he who understands. The purpose of the interpreter is to make himself a *mediator* between the text and all that the text implies. Therefore, the aim of hermeneutics is always to restitute the authentic intention and reestablish the concordance, to fill in the lacunas of the argumentation. This is entirely confirmed by the his/ 69/tory of hermeneutics when we follow closely its major contours: St. Augustine spoke to us of the Old Testament which must be seen through Christian truths; Protestantism resumed this same task during the Reformation; in the age of the Enlightenment we are persuaded that the "rational" meaning of a text offers the first approach to its understanding, and that only the absence of such a "rational" meaning demands an historical interpretation. But is it not curious: while romanticism and Schleiermacher became the messengers of historical self-consciousness, the same romanticism and the same Schleiermacher never even dreamed of attributing to their own tradition the value of a true foundation.

Yet, among Schleiermacher's immediate predecessors, there is one, the philologist Friedrich Ast, who had clear views of this hermeneutical task. According to him, hermeneutics plays a mediating role: that of establishing agreement between the true traditions of antiquity and Christianity. In opposition to the *Aufkärung,* this perspective creates a new situation, in the sense that it was no longer a question of reconciling the authority of tradition with natural reason but of effecting a relation between two different traditions. However, Ast resumes the old tradition to build up an intrinsic and concrete agreement of antiquity with Christianity, and thereby preserves the real task of a non-formal hermeneutics, a forgotten task by the time of Schleiermacher and his successors. If the philologist Ast avoided this forgetfulness, it is by virtue of the spiritual influence of idealistic philosophies and, above all, of Schelling, who inspired him.

/70/ Today, it is through Heidegger's existential analysis that we again discover the deeper meaning of the circular structure of understanding. Here is what we read in Heidegger:

> [The hermeneutic circle] is not to be reduced to the level of a vicious circle or even a circle which is merely tolerated. In the circle is hidden a positive possibility of the most primordial kind of knowing. To be sure, we genuinely take hold of this possibility only when, in our interpretation, we have understood that our first, last, and constant task is never to allow our fore-having, fore-sight, and fore-conceptions to be presented to us by fancies and popular conceptions, but rather to make the scientific theme secure by working out these fore-structures in terms of the things themselves.[23]

Just as they stand, these lines announce not only the conditions imposed on the practice of understanding; they also describe the manner in which interpretation always proceeds when it intends an understanding tempered to the "thing itself." For the very first time the

23. Heidegger, op. cit., p. 153.

positive ontological meaning of the circle that understanding implies is explicitly affirmed. Every authentic interpretation must provide itself against the happenstance arbitration of baroque ideas and against the limitations caused by unconscious habits of thought. It is evident that in order to be authentic the inquiring gaze must be focused on the "thing itself," and in such a manner that it may be grasped, as it were, "in person." Likewise it is evident that an understanding faithful to the meaning of the text, for example, is not a matter of a simple, more or less vague wish /71/ nor of "good and pious intentions," but rather has the same meaning as the program Heidegger designated as the "first, last, and constant task" of interpretative understanding. Now, the circular character of understanding is precisely the outcome of the effort which leads the interpreter to strictly abide by this program, despite any errors he might commit in the course of his investigations.

Let us think once more about textual interpretation. As soon as he discovers some initially understandable elements, the interpreter sketches out the meaning of the whole text. But these first meaningful elements only come to the fore provided that he sets about reading with a more or less definite interest. Understanding the "thing" which arises there, before him, is nothing other than elaborating a preliminary project which will be progressively corrected in the course of the interpretative reading. Let us describe this process, realizing that it is obviously only a kind of "abbreviation," since the process is much more complicated. In the beginning, without the revision of the first project, there is nothing to constitute the basis for a new meaning; but at the same time, discordant projects aspire to constitute themselves as *the* unified meaning until the "first" interpretation is modified and replaces its initial presupposed concepts by more adequate ones. Heidegger described this perpetual oscillation of interpretative visions, that is, understanding being the formative process of a new project. One who follows this course always risks falling under the suggestion of his own rough drafts; he runs the risk that the anticipation which he has prepared may not conform to what the thing is. Therefore, the /72/ constant task of understanding lies in the elaboration of projects that are authentic and more proportionate to its object. In other words, it is a bold venture that awaits its reward in confirmation by the object. What we can term here as objectivity cannot be anything other than the confirmation of an anticipation which results even in

the very course of its elaboration. For how do we judge that an anticipation is arbitrary and inadequate to its task, if not by confronting it
with the only thing which can demonstrate its futility? Every textual
interpretation must begin then with the interpreter's reflection on the
preconceptions which result from the "hermeneutical situation" in
which he finds himself. He must legitimate them, that is, look for their
origin and adequacy.

Under these circumstances we will understand why the task of
hermeneutics as described by Heidegger is not a simple matter of
recommending a method. Quite the contrary, he demands nothing less
than a radical account of actual understanding as everyone who understands has always accomplished it.

To give an example of the procedure that I just spoke about, let us
think of the questions which arise with the analysis of an ancient text
or else when we ask for a translation. It is easily seen that the enterprise
must begin by our attempt to grasp the author's entirely personal
manner of using words and meanings in his text: how arbitrary it
would be to want to understand the text as an exclusive function of
our own vocabulary and particular conceptual baggage. It is immediately evident that our understanding must be guided by the peculiar linguistic customs of the epoch or /73/ author themselves. However, we must ask how this task can be realized *in concreto,* especially
with respect to semantics: how to distinguish between unconventional
language in general and unconventional language specific to the text.
Our reply is to bring out the fact that we get our first initiation
necessarily from the text itself: the experience of an impasse — maybe
the text is totally incomprehensible to us or the response it seems to
offer contradicts our anticipations — this discloses the possibility of an
unconventional linguistic usage.

What is valuable for the implicit aims of a linguistic usage, the
significant tendencies with which the *words* are laden, is even more
valid regarding our anticipations of the *content* of a text, anticipations
which positively determine our preconception of it. Yet, this case is
more complex than the one we have just seen.

It is commonly admitted that when we speak everyday language
we use words in their usual sense. While presupposing *this* we need *not*
presuppose that thoughts (or better, "other people's opinions" [*les dires
d' autrui*]) which have been understood are therefore *of themselves* and

from the mere fact that they have been grasped, organically integrated into my particular system of opinions and expectations. To "grasp" something is not yet to "approve" of it. It is always implied — *to begin with* — that I acquaint myself with "other people's opinions" without committing my own.

This distinction must be maintained. Nevertheless, it must be added that it practically never happens that in taking cognizance of "other people's opinions" I do not feel myself /74/ *ipso facto* invited to take a position on their subject matter; and furthermore, it is usually a matter of feeling invited to take a favorable position. We see in what sense we are going to be able to say that the hermeneutical intention always implies that it slips into a question of another order: that is, what is the "acceptable" meaning of a stated "opinion," the "integratable" meaning of a signification? It is evident that in a concrete situation the two moments are inseparable: the "latter" moment, which is more than a pure and simple "grasping," even determines *in every case* the concrete character of "grasping," and it is precisely into this nexus that the hermeneutical problem is inserted.

What in fact are the implications of this description? — But do not make me say what I have not in fact said; and I have *not* said that when we listen to someone or when we read we ought to forget our own opinions or shield ourselves against forming an anticipatory idea about the content of the communication. In reality, to be open to "other people's opinions," to a text, and so forth, implies right off that they are *situated* in my system of opinions, or better, that I situate myself in relation to them. In other words, it is of course true — and everyone admits it — that other people's opinions can have "in themselves" an indefinite manifold of different meanings (in contrast to the relatively perfect concordance that dictionary words present); *in concreto,* however, when we listen to someone or read a text we discriminate, from our own standpoint, among the different possible meanings — namely, what *we* consider possible — and we reject the remainder which seem to us "unquestionably absurd." On these grounds, and despite the /75/ best presumptions attached to a "literal" reading, we are naturally tempted to sacrifice, in the name of "impossibility," everything that we totally fail to integrate into our system of anticipations.

The authentic intention of understanding, however, is this: in reading a text, in wishing to understand it, what we always expect is that it will *inform* us of something. A consciousness formed by the authentic hermeneutical attitude will be receptive to the origins and entirely foreign features of that which comes to it from outside its own horizons. Yet this receptivity is not acquired with an objectivist "neutrality": it is neither possible, necessary, nor desirable that we put ourselves within brackets. The hermeneutical attitude supposes only that we self-consciously designate our opinions and prejudices and qualify them as such, and in so doing strip them of their extreme character. In keeping to this attitude we grant the text the opportunity to appear as an authentically different being and to manifest its own truth, over and against our own preconceived notions.

The phenomenological descriptions of Heidegger are perfectly correct when in the heart of alleged "immediate givens" he emphasizes the anticipatory structure constitutive of all understanding. But this is not all. *Being and Time* is also an example of the application to a concrete case of the universal hermeneutical task which derives from the anticipatory structure characteristic of understanding. In *Being and Time* this "concrete case" is the ontological problem. Still, the question posed to ontology must be posed concretely, that is, without /76/ making an abstraction of the layered density [*l' épaisseur*] of the hermeneutical situation which frames the meaning of the question. According to Heidegger, to be able to explain the hermeneutical situation of the "ontological question," that is, its implicit "fore-having, fore-sight, and fore-conceptions," it is indispensable to reexamine the general "ontological question" in a concrete way. For this reason he systematically addresses the question to the decisive moments in the history of metaphysics. From all evidence, Heidegger's approach serves this universal task, which appears in all its exigencies only to an historical-hermeneutical consciousness.

Consequently there is a strong need to elaborate a consciousness which directs and controls the anticipations involved in our cognitive approaches. Thus we are assured of a truly valid understanding, since it is intimately linked to the immediate object of our intentions. This is what Heidegger means when he claims that we "make the scientific theme secure by working out these fore-structures in terms of the 'things themselves,'" for which they constitute the horizon.

Certainly no one will accuse us of unbridled exaggeration when we conclude by these analyses that historical consciousness is no longer an unbounded projection. It is indispensible that consciousness take account of its secular prejudices and prevailing anticipations. Without this "purification," the illumination we gain by historical consciousness /77/ is but dim and ineffective. Without it our knowledge of the historically "other" is but a simple reduction. A cognitive procedure which involves prejudices or anticipations, but also preconceptions about method or what "must" be an historical fact, such a procedure flattens experience and inevitably leads to a betrayal of what is specifically "other."

We will now examine how to develop in the hermeneutical domain what we have just established regarding an historically "operative" consciousness. On this point, too, the Heideggerian description marks an important turning point. The pre-Heideggerian theories confined themselves to the framework of a purely formal relation between the whole and the parts. From a subjective point of view, we can express the same thing by characterizing the hermeneutical circle as a dialectic between the "divination" of the meaning of the whole and its subsequent articulation in the parts. In other words, according to the romantic theories, the circular movement is not a result, but a deficiency — however necessary — of inquiry. Having wandered through a text in all its directions and various articulations, the circular movement finally disappears in the light of a perfect understanding. For Schleiermacher this theory of hermeneutical understanding reaches its apogee in the idea of a pure, divinatory act, a purely subjective function. Obviously, such a notion of hermeneutical understanding is inclined to violate the genuinely foreign and mysterious which lies hidden in texts. In contrast, Heidegger, in his description of the interpretative circle, vigorously insists upon the fact that /78/ understanding a text *never ceases* to be determined by the anticipatory impulses of pre-understanding.

Let us take this one step further. I have just said that all understanding can be characterized as a system of circular relations between the whole and its parts. However, this sort of characterization must be completed by a supplementary determination: I will explain it by speaking of the anticipation of "perfect coherence." To begin with, this perfect coherence can be understood in the sense of an anticipation of a purely formal nature: it is an "idea." It is, nevertheless, always at work in achieving understanding. It signifies that nothing is really understandable unless it is actually presented in the form of a coherent meaning. Thus, for example, it is implicit from the outset in our intention of reading a text that we consider the text to be "coherent," unless this presupposition proves untenable, in other words, as long as the message of the text is not denounced as incomprehensible. It is at just this instant that doubt appears and we set to work with our critical instruments. We need not specify here the rules of this critical examination since in every respect their justification is inseparable from the concrete understanding of a text. Thus our understanding is guided by the anticipation of perfect coherence, and this anticipation shows that it possesses a content which is not merely formal. In fact, it is not only the unity of an *immanent* meaning which is presupposed in the concrete operations of understanding: every textual understanding presupposes that it is guided by *transcendent* expectations, /79/ expectations whose origins must be looked for in the relation between the intentional object of the text and the *truth*.

When we receive a letter we see what is communicated through the eyes of our correspondent, but while seeing things through his eyes, it is not his personal opinions, but, rather, the event itself that we believe we ought to know by this letter. In reading a letter, to aim at the personal *thoughts* of our correspondent and not at the matters *about which* he reports is to contradict what is meant by a letter. Likewise, the anticipations implied by our understanding of an historical document emanate from our relations to "things" and not the way these "things" are transmitted to us. Just as we give credence to the news in a letter, because we assume that our correspondent personally witnessed the event or has validly learned of it, in the same way we are open to the possibility that the transmitted text may offer a more authentic picture of the "thing itself" than our own speculations. Only the disappointment of having let the text speak for itself and having then arrived at a bad result could prompt us to attempt "understanding" it by recourse to a supplementary psychological or historical point of view.

Thus, the anticipation of perfect coherence presupposes not only that the text is an adequate expression of a thought, but also that it really transmits to us the *truth*. This confirms that the primordial significance of the idea of understanding is that of "knowing about something" and that only in a derivative sense does it mean understanding the intentions of another as personal opinions. Thus we come back to the original conditions of every hermeneutics: /80/ it must be a shared and comprehensible reference to the "things in themselves." It is this condition which determines the possibility that a unified meaning can be aimed at, and thus also the possibility that the anticipation of perfect coherence may actually be applicable.

We have emphasized the role, within our cognitive approach, played by certain absolutely fundamental anticipations, that is, anticipations *common* to us all. We are now in a position to determine more precisely the meaning of the phenomenon of "affinity," that is to say, the factor of tradition in a historical-hermeneutical attitude. Hermeneutics must start from the fact that understanding is related to "the thing itself" as manifest in the tradition, and at the same time to a tradition from where "the thing" can speak to me. On the other hand, he who achieves hermeneutical understanding must realize that our relation to "things" is not "a matter of course" and unproblematic. We found the hermeneutical task precisely on the tension which exists between the "familiar" and the "foreign" character of the message transmitted to us by tradition. But this tension is not as it was for Schleiermacher, that is, a psychological tension. It is, on the contrary, the *meaning* and *structure* of hermeneutical historicity. It is not some psychic state, but the very "thing" delivered over by tradition which is the object of hermeneutical inquiry. By a relation to both the "familiar" and the "foreign" character of historical messages, hermeneutics claims a "central situation." The interpreter is torn between his belongingness to a tradition and his distance from the objects which are the theme of his investigation.

/81/ This "hermeneutical situation," by which hermeneutics is henceforth placed "in the middle of things," serves to emphasize a phenomenon which has received scant attention thus far. It is the question of *temporal distance* and its meaning for understanding. Contrary to what we often imagine, time is not a chasm which we could bridge over in order to recover the past; in reality, it is the ground which supports the arrival of the past and where the present takes its roots. "Temporal distance" is not a distance in the sense of a distance to be bridged or overcome. This was the naive prejudice of historicism. It believed it could reach the solid terrain of historical objectivity by striving to place itself within the vantage point of a past age and think with the concepts and representations particular to that epoch. Actually, it is rather a matter of considering "temporal distance" as a fundament of positive and productive possibilities for understanding. It is not a distance to be overcome, but a living continuity of elements which cumulatively become a tradition, a tradition which is the light wherein all that we carry with us from our past, everything transmitted to us, makes its appearance.

It is not an exaggeration to speak of the productivity of the historical process. We all know how we make more or less arbitrary judgments when our ideas are not clarified by the passage of time. Limiting ourselves to an example, let us think of the uncertainty which characterizes our esthetic standpoint in the face of contemporary art. It is obviously a matter of uncontrollable prejudices which conceal the real /82/ content — authentic or not — of these works. Momentary relations must be erased in order to know if it is a question of masterpieces or not and if we can discover the true sense enabling contemporary art to enter an ongoing tradition. Obviously, this does not happen from one moment to another, but is developed in an indefinite process. The "temporal distance" which produces the filter is not of a definite magnitude, but evolves in a continuous movement of universalization. Universality purified by time is a second productive aspect of temporality. Its work develops a new set of "prejudices." It is a matter of "prejudices" which are neither partial nor particular, but which constitute, on the contrary, the legitimate guiding for genuine understanding.

This is yet another specification of the hermeneutical task. Only by virtue of the phenomenon and clarified concept of "temporal distance" can the specifically *critical* task of hermeneutics be resolved, that is, of knowing how to distinguish between blind prejudices and those which illuminate, between false prejudices and true prejudices. We must raise to a conscious level the prejudices which govern understanding and in this way realize the possibility that "*other* aims" emerge in their own right from tradition — which is nothing other than realizing the possibility that we can understand something in its *otherness*.

To denouce something as prejudice is to suspend its presumed validity; in fact a prejudice in the strict sense of that term cannot get hold of us unless we are sufficiently unconscious of it. But we cannot successfully take a prejudice into account so long as it is simply at /83/ work; it must be somehow provoked. Now this provocation of our prejudices is precisely the fruit of a renewed encounter with a tradition which was itself, perhaps, at their origin. And, in fact, what demands our efforts at understanding is manifest before and in itself in its character of otherness. And this leads us back to a point we made above: we must realize that every understanding begins with the fact that something *calls out* to us. And since we know the precise meaning of this affirmation, we claim *ipso facto* the bracketing of prejudices. Thus we arrive at our first conclusion: bracketing our judgments in general and, naturally first of all our own prejudices, will end by imposing upon us the demands of a radical reflection on the idea of *questioning* as such.

The essence of questioning is to lay bare and keep alert for possibilities. We will shortly see in what sense. When one of our convictions or opinions becomes problematic as a consequence of new hermeneutical information, and though it is disclosed as prejudice, this does not imply that it is automatically replaced by a sort of "definitive truth"; this was the naive thesis of historical objectivism. Such a thesis forgets that the displaced conviction and the "truth" which denounces and replaces it are both members of an uninterrupted chain of events. The "former" prejudice is not simply cast aside. For in reality it has an /84/ important role to play later on, although a different one than while it was still only implicit. It must also be said that the denouced prejudice can only play its new role if it is exploited to the maximum. It is a difficult task to replace a conviction, to denouce it as a prejudice; this is precisely because whatever replaced it cannot present its credentials until the position under assault is itself unmasked and denounced as prejudice. Every "new" position which replaces another continues to need the "former" because it cannot itself be explained so long as it knows neither *in* what nor *by* what it is opposed.

We see that there are dialectical relations between the "former" and the "new," between, on the one hand, the prejudice organically a part of my particular system of convictions or opinions, that is, the implicit prejudice, and on the other hand, the new element which denounces it, that is, the foreign element which provokes my system or one of its elements. The same can be said of the relation between "my own" opinion *in the process* of losing its implicit persuasive force by being exposed as prejudice, and the new element which, for the moment, is still external to my system of opinions, but is *in the process* of becoming "my own" though being disclosed as truly "other" than "my own" former opinion. This is to say that there are dialectical relations between the inauthentically "mine" and the authentically "mine" (the implicit prejudice in the process of being exposed as prejudice). In other words, the relation is between "my own" in the process of becoming authentic through the new hermeneutical information which provoked it, and the hermeneutical information itself, that is, the information in the process of entering into my system of opinions and /85/ convictions — in the process of becoming "mine"; that is to say that this new hermeneutical information gains entrance into my system by its opposition to the denounced prejudice and by this opposition it is revealed *as strangely "other."* The universal mediator of this dialectic is that denoucing an opinion as prejudice and disclosure of the truly different in hermeneutical information transforms an implicit "mine" into an authentic "mine," makes an inadmissable "other" into a genuine "other" and thus assimilable in its otherness.

Historical objectivism is *naive* because it never follows its reflections to their conclusion. In its trusting blindness to the presuppositions of its method, it totally forgets the historicity which is its "own." An historical consciousness which proposes the task of being truly concrete must *already* consider *itself* as an essentially historical phenomenon. However, to *define* consciousness as historical consciousness or to grant that it is such remains a mere verbalization so long as historical consciousness is not yet *actualized*: that is, we must question it and question it *radically*. There is a notion of the "historical object" which is simply the naive correlative of the thought of historical objectivism. For historical objectivism the historicity of the object is an illusion to be overcome; outside of these illusions the "true" object is no longer historical! Or, in other words, for historical objectivism the "historical object" is a mixture of the "in-itself" and the "for-us"; a mélange of the "true a-historical object" and "our historical illusions." Radical questioning denounces the notion of an "historical object" so characterized as a construction of objectivistic thought, motivated—I say /86/ *motivated,* an implicit motivation—by the *primordial* historicity of knowledge and the historical object which together have affinities. The notion of "historical illusions" was the result of a "true and a-historical object" is the result of an objectivistic or naturalistic interpretation; furthermore, the two interpretations are interdependent: they are the mutual complements of one another.

Not only the concept, but even the expression "historical object" seems useless to me. What we mean to designate by this phrase is not an "object" at all, but a "unity" of "mine" and "other." I repeat again what I have often insisted upon: every hermeneutical understanding begins and ends with the "thing itself." But it is necessary to guard against, on the one hand, a misunderstanding of the role of "temporal distance" which is between the beginning and the end, and, on the other hand, an idealizing objectification of the "thing itself," as historical objectivism has done. The de-specialization of "temporal distance" and the de-idealization of the "thing itself" allows us to understand how it is possible to know in the "historical object" *the genuinely "other" despite "my own" convictions and opinions*; that is to say, how it is possible to know them *both.* Thus it is more true to state that the historical object, in the authentic sense of that term, is not an "object" but the "unity" of one with the other. It is the relationship, that is, "affinity," through which they both manifest themselves: the historical reality on the one hand and the reality of historical understanding on the other. It is this "unity" which is primordial historicity where knowledge and the historical object manifest themselves in their "affiliation" [*d'une manière 'affine'*]. /87/ An object which comes to us through history is not only an object which one discerns from afar, but is the "center" in which historically operative being and historically operative consciousness appear.

I will say then that the condition for hermeneutics to think about historical reality properly so called, comes to us from what I call the *principle of historical productivity.* Properly understood, this effectuates a mediation between the once and the now; it develops in itself all the continual series of perspectives through which the past presents and addresses itself to us. In this radical and universal sense, historical self-consciousness is not the abandonment of philosophy's eternal task, but is the path granted to us for reaching the truth, which is always our goal. And I see in the relation of all understanding to language, the way in which consciousness opens out to historical productivity.[24]

24. The systematic implications of an historically operative hermeneutics, such as has just been sketched here, and the centrality of the phenomenon of language, are illuminated in the third part (pp. 361–465) of the author's *Wahrheit und Methode, Grundzuge einer philosophischen Hermeneutik* (Tübingen: J. C. B. Mohr, 1960, 1965).

PART TWO

Context as World:
Interpretations

Chapter Four

The Search for Paradigms as a Hindrance to Understanding

ALBERT O. HIRSCHMAN

A recent journal article argued forcefully against the "collection of empirical materials as an end in itself and without sufficient theoretical analysis to determine appropriate criteria of selection."[1] The present essay presents a complementary critique of the opposite failing. Its target is the tendency toward compulsive and mindless theorizing — a disease at least as prevalent and debilitating, so it seems to me, as the spread of mindless number work in the social sciences.

While the latter phenomenon has been caused largely by the availability of the computer, several factors are responsible for the compulsion to theorize, which is often so strong as to induce mindlessness. In the academy, the prestige of the theorist is towering. Further, extravagant use of language intimates that theorizing can rival sensuous delights: what used to be called an interesting or valuable theoretical point is commonly referred to today as a "stimulating" or even "exciting" theoretical "insight." Moreover, insofar as the social sciences in the United States are concerned, an important role has no doubt been played by the desperate need, on the part of the hegemonic power, for shortcuts to the understanding of multifarious reality that must be coped with and controlled and therefore be understood at once. In-

Originally published in *World Politics* 22, no. 3 (March 1970). Copyright © by Princeton University Press. Reprinted by permission.

1. Oran R. Young, "Professor Russett: Industrious Tailor to a Naked Emperor," *World Politics* 21 (April 1969): 489–90.

terestingly enough, revolutionaries experience the same compulsion:
while they are fond of quoting Marx to the approximate effect that
interpreting the world is not nearly as important as changing it, they
are well aware of the enormous strength that is imparted to revolutionary determination by the conviction that one has indeed fully
understood social reality and its "laws of change." As a result of these
various factors, the quick theoretical fix has taken its place in our
culture alongside the quick technical fix.

In the following pages, I do not have a central epistemological
theorem to offer that would permit us to differentiate between good
and bad theorizing, or between fruitful and sterile paradigmatic thinking. My accent throughout is on the kind of *cognitive style* that hinders,
or promotes, understanding. I introduce the topic by a critical look at
two books that exemplify opposite styles. Subsequently, I make an
attempt to delineate various areas in which an impatience for theoretical formulation leads to serious pitfalls. Theorizing about Latin American society and economy, on the part of both Latin Americans and
outside observers, receives special attention because it has been particularly marked by the cognitive style I find unfortunate.

I

John Womack's *Zapata and the Mexican Revolution*[2] and James L.
Payne's *Patterns of Conflict in Colombia*[3] are the two books I shall use to
open the argument. They have in common that they are both by
young North American scholars; both, in fact, were originally written
as doctoral dissertations; and they both reached my desk early in 1969.
But this is where any possible resemblance ends. At this point I should
state that both books aroused in me unusually strong feelings: I found
Womack's way of telling the Zapata story extraordinarily appealing,
while I was strongly repelled by Payne's book in spite of its crispness,
cleverness, and occasional flashes of wit. There are of course many
striking contrasts between the two books that can account for these
opposite reactions, not the least perhaps being that Womack obviously
fell in love with revolutionary Mexico and the Zapatistas whereas
Payne's treatment exudes dislike and contempt for Colombians in
general, and for Colombian politicians in particular. But the more

2. New York: Knopf, 1969.
3. New Haven: Yale University Press, 1968.

important, and not necessarily related, difference is in the cognitive styles of the two authors. Within the first few pages of his book Payne presents us triumphantly with the key to the full and complete understanding of the Colombian political system. The rest of the book is a demonstration that the key indeed unlocks all conceivable doors of Colombian political life, past, present, and future. Womack, on the other hand, abjures any pretense at full understanding right in the preface, where he says that his book "is not an analysis but a story because the truth of the revolution in Morelos is in the feeling of it which I could not convey through defining its factors but only through telling of it." "The analysis that I could do," he continues, "and that I thought pertinent I have tried to weave into the narrative, so that it would issue at the moment right for understanding it."[4] And indeed what is remarkable about the book is the continuity of the narrative and the almost complete, one might say Flaubertian, absence from its pages of the author who could have explained, commented, moralized, or drawn conclusions. Yet whoever reads through the book will have gained immeasurably in his understanding not only of the Mexican Revolution, but of peasant revolutions everywhere, and Womack's very reticence and self-effacement stimulate the reader's curiosity and imagination. Payne's book, on the contrary, obviously explains far too much and thereby succeeds only in provoking the reader's resistance and incredulity; the only curiosity it provokes is about the kind of social science that made an obviously gifted young man go so wrong.

Here, then, is the experience behind the title of this essay: understanding as a result of one book without the shadow of a paradigm; and frustration as a result of another in which one paradigm is made to spawn thirty-four hypotheses (reproduced, for the convenience of the reader, in the book's appendix) covering all aspects of political behavior in Colombia and, incidentally, the United States as well.

Perhaps I should explain briefly what Mr. Payne's basic "insight" or paradigm consists in: politicians in Colombia, he has found out through questionnaires, interviews, and similar devices, are motivated primarily by status considerations rather than by genuine interest in programs and policies, as is predominantly and fortunately the case in

4. Womack, *Zapata*, p. x.

the United States. He uses the neutral-sounding terms "status incentive" and "program incentive"; the former characteristically motivates Colombian political leaders whereas the latter animates their North American counterparts. In plain language, occasionally used by the author, Colombian politicians are selfish,[5] ambitious, unscrupulous, unprincipled, exceedingly demagogic—interested exclusively in increasing their own power, always ready to betray yesterday's friends and allies, and, to top it all, incapable of having friendly personal relations with anyone because they feel comfortable only with abject supplicants.[6] On the other hand, there is the politician with a program incentive whose preferred habitat is the United States of America. *He* enjoys working on concrete policies and achieving a stated goal; hence he is principled, willing to defend unpopular causes, always ready to come to constructive agreements, hardworking, and generally lovable.

For a North American to contrast Colombian and United States politicians in terms of such invidious stereotypes is, to say the least, a distasteful spectacle. We must of course allow for the possibility that truth, as unearthed by the scholar, turns out to be distasteful. But Payne does not betray any sense of realizing the unpleasantness of his discovery. On the contrary, he evidently draws much satisfaction from the edifice he has built and takes good care to make sure that there will be no escape from it. At various points he assures us that Colombians are like that; that, as he put it in a subtitle, they are not "on the brink of anything"; that it is futile to expect any change in the pattern of Colombian politics from such incidental happenings as industrialization or urbanization or agrarian reforms: like the three characters in Sartre's *Huis Clos,* the twenty million Colombians will just have to go on living in their self-made hell while Mr. Payne, after his seven-month diagnostic visit (from February to September 1965, as he informs us in the preface), has returned to his own, so much more fortunate section of the hemisphere.

It is easy to show that the Payne model is as wrong as it is outrageous. In the first place, it is unable to explain the very wide swings of Colombian politics; after all, during almost all of the first half of the twentieth century Colombia stood out as a "stable" democracy with

5. Payne, *Patterns,* p. 70.   6. Ibid., p. 12.

peaceful transfers of power from one party to another; throughout the Great Depression of the thirties when almost all other Latin American countries experienced violent political convulsions, constitutional government continued in spite of much social unrest.

This experience is hard to explain by a theory that holds that vicious political infighting, untrammeled by any concern with programs or loyalty, holds continuous sway throughout the body politic. Moreover, such a theory ought to take a good look at—and give a special weight to—the body's head: if Payne had done that he might have noticed that his stereotype, the politician with a status incentive, simply does not apply to a number of the most outstanding leaders and recent presidents of Colombia—there is no need to mention names, but it is amusing to quote, in contrast, from a recent portrait of a contemporary president of the United States: "His preoccupation seems to have been success—in this case the achievement of power rather than its use for political purposes."[7]

Supposing even that the diagnosis is essentially correct and that politicians in Colombia are more interested in the quest for power per se than in the use of this power for the carrying out of specific programs—what does this "insight" explain? Suppose that we find, as Payne indeed does, that those self-seeking politicians frequently switched sides or vote for demagogic measures, does this finding teach us anything fundamental about the political system, its ability to accomodate change, to solve newly arising problems, to assure peace, justice, and development? It does nothing of the sort, but at best leaves us with the proposition, which incidentally is both platitudinous and wrong, that if the politicians are vicious, the ensuing politics are likely to be vicious too!

Let us pass now from the paradigms of James Payne to John Womack, who has rigorously excluded from his universe any semblance of a paradigm. It is of course impossible to do justice to his narrative. I shall refer here only to one particular turn of the events he describes in order to show how he invites speculation and thereby contributes to the possibility of understanding.

It has perhaps not been sufficiently remarked that the book has *two* protagonists: Zapata dominates the action during the first nine chap-

7. Nora Beloff and Michael Davie, "Getting to Know Mr. Nixon," *The Observer*, 23 February 1969.

ters, but in the important last two chapters (eighty pages) the leading figure is Gildardo Magaña who became Zapata's ranking secretary after mid-1917 and, after a brief fight for the succession, the chief of the Zapatista movement following Zapata's death in April 1919. Womack honors Magaña with one of his too-rare character portraits: "From these stresses [of his youth] Gildardo Magaña somehow emerged strong and whole. What he had learned was to mediate: not to compromise, to surrender principle and to trade concessions, but to detect reason in all claims in conflict, to recognize the particular legitimacy of each, to sense where the grounds of concord were, and to bring contestants into harmony there. Instinctively he thrived on arguments, which he entered not to win but to conciliate."[8]

Womack then relates the exploits of Magaña as a resourceful negotiator of ever new alliances and contrasts him with the rigid and sectarian Palafox, Zapata's earlier principal secretary, who "seemed in retrospect the individual responsible for the Zapatistas' present plight — the man they could blame for their disastrous involvement with Villa in 1914, their alienation of worthy chiefs in the constitutionalist party, and their abiding reputation as the most intransigent group in the revolutionary movement."[9]

After the murder of Zapata, Magaña maneuvered tactfully and successfully among the various chiefs. After six months, the succession crisis was over and Magaña was recognized as commander-in-chief, with the movement virtually intact. Womack then traces the complex events through which the Zapatistas, as he puts it in the title of his last chapter, "Inherit Morelos" — that is, how they manage, by alternately fighting and negotiating and by backing Obregón at the right moment, to pass from outlaws into local administrators and members of a national coalition. "So ended the year 1920, in peace, with populist agrarian reform instituted as a national policy, and with the Zapatista movement established in Morelos politics. In the future through thick and thin these achievements would last. This was the claim Zapata, his chiefs, and their volunteers had forced, *and Magaña had won and secured.*"[10]

Twice Womack implies that this outcome was due not only to the presence of Magaña, but perhaps also to the absence of Zapata from

8. Womack, *Zapata*, p. 290.   9. Ibid., p. 306.
10. Ibid., p. 369; my italics.

the scene. There is first the "extraordinary maneuver" by which
Magaña offered the Carranza government the Zapatistas' support
when United States intervention threatened in the Jenkins case in 1919.
Womack says here flatly, "Had Zapata lived, Zapatista strategy could
not have been so flexible."[11] Then again at the celebration of Obregón's
victory, on 2 June 1920,

> twenty thousand Agua Prieta partisans marched in review through the
> Zócalo, among them the forces from Morelos. And watching with the
> honored new leaders from a balcony of the Palacio National . . . stood the
> squat, swarthy de la O, frowning into the sun. From an angle he looked
> almost like Zapata, dead now for over a year. (If de la O had been killed
> and Zapata had lived, Zapata would probably have been there in his
> place, with the same uncomfortable frown, persuaded by Magaña to join
> the boom for Obregón but probably worrying, as Magaña was not,
> about when he might have to revolt again.)[12]

Out of these bits and pieces, there emerges a proposition or
hypothesis that must have been on Womack's mind, but that he allows
the reader to formulate: did the comparative success of the Morelos
uprising within the Mexican Revolution rest on the *alternating* leadership, first of the charismatic, revolutionary Zapata and then of the
skillful, though highly principled, negotiator Magaña? And what are
the "lessons" of this story for other revolutions and, in particular, for
revolutionary movements that are confined to a limited portion or
sector of a nation-state?

The historian is probably ambivalent about such questions. He
revels in the uniqueness of the historical event, yet he constantly intimates that history holds the most precious lessons. And I believe he is
right on both counts! Perhaps the rest of this essay will show why this
is not a self-contradictory position.

II

First let me return briefly to the comparison of Payne and
Womack. What strikes the reader of the two books most is, as I said
before, the difference in cognitive style: Payne, from the first page to
the last, breathes brash confidence that he has achieved complete
understanding of his subject, whereas Womack draws conclusions
with the utmost diffidence and circumspection. His respect for the

11. Ibid., p. 348.   12. Ibid., p. 365.

autonomy of the actors whose deeds he recounts is what gives his book its special appeal and probably contributed to the spectacular accolade he received from Carlos Fuentes in the *New York Review of Books.*[13] For it is today a most unusual restraint. I believe that the countries of the Third World have become fair game for the model builders and paradigm molders, to an intolerable degree. During the nineteenth century several "laws" were laid down for the leading industrial countries whose rapid development was disconcerting to numerous thinkers who were strongly affected by what Flaubert called "la rage de vouloir conclure."[14] Having been proven wrong by the unfolding events in almost every instance, the lawmakers then migrated to warmer climes, that is, to the less developed countries. And here they really came into their own. For the less developed, dependent countries had long been objects of history — so that to treat them as objects of iron law or rigid models from whose working there is no escape came naturally to scholars who turned their attention to them. Soon we were witnesses to a veritable deluge of paradigms and models, from the vicious circle of poverty, low-level equilibrium traps, and uniform stage sequences of the economist, to the traditional or non-achievement-oriented or status-hungry personality of the sociologist, psychologist, or political scientist. A psychologist may find it interesting some day to inquire whether these theories were inspired primarily by compassion or by contempt for the underdeveloped world. The result, in any case, is that the countries of Latin America, for example, appear to any contemporary, well-read observer far more constrained than, say, the United States or France or the USSR.[15] Latin American societies seem somehow less complex and their "laws of movement" more intelligible, their medium-term future more predictable or at least formulable in terms of clearcut simple alternatives (such as "reform or revolution?"), and their average citi-

13. 13 March 1969.
14. I have long looked for a good translation of this key concept into English. It now strikes that an apt, if free, rendering of Flaubert's meaning would be "the compulsion to theorize" — which is the subject and might have been the title of the present essay.
15. Lévi-Strauss's structualist anthropology has had similar effect, as it "has on the whole refrained from attempting to impose totalizing structures on the so-called higher civilizations" (Benjamin I. Schwartz, "A Brief Defense of Political and Intellectual History with Particular Reference to Non-Western Cultures," *Daedalus* [Winter 1971], p. 110).

zens more reducible to one or a very few stereotypes. Of course, all of this is so exclusively because our paradigmatic thinking makes it so. Mr. Payne is merely the latest in a long line of "law" makers, model builders, and paradigm molders who have vied with one another in getting an iron grip on Latin American reality. And it must now be said that Latin American social scientists have themselves made an important contribution to this headlong rush toward the all-revealing paradigm.

Elsewhere I have described as "the age of self-incrimination" one phase of the efforts of Latin Americans at understanding their own reality and the lag of their countries behind Europe and the United States. Incidentally, traces of this phase can be found in a few contemporary Latin American intellectuals, and they, jointly with their bygone confrères, provide Payne with some telling quotations about the despicable character of Colombian politicians and politics. By and large, the phase has fortunately passed; it has, however, been replaced by a somewhat related phase that might be called the age of the *action-arousing gloomy vision:* on the basis of some model or paradigm, the economic and social reality of Latin America is explained and the laws of movement of economy and society are formulated in such a way that current trends (of terms of trade, or of income distribution, or of population growth) are shown to produce either stagnation, or, more usually, deterioration and disaster. The art of statistical projection has made a potent contribution to this type of forecast, which is then supposed to galvanize men into action designed to avert the threatened disaster through some fairly fundamental "structural changes."

Now I believe that this strategy for socioeconomic change has sometimes been and can on occasion again be extremely useful in just this way. But for several reasons I would caution against the exclusive reliance on it that has recently characterized Latin American social and economic thought.

There is a world of difference, by the way, between this action-arousing gloomy vision and the Marxian perspective on capitalist evolution. In the Marxian perspective, events in the absence of revolution were not at all supposed to move steadily downhill. On the contrary, capitalist development, while punctuated by crises and accompanied by increasing misery of the proletariat, was nevertheless expected to be going forward apace. It was in fact the genius of Marxism — which explains a large part of its appeal—that it was able to view both the advances and the setbacks of economic development under the capitalist system as helping toward its eventual overthrow.

My first criticism of the vision ties in directly with my dislike of paradigms laying down excessive constraints on the conceivable moves of individuals and societies. Why should all of Latin America find itself constantly impaled on the horns of some fateful and unescapable dilemma? Even if one is prepared to accept Goldenweiser's "principle of limited possibilities" in a given environment, any theory or model or paradigm propounding that there are only two possibilities—disaster or one particular road to salvation—should be prima facie suspect. After all, there *is* at least temporarily, such a place as purgatory!

The second reason for which I would advocate a de-emphasis of the action-arousing gloomy vision is that it creates more gloom than action. The spread of gloom is certain and pervasive, but the call to action may or may not be heard. And since the theory teaches that in the normal course of events things will be increasingly unsatisfactory, it is an invitation *not* to watch out for possible positive developments. On the contrary, those imbued with the gloomy vision will attempt to prove year by year that Latin America is going from bad to worse; a year like 1968—and this may hold for 1969 as well—when the economic performance of the three large and of several small countries was little short of brilliant, will come as a distinct embarrassment.

Frequently, of course, the theories I am criticizing are the result of wishful thinking: would it not be reassuring if a society that has been unable to meet some standard of social justice or if an oppressive political regime were ipso facto condemned to economic stagnation and deterioration? For that very reason we should be rather on our guard against any theory purporting to prove what would be so reassuring.

But the propensity to see gloom and failure everywhere is not engendered only by the desire to reprove further an oppressive regime or an unjust society. It may also be rooted in the fact that one has come to expect his country to perform poorly because of its long history of backwardness and dependence; hence any evidence that the country may possibly be doing better or may be emerging from its backwardness is going to be dissonant with previous cognitions and is therefore likely to be suppressed; on the contrary, evidence that nothing at all has changed will be picked up, underlined, and even greeted, for it does not necessitate any change in the preexisting cognitions to which one has become comfortably adjusted. This is so because people who have a low self-concept and expect failure apparently feel some discomfort when they suddenly perform well, as psychologists have shown. [16] In this manner, social psychology provides a clue to a Latin American phenomenon that has long puzzled me, yet has struck me with such force that I have invented a name for it — the "failure complex" or "fracasomania."

Finally, the paradigm-based gloomy vision can be positively harmful. When it prevails, hopeful developments either will be not perceived at all or will be considered exceptional and purely temporary. In these circumstances, they will not be taken advantage of as elements on which to build. To give an example: the rise of the fishmeal industry in Peru and the similarly spectacular growth of banana planting in Ecuador from about 1950 to the mid-sixties contradicted the doctrine that the era of export-promoted growth had ended in Latin America. As a result, economists first ignored these booms, then from year to year predicted their imminent collapse. It is quite possible that particularly the latter attitude held down the portion of the bonanza that the two countries might otherwise have set aside for long-term economic and social capital formation; for why bother to exert oneself and, in the process, antagonize powerful interests if the payoff is expected to be so limited and short-lived? More recently, another theory of gloom has been widely propagated: it seems that now the opportunities for import-substituting industrialization have also become "exhausted" even though it can be argued that, just as earlier in the case of *desarrollo hacia afuera,* there is still much life left in *desarrollo hacia adentro.*[17] Again, if the exhaustion thesis is wholly accepted it may weaken the search for and prevent the discovery of new industrial opportunities.

In all these matters I would suggest a little more "reverence for life," a little less straitjacketing of the future, a little more allowance for

16. Elliott Aronson, "Dissonance Theory: Progress and Problems," in R. P. Abelson et al., eds., *Theories of Cognitive Consistency: A Source Book* (Chicago: Rand McNally, 1968), p. 24.

17. The Spanish terms *desarrollo hacia afuera* and *desarrollo hacia adentro* are convenient shorthand expressions for growth through the expansion of exports and of the domestic market, respectively.

the unexpected — and a little less wishful thinking. This is simply a matter, once again, of cognitive style. With respect to actual socioeconomic analysis, I am of course not unaware that without models, paradigms, ideal types, and similar abstractions we cannot even start to think. But cognitive style, that is, the kind of paradigms we search out, the way we put them together, and the ambitions we nurture for their powers — all this can make a great deal of difference.

III

In trying to spell out these notions in greater detail I shall make three principal points. In the first place, I shall explain why the gloomy vision is in a sense the first stage of any reflections about a backward reality, and shall make a plea for not getting stuck in that stage. I shall then attempt to show that in evaluating the broader social and political consequences of some ongoing event we must be suspicious of paradigms that pretend to give a clearcut answer about the desirable or undesirable nature of these consequences. And finally, I shall suggest that large-scale social change typically occurs as a result of a unique constellation of highly disparate events and is therefore amenable to paradigmatic thinking only in a very special sense.

The initial effort to understand reality will almost inevitably make it appear more solidly entrenched than before. The immediate effect of social analysis is therefore to convert the real into the rational or the contingent into the necessary. Herein, rather than in any conservatism of "bourgeois" social scientists, probably lies the principal explanation of that much commented-upon phenomenon — the conservative bias of social science in general, and of functional analysis in particular. This very conservatism takes, however, a strange turn when the target of the social scientists is a society that is viewed from the outset as backward or unjust or oppressive. For analysis will then make it appear, at least to start with, that the backwardness, injustice and oppression are in reality far more deep-rooted than had been suspected. This is the origin of all the vicious circle and vicious personality theories that seem to make any change impossible in the absence of either revolution, highly competent central planning with massive injection of foreign aid, or massive abduction of the young generation so that it may be steeped elsewhere in creativity and achievement motivation.[18]

18. It is only fair to note that, in his more recent work on achievement motivation, David McClelland has changed his earlier views on these matters. Thus he writes (after

Interestingly enough then, the same analytical turn of mind that leads to a conservative bias in the case of a society that we approach without a strong initial commitment to change, leads to a revolutionary or quasi-revolutionary stance in the case of societies that are viewed from the outset as unsatisfactory. In the case of the former, the analyst, like the ecologist, often becomes enamored of all the fine latent functions he uncovers, whereas in the latter case he despairs of the possibility of change (except for the most massive and revolutionary varieties) because of all the interlocking vicious circles he has come upon.

Fortunately these initial effects of social science analysis wear off after a while. In the case of the backward countries, the realization will dawn that certain so-called attributes of backwardness are not necessarily obstacles, but can be lived with and sometimes can be turned into positive assets. I have elsewhere attempted to bring together the accumulating evidence for this sort of phenomenon. This evidence, then, should make us a bit wary when new vicious circles or new development-obstructing personality types or new dead ends are being discovered. Though such discoveries are bound to occur and can be real contributions to understanding, they carry an obligation to look for ways in which they may play not a reinforcing but a neutral or debilitating role insofar as system maintenance is concerned. Perhaps social scientists could pass a rule, such as has long existed in the British Parliament, by which an M.P. proposing a new item of public expenditure must also indicate the additional revenue through which he expects the nation to finance it. Similarly it might be legislated by an assembly of social scientists that anyone who believes he has discovered a new obstacle to development is under an obligation to look for ways in which this obstacle can be overcome or can possibly be lived with or can, in certain circumstances, be transformed into a blessing in disguise.

IV

A related element of the cognitive style I am advocating derives from the recognition of one aspect of the unfolding of social events that makes prediction exceedingly difficult and contributes to that

having given cogent reasons for doing so): "To us it is no longer a self-evident truth that it is easier to produce long-range personality transformations in young children than it is in adults." David C. McClelland and David G. Winter, *Motivating Economic Achievement* (New York: Free Press, 1969), p. 356.

peculiar open-endedness of history that is the despair of the
paradigm-obsessed social scientist. Situations in which the expertise of
the social scientist is solicited frequently have the following structure:
some new event or bundle of events such as industrialization, urbanization, rapid population growth, and so forth, has happened or is
happening before our eyes, and we would like to know what its
consequences are for a number of social and political system characteristics, such as integration of marginal or oppressed groups, loss of
authority on the part of traditional elites, political stability or crisis,
likely level of violence or of cultural achievement, and so on. Faced
with the seemingly reasonable demand for enlightenment on the part
of the layman and the policy maker, and propelled also by his own
curiosity, the social scientist now opens his paradigm box to see how
best to handle the job at hand. To his dismay, he then finds, provided
he looks carefully, that he is faced with an embarrassment of riches:
various available paradigms will produce radically different answers.
The situation can be compared, in a rough way, with the quandary the
forecasting economist has long experienced: the magnitudes that are of
most interest to the policy makers, such as the prospective deficit or
surplus in the balance of payments or the budget, or the inflationary or
deflationary gap, or the rate of unemployment, are usually — and
maddeningly — differences between gross magnitudes. Hence, even if
the gross magnitudes are estimated with an acceptable margin of error,
the estimate of the difference may be off by a very large percentage
and may easily be even of the wrong sign. The hazards in forecasting
qualitative social events on the basis of perfectly respectable and reliable paradigms can be rather similar. Take the question: what is the
effect of industrialization and economic development on a society's
propensity for civil war, or for external adventure, or for genocide, or
for democracy? As with the effect, say, of accelerated growth on the
balance of payments, the answer must be: it depends on the balance of
the contending forces that are set in motion. Industrialization creates
new tensions, but may allay old ones; it may divert the minds of the
elite from external adventure while creating new capabilities for such
adventure, and so forth. Thus the outcome is here also a difference
whose estimate is necessarily subject to a particularly high degree of
error. This ambiguous situation, incidentally, characterizes also less
crucial, more "middle-range" causal relationships. An example is the

effect of bigness and diversity of an organization on innovation. As James Q. Wilson has argued, bigness and diversity increase the probability that members will conceive of and propose major innovations; but they also increase the probability that any one innovation that is proposed will be turned down. Again the net effect is in doubt.[19]

Wilson's dilemma is the sort of cognitive style in paradigmatic thinking that is not often met with; ordinarily social scientists are happy enough when they have gotten hold of one paradigm or line of causation. As a result, their guesses are often farther off the mark than those of the experienced politician whose intuition is more likely to take a variety of forces into account.

V

Finally, the ability of paradigmatic thinking to illuminate the paths of change is limited in yet another, perhaps more fundamental way. In the context of most Latin American societies, many of us are concerned with the bringing about of large-scale change to be carried through in a fairly brief period of time. But ordinarily the cards are stacked so much against the accomplishment of large-scale change that when it happens, be it a result of revolution or reform or some intermediate process, it is bound to be an unpredictable and nonrepeatable event, unpredictable because it took the very actors by surprise and nonrepeatable because once the event has happened everybody is put on notice and precautions will be taken by various parties so that it will not happen again. The uniqueness and scientific opaqueness of the large-scale changes that occur when history "suddenly accelerates" have often been remarked upon. Womack brings this out as well as anyone in his narrative of the Mexican Revolution. I shall invoke the authority of two recent commentators belonging to rather different camps. The first is the anthropologist Max Gluckman, who addresses himself to "radical change" after having defended anthropology against the charge that it is not interested in change. He writes, "The source of radical change escapes these analyses [of other kinds of change]. Perhaps this is inevitable because social anthropology aims to be specific. Scientific method cannot deal with unique complexes of

19. James Q. Wilson, "Innovation in Organization: Notes Toward a Theory," in James D. Thompson, ed., *Approaches to Organizational Design* (Pittsburgh: University of Pittsburgh Press, 1966), pp. 193–218.

many events. The accounts of the actual course of events which produce change therefore necessarily remain historical narrative."[20]

Perhaps a more significant witness, because as a Marxist he should
be an inveterate paradigm-lover, is Louis Althusser. In his remarkable
essay, "Contradiction and Over-determination," Althusser makes
much of some striking statements of Lenin's about the unique constellation of events that made possible the Russian Revolution of 1917.
The key passage from Lenin reads: "If the revolution has triumphed so
rapidly it is exclusively because, as a result of a historical situation of
extreme originality, a number of completely distinct currents, a
number of totally heterogeneous class interests, and a number of completely opposite social and political tendencies have become fused with
remarkable coherence."[21]

On the basis of Lenin's testimony Althusser then proceeds to explain that revolutions never arise purely out of the basic economic
contradictions that Marx stressed, but only when these contradictions
are "fused" in some unique manner with a number of other determinants. This fusion or embedding is the phenomenon he calls "over-
determination" of revolutions. Actually this is a poor term (as he
himself recognizes) for it could imply that, had one of the many
circumstantial factors not been present, the revolution would still have
taken place. But the whole context of the essay, and certainly the
quotations from Lenin, exclude this interpretation. On the contrary, it
is quite clear that even with all these converging elements the revolution won by an exceedingly narrow margin. Thus, while a surprising
number of heterogeneous elements almost miraculously conspired to
bring the revolution about, every single one of them was still absolutely indispensable to its success. Uniqueness seems a better term for
this phenomenon than overdetermination.

Incidentally, this interpretation of revolutions undermines the revolutionary's usual critique of the advocacy of reform. This critique is
generally based on the high degree of improbability that a ruling
group will ever tolerate or even connive at the elimination or destruction of its own privileges; the only way to achieve this end is by
smashing the "system" through revolutionary assault. But with the
view of revolutions as overdetermined or unique events, it turns out

20. *Politics, Law and Ritual in Tribal Society* (Chicago: Aldine, 1965), p. 286.
21. As quoted in Althusser, *Pour Marx* (Paris: Maspero, 1966), p. 98.

to be a toss-up which form of large-scale change is more unlikely — so we may as well be on the lookout for whatever rare openings in either direction appear on the horizon.

In sum, he who looks for large-scale social change must be possessed, with Kierkegaard, by "the passion for what is possible" rather than rely on what has been certified as probable by factor analysis.

This view of large-scale social change as a unique, nonrepeatable, and *ex ante* highly improbable complex of events is obviously damaging to the aspirations of anyone who would explain and predict these events through "laws of change." Once again, there is no denying that such "laws" or paradigms can have considerable utility. They are useful for the apprehending of many elements of the complex and often are stimuli to action before the event and indispensable devices for achieving a beginning of understanding after the event has happened. That is much, but that is all. The architect of social change can never have a reliable blueprint. Not only is each house he builds different from any other that was built before, but it also necessarily uses new construction materials and even experiments with untested principles of stress and structure. Therefore what can be most usefully conveyed by the builders of one house is an understanding of the experience that made it all possible to build under these trying circumstances. It is, I believe, in this spirit that Womack makes that, at first sight rather shocking, statement, "the truth of the revolution in Morelos is in the feeling of it." Perhaps he means not only the truth, but also the principal lesson.

Chapter Five

Deep Play: Notes on the Balinese Cockfight

CLIFFORD GEERTZ

THE RAID

Early in April of 1958, my wife and I arrived, malarial and diffi-
dent, in a Balinese village we intended, as anthropologists, to study. A
small place, about five hundred people, and relatively remote, it was
its own world. We were intruders, professional ones, and the villagers
dealt with us as Balinese seem always to deal with people not part of
their life who yet press themselves upon them: as though we were not
there. For them, and to a degree for ourselves, we were nonpersons,
specters, invisible men.

We moved into an extended family compound (that had been arranged before through the provincial government) belonging to one
of the four major factions in village life. But except for our landlord
and the village chief, whose cousin and brother-in-law he was, everyone ignored us in a way only a Balinese can do. As we wandered
around, uncertain, wistful, eager to please, people seemed to look
right through us with a gaze focused several yards behind us on some
more actual stone or tree. Almost nobody greeted us; but nobody
scowled or said anything unpleasant to us either, which would have
been almost as satisfactory. If we ventured to approach someone
(something one is powerfully inhibited from doing in such an atmosphere), he moved, negligently but definitely, away. If, seated or lean-

Originally published in *Daedalus*, the Journal of the American Academy of Arts and
Sciences, Boston, Massachusetts, vol. 101, no. 1 (Winter 1972). Reprinted by permission.

ing against a wall, we had him trapped, he said nothing at all, or mumbled what for the Balinese is the ultimate nonword — "yes." The indifference, of course, was studied; the villagers were watching every move we made, and they had an enormous amount of quite accurate information about who we were and what we were going to be doing. But they acted as if we simply did not exist, which, in fact, as this behavior was designed to inform us, we did not, or anyway not yet.

This is, as I say, general in Bali. Everywhere else I have been in Indonesia, and more latterly in Morocco, when I have gone into a new village, people have poured out from all sides to take a very close look at me, and often an all-too-probing feel as well. In Balinese villages, at least those away from the tourist circuit, nothing happens at all. People go on pounding, chatting, making offerings, staring into space, carrying baskets about while one drifts around feeling vaguely disembodied. And the same thing is true on the individual level. When you first meet a Balinese, he seems virtually not to relate to you at all; he is, in the term Gregory Bateson and Margaret Mead made famous, "away."[1] Then — in a day, a week, a month (with some people the magic moment never comes) — he decides, for reasons I have never quite been able to fathom, that you *are* real, and then he becomes a warm, gay, sensitive, sympathetic, though, being Balinese, always precisely controlled, person. You have crossed, somehow, some moral or metaphysical shadow line. Though you are not exactly taken as a Balinese (one has to be born to that), you are at least regarded as a human being rather than a cloud or a gust of wind. The whole complexion of your relationship dramatically changes to, in the majority of cases, a gentle, almost affectionate one — a low-keyed, rather playful, rather mannered, rather bemused geniality.

My wife and I were still very much in the gust-of-wind stage, a most frustrating, and even, as you soon begin to doubt whether you are really real after all, unnerving one, when, ten days or so after our arrival, a large cockfight was held in the public square to raise money for a new school.

Now, a few special occasions aside, cockfights are illegal in Bali under the Republic (as, for not altogether unrelated reasons, they were under the Dutch), largely as a result of the pretensions to puritanism

1. G. Bateson and M. Mead, *Balinese Character: A Photographic Analysis* (New York, 1942), p. 68.

radical nationalism tends to bring with it. The elite, which is not itself so very puritan, worries about the poor, ignorant peasant gambling all his money away, about what foreigners will think, about the waste of time better devoted to building up the country. It sees cockfighting as "primitive," "backward," "unprogressive," and generally unbecoming an ambitious nation. And, as with those other embarrassments — opium smoking, begging, or uncovered breasts — it seeks, rather unsystematically, to put a stop to it.

Of course, like drinking during Prohibition or, today, smoking marihuana, cockfights, being a part of "The Balinese Way of Life," nonetheless go on happening, and with extraordinary frequency. And, as with Prohibition or marihuana, from time to time the police (who, in 1958 at least, were almost all not Balinese but Javanese) feel called upon to make a raid, confiscate the cocks and spurs, fine a few people, and even now and then expose some of them in the tropical sun for a day as object lessons which never, somehow, get learned, even though occasionally, quite occasionally, the object dies.

As a result, the fights are usually held in a secluded corner of a village in semisecrecy, a fact which tends to slow the action a little — not very much, but the Balinese do not care to have it slowed at all. In this case, however, perhaps because they were raising money for a school that the government was unable to give them, perhaps because raids had been few recently, perhaps, as I gathered from subsequent discussion, there was a notion that the necessary bribes had been paid, they thought they could take a chance on the central square and draw a larger and more enthusiastic crowd without attracting the attention of the law.

They were wrong. In the midst of the third match, with hundreds of people, including, still transparent, myself and my wife, fused into a single body around the ring, a superorganism in the literal sense, a truck full of policemen armed with machine guns roared up. Amid great screeching cries of "pulisi! pulisi!" from the crowd, the policemen jumped out, and, springing into the center of the ring, began to swing their guns around like gangsters in a motion picture, though not going so far as actually to fire them. The superorganism came instantly apart as its components scattered in all directions. People raced down the road, disappeared headfirst over walls, scrambled under platforms, folded themselves behind wicker screens, scuttled up coconut trees. Cocks armed with steel spurs sharp enough to cut off a finger or run a hole through a foot were running wildly around. Everything was dust and panic.

On the established anthropological principle, "When in Rome," my wife and I decided, only slightly less instantaneously than everyone else, that the thing to do was run too. We ran down the main village street, northward, away from where we were living, for we were on that side of the ring. About halfway down another fugitive ducked suddenly into a compound — his own, it turned out — and we, seeing nothing ahead of us but rice fields, open country, and a very high volcano, followed him. As the three of us came tumbling into the courtyard, his wife, who had apparently been through this sort of thing before, whipped out a table, a tablecloth, three chairs, and three cups of tea, and we all, without any explicit communication whatsoever, sat down, commenced to sip tea, and sought to compose ourselves.

A few moments later, one of the policemen marched importantly into the yard, looking for the village chief. (The chief had not only been at the fight, he had arranged it. When the truck drove up he ran to the river, stripped off his sarong, and plunged in so he could say, when at length they found him sitting there pouring water over his head, that he had been away bathing when the whole affair had occurred and was ignorant of it. They did not believe him and fined him three hundred rupiah, which the village raised collectively.) Seeing me and my wife, "White Men," there in the yard, the policeman performed a classic double take. When he found his voice again he asked, approximately, what in the devil did we think we were doing there. Our host of five minutes leaped instantly to our defense, producing an impassioned description of who and what we were, so detailed and so accurate that it was my turn, having barely communicated with a living human being save my landlord and the village chief for more than a week, to be astonished. We had a perfect right to be there, he said, looking the Javanese upstart in the eye. We were American professors; the government had cleared us; we were there to study culture; we were going to write a book to tell Americans about Bali. And we had all been there drinking tea and talking about cultural matters all afternoon and did not know anything about any cockfight. Moreover, we had not seen the village chief all day; he must have gone to town. The policeman retreated in rather total disarray. And, after a decent interval, bewildered but relieved to have survived and stayed out of jail, so did we.

The next morning the village was a completely different world for us. Not only were we no longer invisible, we were suddenly the center of all attention, the object of a great outpouring of warmth, interest, and most especially, amusement. Everyone in the village knew we had fled like everyone else. They asked us about it again and again (I must have told the story, small detail by small detail, fifty times by the end of the day), gently, affectionately, but quite insistently teasing us: "Why didn't you just stand there and tell the police who you were?" "Why didn't you just say you were only watching and not betting?" "Were you really afraid of those little guns?" As always, kinesthetically minded and, even when fleeing for their lives (or, as happened eight years later, surrendering them), the world's most poised people, they gleefully mimicked, also over and over again, our graceless style of running and what they claimed were our panic-stricken facial expressions. But above all, everyone was extremely pleased and even more surprised that we had not simply "pulled out our papers" (they knew about those too) and asserted our Distinguished Visitor status, but had instead demonstrated our solidarity with what were now our covillagers. (What we had actually demonstrated was our cowardice, but there is fellowship in that too.) Even the Brahmana priest, an old, grave, halfway-to-heaven type who because of its associations with the underworld would never be involved, even distantly, in a cockfight, and was difficult to approach even to other Balinese, had us called into his courtyard to ask us about what had happened, chuckling happily at the sheer extraordinariness of it all.

In Bali, to be teased is to be accepted. It was the turning point so far as our relationship to the community was concerned, and we were quite literally "in." The whole village opened up to us, probably more than it ever would have otherwise (I might actually never have gotten to that priest, and our accidental host became one of my best informants), and certainly very much faster. Getting caught, or almost caught, in a vice raid is perhaps not a very generalizable recipe for achieving that mysterious necessity of anthropological field work, rapport, but for me it worked very well. It led to a sudden and un-

usually complete acceptance into a society extremely difficult for outsiders to penetrate. It gave me the kind of immediate, inside-view
grasp of an aspect of "peasant mentality" that anthropologists not
fortunate enough to flee headlong with their subjects from armed
authorities normally do not get. And, perhaps most important of all,
for the other things might have come in other ways, it put me very
quickly on to a combination emotional explosion, status war, and
philosophical drama of central significance to the society whose inner
nature I desired to understand. By the time I left I had spent about as
much time looking into cockfights as into witchcraft, irrigation, caste,
or marriage.

OF COCKS AND MEN

Bali, mainly because it is Bali, is a well-studied place. Its mythol-
ogy, art, ritual, social organization, patterns of child rearing, forms of
law, even styles of trance, have all been microscopically examined for
traces of that elusive substance Jane Belo called "The Balinese
Temper."[2] But, aside from a few passing remarks, the cockfight has
barely been noticed, although as a popular obsession of consuming
power it is at least as important a revelation of what being a Balinese
"is really like" as these more celebrated phenomena.[3] As much of
America surfaces in a ball park, on a golf links, at a race track, or
around a poker table, much of Bali surfaces in a cock ring. For it is
only apparently cocks that are fighting there. Actually, it is men.

To anyone who has been in Bali any length of time, the deep
psychological identification of Balinese men with their cocks is unmistakable. The double entendre here is deliberate. It works in exactly the
same way in Balinese as it does in English, even to producing the same
tired jokes, strained puns, and uninventive obscenities. Bateson and
Mead have even suggested that, in line with the Balinese conception of
the body as a set of separately animated parts, cocks are viewed as
detachable, self-operating penises, ambulant genitals with a life of
their own.[4] And while I do not have the kind of unconscious material
either to confirm or disconfirm this intriguing notion, the fact that

2. J. Belo, "The Balinese Temper," in *Traditional Balinese Culture,* edited by J. Belo
(New York, 1970, originally published in 1935), pp. 85–110.
    3. The best discussion of cockfighting is again Bateson and Mead's *Balinese Charac-
ter,* pp. 24–25, 140; but it, too, is general and abbreviated.
    4. Ibid., pp. 25–26. The cockfight is unusual within Balinese culture in being a
single-sex public activity from which the other sex is totally and expressly excluded.

they are masculine symbols par excellence is about as indubitable, and to the Balinese about as evident, as the fact that water runs downhill.

The language of everyday moralism is shot through, on the male side of it, with roosterish imagery. *Sabung,* the work for cock (and one which appears in inscriptions as early as A.D. 922), is used metaphorically to mean "hero," "warrior," "champion," "man of parts," "political candidate," "bachelor," "dandy," "lady-killer," or "tough guy." A pompous man whose behavior presumes above his station is compared to a tailless cock who struts about as though he had a large, spectacular one. A desperate man who makes a last, irrational effort to extricate himself from an impossible situation is likened to a dying cock who makes one final lunge at his tormentor to drag him along to a common destruction. A stingy man, who promises much, gives little, and begrudges that, is compared to a cock which, held by the tail, leaps at another without in fact engaging him. A marriageable young man still shy with the opposite sex or someone in a new job anxious to make a good impression is called "a fighting cock caged for the first time."[5] Court trials, wars, political contests, inheritance disputes, and street arguments are all compared to cockfights.[6] Even the very island itself is perceived from its shape as a small, proud cock, poised, neck extended, back taut, tail raised, in eternal challenge to large, feckless, shapeless Java.[7]

But the intimacy of men with their cocks is more than metaphori-

---

Sexual differentiation is culturally extremely played down in Bali and most activities, formal and informal, involve the participation of men and women on equal ground, commonly as linked couples. From religion, to politics, to economics, to kinship, to dress, Bali is a rather "unisex" society, a fact both its customs and its symbolism clearly express. Even in contexts where women do not in fact play much of a role — music, painting, certain agricultural activities — their absence, which is only relative in any case, is more a mere matter of fact that socially enforced. To this general pattern, the cockfight, entirely of, by, and for men (women — at least Balinese women — do not even watch), is the most striking exception.

5. C. Hooykass, *The Lay of the Jaya Prana* (London, 1958), p. 39. The lay has a stanza (no. 17) comparing the reluctant bridegroom to a caged cock. Jaya Prana, the subject of a Balinese Uriah myth, responds to the lord who has offered him the loveliest of six hundred servant girls: "Godly King, my Lord and Master/I beg you, give me leave to go/such things are not yet in my mind;/like a fighting cock encaged/indeed I am on my mettle/I am alone/as yet the flame has not been fanned."

6. For these, see V. E. Korn, *Het Adatrecht van Bali,* 2nd. ed. (The Hague, 1932), index under *toh.*

7. There is indeed a legend to the effect that the separation of Java and Bali is due to the action of a powerful Javanese religious figure who wished to protect himself against a Balinese culture hero (the ancestor of two Ksatria castes) who was a passionate cockfighting gambler. See C. Hooykass, *Agama Tirtha* (Amsterdam, 1964), p. 184.

cal. Balinese men, or anyway a large majority of Balinese men, spend an enormous amount of time with their favorites, grooming them, feeding them, discussing them, trying them out against one another, or just gazing at them with a mixture of rapt admiration and dreamy self-absorption. Whenever you see a group of Balinese men squatting idly in the council shed or along the road in their hips down, shoulders forward, knees up fashion, half or more of them will each have a rooster in his hands, holding it between his thighs, bouncing it gently up and down to strengthen its legs, ruffling its feathers with abstract sensuality, pushing it out against a neighbor's rooster to rouse its spirit, withdrawing it toward his loins to calm it again. Now and then, to get a feel for another bird, a man will fiddle this way with someone else's cock for a while, but usually by moving around to squat in place behind it, rather than just having it passed across to him as though it were merely an animal.

In the houseyard, the high-walled enclosures where the people live, fighting cocks are kept in wicker cages, moved frequently about so as to maintain the optimum balance of sun and shade. They are fed a special diet, which varies somewhat according to individual theories but which is mostly maize, sifted for impurities with far more care than it is when mere humans are going to eat it, and offered to the animal kernel by kernel. Red pepper is stuffed down their beaks and up their anuses to give them spirit. They are bathed in the same ceremonial preparation of tepid water, medicinal herbs, flowers, and onions in which infants are bathed, and for a prize cock just about as often. Their combs are cropped, their plumage dressed, their spurs trimmed, and their legs massaged, and they are inspected for flaws with the squinted concentration of a diamond merchant. A man who has a passion for cocks, an enthusiast in the literal sense of the term, can spend most of his life with them, and even those, the overwhelming majority, whose passion though intense has not entirely run away with them, can and do spend what seems not only to an outsider, but also to themselves, an inordinate amount of time with them. "I am cock crazy," my landlord, a quite ordinary *afficionado* by Balinese standards, used to moan as he went to move another cage, give another bath, or conduct another feeding. "We're all cock crazy."

The madness has some less visible dimensions, however, because although it is true that cocks are symbolic expressions or magnifications of their owner's self, the narcissistic male ego writ out in Aesopian terms, they are also expressions—and rather more immediate ones—of what the Balinese regard as the direct inversion, aesthetically, morally, and metaphysically, of human status: animality.

The Balinese revulsion against any behavior regarded as animal-like can hardly be overstressed. Babies are not allowed to crawl for that reason. Incest, though hardly approved, is a much less horrifying crime than bestiality. (The appropriate punishment for the second is death by drowning, for the first being forced to live like an animal.)[8] Most demons are represented—in sculpture, dance, ritual, myth—in some real or fantastic animal form. The main puberty rite consists in filing the child's teeth so they will not look like animal fangs. Not only defecation but eating is regarded as a disgusting, almost obscene activity, to be conducted hurriedly and privately, because of its association with animality. Even falling down or any form of clumsiness is considered to be bad for these reasons. Aside from cocks and a few domestic animals—oxen, ducks—of no emotional significance, the Balinese are aversive to animals and treat their large number of dogs not merely callously but with a phobic cruelty. In identifying with his cock, the Balinese man is identifying not just with his ideal self, or even his penis, but also, and at the same time, with what he most fears, hates, and ambivalence being what it is, is fascinated by—"The Powers of Darkness."

The connection of cocks and cockfighting with such Powers, with the animalistic demons that threaten constantly to invade the small, cleared-off space in which the Balinese have so carefully built their lives and devour its inhabitants, is quite explicit. A cockfight, any cockfight, is in the first instance a blood sacrifice offered, with the appropriate chants and oblations, to the demons in order to pacify their ravenous, cannibal hunger. No temple festival should be conducted until one is made. (If it is omitted, someone will inevitably fall into a trance and command with the voice of an angered spirit that the oversight be immediately corrected.) Collective responses to natural evils—illness, crop failure, volcanic eruptions—almost always in-

8. An incestuous couple is forced to wear pig yokes over their necks and crawl to a pig trough and eat with their mouths there. On this, see J. Belo, "Customs Pertaining to Twins in Bali," in *Traditional Balinese Culture,* edited by J. Belo, p. 49; on the abhorrence of animality generally, Bateson and Mead, *Balinese Character,* p. 22.

volve them. And that famous holiday in Bali, "The Day of Silence" (*Njepi*), when everyone sits silent and immobile all day long in order to avoid contact with a sudden influx of demons chased momentarily out of hell, is preceded the previous day by large-scale cockfights (in this case legal) in almost every village on the island.

In the cockfight, man and beast, good and evil, ego and id, the creative power of aroused masculinity and the destructive power of loosened animality fuse in a bloody drama of hatred, cruelty, violence, and death. It is little wonder that when, as is the invariable rule, the owner of the winning cock takes the carcass of the loser — often torn limb from limb by its enraged owner — home to eat, he does so with a mixture of social embarrassment, moral satisfaction, aesthetic disgust, and cannibal joy. Or that a man who has lost an important fight is sometimes driven to wreck his family shrines and curse the gods, an act of metaphysical (and social) suicide. Or that in seeking earthly analogues for heaven and hell the Balinese compare the former to the mood of a man whose cock has just won, the latter to that of a man whose cock has just lost.

THE FIGHT

Cockfights (*tetadjen; sabungan*) are held in a ring about fifty feet square. Usually they begin toward late afternoon and run three or four hours until sunset. About nine or ten separate matches (*sehet*) compose a program. Each match is precisely like the others in general pattern: there is no main match, no connection between individual matches, no variation in their format, and each is arranged on a completely ad hoc basis. After the fight has ended and the emotional debris is cleaned away — the bets have been paid, the curses cursed, the carcasses possessed — seven, eight, perhaps even a dozen men slip negligently into the ring with a cock and seek to find there a logical opponent for it. This process, which rarely takes less than ten minutes, and often a good deal longer, is conducted in a very subdued, oblique, even dissembling manner. Those not immediately involved give it at best but disguised, sidelong attention; those who, embarrassedly, are, attempt to pretend somehow that the whole thing is not really happening.

A match made, the other hopefuls retire with the same deliberate indifference, and the selected cocks have their spurs (*tadji*) affixed — razor sharp, pointed steel swords, four or five inches long. This is a delicate job which only a small proportion of men, a half-dozen or so in most villages, know how to do properly. The man who attaches the spurs also provides them, and if the rooster he assists wins, its owner awards him the spur-leg of the victim. The spurs are affixed by winding a long length of string around the foot of the spur and the leg of the cock. For reasons I shall come to presently, it is done somewhat differently from case to case, and is an obsessively deliberate affair. The lore about spurs is extensive—they are sharpened only at eclipses and the dark of the moon, should be kept out of the sight of women, and so forth. And they are handled, both in use and out, with the same curious combination of fussiness and sensuality the Balinese direct toward ritual objects generally.

The spurs affixed, the two cocks are placed by their handlers (who may or may not be their owners) facing one another in the center of the ring.[9] A coconut pierced with a small hole is placed in a pail of water, in which it takes about twenty-one seconds to sink, a period known as a *tjeng* and marked at the beginning and the end by the beating of a slit gong. During these twenty-one seconds the handlers (*pengangkeb*) are not permitted to touch their roosters. If, as sometimes happens, the animals have not fought during this time, they are picked up, fluffed, pulled, prodded, and otherwise insulted, and put back in the center of the ring and the process begins again. Sometimes they refuse to fight at all, or one keeps running away, in which case they are imprisoned together under a wicker cage, which usually gets them engaged.

Most of the time, in any case, the cocks fly almost immediately at one another in a wing-beating, head-thrusting, leg-kicking explosion of animal fury so pure, so absolute, and in its own way so beautiful, as to be almost abstract, a Platonic concept of hate. Within moments one or the other drives home a solid blow with his spur. The handler

9. Except for unimportant, small-bet fights (on the question of fight "importance," see below) spur affixing is usually done by someone other than the owner. Whether the owner handles his own cock or not more or less depends on how skilled he is at it, a consideration whose importance is again relative to the importance of the fight. When spur affixers and cock handlers are someone other than the owner, they are almost always a quite close relative—a brother or a cousin—or a very intimate friend of his. They are thus almost extensions of his personality, as the fact that all three will refer to the cock as "mine," say "I" fought So-and-So, and so on, demonstrates. Also, owner-handler-affixer triads tend to be fairly fixed, though individuals may participate in several and often exchange roles within a given one.

whose cock has delivered the blow immediately picks it up so that it will not get a return blow, for if he does not the match is likely to end in a mutually mortal tie as the two birds wildly hack each other to pieces. This is particularly true if, as often happens, the spur sticks in its vicitim's body, for then the aggressor is at the mercy of his wounded foe.

With the birds again in the hands of their handlers, the coconut is now sunk three times after which the cock which has landed the blow must be set down to show that he is firm, a fact he demonstrates by wandering idly around the ring for a coconut sink. The coconut is then sunk twice more and the fight must recommence.

During this interval, slighty over two minutes, the handler of the wounded cock has been working frantically over it, like a trainer patching a mauled boxer between rounds, to get it in shape for a last, desperate try for victory. He blows in its mouth, putting the whole chicken head in his mouth and sucking and blowing, fluffs it, stuffs its wounds with various sorts of medicines, and generally tries anything he can think of to arouse the last ounce of spirit which may be hidden somewhere within it. By the time he is forced to put it back down he is usually drenched in chicken blood, but, as in prize fighting, a good handler is worth his weight in gold. Some of them can virtually make the dead walk, at least long enough for the second and final round.

In the climactic battle (if there is one; sometimes the wounded cock simply expires in the handler's hands or immediately as it is placed down again), the cock who landed the first blow usually proceeds to finish off his weakened opponent. But this is far from an inevitable outcome, for if a cock can walk, he can fight, and if he can fight, he can kill, and what counts is which cock expires first. If the wounded one can get a stab in and stagger on until the other drops, he is the official winner, even if he himself topples over an instant later.

Surrounding all this melodrama — which the crowd packed tight around the ring follows in near silence, moving their bodies in kinesthetic sympathy with the movement of the animals, cheering their champions on with wordless hand motions, shiftings of the shoulders, turning of the head, falling back en masse as the cock with the murderous spurs careens toward one side of the ring (it is said that spectators sometimes lose eyes and fingers from being too attentive), surging forward again as they glance off toward another — is a vast body of extraordinarily elaborate and precisely detailed rules.

These rules, together with the developed lore of cocks and cock-fighting which accompanies them, are written down in palm-leaf manuscripts (*lontar; rontal*) passed on from generation to generation as part of the general legal and cultural tradition of the villages. At a fight, the umpire, (*saja komong; djuru kembar*) — the man who manages the coconut — is in charge of their application and his authority is absolute. I have never seen an umpire's judgment questioned on any subject, even by the more despondent losers, nor have I ever heard, even in private, a charge of unfairness directed against on, or, for that matter, complaints about umpires in general. Only exceptionally well trusted, solid, and, given the complexity of the code, knowledgeable citizens perform this job, and in fact men will bring their cocks only to fights presided over by such men. It is also the umpire to whom accusations of cheating, which, though are in the extreme, occasionally arise, are referred; and it is he who in the not infrequent cases where the cocks expire virtually together decides which (if either, for, though the Balinese do not care for such an outcome, there can be ties) went first. Likened to a judge, a king, a priest, and a policeman, he is all of these, and under his assured direction the animal passion of the fight proceeds within the civic certainty of the law. In the dozens of cockfights I saw in Bali, I never once saw an altercation about rules. Indeed, I never saw an open altercation other than those between cocks, at all.

This crosswise doubleness of an event which, taken as a fact of nature, is rage untrammeled and, taken as a fact of culture, is form perfected, defines the cockfight as a sociological entity. A cockfight is what, searching for a name for something not vertebrate enough to be called a group and not structureless enough to be called a crowd, Erving Goffman has called a "focused gathering" — a set of persons engrossed in a common flow of activity and relating to one another in terms of that flow.[10] Such gatherings meet and disperse; the participants in them fluctuate; the activity that focuses them is discrete — a particulate process that reoccurs rather than a continuous one that endures. They take their form from the situation that evokes them, the floor on which they are placed, as Goffman puts it; but it is a form, and an articulate one, nonetheless. For the situation, the floor is itself created, in jury deliberations, surgical operations, block meetings,

10. E. Goffman, *Encounters: Two Studies in the Sociology of Interaction* (Indianapolis, 1961), pp. 9–10.

sit-ins, cockfights, by the cultural preoccupations—here, as we shall see, the celebration of status rivalry—which not only specify the focus but, assembling actors and arranging scenery, bring it actually into being.

In classical times (that is to say, prior to the Dutch invasion of 1908), when there were no bureaucrats around to improve popular morality, the staging of a cockfight was an explicitly societal matter. Bringing a cock to an important fight was, for an adult male, a compulsory duty of citizenship; taxation of fights, which were usually held on market day, was a major source of public revenue; patronage of the art was a stated responsibility of princes; and the cock ring, or *wantilan,* stood in the center of the village near those other monuments of Balinese civility—the council house, the origin temple, the marketplace, the signal tower, and the banyan tree. Today, a few special occasions aside, the newer rectitude makes so open a statement of the connection between the excitements of collective life and those of blood sport impossible, but, less directly expressed, the connection itself remains intimate and intact. To expose it, however, it is necessary to turn to the aspect of cockfighting around which all the others pivot, and through which they exercise their force, an aspect I have thus far studiously ignored. I mean, of course, the gambling.

ODDS AND EVEN MONEY

The Balinese never do anything in a simple way that they can contrive to do in a complicated one, and to this generalization cockfight wagering is no exception.

In the first place, there are two sorts of bets, or *toh*.[11] There is the single axial bet in the center between the principals (*toh ketengah*), and there is the cloud of peripheral ones around the ring between members of the audience (*toh kesasi*). The first is typically large, the second typically small. The first is collective, involving coalitions of bettors

11. This word, which literally means an indelible stain or mark, as in a birthmark or a vein in a stone, is used as well for a deposit in a court case, for a pawn, for security offered in a loan, for a stand-in for someone else in a legal or ceremonial context, for an earnest advanced in a business deal, for a sign placed in a field to indicate its ownership is in dispute, and for the status of an unfaithful wife from whose lover her husband must gain satisfaction or surrender her to him. See Korn, *Het adatrecht van Bali*; Th. Pigeaud, *Javaans-Nederlands Handwoordenboek* (Groningen, 1938); H. H. Juynboll, *Oudjavaansche-Nederlandsche Woordenlijst* (Leiden, 1923).

clustering around the owner; the second is individual, man to man. The first is a matter of deliberate, very quiet, almost furtive arrangement by the coalition members and the umpire huddled like conspirators in the center of the ring; the second is a matter of impulsive shouting, public offers, and public acceptances by the the excited throng around its edges. And most curiously, and as we shall see most revealingly, *where the first is always, without exception, even money, the second, equally without exception, is never such.* What is a fair coin in the center is a biased one on the side.

The center bet is the official one, hedged in again with a webwork of rules, and is made between the two cock owners, with the umpire as overseer and public witness.[12] This bet, which, as I say, is always relatively and sometimes very large, is never raised simply by the owner in whose name it is made, but by him together with four or five, sometimes seven or eight, allies — kin, village mates, neighbors, close friends. He may, if he is not especially well-to-do, not even be the major contributor; though, if only to show that he is not involved in any chicanery, he must be a significant one.

Of the fifty-seven matches for which I have exact and reliable data on the center bet, the range is from fifteen ringgits to five hundred, with a mean at eighty-five and with the distribution being rather noticeably trimodal: small fights (15 ringgits either side of 35) accounting for about 45 percent of the total number; medium ones (20 ringgits either side of 70) for about 25 percent; and large (75 ringgits either side of 175) for about 20 percent, with a few very small and very large ones out at the extremes. In a society where the normal daily wage of a manual laborer — a brickmaker, an ordinary farmworker, a market porter — was about three ringgits a day, and considering the fact that fights were held on the average about every two-and-a-half days in the immediate area I studied, this is clearly serious gambling, even if the bets are pooled rather than individual efforts.

The side bets are, however, something else altogether. Rather than the solemn, legalistic pactmaking of the center, wagering takes place

12. The center bet must be advanced in cash by both parties prior to the actual fight. The umpire holds the stakes until the decision is rendered and then awards them to the winner, avoiding, among other things, the intense embarrassment both winner and loser would feel if the latter had to pay off personally following his defeat. About ten percent of the winner's receipts are subtracted for the umpire's share and that of the fight sponsors.

rather in the fashion in which the stock exchange used to work when it was out on the curb. There is a fixed and known odds paradigm which runs in a continuous series from ten-to-nine at the short end to two-to-one at the long: 10–9, 9–8, 8–7, 7–6, 6–5, 5–4, 4–3, 3–2, 2–1. The man who wishes to back the *underdog cock* (leaving aside how favorites, *kebut,* and underdogs, *ngai,* are established for the moment) shouts the short-side number indicating the odds he wants *to be given.* That is, if he shouts *gasal,* "five," he wants the underdog at five-to-four (or, for him, four-to-five); if he shouts "four," he wants it at four-to-three (again, he putting up the "three"); if "nine," at nine-to-eight, and so on. A man backing the favorite, and thus considering giving odds if he can get them short enough, indicates the fact by crying out the color-type of that cock — "brown," "speckled," or whatever.[13]

As odds-takers (backers of the underdog) and odds-givers (backers of the favorite) sweep the crowd with their shouts, they begin to focus in on one another as potential betting pairs, often from far across the ring. The taker tries to shout the giver into longer odds, the giver to shout the taker into shorter ones.[14] The taker, who is the wooer in this

13. Actually, the typing of cocks, which is extremely elaborate (I have collected more than twenty classes, certainly not a complete list), is based not on color alone but on a series of independent, interacting dimensions, which include — besides color — size, bone thickness, plumage, and temperament. (But *not* pedigree. The Balinese do not breed cocks to any significant extent, nor, so far as I have been able to discover, have they ever done so. The *asil,* or jungle cock, which is the basic fighting strain everywhere the sport is found, is native to southern Asia, and one can buy a good example in the chicken section of almost any Balinese market for anywhere from four to five ringgits up to fifty or more.) The color element is merely the one normally used as the type name, except when the two cocks of different types — as on principle they must be — have the same color, in which case a secondary indication from one of the other dimensions ("large speckled" v. "small speckled," etc.) is added. The types are coordinated with various cosmological ideas which help shape the making of matches, so that, for example, you fight a small, headstrong, speckled brown-on-white cock with flat-lying feathers and thin legs from the east side of the ring on a certain day of the complex Balinese calendar, and a large, cautious, all-black cock with tufted feathers and stubby legs from the north side on another day, and so on. All this is again recorded in palm-leaf manuscripts and endlessly discussed by the Balinese (who do not all have identical systems), and a full-scale componential-cum-symbolic analysis of cock classifications would be extremely valuable both as an adjunct to the description of the cockfight and in itself. But my data on the subject, though extensive and varied, do not seem to be complete and systematic enough to attempt such an analysis here. For Balinese cosmological ideas more generally, see Belo, ed., *Traditional Balinese Culture,* and J. L. Swellengrebel, ed., *Bali: Studies in Life, Thought, and Ritual* (The Hague, 1960).

14. For purposes of ethnographic completeness, it should be noted that it is possible for the man backing the favorite — the odds-giver — to make a bet in which he wins if his

situation, will signal how large a bet he wishes to make at the odds he is shouting by holding a number of fingers up in front of his face and vigorously waving them. If the giver, the wooed, replies in kind, the bet is made; if he does not, they unlock gazes and the search goes on.

The side betting, which takes place after the center bet has been made and its size announced, consists then in a rising crescendo of shouts as backers of the underdog offer their propositions to anyone who will accept them, while those who are backing the favorite but do not like the price being offered, shout equally frenetically the color of the cock to show they too are desperate to bet but want shorter odds.

Almost always odds–calling, which tends to be very consensual in that at any one time almost all callers are calling the same thing, starts off toward the long end of the range—five-to-four or four-to-three—and then moves, also consensually, toward the short end with greater or lesser speed and to a greater or lesser degree. Men crying "five" and finding themselves answered only with cries of "brown" start crying "six," either drawing the other callers fairly quickly with them or retiring from the scene as their too-generous offers are snapped up. If the change is made and partners are still scarce, the procedure is repeated in a move to "seven," and so on, only rarely, and in the very largest fights, reaching the ultimate "nine" or "ten" levels. Occasionally, if the cocks are clearly mismatched, there may be no upward movement at all, or even a movement down the scale to four-to-three, three-to-two, very, very rarely two-to-one, a shift which is accompanied by a declining number of bets as a shift upward is accompanied by an increasing number. But the general pattern is for the betting to move a shorter or longer distance up the scale toward the, for sidebets, nonexistent pole of even money, with the over-whelming majority of bets falling in the four-to-three to eight-to-seven range.[15]

---

cock wins or there is a tie, a slight shortening of the odds (I do not have enough cases to be exact, but ties seem to occur about once every fifteen or twenty matches). He indicates his wish to do this by shouting *sapih* ("tie") rather than the cock-type, but such bets are in fact infrequent.

15. The precise dynamics of the movement of the betting is one of the most intriguing, most complicated, and, given the hectic conditions under which it occurs, most difficult to study, aspects of the fight. Motion picture recording plus multiple observers would probably be necessary to deal with it effectively. Even impressionisti-cally—the only approach open to a lone ethnographer caught in the middle of all this—it is clear that certain men lead both in determining the favorite (that is, making

As the moment for the release of the cocks by the handlers approaches, the screaming, at least in a match where the center bet is large, reaches almost frenzied proportions as the remaining unfulfilled bettors try desperately to find a last-minute partner at a price they can live with. (Where the center bet is small, the opposite tends to occur: betting dies off, trailing into silence, as odds lengthen and people lose interest.) In a large-bet, well-made match—the kind of match the Balinese regard as "real cockfighting"—the mob scene quality, the sense that sheer chaos is about to break loose, with all those waving, shouting, pushing, clambering men is quite strong, an effect which is only heightened by the intense stillness that falls with instant suddenness, rather as if someone had turned off the current, when the slit gong sounds, the cocks are put down, and the battle begins.

When it ends, anywhere from fifteen seconds to five minutes later, *all bets are immediately paid.* There are absolutely no IOUs, at least to a betting opponent. One may, of course, borrow from a friend before offering or accepting a wager, but to offer or accept it you must have the money already in hand and, if you lose, you must pay it on the spot, before the next match begins. This is an iron rule, and as I have never heard of a disputed umpire's decision (though doubtless there must sometimes be some), I have also never heard of a welshed bet, perhaps because in a worked-up cockfight crowd the consequences might be, as they are reported to be sometimes for cheaters, drastic and immediate.

It is, in any case, this formal asymmetry between balanced center bets and unbalanced side ones that poses the critical analytical problem for a theory which sees cockfight wagering as the link connnecting the fight to the wider world of Balinese culture. It also suggests the way to go about solving it and demonstrating the link.

The first point that needs to be made in this connection is that the higher the center bet, the more likely the match will in actual fact be an even one. Simple considerations of rationality suggest that. If you are

---

the opening cock-type calls which always initiate the process) and in directing the movement of the odds, these "opinion leaders" being the more accomplished cockfighters-cum-solid-citizens to be discussed below. If these men begin to change their calls, others follow; if they begin to make bets, so do others and—though there are always a large number of frustrated bettors crying for shorter or longer odds to the end—the movement more or less ceases. But a detailed understanding of the whole process awaits what, alas, it is not very likely ever to get: a decision theorist armed with precise observations of individual behavior.

betting fifteen ringgits on a cock, you might be willing to go along with even money even if you feel your animal somewhat the less promising. But if you are betting five hundred you are very, very likely to be loathe to do so. Thus, in large-bet fights, which of course involve the better animals, tremendous care is taken to see that the cocks are about as evenly matched as to size, general condition, pugnacity, and so on as is humanly possible. The different way of adjusting the spurs of the animals are often employed to secure this. If one cock seems stronger, an agreement will be made to position his spur at a slightly less advantageous angle—a kind of handicapping, at which spur affixers are, so it is said, extremely skilled. More care will be taken, too, to employ skillful handlers and to match them exactly as to abilities.

In short, in a large-bet fight the pressure to make the match a genuinely fifty-fifty proposition is enormous, and is consciously felt as such. For medium fights the pressure is somewhat less, and for small ones less yet, though there is always an effort to make things at least approximately equal, for even at fifteen ringgits (five days' work) no one wants to make an even money bet in a clearly unfavorable situation. And, again, what statistics I have tend to bear this out. In my fifty-seven matches, the favorite won thirty-three times overall, the underdog twenty-four, a 1.4:1 ratio. But if one splits the figures at sixty ringgits center bets, the ratios turn out to be 1.1:1 (twelve favorites, eleven underdogs) for those above this line, and 1.6:1 (twenty-one and thirteen) for those below it. Or, if you take the extremes, for very large fights, those with center bets over a hundred ringgits the ratio is 1:1 (seven and seven); for very small fights, those under forty ringgits, it is 1.9:1 (nineteen and ten).[16]

Now, from this proposition—that the higher the center bet the more exactly a fifty-fifty proposition the cockfight is—two things more or less immediately follow: (1) the higher the center bet is, the

16. Assuming only binomial variability, the departure from a fifty-fifty expectation in the sixty-ringgits-and-below case is 1.38 standard deviations, or (in a one direction test) an eight in one hundred possibility by chance alone; for the below-forty-ringgits case it is 1.65 standard deviations, or about five in one hundred. The fact that these departures though real are not extreme merely indicates, again, that even in the smaller fights the tendency to match cocks at least reasonably evenly persists. It is a matter of relative relaxation of the pressures toward equalization, not their elimination. The tendency for high-bet contests to be coin-flip propositions is, of course, even more striking, and suggests the Balinese know quite well what they are about.

greater the pull on the side betting toward the short-odds end of the wagering spectrum, and vice versa; (2) the higher the center bet is, the greater the volume of side betting, and vice versa.

The logic is similar in both cases. The closer the fight is in fact to even money, the less attractive the long end of the odds will appear and, therefore, the shorter it must be if there are to be takers. That this is the case is apparent from mere inspection, from the Balinese's own analysis of the matter, and from what more systematic observations I was able to collect. Given the difficulty of making precise and complete recordings of side betting, this argument is hard to cast in numerical form, but in all my cases the odds-giver, odds-taker consensual point, a quite pronounced mini-max saddle where the bulk (at a guess, two-thirds to three-quarters in most cases) of the bets are actually made, was three or four points further along the scale toward the shorter end for the large-center-bet fights than for the small ones, with medium ones generally in between. In detail, the fit is not, of course, exact, but the general pattern is quite consistent: the power of the center bet to pull the side bets toward its own even-money pattern is directly proportional to its size, because its size is directly proportional to the degree to which the cocks are in fact evenly matched. As for the volume question, total wagering is greater in large-center-bet fights because such fights are considered more "interesting," not only in the sense that they are less predictable, but, more crucially, that more is at stake in them — in terms of money, in terms of the quality of the cocks, and consequently, as we shall see, in terms of social prestige.[17]

The paradox of fair coin in the middle, biased coin on the outside is thus a merely apparent one. The two betting systems, though for-

17. The reduction in wagering in smaller fights (which, of course, feeds on itself; one of the reasons people find small fights uninteresting is that there is less wagering in them, and contrariwise for large ones) takes place in three mutually reinforcing ways. First, there is a simple withdrawal of interest as people wander off to have a cup of coffee or chat with a friend. Second, the Balinese do not mathematically reduce odds, but bet directly in terms of stated odds as such. Thus, for a nine-to-eight bet, one man wagers nine ringgits, the other eight; for five-to-four, one wagers five, the other four. For any given currency unit, like the ringgit, therefore, 6.3 times as much money is involved in a ten-to-nine bet as in a two-to-one bet, for example, and, as noted, in small fights betting settles toward the longer end. Finally, the bets which are made tend to be one- rather than two-, three-, or in some of the very largest fights, four- or five-finger ones. (The fingers indicate the *multiples* of the stated bet odds at issue, not absolute figures. Two fingers in a six-to-five situation means a man wants to wager ten ringgits on the underdog against twelve, three in an eight-to-seven situation, twenty-one against twenty-four, and so on.)

mally incongruent, are not really contradictory to one another, but are part of a single larger system in which the center bet is, so to speak, the "center of gravity," drawing, the larger it is the more so, the outside bets toward the short-odds end of the scale. The center bet thus "makes the game," or perhaps better, defines it, signals what, following a notion of Jeremy Bentham's, I am going to call its "depth."

The Balinese attempt to create an interesting, if you will, "deep," match by making the center bet as large as possible so that the cocks matched will be as equal and as fine as possible, and the outcome, thus, as unpredictable as possible. They do not always succeed. Nearly half the matches are relatively trivial, relatively uninteresting—in my borrowed terminology, "shallow"—affairs. But that fact no more argues against my interpretation than the fact that most painters, poets, and playwrights are mediocre argues against the view that artistic effort is directed toward profundity and, with a certain frequency, approximates it. The image of artistic technique is indeed exact: the center bet is a means, a device, for creating "interesting," "deep" matches, *not* the reason, or at least not the main reason, *why* they are interesting, the source of their fascination, the substance of their depth. The question of why such matches are interesting—indeed, for the Balinese, exquisitely absorbing—takes us out of the realm of formal concerns into more broadly sociological and social-psychological ones, and to a less purely economic idea of what "depth" in gaming amounts to.[18]

18. Besides wagering there are other economic aspects of the cockfight, especially its very close connection with the local market system which, though secondary both to its motivation and to its function, are not without importance. Cockfights are open events to which anyone who wishes may come, sometimes from quite distant areas, but well over 90 percent, probably over 95, are very local affairs, and the locality concerned is defined not by the village, nor even by the administrative district, but by the rural market system. Bali has a three-day market week with the familiar "solar-system" type of rotation. Though the markets themselves have never been very highly developed, small morning affairs in a village square, it is the microregion such rotation rather generally marks out—ten or twenty square miles, seven or eight neighboring villages (which in contemporary Bali is usually going to mean anywhere from five to ten or eleven thousand people)—from which the core of any cockfight audience, indeed virtually all of it, will come. Most of the fights are in fact organized and sponsored by small combines of petty rural merchants under the general premise, very strongly held by them and indeed by all Balinese, that cockfights are good for trade because "they get money out of the house, they make it circulate." Stalls selling various sorts of things as well as assorted sheer-chance gambling games are set up around the edge of the area so that this even takes on the quality of a small fair. This connection of cockfighting with markets and market sellers is very old, as, among other things, their conjunction in

PLAYING WITH FIRE

Bentham's concept of "deep play" is found in his *The Theory of Legislation*.[19] By it he means play in which the stakes are so high that it is, from his utilitarian standpoint, irrational for men to engage in it at all. If a man whose fortune is a thousand pounds (or ringgits) wagers five hundred of it on an even bet, the marginal utility of the pound he stands to win is clearly less than the marginal disutility of the one he stands to lose. In genuine deep play, this is the case for both parties. They are both in over their heads. Having come together in search of pleasure they have entered into a relationship which will bring the participants, considered collectively, net pain rather than net pleasure. Bentham's conclusion was, therefore, that deep play was immoral from first principles and, a typical step for him, should be prevented legally.

But more interesting than the ethical problem, at least for our concerns here, is that despite the logical force of Bentham's analysis men do engage in such play, both passionately and often, and even in the face of law's revenge. For Bentham and those who think as he does (nowadays mainly lawyers, economists, and a few psychiatrists), the explanation is, as I have said, that such men are irrational — addicts, fetishists, children, fools, savages, who need only to be protected against themselves. But for the Balinese, though naturally they do not formulate it in so many words, the explanation lies in the fact that in such play, money is less a measure of utility, had or expected, than it is a symbol of moral import, perceived or imposed.

It is, in fact, in shallow games, ones in which smaller amounts of money are involved, that increments and decrements of cash are more nearly synonyms for utility and disutility, in the ordinary, unexpanded sense — for pleasure and pain, happiness and unhappiness. In deep ones, where the amounts of money are great, much more is at stake than material gain: namely, esteem, honor, dignity, respect — in a word, though in Bali a profoundly freighted word, status.[20] It is at

---

inscriptions [R. Goris, *Prasasti Bali*, 2 vols. (Bandung, 1954)] indicates. Trade has followed the cock for centuries in rural Bali, and the sport has been one of the main agencies of the island's monetization.

19. The phrase is found in the Hildreth translation, International Library of Psychology (1931), note to p. 106; see L. L. Fuller, *The Morality of Law* (New Haven, 1964), pp. 6ff.

20. Of course, even in Bentham, utility is not normally confined as a concept to

stake symbolically, for (a few cases of ruined addict gamblers aside) no one's status is actually altered by the outcome of a cockfight; it is only, and that momentarily, affirmed or insulted. But for the Balinese, for whom nothing is more pleasurable than an affront obliquely delivered or more painful than one obliquely received—particularly when mutual acquaintances, undeceived by surfaces, are watching—such appraisive drama is deep indeed.

This, I must stress immediately, is *not* to say that the money does not matter, or that the Balinese is no more concerned about losing five hundred ringgits than fifteen. Such a conclusion would be absurd. It is because money *does,* in this hardly unmaterialistic society, matter and matter very much that the more of it one risks, the more of a lot of other things, such as one's pride, one's poise, one's dispassion, one's masculinity, one also risks, again only momentarily but again very publicly as well. In deep cockfights an owner and his collaborators, and, as we shall see, to a lesser but still quite real extent also their backers on the outside, put their money where their status is.

It is in large part *because* the marginal disutility of loss is so great at the higher levels of betting that to engage in such betting is to lay one's public self, allusively and metaphorically, through the medium of one's cock, on the line. And though to a Benthamite this might seem merely to increase the irrationality of the enterprise that much further, to the Balinese what it mainly increases is the meaningfulness of it all. And as (to follow Weber rather than Bentham) the imposition of meaning on life is the major end and primary condition of human existence, that access of significance more than compensates for the economic costs involved.[21] Actually, given the even-money quality of

---

monetary losses and gains, and my argument here might be more carefully put in terms of a denial that for the Balinese, as for any people, utility (pleasure, happiness ...) is merely identifiable with wealth. But such terminological problems are in any case secondary to the essential point: the cockfight is not roulette.

21. M. Weber, *The Sociology of Religion* (Boston, 1963). There is nothing specifically Balinese, of course, about deepening significance with money, as Whyte's description of corner boys in a working-class district of Boston demonstrates: "Gambling plays an important role in the lives of Cornerville people. Whatever game the corner boys play, they nearly always bet on the outcome. When there is nothing at stake, the game is not considered a real contest. This does not mean that the financial element is all-important. I have frequently heard men say that the honor of winning was much more important than the money at stake. The corner boys consider playing for money the real test of skill and, unless a man performs well when money is at stake, he is not considered a good competitor." W. F. Whyte, *Street Corner Society,* 2nd ed. (Chicago, 1955), p. 140.

the larger matches, important changes in material fortune among those who regularly participate in them seem virtually nonexistent, because matters more or less even out over the long run. It is, actually, in the smaller, shallow fights, where one finds the handful of more pure, addict-type gamblers involved — those who *are* in it mainly for the money — that "real" changes in social position, largely downward, are affected. Men of this sort, plungers, are highly dispraised by "true cockfighters" as fools who do not understand what the sport is all about, vulgarians who simply miss the point of it all. They are, these addicts, regarded as fair game for the genuine enthusiasts, those who do understand, to take a little money away from — something that is easy enough to do by luring them, through the force of their greed, into irrational bets on mismatched cocks. Most of them do indeed manage to ruin themselves in a remarkably short time, but there always seems to be one or two of them around, pawning their land and selling their clothes in order to bet, at any particular time.[22]

This graduated correlation of "status gambling" with deeper fights and, inversely, "money gambling" with shallower ones is in fact quite general. Bettors themselves form a sociomoral hierarchy in these terms. As noted earlier, at most cockfights there are, around the very edges of the cockfight area, a large number of mindless, sheer-chance-type gambling games (roulette, dice throw, coin-spin, pea-under-the-shell) operated by concessionaires. Only women, children, adolescents, and various other sorts of people who do not (or not yet) fight cocks — the extremely poor, the socially despised, the personally idiosyncratic — play at these games, at, of course, penny ante levels. Cockfighting men would be ashamed to go anywhere near them. Slightly above these people in standing are those who though they do

22. The extremes to which this madness is conceived on occasion to go — and the fact that it is considered madness — is demonstrated by the Balinese folk tale *I Tuhung Kuning*. A gambler becomes so deranged by his passion that, leaving on a trip, he orders his pregnant wife to take care of the prospective newborn if it is a boy but to feed it as meat to his fighting cocks if it is a girl. The mother gives birth to a girl, but rather than giving the child to the cocks she gives them a large rat and conceals the girl with her own mother. When the husband returns, the cocks, crowing a jingle, inform him of the deception and, furious, he sets out to kill the child. A goddess descends from heaven and takes the girl up to the skies with her. The cocks die from the food given them, the owner's sanity is restored, the goddess brings the girl back to the father, who reunites him with his wife. The story is given as "Geel Komkommertje" in J. Hooykaas-van Leeuwen Boomkamp, *Sprookjes en Verhalen van Bali* (The Hague, 1956), pp. 19–25.

not themselves fight cocks, bet on the smaller matches around the edges. Next, there are those who fight cocks in small, or occasionally medium matches, but have not the status to join the large ones, though they may bet from time to time on the side in those. And finally, there are those, the really substantial members of the community, the solid citizenry around whom local life revolves, who fight in the larger fights and bet on them around the side. The focusing element in these focused gatherings, these men generally dominate and define the sport as they dominate and define the society. When a Balinese male talks, in that almost venerative way, about "the true cockfighter," the *bebatoh* ("bettor") or *djuru kurung* ("cage keeper"), it is this sort of person, not those who bring the mentality of the pea-and-shell game into the quite different, inappropriate context of the cockfight, the driven gambler (*potét,* a word which has the secondary meaning of thief or reprobate), and the wistful hanger-on, that they mean. For such a man, what is really going on in a match is something rather closer to an *affaire d'honneur* (though, with the Balinese talent for practical fantasy, the blood that is spilled is only figuratively human) than to the stupid, mechanical crank of a slot machine.

What makes Balinese cockfighting deep is thus not money in itself, but what, the more of it that is involved the more so, money causes to happen: the migration of the Balinese status hierarchy into the body of the cockfight. Psychologically an Aesopian representation of the ideal/demonic, rather narcissistic, male self, sociologically it is an equally Aesopian representation of the complex fields of tension set up by the controlled, muted, ceremonial, but for all that deeply felt, interaction of those selves in the context of everyday life. The cocks may be surrogates for their owners' personalities, animal mirrors of psychic form, but the cockfight is — or more exactly, deliberately is made to be — a simulation of the social matrix, the involved system of cross-cutting, overlapping, highly corporate groups — villages, kin-groups, irrigation societies, temple congregations, "castes" — in which its devotees live.[23] And as prestige, the necessity to affirm it, defend it,

23. For a fuller description of Balinese rural social structure, see C. Geertz, "Form and Variation in Balinese Village Structure," *American Anthropologist* 61 (1959): 94–108; "Tihingan, A Balinese Village," in R. M. Koentjaraningrat, *Villages in Indonesia* (Ithaca, 1967), pp. 210–243; and, though it is a bit off the norm as Balinese villages go, V. E. Korn, *De Dorpsrepubliek tnganan Pagringsingan* (Santpoort, Netherlands, 1933).

celebrate it, justify it, and just plain bask in it (but not, given the strongly ascriptive character of Balinese stratification, to seek it), is perhaps the central driving force in the society, so also —ambulant penises, blood sacrifices, and monetary exchanges aside —is it of the cockfight. This apparent amusement and seeming sport is, to take another phrase from Erving Goffman, "a status bloodbath."[24]

The easiest way to make this clear, and at least to some degree to demonstrate it, is to invoke the village whose cockfighting activities I observed the closest —the one in which the raid occurred and from which my statistical data are taken.

Like all Balinese villages, this one —Tihingan, in the Klungkung region of southeast Bali —is intricately organized, a labyrinth of alliances and oppositions. But, unlike many, two sorts of corporate groups, which are also status groups, particularly stand out, and we may concentrate on them, in a part-for-whole way, without undue distortion.

First, the village is dominated by four large, patrilineal, partly endogamous descent groups which are constantly vying with one another and form the major factions in the village. Sometimes they group two and two, or rather the two larger ones versus the two smaller ones plus all the unaffiliated people; sometimes they operate independently. There are also subfactions within them, subfactions within the subfactions, and so on to rather fine levels of distinction. And second, there is the village itself, almost entirely endogamous, which is opposed to all the other villages round about in its cockfight circuit (which, as was explained, is the market region), but which also forms alliances with certain of these neighbors against certain others in various supravillage political and social contexts. The exact situation is thus, as everywhere in Bali, quite distinctive; but the general pattern of a tiered hierarchy of status rivalries between highly corporate but various based groupings (and, thus, between the members of them) is entirely general.

Consider, then, as support of the general thesis that the cockfight, and especially the deep cockfight, is fundamentally a dramatization of status concerns, the following facts, which to avoid extended ethnographic description I shall simply pronounce to be facts —though the

24. Goffman, *Encounters,* p. 78.

concrete evidence, examples, statements, and numbers that could be brought to bear in support of them, is both extensive and unmistakable:

1. A man virtually never bets against a cock owned by a member of his own kingroup. Usually he will feel obliged to bet for it, the more so the closer the kin tie and the deeper the fight. If he is certain in his mind that it will not win, he may just not bet at all, particularly if it is only a second cousin's bird or if the fight is a shallow one. But as a rule he will feel he must support it and, in deep games, nearly always does. Thus the great majority of the people calling "five" or "speckled" so demonstratively are expressing their allegiance to their kinsman, not their evaluation of his bird, their understanding of probability theory, or even their hopes of unearned income.

2. This principle is extended logically. If your kingroup is not involved you will support an allied kingroup against an unallied one in the same way, and so on through the very involved networks of alliances which, as I say, make up this, as any other, Balinese village.

3. So, too, for the village as a whole. If an outsider cock is fighting any cock from your village, you will tend to support the local one. If, what is a rarer circumstance but occurs every now and then, a cock from outside your cockfight circuit is fighting one inside it, you will also tend to support the "home bird."

4. Cocks which come from any distance are almost always favorites, for the theory is the man would not have dared to bring it if it was not a good cock, the more so the further he has come. His followers are, of course, obliged to support him, and when the more grand-scale legal cockfights are held (on holidays, and so on) the people of the village take what they regard to be the best cocks in the village, regardless of ownership, and go off to support them, although they will almost certainly have to give odds on them and to make large bets to show that they are not a cheapskate village. Actually, such "away games," though infrequent, tend to mend the ruptures between village members that the constantly occurring "home games," where village factions are opposed rather than united, exacerbate.

5. Almost all matches are sociologically relevant. You seldom get two outsider cocks fighting, or two cocks with no particular group backing, or with group backing which is mutually unrelated in any

clear way. When you do get them, the game is very shallow, betting very slow, and the whole thing very dull, with no one save the immediate principals and an addict gambler or two at all interested.

6. By the same token, you rarely get two cocks from the same group, even more rarely from the same subfaction, and virtually never from the same sub-subfaction (which would be in most cases one extended family) fighting. Similarly, in outside village fights two members of the village will rarely fight against one another, even though, as bitter rivals, they would do so with enthusiasm on their home grounds.

7. On the individual level, people involved in an institutionalized hostility relationship, called *puik,* in which they do not speak or otherwise have anything to do with each other (the causes of this formal breaking of relations are many: wife-capture, inheritance arguments, political differences) will bet very heavily, sometimes almost maniacally, against one another in what is a frank and direct attack on the very masculinity, the ultimate ground of his status, of the opponent.

8. The center bet coalition is, in all but the shallowest games, *always* made up by structural allies—no "outside money" is involved. What is "outside" depends upon the context, of course, but given it, no outside money is mixed in with the main bet; if the principals cannot raise it, it is not made. The center bet, again especially in deeper games, is thus the most direct and open expression of social opposition, which is one of the reasons why both it and matchmaking are surrounded by such an air of unease, furtiveness, embarrassment, and so on.

9. The rule about borrowing money—that you may borrow *for* a bet but not *in* one—stems (and the Balinese are quite conscious of this) from similar considerations: you are never at the *economic* mercy of your enemy that way. Gambling debts, which can get quite large on a rather short-term basis, are always to friends, never to enemies, structurally speaking.

10. When two cocks are structurally irrelevant or neutral so far as *you* are concerned (though, as mentioned, they almost never are to each other) you do not even ask a relative or a friend whom he is betting on, because if you know how he is betting and he knows you know, and you go the other way, it will lead to strain. This rule is explicit and rigid; fairly elaborate, even rather artificial precautions are

taken to avoid breaking it. At the very least you must pretend not to notice what he is doing, and he what you are doing.

11. There is a special word for betting against the grain, which is also the word for "pardon me" (*mpura*). It is considered a bad thing to do, though if the center bet is small it is sometimes all right as long as you do not do it too often. But the larger the bet and the more frequently you do it, the more the "pardon me" tack will lead to social disruption.

12. In fact, the institutionalized hostility relation, *puik,* is often formally initiated (though its causes always lie elsewhere) by such a "pardon me" bet in a deep fight, putting the symbolic fat in the fire. Similarly, the end of such a relationship and resumption of normal social intercourse is often signalized (but, again, not actually brought about) by one or the other of the enemies supporting the other's bird.

13. In sticky, cross-loyalty situations, of which in this extraordinarily complex social system there are of course many, where a man is caught between two more or less equally balanced loyalties, he tends to wander off for a cup of coffee or something to avoid having to bet, a form of behavior reminiscent of that of American voters in similar situations.[25]

14. The people involved in the center bet are, especially in deep fights, virtually always leading members of their group—kinship, village, or whatever. Further, those who bet on the side (including these people) are, as I have already remarked, the more established members of the village—the solid citizens. Cockfighting is for those who are involved in the everyday politics of prestige as well, not for youth, women, subordinates, and so forth.

15. So far as money is concerned, the explicitly expressed attitude toward it is that it is a secondary matter. It is not, as I have said, of no importance; Balinese are no happier to lose several weeks' income than anyone else. But they mainly look on the monetary aspects of the cockfight as self-balancing, a matter of just moving money around, circulating it among a fairly well-defined group of serious cockfighters. The really important wins and losses are seen mostly in other terms, and the general attitude toward wagering is not any hope of cleaning up, of making a killing (addict gamblers again excepted),

25. B. R. Berelson, P. F. Lazersfeld, and W. N. McPhee, *Voting: A Study of Opinion Formation in a Presidential Campaign* (Chicago, 1954).

but that of the horse-player's prayer: "Oh, God, please let me break even." In prestige terms, however, you do not want to break even, but, in a momentary, punctuate sort of way, win utterly. The talk (which goes on all the time) is about fights against such-and-such a cock of So-and-So which your cock demolished, not on how much you won, a fact people, even for large bets rarely remember for any length of time, though they will remember the day they did in Pan Loh's finest cock for years.

16. You must bet on cocks of your own group aside from mere loyalty considerations, for if you do not people generally will say, "What! Is he too proud for the likes of us? Does he have to go to Java or Den Pasar [the capital town] to bet, he is such an important man?" Thus there is a general pressure to bet not only to show that you are important locally, but that you are not so important that you look down on everyone else as unfit even to be rivals. Similarly, home team people must bet against outside cocks or the outsiders will accuse them — a serious charge — of just collecting entry fees and not really being interested in cockfighting, as well as again being arrogant and insulting.

17. Finally, the Balinese peasants themselves are quite aware of all this and can and, at least to an ethnographer, do state most of it in approximately the same terms as I have. Fighting cocks, almost every Balinese I have ever discussed the subject with has said, is like playing with fire only not getting burned. You activate village and kingroup rivalries and hostilities, but in "play" form, coming dangerously and entrancingly close to the expression of open and direct interpersonal and intergroup aggression (something which, again, almost never happens in the normal course of ordinary life), but not quite, because, after all, it is "only a cockfight."

More observations of this sort could be advanced, but perhaps the general point is, if not made, at least well delineated, and the whole argument thus far can be usefully summarized in a formal paradigm:

The More a Match Is . . .
    1. Between near status equals (and/or personal enemies)
    2. Between high status individuals

The Deeper the Match.

The Deeper the Match . . .

1. The closer the identification of cock and man (or, more properly, the deeper the match the more the man will advance his best, most closely-identified-with cock).
2. The finer the cocks involved and the more exactly they will be matched.
3. The greater the emotion that will be involved and the more general absorption in the match.
4. The higher the individual bets center and outside, the shorter the outside bet odds will tend to be, and the more betting there will be overall.
5. The less an "economic" and the more a "status" view of gaming will be involved, and the "solider" the citizens who will be gaming.[26]

Inverse arguments hold for the shallower the fight, culminating, in a reversed-signs sense, in the coin-spinning and dice-throwing amusements. For deep fights there are no absolute upper limits, though there are of course practical ones, and there are a great many legend-like tales of great Duel-in-the-Sun combats between lords and princes in classical times (for cockfighting has always been as much an elite concern as a popular one), far deeper than anything anyone, even aristocrats, could produce today anywhere in Bali.

Indeed, one of the great culture heroes of Bali is a prince, called after his passion for the sport, "The Cockfighter," who happened to be away at a very deep cockfight with a neighboring prince when the whole of his family—father, brothers, wives, sisters—were assassinated by commoner usurpers. Thus spared, he returned to dispatch the upstart, regain the throne, reconstitute the Balinese high tradition, and build its most powerful, glorious, and prosperous state. Along with everything else that the Balinese see in fighting cocks—themselves, their social order, abstract hatred, masculinity, demonic power—they also see the archetype of status virtue, the arrogant, resolute, honor-mad player with real fire, the ksatria prince.[27]

26. As this is a formal paradigm, it is intended to display the logical, not the causal, structure of cockfighting. Just which of these considerations leads to which, in what order, and by what mechanisms, is another matter—one I have attempted to shed some light on in the general discussion.

27. In another of Hooykaas-van Leeuwen Boomkamp's folk tales ("De Gast,"

FEATHERS, BLOOD, CROWDS, AND MONEY

"Poetry makes nothing happen," Auden says in his elegy of Yeats, "it survives in the valley of its saying . . . a way of happening, a mouth." The cockfight too, in this colloquial sense, makes nothing happen. Men go on allegorically humiliating one another and being allegorically humiliated by one another, day after day, glorying quietly in the experience if they have triumphed, crushed only slightly more openly by it if they have not. *But no one's status really changes.* You cannot ascend the status ladder by winning cockfights; you cannot, as an individual, really ascend it at all. Nor can you descend it that way.[28] All you can do is enjoy and savor, or suffer and withstand, the con-

---

Sprookjes en Verhalen van Bali, pp. 172–180), a low-caste *Sudra,* a generous, pious, and carefree man who is also an accomplished cockfighter, loses, despite his accomplishment, fight after fight until he is not only out of money but down to his last cock. He does not despair, however—"I bet," he says, "upon the Unseen World."

His wife, a good and hard-working woman, knowing how much he enjoys cockfighting, gives him her last "rainy day" money to go and bet. But, filled with misgivings due to his run of ill luck, he leaves his own cock at home and bets merely on the side. He soon loses all but a coin or two and repairs to a food stand for a snack, where he meets a decrepit, odorous, and generally unappetizing old beggar leaning on a staff. The old man asks for food, and the hero spends his last coins to buy him some. The old man then asks to pass the night with the hero, which the hero gladly invites him to do. As there is no food in the house, however, the hero tells his wife to kill the last cock for dinner. When the old man discovers this fact, he tells the hero he has three cocks in his own mountain hut and says the hero may have one of them for fighting. He also asks for the hero's son to accompany him as a servant, and, after the son agrees, this is done.

The old man turns out to be Siva and, thus, to live in a great palace in the sky, though the hero does not know this. In time, the hero decides to visit his son and collect the promised cock. Lifted up into Siva's presence, he is given the choice of three cocks. The first crows: "I have beaten fifteen opponents." The second crows, "I have beaten twenty-five opponents." The third crows, "I have beaten the king." "That one, the third, is my choice," says the hero, and returns with it to earth.

When he arrives at the cockfight, he is asked for an entry fee and replies, "I have no money; I will pay after my cock has won." As he is known never to win, he is let in because the king, who is there fighting, dislikes him and hopes to enslave him when he loses and cannot pay off. In order to insure that this happens, the king matches his finest cock against the hero's. When the cocks are placed down, the hero's flees, and the crowd, led by the arrogant king, hoots in laughter. The hero's cock then flies at the king himself, killing him with a spur stab in the throat. The hero flees. His house is encircled by the king's men. The cock changes into a Garuda, the great mythic bird of Indic legend, and carries the hero and his wife to safety in the heavens.

When the people see this, they make the hero king and his wife queen and they return as such to earth. Later their son, released by Siva, also returns and the hero-king announces his intentions to enter a hermitage. ("I will fight no more cockfights. I have bet on the Unseen and won.") He enters the hermitage and his son becomes king.

28. Addict gamblers are really less declassed (for their status is, as everyone else's inherited) than merely impoverished and personally disgraced. The most prominent addict gambler in my cockfight circuit was actually a very high caste *satria* who sold off

cocted sensation of drastic and momentary movement along an aesthetic semblance of that ladder, a kind of behind-the-mirror status
jump which has the look of mobility without its actuality.

Like any art form — for that, finally, is what we are dealing with —
the cockfight renders ordinary, everyday experience comprehensible
by presenting it in terms of acts and objects which have had their
practical consequences removed and been reduced (or, if you prefer,
raised) to the level of sheer appearances, where their meaning can be
more powerfully articulated and more exactly perceived. The cockfight is "really real" only to the cocks — it does not kill anyone, cas-
trate anyone, reduce anyone to animal status, alter the hierarchical
relations among people, or refashion the hierarchy; it does not even
redistribute income in any significant way. What it does is what, for
other peoples with other temperaments and other conventions, *Lear*
and *Crime and Punishment* do; it catches up these themes — death, masculinity, rage, pride, loss, beneficence, chance — and, ordering them
into an encompassing structure, presents them in such a way as to
throw into relief a particular view of their essential nature. It puts a
construction on them, makes them, to those historically positioned to
appreciate the construction, meaningful — visible, tangible, grasp-
able — "real," in an ideational sense. An image, fiction, a model, a
metaphor, the cockfight is a means of expression; its function is neither
to assuage social passions nor to heighten them (though, in its
playing-with-fire way it does a bit of both), but, in a medium of
feathers, blood, crowds, and money, to display them.

The question of how it is that we perceive qualities in things —
paintings, books, melodies, plays — that we do not feel we can assert
literally to be there has come, in recent years, into the very center of
aesthetic theory.[29] Neither the sentiments of the artist, which remain
his, nor those of the audience, which remain theirs, can account for the
agitation of one painting or the serenity of another. We attribute gran-
deur, wit, despair, exuberance to strings of sounds; lightness, energy,

---

most of his considerable lands to support his habit. Though everyone privately regarded
him as a fool and worse (some, more charitable, regarded him as sick), he was publicly
treated with the elaborate deference and politeness due his rank.

29. For four, somewhat variant, treatments, see S. Langer, *Feeling and Form* (New
York, 1953); R. Wollheim, *Art and Its Objects* (New York, 1968); N. Goodman, *Lan-
guages of Art* (Indianapolis, 1968); M. Merleau-Ponty, "The Eye and the Mind," in his
The Primacy of Perception (Evanston, Ill., 1964), pp. 159–190.

violence, fluidity to blocks of stone. Novels are said to have strength, buildings eloquence, plays momentum, ballets repose. In this realm of eccentric predicates, to say that the cockfight, in its perfected cases at least, is "disquietful" does not seem at all unnatural, merely, as I have just denied it practical consequence, somewhat puzzling.

The disquietfulness arises, "somehow," out of a conjunction of three attributes of the fight: its immediate dramatic shape; its metaphoric content; and its social context. A cultural figure against a social ground, the fight is at once a convulsive surge of animal hatred, a mock war of symbolical selves, and a formal simulation of status tensions, and its aesthetic power derives from its capacity to force together these diverse realities. The reason it is disquietful is not that it has material effects (it has some, but they are minor); the reason that it is disquietful is that, joining pride to selfhood, selfhood to cocks, and cocks to destruction, it brings to imaginative realization a dimension of Balinese experience normally well obscured from view. The transfer of a sense of gravity into what is in itself a rather blank and unvarious spectacle, a commotion of beating wings and throbbing legs, is effected by interpreting it as expressive of something unsettling in the way its authors and audience live, or, even more ominously, what they are.

As a dramatic shape, the fight displays a characteristic that does not seem so remarkable until one realizes that it does not have to be there: a radically atomistical structure.[30] Each match is a world unto itself, a particulate burst of form. There is the matchmaking, there is the betting, there is the fight, there is the result — utter triumph and utter defeat — and there is the hurried, embarrassed passing of money. The loser is not consoled. People drift away from him, look around him,

30. British cockfights (the sport was banned there in 1840) indeed seem to have lacked it, and to have generated, therefore, a quite different family of shapes. Most British fights were "mains," in which a preagreed number of cocks were aligned into two teams and fought serially. Score was kept and wagering took place both on the individual matches and on the main as a whole. There were also "battles Royales," both in England and on the Continent, in which a large number of cocks were let loose at once with the one left standing at the end the victor. And in Wales, the so-called Welsh main followed an elimination pattern, along the lines of a present-day tennis tournament, winners proceeding to the next round. As a genre, the cock fight has perhaps less compositional flexibility than, say, Latin comedy, but it is not entirely without any. On cockfighting more generally, see A. Ruport, *The Art of Cockfighting* (New York, 1949); G. R. Scott, *History of Cockfighting* (London, 1957); and L. Fitz-Barnard, *Fighting Sports* (London, 1921).

leave him to assimilate his momentary descent into nonbeing, reset his face, and return, scarless and intact, to the fray. Nor are winners congratulated, or events rehashed; once a match is ended the crowd's attention turns totally to the next, with no looking back. A shadow of the experience no doubt remains with the principals, perhaps even with some of the witnesses of a deep fight, as it remains with us when we leave the theater after seeing a powerful play well performed; but it quite soon fades to become at most a schematic memory — a diffuse glow or an abstract shudder — and usually not even that. Any expressive form lives only in its own present — the one it itself creates. But, here, that present is severed into a string of flashes, some more bright than others, but all of them disconnected, aesthetic quanta. Whatever the cockfight says, it says in spurts.

But the Balinese live in spurts. Their life, as they arrange it and perceive it, is less a flow, a directional movement out of the past, through the present, toward the future than an on-off pulsation of meaning and vacuity, an arhythmic alternation of short periods when "something" (that is, something significant) is happening, and equally short ones where "nothing" (that is, nothing much) is — between what they themselves call "full" and "empty" times, or, in another idiom, "junctures" and "holes." In focusing activity down to a burning-glass dot, the cockfight is merely being Balinese in the same way in which everything from the monadic encounters of everyday life, through the clanging pointillism of *gamelan* music, to the visiting-day-of-the-gods temple celebrations are. It is not an imitation of the punctuateness of Balinese social life, nor a depiction of it, nor even an expression of it; it is an example of it, carefully prepared.[31]

If one dimension of the cockfight's structure, its lack of temporal directionality, makes it seem a typical segment of the general social life, however, the other, its flat-out, head-to-head (or spur-to-spur) aggressiveness, makes it seem a contradiction, a reversal, even a subversion of it. In the normal course of things, the Balinese are shy to the point of obsessiveness of open conflict. Oblique, cautious, subdued, controlled, masters of indirection and dissimulation — what they call

---

31. For the necessity of distinguishing among "description," "representation," "exemplification," and "expression" (and the irrelevance of "imitation" to all of them) as modes of symbolic reference, see Goodman, *Languages of Art,* pp. 61–110, 45–91, 225–241.

alus, "polished," "smooth" — they rarely face what they can turn away from, rarely resist what they can evade. But here they portray themselves as wild and murderous, with manic explosions of instinctual cruelty. A powerful rendering of life as the Balinese most deeply do not want it (to adapt a phrase Frye has used of Gloucester's blinding) is set in the context of a sample of it as they do in fact have it.[32] And, because the context suggests that the rendering, if less than a straightforward description, is nonetheless more than an idle fancy, it is here that the disquietfulness — the disquietfulness of the *fight,* not (or, anyway, not necessarily) its patrons, who seem in fact rather thoroughly to enjoy it — emerges. The slaughter in the cock ring is not a depiction of how things literally are among men, but, what is almost worse, of how, from a particular angle, they imaginatively are.[33]

The angle, of course, is stratificatory. What, as we have already seen, the cockfight talks most forcibly about is status relationships, and what it says about them is that they are matters of life and death. That prestige is a profoundly serious business is apparent everywhere one looks in Bali — in the village, the family, the economy, the state. A peculiar fusion of Polynesian title ranks and Hindu castes, the hierarchy of pride is the moral backbone of the society. But only in the cockfight are the sentiments upon which that hierarchy rests revealed in their natural colors. Enveloped elsewhere in a haze of etiquette, a thick cloud of euphemism and ceremony, gesture and allusion, they are here expressed in only the thinnest disguise of an animal mask, a mask which in fact demonstrates them far more effectively than it conceals them. Jealousy is as much a part of Bali as poise, envy as

32. N. Frye, *The Educated Imagination* (Bloomington, Ind., 1964), p. 99.
33. There are two other Balinese values and disvalues which, connected with punctuate temporality on the one hand and unbridled aggressiveness on the other, reinforce the sense that the cockfight is at once continuous with ordinary social life and a direct negation of it: what the Balinese call *ramé,* and what they call *paling. Ramé* means crowded, noisy, and active, and is a highly sought-after social state: crowded markets, mass festivals, busy streets are all *ramé,* as, of course, is, in the extreme, a cockfight. *Ramé* is what happens in the "full" times (its opposite, *sepi,* "Quiet," is what happens in the "empty" ones). *Paling* is social vertigo, the dizzy, disoriented, lost, turned-around feeling one gets when one's place in the coordinates of social space is not clear, and it is a tremendously disfavored, immensely anxiety-producing state. Balinese regard the exact maintenance of spatial orientation ("not to know where north is" is to be crazy), balance, decorum, status relationships, and so forth, as fundamental to ordered life *(krama)* and *paling,* the sort of whirling confusion of position the scrambling cocks exemplify as its profoundest enemy and contradiction. On *ramé,* see Bateson and Mead, *Balinese Character,* pp. 3, 64; on *paling,* ibid., p. 11, and Belo, ed., *Traditional Balinese Culture,* pp. 90ff.

grace, brutality as charm; but without the cockfight the Balinese would have a much less certain understanding of them, which is, presumably, why they value it so highly.

Any expressive form works (when it works) by disarranging semantic contexts in such a way that properties conventionally ascribed to certain things are unconventionally ascribed to others, which are then seen actually to possess them. To call the wind a cripple, as Stevens does, to fix tone and manipulate timbre, as Schoenberg does, or, closer to our case, to picture an art critic as a dissolute bear, as Hogarth does, is to cross conceptual wires; the established conjunctions between objects and their qualities are altered, and phenomena — fall weather, melodic shape, or cultural journalism — are clothed in signifiers which normally point to other referents.[34] Similarly, to connect — and connect, and connect — the collision of roosters with the divisiveness of status is to invite a transfer of perceptions from the former to the latter, a transfer which is at once a description and a judgment. (Logically, the transfer could, of course, as well go the other way; but, like most of the rest of us, the Balinese are a great deal more interested in understanding men than they are in understanding cocks.)

What sets the cockfight apart from the ordinary course of life, lifts it from the realm of the everyday practical affairs, and surrounds it with an aura of enlarged importance is not, as functionalist sociology would have it, that it reinforces status discriminations (such reinforcement is hardly necessary in a society where every act proclaims them), but that it provides a metasocial commentary upon the whole matter of assorting human beings into fixed hierarchical ranks and then organizing the major part of collective existence around that

34. The Stevens reference is to his "The Motive for Metaphor" ("You like it under the trees in autumn,/Because everything is half dead./The wind moves like a cripple among the leaves/And repeats words without meaning") [Copyright 1947 by Wallace Stevens, reprinted from *The Collected Poems of Wallace Stevens* by permission of Alfred A. Knopf, Inc., and Faber and Faber Ltd.]; the Schoenberg reference is to the third of his *Five Orchestral Pieces* (Opus 16), and is borrowed from H. H. Drager, "The Concept of 'Tonal Body,' " in *Reflections on Art,* ed. S. Langer (New York, 1961), p. 174. On Hogarth, and on this whole problem — there called "multiple matrix matching" — see E. H. Gombrich, "The Use of Art for the Study of Symbols," in *Psychology and the Visual Arts,* edited by J. Hogg (Baltimore, 1969), pp. 149–170. The more usual term for this sort of semantic alchemy is "metaphorical transfer," and good technical discussions of it can be found in M. Black, *Models and Metaphors* (Ithaca, N.Y., 1962), pp. 25ff; Goodman, *Language as Art,* pp. 44ff; and W. Percy, "Metaphor as Mistake," *Sewanee Review* 66 (1958): 78–99.

assortment. Its function, if you want to call it that, is interpretive: it is a Balinese reading of Balinese experience, a story they tell themselves about themselves.

SAYING SOMETHING OF SOMETHING

To put the matter this way is to engage in a bit of metaphorical refocusing of one's own, for it shifts the analysis of cultural forms from an endeavor in general parallel to dissecting an organism, diagnosing a symptom, deciphering a code, or ordering a system — the dominant analogies in contemporary anthropology — to one in general parallel with penetrating a literary text. If one takes the cockfight, or any other collectively sustained symbolic structure, as a means of "saying something of something" (to invoke a famous Aristotelian tag), then one is faced with a problem not in social mechanics but social semantics.[35] For the anthropologist, whose concern is with formulating sociological principles, not with promoting or appreciating cockfights, the question is, what does one learn about such principles from examining culture as an assemblage of texts?

Such an extention of the notion of a text beyond written material, and even beyond verbal, is, though metaphorical, not, or course, all that novel. The *interpretatio naturae* tradition of the Middle Ages, which, culminating in Spinoza, attempted to read nature as Scripture, the Nietszchean effort to treat value systems as glosses on the will to power (or the Marxian one to treat them as glosses on property relations), and the Freudian replacement of the enigmatic text of the manifest dream with the plain one of the latent, all offer precedents, if not equally recommendable ones.[36] But the idea remains theoretically undeveloped; and the more profound corollary, so far as anthropology is concerned, that cultural forms can be treated as texts, as imaginative works built out of social materials, has yet to be systematically exploited.[37]

---

35. The tag is from the second book of the *Organon, On Interpretation*. For a discussion of it, and for the whole argument for freeing "the notion of text . . . from the notion of scripture or writing" and constructing, thus, a general hermeneutics, see P. Ricoeur, *Freud and Philosophy* (New Haven, 1970), pp. 20ff.

36. Ibid.

37. Lévi-Strauss' "structuralism" might seem an exception. But it is only an apparent one, for, rather than taking myths, totem rites, marriage rules, or whatever as texts to interpret, Lévi-Strauss takes them as ciphers to solve, which is very much not the same thing. He does not seek to understand symbolic forms in terms of how they

In the case at hand, to treat the cockfight as a text is to bring out a feature of it (in my opinion, the central feature of it) that treating it as a rite or a pastime, the two most obvious alternatives, would tend to obscure: its use of emotion for cognitive ends. What the cockfight says it says in a vocabulary of sentiment — the thrill of risk, the despair of loss, the pleasure of triumph. Yet what it says is not merely that risk is exciting, loss depressing, or triumph gratifying, banal tautologies of affect, but that it is of these emotions, thus exampled, that society is built and individuals are put together. Attending cockfights and participating in them is, for the Balinese, a kind of sentimental education. What he learns there is what his culture's ethos and his private sensibility (or, anyway, certain aspects of them) look like when spelled out externally in a collective text; that the two are near enough alike to be articulated in the symbolics of a single such text; and — the disquieting part — that the text in which this revelation is accomplished consists of a chicken hacking another mindlessly to bits.

Every people, the proverb has it, loves its own form of violence. The cockfight is the Balinese reflection on theirs: on its look, its uses, its force, its fascination. Drawing on almost every level of Balinese experience, it brings together themes — animal savagery, male narcissism, opponent gambling, status rivalry, mass excitement, blood sacrifice — whose main connection is their involvement with rage and the fear of rage, and, binding them into a set of rules which at once contains them and allows them play, builds a symbolic structure in which, over and over again, the reality of their inner affiliation can be intelligibly felt. If, to quote Northrup Frye again, we go to see *Macbeth* to learn what a man feels like after he has gained a kingdom and lost his soul, Balinese go to cockfights to find out what a man, usually composed, aloof, almost obsessively self-absorbed, a kind of moral autocosm, feels like when, attacked, tormented, challenged, insulted, and driven in result to the extremes of fury, he has totally triumphed or been brought totally low. The whole passage, as it takes us back to Aristotle (though to the *Poetics* rather than the *Hermeneutics*), is worth quotation:

---

function in concrete situations to organize perceptions (meanings, emotions, concepts, attitudes); he seeks to understand them entirely in terms of their internal structure, *indépendent de tout sujet, de tout objet, et de toute contexte.*

But the poet [as opposed to the historian], Aristotle says, never makes any real statements at all, certainly no particular or specific ones. The poet's job is not to tell you what happened, but what happens: not what did take place, but the kind of thing that always does take place. He gives you the typical, recurring, or what Aristotle calls universal event. You wouldn't go to *Macbeth* to learn about the history of Scotland — you go to it to learn what a man feels like after he's gained a kingdom and lost his soul. When you meet such a character as Micawber in Dickens, you don't feel that there must have been a man Dickens knew who was exactly like this: you feel that there's a bit of Micawber in almost everybody you know, including yourself. Our impressions of human life are picked up one by one, and remain for most of us loose and disorganized. But we constantly find things in literature that suddenly coordinate and bring into focus a great many such impressions, and this is part of what Aristotle means by the typical or universal human event.[38]

It is this kind of bringing of assorted experiences of everyday life to focus that the cockfight, set aside from that life as "only a game" and reconnected to it as "more than a game," accomplishes, and so creates what, better than typical or universal, could be called a paradigmatic human event — that is, one that tells us less what happens than the kind of thing that would happen if, as is not the case, life were art and could be as freely shaped by styles of feeling as *Macbeth* and *David Copperfield* are.

Enacted and re-enacted, so far without end, the cockfight enables the Balinese, as, read and reread, *Macbeth* enables us, to see a dimension of his own subjectivity. As he watches fight after fight, with the active watching of an owner and a bettor (for cockfighting has no more interest as a pure spectator sport than does croquet or dog racing), he grows familiar with it and what it has to say to him, much as the attentive listener to string quartets or the absorbed viewer of still life grows slowly more familiar with them in a way which opens his subjectivity to himself.[39]

38. Frye, *The Educated Imagination*, pp. 63–64.

39. The use of the, to Europeans, "natural" visual idion for perception — "see," "watches," and so forth — is more than usually misleading here, for the fact that, as mentioned earlier, Balinese follow the progress of the fight as much (perhaps, as fighting cocks are actually rather hard to see except as blurs of motion, more) with their bodies as with their eyes, moving their limbs, heads, and trunks in gestural mimicry of the cocks' maneuvers, means that much of the individual's experience of the fight is kinesthetic rather than visual. If ever there was an example of Kenneth Burke's definition of a symbolic act as "the dancing of an attitude" (*The Philosophy of Literary Form*, rev. ed. [New York, 1957], p. 9) the cockfight is it. On the enormous role of kinesthetic

Yet, because—in another of those paradoxes, along with painted feelings and unconsequenced acts, which haunt aesthetics—that subjectivity does not properly exist until it is thus organized, art forms generate and regenerate the very subjectivity they pretend only to display. Quartets, still lifes, and cockfights are not merely reflections of a preexisting sensibility analogically represented; they are positive agents in the creation and maintenance of such a sensibility. If we see ourselves as a pack of Micawbers, it is from reading too much Dickens (if we see ourselves as unillusioned realists, it is from reading to little); and similarly for Balinese, cocks, and cockfights. It is in such a way, coloring experience with the light they cast it in, rather than through whatever material effects they may have, that the arts play their role, as arts, in social life.[40]

In the cockfight, then, the Balinese forms and discovers his temperament and his society's temper at the same time. Or, more exactly, he forms and discovers a particular facet of them. Not only are there a great many other cultural texts providing commentaries on status hierarchy and self-regard in Bali, but there are a great many other critical sectors of Balinese life besides the stratificatory and the agonistic that receive such commentary. The ceremony consecrating a Brahmana priest, a matter of breath control, postural immobility, and vacant concentration upon the depths of being, displays a radically different, but to the Balinese equally real, property of social hierarchy—its reach toward the numinous transcendent. Set not in the matrix of the kinetic emotionality of animals, but in that of the static passionlessness of divine mentality, it expresses tranquility not disquiet. The mass festivals at the village temples, which mobilize the

---

perception in Balinese life, Bateson and Mead, *Balinese Character,* pp. 84–88; on the active nature of aesthetic perception in general, Goodman, *Language of Art,* pp. 241–244.

40. All this coupling of the occidental great with the oriental lowly will doubtless disturb certain sorts of aestheticians as the earlier efforts of anthropologists to speak of Christianity and totemism in the same breath disturbed certain sorts of theologians. But as ontological questions are (or should be) bracketed in the sociology of religion, judgmental ones are (or should be) bracketed in the sociology of art. In any case, the attempt to deprovincialize the concept of art is but part of the general anthropological conspiracy to deprovincialize all important social concepts—marriage, religion, law, rationality—and though this is a threat to aesthetic theories which regard certain works of art as beyond the reach of sociological analysis, it is no threat to the conviction, for which Robert Graves claims to have been reprimanded at his Cambridge tripos, that some poems are better than others.

whole local population in elaborate hostings of visiting gods — songs, dances, compliments, gifts — assert the spiritual unity of village mates against their status inequality and project a mood of amity and trust.[41] The cockfight is not the master key to Balinese life, any more than bullfighting is to Spanish. What it says about that life is not unqualified nor even unchallenged by what other equally eloquent cultural statements say about it. But there is nothing more surprising in this than in the fact that Racine and Molière were contemporaries, or that the same people who arrange chrysanthemums cast swords.[42]

The culture of a people is an ensemble of texts, themselves ensembles, which the anthropologist strains to read over the shoulders of those to whom they properly belong. There are enormous difficulties in such an enterprise, methodological pitfalls to make a Freudian quake, and some moral perplexities as well. Nor is it the only way that symbolic forms can be sociologically handled. Functionalism lives, and so does psychologism. But to regard such forms as "saying something of something," and saying it to somebody, is at least to open up the possibility of an analysis which attends to their substance rather than to reductive formulas professing to account for them.

As in more familiar exercises in close reading, one can start anywhere in a culture's repertoire of forms and end up anywhere else. One can stay, as I have here, within a single, more or less bounded form, and circle steadily within it. One can move between forms in

41. For the consecration ceremony, see V. E. Korn, "The Consecration of the Priest," in Swellengrebel, ed., *Bali: Studies,* pp. 131–154; for (somewhat exaggerated) village communion, R. Goris, "The Religious Character of the Balinese Village," ibid., pp. 79–100.

42. That what the cockfight has to say about Bali is not altogether without perception, and the disquiet it expresses about the general pattern of Balinese life is not wholly without reason, is attested by the fact that in two weeks of December 1965, during the upheavals following the unsuccessful coup in Djakarta, between forty and eighty thousand Balinese (in a population of about two million) were killed, largely by one another — the worst outburst in the country. [J. Hughes, *Indonesian Upheaval* (New York, 1967), pp. 173–183. Hughes' figures are, of course, rather casual estimates, but they are not the most extreme.] This is not to say, of course, that the killings were caused by the cockfight, could have been predicted on the basis of it, or were some sort of enlarged version of it with real people in the place of the cocks — all of which is nonsense. It is merely to say that if one looks at Bali not just through the medium of its dances, its shadow-plays, its sculpture, and its girls, but — as the Balinese themselves do — also through the medium of its cockfight, the fact that the massacre occurred seems, if no less appalling, less like a contradiction to the laws of nature. As more than one real Gloucester has discovered, sometimes people actually get life precisely as they most deeply do not want it.

search of broader unities or informing contrasts. One can even compare forms from different cultures to define their character in reciprocal relief. But whatever the level at which one operates, and however intricately, the guiding principle is the same: societies, like lives, contain their own interpretations. One has only to learn how to gain access to them.

Chapter Six

From the Native's Point of View:
On the Nature of
Anthropological Understanding

CLIFFORD GEERTZ

Several years ago a minor scandal erupted in anthropology: one of its ancestral figures told the truth in a public place. As befits an ancestor, he did it posthumously and through his widow's decision rather than his own, with the result that a number of the sort of right-thinking types who are always with us immediately rose to cry that she—an in-marrier anyway—had betrayed clan secrets, profaned an idol, and let down the side. What will the children think, to say nothing of the laymen? But the disturbance was not much lessened by such ceremonial wringing of the hands; the damn thing was, after all, already printed. In much the same way that James Watson's *The Double Helix* exposed the nature of research in biophysics, Bronislaw Malinowski's *A Diary in the Strict Sense of the Term* rendered the established image of how anthropological work is conducted fairly well implausible. The myth of the chameleon field-worker perfectly self-tuned to his exotic surroundings—a walking miracle of empathy, tact, patience, and cosmopolitanism—was demolished by the man who had perhaps done the most to create it.

The squabble that surrounded the publication of the *Diary* concentrated, naturally, on inessentials and, as was only to be expected, missed the point. Most of the shock seems to have arisen from the

Reprinted by permission from *Meaning in Anthropology,* ed. Keith H. Basso and Henry A. Selby, School of American Research Advanced Seminar Series (Albuquerque: University of New Mexico Press), 1976. Courtesy School of American Research.

mere discovery that Malinowski was not, to put it delicately, an un-
mitigated nice guy. He had rude things to say about the natives he was
living with and rude words to say it in. He spent a great deal of his
time wishing he were elsewhere. And he projected an image of a man
as little complaisant as the world has seen. (He also projected an image
of a man consecrated to a strange vocation to the point of self-
immolation, but that was less noted.)

The discussion eventually came down to Malinowski's moral
character or lack of it; ignored was the genuinely profound question
his book raised, namely, if anthropological understanding does not
stem, as we have been taught to believe, from some sort of extraordinary sensibility, an almost preternatural capacity to think, feel, and
perceive like a native (a word, I should hurry to say, I use here "in the
strict sense of the term"), then how is anthropological knowledge of
the way natives think, feel, and perceive possible? The issue the *Diary*
presents, with a force perhaps only a working ethnographer can fully
appreciate, is not moral; it is epistemological. If we are going to
cling—as in my opinion, we must—to the injunction to see things
from the native's point of view, what is our position when we can no
longer claim some unique form of psychological closeness, a sort of
transcultural identification, with our subjects? What happens to *Verstehen* when *Einfülen* disappears?

As a matter of fact, this general problem has been exercising
methodological discussion in anthropology for the last ten or fifteen
years; Malinowski's voice from the grave merely dramatized it as a
human dilemma over and above a professional one. The formulations
have been various: "inside" versus "outside," or "first person" versus
"third person" descriptions; "phenomenological" versus "objectivist,"
or "cognitive" versus "behavioral" theories; or, perhaps most commonly, "emic" versus "etic" analyses, this last deriving from the distinction in linguistics between phonemics and phonetics—phonemics
classifying sounds according to their internal function in language,
phonetics classifying them according to their acoustic properties as
such. But perhaps the simplest and most directly appreciable way to
put the matter is in terms of a distinction formulated, for his own
purposes, by the psychoanalyst Heinz Kohut—a distinction between
what he calls "experience-near" and "experience-distant" concepts.

An experience-near concept is roughly, one which an individual—a patient, a subject, in our case an informant—might himself

naturally and effortlessly use to define what he or his fellows see, feel, think, imagine, and so on, and which he would readily understand when similarly applied by others. An experience-distant concept is one which various types of specialists — an analyst, an experimenter, an ethnographer, even a priest or an ideologist — employ to forward their scientific, philosophical, or practical aims. "Love" is an experience-near concept; "object cathexis" is an experience-distant one. "Social stratification" and perhaps for most peoples in the world even "religion" (and certainly, "religious system") are experience-distant; "caste" and "nirvana" are experience-near, at least for Hindus and Buddhists.

Clearly, the matter is one of degree, not polar opposition: "fear" is experience-nearer than "phobia," and "phobia" experience-nearer than "ego dyssyntonic." And the difference is not, at least so far as anthropology is concerned (the matter is otherwise in poetry and physics), a normative one, in the sense that one sort of concept as such is to be preferred over the other. Confinement to experience-near concepts leaves an ethnographer awash in immediacies as well as entangled in vernacular. Confinement to experience-distant ones leaves him stranded in abstractions and smothered in jargon. The real question, and the one Malinowski raised by demonstrating that, in the case of "natives," you don't have to be one to know one, is what roles the two kinds of concepts play in anthropological analysis. To be more exact: How, in each case, should they be deployed so as to produce an interpretation of the way a people live which is neither imprisoned within their mental horizons, an ethnography of witchcraft as written by a witch, nor systematically deaf to the distinctive tonalities of witchcraft as written by a geometer?

Putting the matter this way — in terms of how anthropological analysis is to be conducted and its results framed, rather than what psychic constitution anthropologists need to have — reduces the mystery of what "seeing things from the native's point of view" means. But it does not make it any easier nor does it lessen the demand for perceptiveness on the part of the field-worker. To grasp concepts which, for another people, are experience-near, and to do so well enough to place them in illuminating connection with those experience-distant concepts that theorists have fashioned to capture the general features of social life, is clearly a task at least as delicate, if a bit less magical, as putting oneself into someone else's skin. The trick

is not to achieve some inner correspondence of spirit with your informants; preferring, like the rest of us, to call their souls their own, they
are not going to be altogether keen about such an effort anyhow. The
trick is to figure out what the devil they think they are up to.

In one sense, of course, no one knows this better than they do
themselves; hence the passion to swim in the stream of their experience, and the illusion afterward that one somehow has. But in another
sense, that simple truism is simply not true. People use experience-
near concepts spontaneously, unselfconsciously, as it were, colloqui-
ally; they do not, except fleetingly and on occasion, recognize that
there are any "concepts" involved at all. That is what experience-near
means — that ideas and the realities they disclose are naturally and
indissolubly bound up together. What else could you call a hip-
popotamus? Of course the gods are powerful; why else would we fear
them? The ethnographer does not, and in my opinion, largely cannot,
perceive what his informants perceive. What he perceives — and that
uncertainly enough — is what they perceive "with," or "by means of,"
or "through" or whatever word one may choose. In the country of the
blind, who are not as unobservant as they appear, the one-eyed is not
king but spectator.

Now, to make all this a bit more concrete I want to turn for a
moment to my own work, which whatever its other faults has at least
the virtue of being mine — a distinct advantage in discussions of this
sort. In all three of the societies I have studied intensively, Javanese,
Balinese, and Moroccan, I have been concerned, among other things,
with attempting to determine how the people who live there define
themselves as persons, what enters into the idea they have (but, as I
say, only half-realize they have) of what a self, Javanese, Balinese or
Moroccan style, is. And in each case, I have tried to arrive at this most
intimate of notions not by imagining myself as someone else — a rice
peasant or a tribal sheikh, and then seeing what I thought — but by
searching out and analyzing the symbolic forms — words, images, institutions, behaviors — in terms of which, in each place, people actually represent themselves to themselves and to one another.

The concept of person is, in fact, an excellent vehicle by which to
examine this whole question of how to go about poking into another
people's turn of mind. In the first place, some sort of concept of this
kind, one feels reasonably safe in saying, exists in recognizable form

within all social groups. Various notions of what persons are may be, from our point of view, more than a little odd. People may be conceived to dart about nervously at night, shaped like fireflies. Essential elements of their psyche, like hatred, may be thought to be lodged in granular black bodies within their livers, discoverable upon autopsy. They may share their fates with *doppelganger* beasts, so that when the beast sickens or dies they sicken or die too. But at least some conception of what a human individual is, as opposed to a rock, an animal, a rainstorm, or a god, is, so far as I can see, universal.

Yet, at the same time, as these offhand examples suggest, the actual conceptions involved vary, often quite sharply, from one group to the next. The Western conception of the person as a bounded, unique, more or less integrated motivational and cognitive universe, a dynamic center of awareness, emotion, judgment, and action organized into a distinctive whole and set contrastively both against other such wholes and against a social and natural background is, however incorrigible it may seem to us, a rather peculiar idea within the context of the world's cultures. Rather than attempt to place the experience of others within the framework of such a conception, which is what the extolled "empathy" in fact usually comes down to, we must, if we are to achieve understanding, set that conception aside and view their experiences within the framework of their own idea of what selfhood is. And for Java, Bali, and Morocco, at least, that idea differs markedly not only from our own but, no less dramatically and no less instructively, from one to the other.

MAKING THE SELF "SMOOTH"

In Java, where I worked in the fifties, I studied a small, shabby inland county-seat sort of place: two shadeless streets of whitewashed wooden shops and offices, with even less substantial bamboo shacks crammed in helter-skelter behind them, the whole surrounded by a great half-circle of densely packed rice-bowl villages. Land was short; jobs were scarce; politics was unstable; health was poor; prices were rising; and life was altogether far from promising, a kind of agitated stagnancy in which, as I once put it, thinking of the curious mixture of borrowed fragments of modernity and exhausted relics of tradition that characterized the place, the future seemed about as remote as the past. Yet, in the midst of this depressing scene there was an absolutely

astonishing intellectual vitality—a philosophical passion, and a popular one besides, to track the riddles of existence right down to the
ground. Destitute peasants would discuss questions of freedom of the
will; illiterate tradesmen discoursed on the properties of God; common laborers had theories about the relations between reason and
passion, the nature of time, or the reliability of the senses. And,
perhaps most important, the problem of the self—its nature, function,
and mode of operation—was pursued with the sort of reflective intensity one could find among ourselves in only the most recherché settings indeed.

The central ideas in terms of which this reflection proceeded and
which thus defined its boundaries and the Javanese sense of what a
person is were arranged into two sets of, at base, religious contrasts:
one between "inside" and "outside" and one between "refined" and
"vulgar." These glosses are, of course, crude and imprecise; determining exactly what was signified by the terms involved and sorting out
their shades of meaning was what all the discussion was about. But
together they formed a distinctive conception of the self which, far
from being merely theoretical, was the means by which Javanese in
fact perceive one another, and, of course, themselves.

The "inside" / "outside" words, *batin* and *lair* (terms borrowed, as
a matter of fact, from the Sufi tradition of Muslim mysticism, but
locally reworked) refer on the one hand to the felt realm of human
experience and on the other to the observed realm of human behavior.
These have, one hastens to say, nothing to do with "soul" and "body"
in our sense, for which there are quite other words with quite other
implications. *Batin,* the "inside" word, does not refer to a separate seat
of encapsulated spirituality detached or detachable from the body, or
indeed to a bounded unit at all, but to the emotional life of human
beings taken generally. It consists of the fuzzy, shifting flow of subjective feeling perceived directly in all its phenomenological immediacy
but considered to be, at its roots at least, identical across all individuals, whose individuality it thus effaces. And, similarly, *lair,* the "outside" word, has nothing to do with the body as an object, even an
experienced object. Rather, it refers to that part of human life which,
in our culture, strict behaviorists limit themselves to studying—
external actions, movements, postures, speech—again conceived as in
its essence invariant from one individual to the next. Therefore, these

two sets of phenomena — inward feelings and outward actions — are regarded not as functions of one another but as independent realms of being to be put in proper order independently.

It is in connection with this "proper ordering" that the contrast between *alus,* the word meaning "pure," "refined," "polished," "exquisite," "ethereal," "subtle," "civilized," "smooth," and *kasar,* the word meaning "impolite," "rough," "uncivilized," "coarse," "insensitive," "vulgar," comes into play. The goal is to be *alus* in both separated realms of the self. In the inner realm this is to be achieved through religious discipline, much but not all of it mystical. In the outer realm, it is to be achieved through etiquette, the rules of which, in this instance, are not only extraordinarily elaborate but have something of the force of law. Through meditation the civilized man thins out his emotional life to a kind of constant hum; through etiquette, he both shields that life from external disruptions and regularizes his outer behavior in such a way that it appears to others as a predictable, undisturbing, elegant, and rather vacant set of choreographed motions and settled forms of speech.

There is much to all this because it connects up to both an ontology and an aesthetic. But so far as our problem is concerned, the result is a bifurcate conception of the self, half ungestured feeling and half unfelt gesture. An inner world of stilled emotion and an outer world of shaped behavior confront one another as sharply distinguished realms unto themselves, any particular person being but the momentary locus, so to speak, of that confrontation, a passing expression of their permanent existence, their permanent separation, and their permanent need to be kept in their own separate order. Only when you have seen, as I have, a young man whose wife — a woman he had raised from childhood and who had been the center of his life — has suddenly and inexplicably died, greeting everyone with a set smile and formal apologies for his wife's absence and trying, by mystical techniques, to flatten out, as he himself put it, the hills and valleys of his emotion into an even, level plain ("That is what you have to do," he said to me, "be smooth inside and out") can you come, in the face of our own notions of the intrinsic honesty of deep feeling and the moral importance of personal sincerity, to take the possibility of such a conception of selfhood seriously and to appreciate, however inaccessible it is to you, its own sort of force.

A THEATER OF STATUS

Bali, where I worked both in another small provincial town, though one rather less drifting and dispirited, and, later, in an upland village of highly skilled musical-instrument makers, is in many ways similar to Java, with which it shared a common culture until the fifteenth century. But at a deeper level, having continued Hindu while Java was nominally at least, Islamized, it is quite different. The intricate, obsessive ritual life, Hindu, Buddhist, and Polynesian in about equal proportions (the development of which was more or less cut off in Java, leaving its Indic spirit to turn reflective and phenomenological, even quietistic, in the way I've just described), flourished in Bali to reach levels of scale and flamboyance that have startled the world and made the Balinese a much more dramaturgical people with a self to match. What is philosophy in Java is theater in Bali.

As a result, there is in Bali a persistent and systematic attempt to stylize all aspects of personal expression to the point where anything idiosyncratic, anything characteristic of the individual merely because he is who he is physically, psychologically, or biographically, is muted in favor of his assigned place in the continuing and, so it is thought, never-changing pageant that is Balinese life. It is dramatis personae, not actors, that endure; indeed, it is dramatis personae, not actors, that in the proper sense really exist. Physically men come and go — mere incidents in a happenstance history of no genuine importance, even to themselves. But the masks they wear, the stage they occupy, the parts they play, and, most important, the spectacle they mount remain and constitute not the facade but the substance of things, not least the self. Shakespeare's old-trouper view of the vanity of action in the face of mortality — "all the world's a stage and we but poor players, content to strut our hour" — makes no sense here. There is no make-believe: of course players perish, but the play doesn't, and it is the latter, the performed rather than the performer, that really matters.

Again, all this is realized not in terms of some general mood the anthropologist in his spiritual versatility somehow captures, but through a set of readily observable symbolic forms: an elaborate repertoire of designations and titles. The Balinese have at least a half dozen major sorts of labels, ascriptive, fixed, and absolute, which one person can apply to another (or, of course, to himself) to place him among his fellows. There are birth-order markers, kinship terms, caste titles, sex indicators, teknonyms, and so on, each of which consists not of a mere collection of useful tags but a distinct and bounded, internally very complex, terminological system. To apply one of these designations or titles (or, as is more common, several at once) to a person is to define him as a determinate point in a fixed pattern, as the temporary occupant of a particular, quite untemporary, cultural locus. To identify someone, yourself or anyone else, in Bali is thus to locate him within the familiar cast of characters — "king," "grandmother," "third-born," "Brahman" — of which the social drama is, like some stock company roadshow piece — *Charley's Aunt* or *Springtime for Henry* — inevitably composed.

The drama is, of course, not farce, and especially not transvestite farce, though there are such elements in it. It is an enactment of hierarchy, a theater of status. But that, though critical, is unpursuable here. The immediate point is that, in both their structure and their mode of operation, the terminological systems conduce to a view of the human person as an appropriate representative of a generic type, not a unique creature with a private fate. To see how they do this, how they tend to obscure the mere materialities — biological, psychological, historical — of individual existence in favor of standardized status qualities would involve an extended analysis. But perhaps a single example, the simplest further simplified, will suffice to suggest the pattern.

All Balinese receive what might be called birth-order names. There are four of these, "first-born," "second-born," "third-born," and "fourth-born," after which they recycle, so that the fifth-born child is called again "first-born," the sixth "second-born," and so on. Further, these names are bestowed independently of the fates of the children. Dead children, even still-born ones, count, so that in this still high birth rate — high infant mortality society, the names don't really tell you anything very reliable about the birth-order relations of concrete individuals. Within a set of living siblings, someone called "first-born" may actually be first, fifth-, or ninth-born, or, if somebody is missing, almost anything in between; and someone called "second-born" may in fact be older.

The birth-order naming system does not identify individuals as individuals nor is it intended to; what it does is to suggest that, for all procreating couples, births form a circular succession of "firsts," "seconds," "thirds," and "fourths," an endless four-stage replication of imperishable form. Physically men appear and disappear as the ephemerae they are, but socially the acting figures remain eternally the same as new "firsts," "seconds," and so on; they emerge from the timeless world of the gods to replace those, who, dying, dissolve once more into it. Thus I would argue that all the designation and title systems function in the same way: to represent the most time-saturated aspects of the human condition as but ingredients in an eternal, footlight present.

Nor is this sense the Balinese have of always being on stage a vague and ineffable one either. It is, in fact, exactly summed up in what is surely one of their experience-nearest concepts: *lek*. *Lek* has been variously translated or mistranslated ("shame" is the most common attempt), but what it really means is close to what we call stage fright. Stage fright is the fear that, for want of skill or self-control, or perhaps by mere accident, an aesthetic illusion will not be maintained, the fear that the actor will show through his part. Aesthetic distance collapses; the audience (and the actor) loses sight of Hamlet and gains, uncomfortably for all concerned, a picture of bumbling John Smith painfully miscast as the Prince of Denmark.

In Bali, the case is the same: what is feared is that the public performance to which one's cultural location commits one will be botched and that the personality (as we would call it but the Balinese, of course, not believing in such a thing, would not) of the individual will break through to dissolve his standardized public identity. When this occurs, as it sometimes does the immediacy of the moment is felt with excruciating intensity, and men become suddenly and unwillingly creatural, locked in mutual embarrassment, as though they had happened upon each other's nakedness. It is the fear of *faux pas*, rendered only that much more probable by the extraordinary ritualization of daily life, that keeps social intercourse on its deliberately narrowed rails and protects the dramatistical sense of self against the disruptive threat implicit in the immediacy and spontaneity which even the most passionate ceremoniousness cannot fully eradicate from face-to-face encounters.

A PUBLIC CONTEXT FOR A PRIVATE LIFE

Morocco, mid-Eastern and dry rather than East Asian and wet, extrovert, fluid, activist, masculine, informal to a fault, a wild-west sort of place without the barrooms and the cattle drives, is another kettle of selves altogether. My work there, which began in the mid-sixties, has been centered in a moderately large town or small city in the foothills of the Middle Atlas, about twenty miles south of Fez. It is an old place, probably founded in the tenth century, conceivably even earlier. It has the walls, the gates, the narrow minarets rising to prayer-call platforms of a classical Muslim town, and, from a distance anyway, it is a rather pretty place, an irregular oval of blinding white set in the deep-sea green of an olive-grove oasis, the mountains, bronze and stony here, slanting up immediately behind it.

Close up, it is less prepossessing, though more exciting: a labyrinth of passages and alleyways, three-quarters of them blind, pressed in by wall-like buildings and curbside shops and filled with a simply astounding variety of very emphatic human beings. Arabs, Berbers, and Jews; tailors, herdsmen, and soldiers; people out of offices, people out of markets, people out of tribes; rich, super-rich, poor, super-poor; locals, immigrants, mimic Frenchmen, unbending medievalists, and somewhere, according to the official government census for 1960, an unemployed Jewish airplane pilot—the town houses one of the finest collections of rugged individuals I, at least, have ever come up against. Next to Sefrou (the name of the place), Manhattan seems almost monotonous.

Yet, no society consists of anonymous eccentrics bouncing off one another like billiard balls, and Moroccans, too, have symbolic means by which to sort people out from one another and form an idea of what it is to be a person. The main such means—not the only one, but I think the most important and the one I want to talk about particularly here—is a peculiar linguistic form called in Arabic the *nisba*. The word derives from the triliteral root, *n-s-b*, for "ascription," "attribution," "imputation," "relationship," "affinity," "correlation," "connection," "kinship." *Nsīb* means "in-law"; *nsab* means "to attribute or impute to"; *munasāba* means "a relation," "an analogy," "a correspondence"; *mansūb* means "belonging to," "pertaining to"; and so on to at

least a dozen derivatives from *nassāb,* "genealogist," to *nisbiya,* "(physical) relativity."

    Nisba itself, then, refers to a combination morphological, gram-
matical, and semantic process which consists of transforming a noun
into what we would call a relative adjective but what for Arabs becomes just another sort of noun by adding *ī* (f., *īya*): *Sefrū*/Sefrou —
Sefrū-wī/native son of Sefrou; *Sūs*/region of southwestern
Morocco — *Sūsī*/man coming from that region; *Beni Yazgā*/a tribe
near Sefrou — *Yāzgī*/a member of that tribe; *Yahūd*/the Jews as a
people, Jewry — *Yadūdī*/a Jew; *'Adlun*/surname of a prominent Sefrou
family — *'Adlūnī*/ a member of that family. Nor is the procedure confined to this more or less straightforward "ethnicizing" use but is
employed, in a wide range of domains, to attribute relational properties to persons. For example, occupation (*hrār*/silk — *hrārī*/silk merchant); religious sect (*Darqāwā*/a mystical brotherhood — *Darqāwī*/an
adept of that brotherhood); or spiritual status (*'Ali*/the Prophet's son-
in-law — *'Alawī*/ descendant of the Prophet's son-in-law, and thus of
the Prophet).

    Now as once formed, nisbas tend to be incorporated into personal
names — Umar Al-Buhadiwi/Umar of the Buhadu Tribe; Muhammed
Al-Sussi/Muhammed from the Sus region; this sort of adjectival, at-
tributive classification is quite publicly stamped upon an individual's
identity. I was unable to find a single case in which an individual was
generally known, or known about, but his (or her) nisba was not.
Indeed, Sefrouis are far more likely to be ignorant of how well-off a
man is, how long he has been around, what his personal character is,
or where exactly he lives, than they are of what his nisba is — Sussi or
Sefroui, Buhadiwi or Adluni, Harari or Darqawi. (Of women to
whom he is not related, that is very likely to be all he knows — or,
more exactly, is permitted to know). The selves that bump and jostle
each other in the alleys of Sefrou gain their definition from associative
relations they are imputed to have with the society that surrounds
them. They are contextualized persons.

    But the situation is even more radical than this. Nisbas render men
relative to their contexts, but as contexts themselves are relative, so
too are nisbas, and the whole thing rises, so to speak, to the second
power: relativism squared. Thus, at one level, everyone in Sefrou has
the same nisba, or at least the potential of it — namely, Sefroui. How-

ever, within Sefrou such a nisba, precisely because it does not discriminate, will never be heard as part of an individual designation. It is
only outside of Sefrou that the relationship to that particular context
becomes identifying. Inside it, a man is an Adluni, Alawi, Meghrawi,
Ngadi, or whatever; and similar distinctions exist within these
categories: there are, for example, twelve different nisbas (Shakibis,
Zuinis, etc.) by means of which, among themselves, Sefrou Alawis
distinguish one another.

The whole matter is far from regular: what level or sort of nisba is
used and seems relevant and appropriate (relevant and appropriate,
that is, to the users) depends heavily on the situation. A man I knew
who lived in Sefrou and worked in Fez but came from the Beni Yazgha
tribe settled nearby—and from the Hima lineage of the Taghut subfraction within it—was known as a Sefroui to his work fellows in Fez;
a Yazghi to all of us non-Yazghis in Sefrou; an Ydiri to other Beni
Yazghis around, except for those who were themselves of the Wulad
Ben Ydir fraction, who called him a Taghuti. As for the few other
Taghutis, they called him a Himiwi. That's as far as things went here
but not as far as they can go in either direction. Should, by chance, our
friend journey to Egypt he would become a Maghrebi, the nisba
formed from the Arabic word for North Africa. The social contextualization of persons is pervasive and, in its curiously unmethodical
way, systematic. Men do not float as bounded psychic entities, detached from their backgrounds and singularly named. As individualistic, even willful, as the Moroccans in fact are, their identity is an
attribute they borrow from their setting.

Now, as with the Javanese inside/outside, smooth/rough phenomenological sort of reality-dividing, and the absolutizing Balinese title
systems, the nisba way of looking at persons—as though they were
outlines waiting to be filled in—is not an isolated custom but part of a
total pattern of social life. This pattern is, as the others, difficult to
characterize succinctly, but surely one of its outstanding features is a
promiscuous tumbling in public settings of varieties of men kept carefully segregated in private ones—all-out cosmopolitanism in the
streets, strict communalism (of which the famous secluded woman is
only the most striking index) in the home.

This is indeed the so-called mosaic system of social organization so
often held to be characteristic of the Middle East generally: differently

shaped and colored chips jammed in irregularly together to generate an intricate overall design within which their individual distinctiveness remains nonetheless intact. Nothing if not diverse, Moroccan society does not cope with its diversity by sealing it into castes, isolating it into tribes, dividing it into ethnic groups, or covering it over with some common denominator concept of nationality, though, fitfully, all have now and then been tried. It copes with it by distinguishing, with elaborate precision, the contexts — marriage, worship, and to an extent diet, law, and education — within which men are separated by their dissimilitudes, from those — work, friendship, politics, trade — within which, however warily and however conditionally, they are connected by them.

To such a social pattern a concept of selfhood which marks public identity contextually and relativistically, but yet does so in terms — tribal, territorial, linguistic, religious, familial — which grow out of the more private and settled arenas of life and have a deep and permanent resonance there, would seem particularly appropriate. Indeed, it would virtually seem to create it; for it produces a situation in which people interact with one another in terms of categories whose meaning is almost purely positional — location in the general mosaic — leaving the substantive content of the categories, what they mean subjectively as experienced forms of life, aside as something properly concealed in apartments, temples and tents. Nisba discriminations can be more or less specific; they can indicate location within the mosaic roughly or finely; and they can be adapted to almost any changes in circumstance. But they cannot carry with them more than the most sketchy, outline implications concerning what men so named as a rule are like. Calling a man a Sefroui is like calling him a San Franciscan: it classifies him but it doesn't type him; it places him without portraying him.

It is the capacity of the nisba system to do this — to create a framework within which persons can be identified in terms of supposedly immanent characteristics (speech, blood, faith, provenance, and the rest) and yet to minimize the impact of those characteristics in determining the practical relations among such persons in markets, shops, bureaus, fields, cafes, baths, and roadways — that makes it so central to the Moroccan idea of the self. Nisba-type categorization leads, paradoxically, to a hyperindividualism in public relationships because by providing only a vacant sketch (and that shifting) of who the actors are — Yazghis, Adlunis, Buhadiwis, or whatever — it leaves the rest, that is, almost everything, to be filled in by the process of interaction itself. What makes the mosaic work is the confidence that one can be as totally pragmatic, adaptive, opportunistic, and generally *ad hoc* in one's relations with others — a fox among foxes, a crocodile among crocodiles — as one wants without any risk of losing one's sense of who one is. Selfhood is never in danger because, outside the immediacies of procreation and prayer, only its coordinates are asserted.

RELATING PARTS AND WHOLES

Now, without trying to tie up the dozens of loose ends I have not only left dangling in these rather breathless accounts of the senses of selfhood of nearly ninety million people but have doubtless frazzled even more, let us return to the question of what all this can tell us, or could if it were done adequately, about "the native's point of view" in Java, Bali, and Morocco. In describing symbol uses, are we describing perceptions, sentiments, outlooks, experiences? If so, in what sense is this being done? What do we claim when we assert that we understand the semiotic means by which, in this case, persons are defined to one another? That we know words or that we know minds?

In answering this question, it is necessary I think first to notice the characteristic intellectual movement, the inward conceptual rhythm, in each of these analyses and indeed in all similar analyses including those of Malinowski — namely, a continuous dialectical tacking between the most local of local detail and the most global of global structure in such a way as to bring both into view simultaneously. In seeking to uncover the Javanese, Balinese, or Moroccan sense of self, one oscillates restlessly between the sort of exotic minutiae (lexical antitheses, categorical schemes, morphophonemic transformations) that makes even the best ethnographies a trial to read and the sort of sweeping characterizations ("quietism," "dramatism," "contextualism") that makes all but the most pedestrian of them somewhat implausible. Hopping back and forth between the whole conceived through the parts which actualize it and the parts conceived through the whole which motivates them, we seek to turn them, by a sort of intellectual perpetual motion, into explications of one another.

All this is, of course, but the now familiar trajectory of what

Dilthey called the hermeneutic circle, and my argument here is merely that it is as central to ethnographic interpretation, and thus to the penetration of other people's modes of thought, as it is to literary, historical, philological, psychoanalytic, or biblical interpretation, or for that matter to the informal annotation of everyday experience we call common sense. In order to follow a baseball game one must understand what a bat, a hit, an inning, a left fielder, a squeeze play, a hanging curve, or a tightened infield are, and what the game in which these "things" are elements is all about.

When an *explication de texte* critic like Leo Spitzer attempts to interpret Keats's "Ode on a Grecian Urn," he does so by repetitively asking himself the alternating questions "What is the whole poem about?" and "What exactly has Keats seen (or chosen to show us) depicted on the urn he is describing?" At the end of an advancing spiral of general observations and specific remarks he emerges with a reading of the poem as an assertion of the triumph of the aesthetic mode of perception over the historical.

In the same way, when a meanings-and-symbols ethnographer like myself attempts to find out what some pack of natives conceive a person to be, he moves back and forth between asking himself, "What is the general form of their life?" and "What exactly are the vehicles in which that form is embodied?" emerging at the end of a similar sort of spiral with the notion that they see the self as a composite, a persona, or a point in a pattern.

You can no more know what *lek* is if you don't know what Balinese dramatism is than you can know what a catcher's mitt is if you don't know what baseball is. And you can no more know what mosaic social organization is if you don't know what a nisba is than you can know what Keats's Platonism is if you are unable to grasp, to use Spitzer's own formulation, the "intellectual thread of thought" captured in such fragment phrases as "Attic shape," "silent form," "bride of quietness," "cold pastoral," "silence and slow time," "peaceful citadel," and "ditties of no tone."

In short, accounts of other peoples' subjectivities can be built up without recourse to pretensions to more-than-normal capacities for ego-effacement and fellow-feeling. Normal capacities in these respects are, of course, essential, as is their cultivation, if we expect people to tolerate our intrusions into their life at all and accept us as persons worth talking to. I am certainly not arguing for insensitivity here and hope I have not demonstrated it.

But whatever accurate or half-accurate sense one gets of what one's informants are "really like" comes not from the experience of that acceptance as such, which is part of one's own biography, not of theirs, but from the ability to construe their modes of expression, what I would call their symbol systems, which such an acceptance allows one to work toward developing. Understanding the form and pressure of, to use the dangerous word one more time, natives' inner lives is more like grasping a proverb, catching an allusion, seeing a joke — or, as I have suggested, reading a poem — than it is like achieving communion.

Chapter Seven

Normal Circumstances, Literal Language, Direct Speech Acts, the Ordinary, the Everyday, the Obvious, What Goes Without Saying, and Other Special Cases

STANLEY FISH

I

On May Day, 1977, Pat Kelly, an outfielder for the Baltimore Orioles, hit two home runs in a game against the California Angels. The *Baltimore Sun* devoted three columns to the story, in part because Kelly had rarely displayed such power (he had hit only five home runs in the entire previous season), but largely because of the terms in which he saw his accomplishment. In fact, he didn't see it as his at all but as the working through him of Divine Providence. Two years previously Kelly had experienced a religious conversion. As he reports it, "I had been like a normal ballplayer. I was an extreme party-er, hanging around in bars and chasing all the women. But then this change came over me, and I have dedicated myself to Him." The effects of this change are described by the *Sun* reporter Michael Janofsky, whose comments betray some understandable exasperation:

> It is not even possible to discuss [with Kelly] the events of yesterday's game — or any game — on strictly a baseball level. He does not view his

Originally published in *Critical Inquiry*

home runs as merely a part of athletic competition. They are part of his religious existence.

One assumes that Janofsky had tried to discuss the events of yesterday's game and found that Kelly simply did not recognize the facts to which sports writers' questions routinely refer. These are the facts that exist on "a strictly baseball level," a wonderful phrase that can serve to identify the subject of this paper, a level of observation or discourse at which meanings are obvious and indisputable, the level of the ordinary, the normal, the usual, the everyday, the straightforward, the literal. From Janofsky's point of view it is this level that Kelly has lost, but from Kelly's point of view it has simply been redefined: as Janofsky reports, he now *literally* sees everything as a function of his religious existence; it is not that he allegorizes events after they have been normally perceived but that his normal perception is of events as the evidence of supernatural forces. Kelly played on May first only because the regular right fielder came down with conjunctivitis, and "even that," Janofsky exclaims, "he interpreted as divine intervention." "Interpreted" is not quite right, because it suggests an imposition upon raw data of a meaning not inherent in them, but for Kelly the meaning is prior to the data which will always have the same preread shape. The effort that Janofsky must make before he can read providential design into everyday occurrences is *natural* for the born-again Christian who would now have to make an effort wholly *un*natural in order once again to see a "mere athletic competition."

What this suggests is that categories like "the natural" and "the everyday" are not essential, but conventional. They refer not to properties of the world but to properties of the world as it is given to us by our interpretive assumptions. In the world in which Janofsky is situated as an independent agent amidst equally independent phenomena, Kelly is an anomaly (and therefore noteworthy) because, rather than accepting that world as it is, he populates it with the invisible presences demanded by his belief. That is, Janofsky assumes (without being aware of the assumption) that he speaks from a position above or below or to the side of belief, but in fact he speaks from within an *alternative* belief, one that gives him his world of "natural" causes as surely as Kelly's belief gives him a world alive with divine interventions. At stake here is the status of the ordinary. It would never occur to Janofsky to explain or defend the basis on which he describes events on a "strictly baseball level" (as he asks Kelly to explain and defend his point of view); he is simply describing what is there. That is what the ordinary is, that which appears to be there independently of anything we might say or think about it. It does not require comment (one doesn't write news stories about it), because it is obvious, right there on the surface; anyone can see it. But what anyone sees is not independent of his verbal and mental categories but is in fact a product of them; and it is because these categories, rather than being added to perception, are its content that the entities they bring into being seem to be a part of the world in the sense that they were there before there was anyone to perceive them. In other words, while the ordinary and the obvious are always with us, because we are always in the grip of some belief or other, they can change. They have changed for Kelly and that is why his story can bear the weight I am putting on it. "I had," he says, "been like a normal ballplayer," by which he means that he saw what normal ballplayers see. Now what he just as normally sees are divine interventions. His conversion follows the pattern prescribed by Augustine in *On Christian Doctrine*. The eye that was in bondage to the phenomenal world (had as its constitutive principle the autonomy of that world) has been cleansed and purged and is now capable of seeing what is really there, what is obvious, what anyone who has the eyes can see: "To the healthy and pure internal eye He is everywhere. . . . "[1] He is everywhere, not as the result of an interpretive act self-consciously performed on data otherwise available, but as the result of an interpretive act performed at so deep a level that it is indistinguishable from consciousness itself.

II

I have lingered over this example because it seems to me to bear (however indirectly) on the question most frequently debated in current literary discussions: What is in the text? That question assumes that at some (perhaps molecular) level what is in the text is independent of and prior to whatever people have said about it, and that therefore the text is stable, even though interpretations of it may vary.

1. Saint Augustine, *On Christian Doctrine*, translated by D. W. Robertson, Jr. (New York, 1958) p. 13.

I want to argue that there always is a text (just as there always is an ordinary world) but that what is in it can change, and therefore at no level is it independent of and prior to interpretation. My literary example is Milton's *Samson Agonistes,* a text whose history has a surprising relationship to Pat Kelly's conversion.

Like Milton's other major works, *Samson Agonistes* has received many readings. Among the readings now considered acceptable is one in which Samson's story is seen in relationship to the life of Christ. In its starkest form, the argument for this reading has the air of a paradox: *Samson Agonistes* is about Christ because he is nowhere mentioned. Such an argument seems to fly in the face of the rules of evidence, but in fact it illustrates something very important about evidence: it is always a function of what it is to be evidence for, and is never independently available. That is, the interpretation determines what will count as evidence for it, and the evidence is able to be picked out only because the interpretation has *already* been assumed. In this case, the evidence is evidence for a typological interpretation, and that is why it *is* evidence even if, in some sense, it is not there. Typology is a way of reading the Old Testament as a prefiguration or foreshadowing of events in the life of Christ. It is not, at least in its Protestant version, allegorical, because it insists on respecting the historical reality of the type who is unaware of his significance as an anticipation of one greater than he. In *Paradise Lost,* this significance can be pointed out by the narrator who stands outside the consciousnesses of the characters and therefore can look forward to the new dispensation without violating typological decorum. In *Samson Agonistes,* however, there is no narrator, and the consciousnesses of the characters mark the limits of allowable awareness. It follows (given a disposition to read typology) that the absence of any reference to Christ, rather than being evidence that he is not being referred to, is evidence of Milton's intention to respect typological decorum. As William Madsen puts it,

> Instead of collapsing Samson and Christ, [Milton] is concerned with measuring the distance between the various levels of awareness . . . possible to those living under the old dispensation and the level of awareness revealed by Christ.[2]

2. William Madsen, *From Shadowy Types to Truth* (New Haven and London, 1968), p. 198.

Once this characterization of Milton's intention has been specified, the text will immediately assume the shape that Madsen proceeds to describe:

> If ... Samson is viewed first of all as a concrete individual living in a concrete historical situation, then his significance for the Christian reader lies primarily in his inability to measure up to the heroic norm delineated in *Paradise Regained.*[3]

The fact that this significance is unavailable to the characters is precisely what makes it inescapable for the Christian reader. Moreover, it is not a figurative significance, one that is imposed on the text's literal level; rather it is built into the text as it is *immediately* seen by anyone who operates within Madsen's interpretive assumptions. A reader who was innocent of those assumptions would not see that significance, but he would see some other, and that other would be similarly the product of the assumptions within which *he* was operating. In either case (and in any other that could be imagined) the resulting meaning would be a *literal* one that followed directly upon a determination of what was in the text. The category "in the text" is usually thought to refer to something that is irreducibly there independently of and prior to all interpretive activities. The example of *Samson Agonistes* suggests that what is perceived to be "in the text" is a *function* of interpretive activities, although these activities are performed at so primary a level that the shapes they yield seem to be there before we have done anything. In other words, the category "in the text," like the category of the "ordinary," is always full (because there is never a point at which a set of interpretive assumptions is not in force), but what fills it is not always the same. For some readers this year, Christ is "in the text" of *Samson Agonistes,* for others he is not, and before the typological interpretation of the poem was introduced and developed by Michael Krouse in 1949, he was not "in the text" for anyone. Again, it is important to see that the question of what is in the text cannot be settled by appealing to the evidence since the evidence will have become available only because some determination of what is in the text has already been made. (Otherwise it would be impossible to read.) Indeed the same piece of evidence will not be the same

3. Ibid., pp. 201–2.

when it is cited in support of differing determinations of what is in the text. Thus for one reader the fact that Christ is not mentioned "proves" that he is not in the text, while for another the same "fact" (really not the same) proves that he is. Nor can one descend to a lower level of description and assert that at least *that* fact about the text (that Christ is not mentioned) is beyond dispute; for the two readers I posit would be stipulating two different notions of "mention," and indeed the second reader would be claiming that the mention of Samson *includes* Christ and that thus He is no less mentioned than his Old Testament prefiguration. This does not mean that the text of *Samson Agonistes* is ambiguous or unstable; it is always stable and never ambiguous. It is just that it is stable in more than one direction, as a succession of interpretive assumptions give it a succession of stable shapes. Mine is not an argument for an infinitely plural or an open text, but for a text that is always set; and yet because it is set not for all places or all times but for wherever and however long a particular way of reading is in force, it is a text that can change.

III

Perhaps a shorter example, one taken neither from the sports pages nor from literature but from (if you will pardon the expression) life, will make the point clearer. I have in mind a sign that is affixed in this unpunctuated form to the door of the John Hopkins University Club:

PRIVATE MEMBERS ONLY

I have had occasion to ask several classes what that sign means, and I have received a variety of answers, the least interesting of which is, "Only those who are secretly and not publicly members of this club may enter it." Other answers fall within a predictable and narrow range: "Only the genitalia of members may enter" (this seems redundant), or "You may only bring in your own genitalia," or (and this is the most popular reading, perhaps because of its Disney-like anthropomorphism) "Only genitalia may enter." In every class, however, some Dr. Johnson-like positivist rises to say, "But you're just playing games; everyone knows that the sign really means 'Only those persons who belong to this club may enter it.'" He is of course right. Everyone does know (although as we shall see everyone does not always know the same thing), but we can still inquire into the source of that knowledge. How is it that a text so demonstrably unstable can be stabilized to such a degree that a large number of people know immediately what it means? The answer can be found in the exercise performed by my students. What they did was move the words out of a context (the faculty club door) in which they had a literal and obvious meaning into another context (my classroom) in which the meaning was no less obvious and literal and yet was different. What they did not do was move away from a meaning that was available apart from a context to the various meanings contexts confer. Paradoxically the exercise does not prove that the words can mean anything one likes, but that they always and only mean one thing, although that one thing is not always the same. The one thing they mean will be a function of the shape language *already has* when we come upon it in a situation, and it is the knowledge that is the content of being in a situation that will have stabilized it. In the case of PRIVATE MEMBERS ONLY, the knowledge is the knowledge of what to do with signs on faculty club doors. Those who enter the club do not first perceive the sign in some uninterpreted or acontextual form and *then* construe it so as to conform with the situation; rather, being in the situation means that they have already construed it, even before they see it. That is, to know what to do with signs on faculty club doors is already to have done it because that knowledge will already have been organizing perception.

This is not to say that the knowledge of what to do with the signs on faculty club doors is itself stable, but that in whatever form it takes, it is always stabilizing. In many municipalities a business will incorporate as a club in order to secure certain tax advantages, and in some "dry" states incorporation is a way of circumventing laws that prohibit the public sale of liquor. In such situations the word "private" means "public" (it is not restrictive at all, except in the sense that any business establishment is restrictive), and the sign PRIVATE MEMBERS ONLY would be immediately understood to mean "anyone who has the price may enter." That would then be as literal a reading as "Only those persons who belong to this club may enter it" because to those whose understandings were an extension of the situation they were already in, the words could mean nothing else. It may seem confusing and even contradictory to assert that a text may have more than one literal reading, but that is because we usually reserve "literal" for the

single meaning a text will always (or should always) have, while I am
using "literal" to refer to the different single meanings a text will have
in a succession of different situations. There always is a literal meaning
because in any situation there is always a meaning that seems obvious
in the sense that it is there independently of anything we might do. *But
that only means that we have already done it,* and in another situation,
when we have already done something else, there will be another
obvious, that is, literal, meaning. The stronger sense of literal, in
which "single" is inseparable from "once and for all," would itself
make sense only if there were a meaning that was apprehensible apart
from any situation whatsoever, a meaning that was not the product of
an interpretation but available independently. Every literal meaning
comes to us with that claim, but it is a claim that seems to be support-
able only because an interpretive act is already in force but is so embedded in the situation (its structure *is* the structure of the situation)
that it doesn't seem to be an act at all. We are never not in a situation.
Because we are never not in a situation, we are never not in the act of
interpreting. Because we are never not in the act of interpreting, there
is no possibility of reaching a level of meaning beyond or below
interpretation. But in every situation some or other meaning will
appear to us to be uninterpreted because it is isomorphic with the
interpretive structure the situation (and therefore our perception) already has. Therefore, there always will be a literal reading, but (1) it
will not always be the same one, and (2) it can change.

In this newly defined sense, a literal reading can even be plural, as it
is for my students when they are asked, "What does PRIVATE MEM-
BERS ONLY mean?" Constituting *their* perception is not the knowledge
of what to do with signs on faculty club doors but the knowledge of
what to do with texts written on blackboards by professors of English
literature. That is, professors of English literature do not put things on
boards unless they are to be examples of problematic or ironic or
ambiguous language. Students know that because they know what it
means to be in a classroom, and the categories of understanding that
are the content of that knowledge will be organizing what they see
before they see it. Irony and ambiguity are not properties of language
but are functions of the expectations with which we approach it. If we
expect a text to be ambiguous, we will in the act of reading it imagine
situations in which it means first one thing and then another (there is
no text with which this cannot be done), and those plural meanings

will, in the context of that situation, be that text's literal reading. That is, in a situation in which the obvious (immediately apprehensible) reading is a plural one, meaning more than one thing will be the one thing a text means.

In summary, then, there are two things I do not want to say about PRIVATE MEMBERS ONLY: that it has a literal meaning, and that it doesn't. It does not have a literal meaning in the sense of some irreducible content which survives the sea change of situations; but in each of those situations one meaning (even if it is plural) will seem so obvious that one cannot see how it could be otherwise, and that meaning will be literal.

IV

If the question of what is literal is important in literary discussions, it is the central question in the law where determining what a text (contract, statute, case, precedent, ruling) *says* is the business everyone is in. A close examination of the way that business is conducted will reveal a pattern that should by now be familiar. My example is a case that deals with the probating of wills, *Riggs* v. *Palmer,* New York, 1889.[4] The decision is prefaced by a rehearsal of the facts: "On the thirteenth day of August, 1880, Francis B. Palmer made his last will and testament, in which he gave small legacies to his two daughters, Mrs. Riggs and Mrs. Preston, the plaintiffs in this action, and the remainder to his grandson, the defendant Elmer E. Palmer." In 1882 the elder Palmer married one Mrs. Bressee, and there was some indication that he would alter the will so as to make his new wife the principal beneficiary. It was then that Elmer acted: "He knew," says the court,

> of the provisions made in his favor . . . and that he might prevent his grandfather from revoking such provisions, which he had manifested some intention to do, and to obtain the speedy enjoyment and immediate possession of his property, he willfully murdered him by poisoning him. He now claims the property and the sole question for our determination is, Can he have it? The defendants say that the testator is dead; that his will was made in due form, and has been admitted to probate, and that, therefor it must have effect according to the letter of the law.

It is with this last phrase — "the letter of the law" — that this example

4. Riggs v. Palmer, 115 N.Y. 506, 22 N.E. 188 (1889). All further references to this text will be at 189.

falls into line with the others. Elmer's lawyers have presented the court with a dilemma: either it must decide in favor of their client or it must go against what the law plainly says. The law in this case is a statute that reads as follows:

> All persons, except idiots, persons of unsound mind and infants, may devise their real estate, by a last will and testament, duly executed, according to the provisions of this article.

In effect Elmer and his counsel are arguing that there is nothing in the statute that bars a murderer from inheriting or a victim from bequeathing his property to a murderer, and that therefore his act is irrelevant to the question of probate.

The court begins rather badly by conceding Elmer's basic claim: "It is quite true that statutes regulating the making, proof, and effect of wills, and the devolution of property, if literally construed, and if their force and effect can in no way and under no circumstances be controlled or modified, give this property to the murderer." This would be a damaging admission were it not that as the decision unfolds the court proceeds to take it back. It does this by introducing the notion of purpose and by insisting that the statute be read in its light:

> The purpose of the statutes was to enable testators to dispose all of their bounty at death . . . and in considering and giving effect to them, this purpose must be kept in view. It was the intention of the law-makers that the donees in a will should have the property given to them. But it never could have been their intention that a donee who murdererd the testator to make the will operative should have any benefit under it.

Why could it "never have been their intention"? The court answers that question by invoking as one of the "general fundamental maxims of the common law," the principle that "No one shall be permitted to profit by his own fraud, or take advantage of his own wrong, or found any claim upon his own iniquity, or to acquire property by his own crime. At this point the court's strategy becomes clear. It wants to find a way of reading the statute so that it bars Elmer from inheriting, and the way it finds is to assert that something goes without saying, (that is why it is a matter of common, i.e., unwritten, law) and therefore has been said. The reasoning is the same that yields the typological reading of *Samson Agonistes:* just as the mention of Samson is understood to include a reference to Christ, so is the text of a statute understood (at least under this interpretive assumption) to include a proviso disallowing any claim founded upon the commission of a wrong.

It is a very good argument, and the court errs only in thinking that in order to make it, the literal reading must be set aside. That is, the court apparently believes that only *it* is reading the statute with "a purpose in view" while the defendant is urging a reading of what the words literally express. The truth of the matter is that both are pointing to what the words literally express but in the light of two different purposes. The opposition between a literal and a nonliteral reading could be maintained only if it were possible to conceive of a reading that did not follow from the assumption of some purpose or other, but as Kenneth Abraham observes,

> A statute without a purpose would be meaningless. . . . To speak of the literal meaning of a statute . . . is already to have read it in the light of some purpose, to have engaged in an interpretation.[5]

In other words, any reading that is plain and obvious in the light of some assumed purpose (and it is impossible not to assume one) is a literal reading; but no reading is *the* literal reading in the sense that it is available apart from any purpose whatsoever. If it is assumed that the purpose of probate is to ensure the orderly devolution of property at all costs, then the statute in this case will have the plain meaning urged by the defendant; but if it is assumed that no law ever operates in favor of someone who would profit by his crime, then the "same" statute will have a meaning that is different, but no less plain. In either case the statute will have been literally construed, and what the court will have done is prefer one literal construction to another by invoking one purpose (assumed background) rather than another. It is not that we first read the statute and then know its purpose; we know the purpose first and only then can the statute be read. This is exactly the sequence the court follows, and at one point the principle underlying its procedure is articulated:

> It is a familiar canon of construction that a thing which is within the intention of the makers of a statute is as much within the statute as if it were within the letter; and a thing which is within the letter of the statute is not within the statute, unless it be within the intention of the makers.

5. Kenneth Abraham, "Intention and Authority in Statutory Interpretation" (an unpublished paper).

The rhetoric of this sentence insists upon the distinction between what is intended and what is literally there, but the argument of the sentence takes the distinction away. It is your specification of the makers' intention that tells you what is in the statute, not your literal reading of the statute that informs you as to it makers' intention. This would seem to suggest that one need only recover the makers' intention in order to arrive at the *correct* literal reading; but the documents (including even *verbatim* reports) that would give us that intention are no more available to a literal reading (are no more interpreted) than the literal reading it would yield. However, one specifies what is in a statute — whether by some theory of strict constructionism or by some construction of an original intention — that specification will have the same status as the specification of what is in *Samson Agonistes* or what PRIVATE MEMBERS ONLY means. It can always be made, but as situations and the purposes which inform them change, it will have to be made again.

V

I could imagine someone objecting to the previous pages in the following way: "Aren't you in each of these examples simply talking about ambiguous language, language that can mean more than one thing?" My answer is that the objection would have force only if there were a kind of language to which ambiguous language could be opposed. That is, to label a sentence "ambiguous" will be to distinguish it only if there are sentences that always and only mean one thing, and I would contend that there are no such sentences. I am not saying that sentences always have more than one meaning, but that the sentence which is perceived as having only one meaning will not always have the same one. In other words, I am as willing to say that all sentences are straightforward as I am to say that all sentences are ambiguous. What I am not willing to do is say that any sentence is by right either one or the other. That is, I wish to deny that ambiguity is a property of some sentences and not of others.

Typically, the division of sentences into two classes (ambiguous, nonambiguous) is not defended; it is simply assumed in the course of presenting strings that are asserted to be obviously members of one or the other class. In a recent introduction to transformational grammar the following sentence is offered as an example of one that is ambiguous on its face: "The suit is light."[6] As the authors point out, the reference can be either to the suit's weight or its color, and the situation is not helped, they observe, when the sentence is expanded to read: "The suit is too light to wear." The additional material is not sufficiently disambiguating because the words do not combine in such a way as to make one reading inescapable; but when the sentence is further expanded to read "The suit is too light to wear on such a cold day," the ambiguity, we are told, disappears. In the new sentence, the "semantic environment" specified by "cold day" blocks one of the possible readings of "light," and the result is a perfectly straightforward utterance.

It is an elegant argument, but unfortunately it won't work. It takes only a moment of reflection to imagine a situation in which this sentence would have the reading that is now supposedly blocked. It so happens that I have a weakness for light-colored suits, and I have several that are heavy enough to wear on a cold day. My wife, however, is more conscious of the proprieties of fashion than I am and is likely to say to me, "That suit is too light to wear on such a cold day," and be immediately understood as meaning that the suit is too light in color. M. F. Garrett offers a similar counterexample to a supposedly unambiguous sentence put forward by Jerrold J. Katz and Paul M. Postal: "The stuff is light enough to carry." It is not ambiguous, Katz and Postal say, because "light enough to carry" cannot be understood to mean "light enough in color to be carried." But, objects Garrett, "it does not take an especially tortured context to make this the preferred reading:

> Scene: Highway patrolman lecturing to 3rd grade class.
> Patrolman: "When you are walking on a highway at night, it is important to wear light-colored clothing or carry a light-colored flag so that you will be visible to oncoming cars. For instance (holds up flag), this stuff is light enough to carry."[7]

Katz and Postal might reply that what the counterexample shows is

---

6. John T. Grinder and Suzette Haden Elgin, *Guide to Transformational Grammar* (New York, 1973), p. 117.

7. M. F. Garrett, "Does Ambiguity Complicate the Perception of Sentences?" in *Advances in Psycholinguistics,* edited by G. B. Flores d'Arcias and W. J. M. Levelt (New York, 1970), p. 54.

that the original sentence was not sufficiently explicit. If we were to add more information to it and write (let us say) "This stuff is light enough to carry even for a small child," it will be capable of one reading and of no other. But if this sentence were uttered by a manufacturer's representative, the word "carry" would be understood to mean "stock in inventory," and the speaker would be reminding a potential buyer that small children do not normally wear the darker colors. One could imagine counterexample following upon counterexample, but the result would always be the same; for no degree of explicitness will ever be sufficient to disambiguate the sentence if by disambiguate we understand *render it impossible to conceive of a set of circumstances in which its plain meaning would be other than it now appears to be.*

The conclusion that Garrett draws from this and other examples is that all sentences are ambiguous, but then he is faced with the problem of explaining the fact that "we simply don't notice most of the ambiguities we encounter."[8] It is a problem because Garrett has moved away from one version of an error only to embrace another. He correctly sees that no sentence always means the same thing, but this leads him to affirm that every sentence has more than one meaning. What he does not realize is that these positions are the same position in that they both assume a stage in the life of sentences *before* they are perceived in a context. It is just that in one position that stage is characterized by timeless stability (means only one thing), in the other by a timeless instability (means more than one thing). The truth is that there is no such stage. A sentence is never apprehended independently of the context in which it is perceived, and therefore we never know a sentence except in the stabilized form a context has *already* conferred. But since a sentence can appear in more than one context, its stabilized form will not always be the same. It follows then that while no sentence is ambiguous in the sense that it has (as a constitutive property) more than one meaning, every sentence is ambiguous in the (undistinguishing) sense that the single meaning it will always have can change. Now, it is sometimes the case that we are asked to imagine first one and then another context in which a sentence will have different single meanings. In that case, we are in a *third* context in which the single meaning the sentence has is that it has more than one single meaning.

8. Ibid., p. 50.

The insight which makes perfect sense of the apparent paradoxes is firmly articulated by Garrett: "We must, I believe, always assume that any sentence is interpreted with respect to some context."[9] Garrett then immediately demonstrates how easy it is to slip away from that insight by declaring that if "a sentence is ambiguous, it is the context which determines what reading will be assigned." In the interval of a typographical space, the contextless utterance has been revived, since, presumably, no context at all has determined that the sentence is ambiguous in the first place. But by Garrett's own axiom, there is no "first place" in the sense of a state in which the natural (acontextual) properties of a sentence can be observed and enumerated. In order for the sentence to be perceived as ambiguous (or to be perceived at all), it must already be in a context, and that context, rather than any natural property, will be responsible for the ambiguity the sentence will then (in a limited sense) have.

VI

A sentence is never not in a context. We are never not in a situation. As statute is never not read in the light of some purpose. A set of interpretive assumptions is always in force. A sentence that seems to need no interpretation is already the product of one. These statements have made my single point from a variety of perspectives, and I am about to make it again with another statement. No sentence is ever apprehended independently of some or other illocutionary force. Illocutionary force is the key term in speech-act theory. It refers to the way an utterance is taken—as an order, a warning, a promise, a proposal, a request and so forth—and the theory's strongest assertion is that no utterance is ever taken purely, that is, without already having been understood as the performance of some illocutionary act. Consider, as an example, the sentence "I will go." Depending on the context in which it is uttered, "I will go" can be understood as a promise, a threat, a warning, a report, a prediction, and so forth, but it will always be understood as one of these, and it will never be an unsituated kernel of pure semantic value. In other words, "I will go" does not have a basic or primary meaning which is then put to various illocutionary uses; rather, "I will go" is known only in its illocutionary

9. Ibid, p. 51.

lives, and in each of them its meaning will be different. Moreover, if the meaning of a sentence is a function of its illocutionary force (the way it is taken), and if illocutionary force varies with circumstances, then illocutionary force is a property not of sentences but of situations. That is, while a sentence will always have an illocutionary force (because otherwise it would not have a meaning), the illocutionary force it has will not always be the same.

My authority for much of the preceding paragraph is John Searle, and therefore it is surprising to find that Searle, along with other speech-act theorists, is committed to a distinction between direct and indirect speech acts. A direct speech act is defined as one whose illocutionary force is a function of its meaning, and the best example of a direct speech act would be an explicit performative, that is, "I promise to pay you five dollars." An indirect speech act is one whose illocutionary force is something other than its literal meaning would suggest. "Can you reach the salt?" is literally a question about the hearer's abilities, but in normal circumstances it is heard as a request. The distinction then is between utterances that mean exactly what they say and utterances that mean something different or additional. As Searle puts it, "in indirect speech acts the speaker communicates to the hearer more than he actually says by way of relying on their mutually shared background information . . . together with the general powers of rationality and inference on the part of the hearer."[10] This assumes, of course, that in the performance of direct speech acts speaker and hearer do *not* rely on their mutually shared background information because what is actually said is available directly (hence the distinction). It is with this assumption that I should like to quarrel, if only because it reinstates what John Austin in *How to Do Things with Words* was at such pains to dislodge, a class of utterances (constructive utterances) that mean independently of situations, purposes, and goals. It seems to me that *all* utterances are understood by way of relying on "shared background information" and that therefore the distinction between direct and indirect speech acts, as it is usually formulated, will not hold.

What I have to show then is that the acts cited as direct are, in fact, indirect, at least according to the theory's definition of the terms. My

10. John R. Searle, *"Indirect Speech Acts,"* in *Syntax and Semantics Volume 3: Speech Acts,* edited by Roger Cole et al. (New York, 1975), pp. 60–61.

argument will take up Searle's as it appears in his first full example. Searle begins by imagining a conversation between two students. Student X says, "Let's go to the movies tonight," and student Y replies, "I have to study for an exam." The first sentence, Searle declares, "constitues a proposal in virtue of its meaning," but the second sentence, which is understood as a rejection of the proposal, is not so understood in virtue of its meaning because "in virtue of its meaning it is simply a statement about Y."[11] It is here, in the assertion that either of these sentences is ever taken in the way it is "in virtue of its meaning," that this account must finally be attacked. For if this were the case, then we would have to say that there is something about the meaning of a sentence that makes it more available for some illocutionary uses than for others, and this is precisely what Searle proceeds to say about "I have to study for an exam":

> Statements of this form do not, in general, constitute rejections of proposals, even in cases in which they are made in response to a proposal. Thus, if Y had said *I have to eat popcorn tonight* or *I have to tie my shoes* in a normal context, neither of these utterances would have been a rejection of the proposal.[12]

At this point my question would be "Normal for whom?" Or, to put it another way: Is it possible to imagine a set of circumstances in which "I have to eat popcorn tonight" would immediately and without any chain of inference be heard as a rejection of X's proposal? It is not only possible; it is easy. Let us suppose that student Y is passionately fond of popcorn and that it is not available in any of the local movie theaters. If student X knows these facts (if he and student Y mutually share background information), then he will hear "I have to eat popcorn tonight" as a rejection of his proposal. Or, let us suppose that student Y is by profession a popcorn taster; that is, he works in a popcorn manufacturing plant and is responsible for quality control. Again if student X knows this, he will hear "I have to eat popcorn tonight" as a rejection of his proposal because it will mean "sorry, I have to work." Or, let us suppose that student Y owns seventy-five pairs of shoes and that he has been ordered by a dormitory housemother to retrieve them from various corners, arrange them neatly in one place, and tie them together in pairs so that they

11. Ibid., pp. 61, 62.   12. Ibid., p. 62.

will not again be separated and scattered. In such a situation "I have to tie my shoes" will constitute a rejection of student X's proposal and will be so heard. Moreover it is not just "I have to eat popcorn" and "I have to tie my shoes" that could be heard as a rejection of the proposal; given the appropriate circumstances *any* sentence ("The Russians are coming," "My pen is blue," "Why do you behave like that?") could be so heard. This does not mean that any sentence is potentially a proposal (that would be the mistake of ascribing properties to sentences) or that it doesn't matter what sentence a speaker utters; it means that for any sentence circumstances could be imagined in which it would be understood as a proposal, and as nothing but a proposal.

The objection to these examples (which could easily be multiplied) is obvious: they have reference to *special* contexts, while Searle is talking about what sentences mean in a *normal* context. But for those who are in the contexts I describe, the meanings I specify would be the normal ones because they would be the only ones. Searle's argument will hold only if the category "normal" is transcendental, if what fills it is always the same, whatever the circumstances. But what is normal (like what is ordinary, literal, everyday) is a *function* of circumstances in that it depends on the expectations and assumptions that happen to be in force. Any other sense of normal would require that the circumstances be not circumstantial but essential (always in force), and that would be a contradiction in terms. In other words, "normal" is context specific and to speak of a normal context is to be either redundant (because whatever in a given context goes without saying *is* the normal) or incoherent (because it would refer to a context whose claim was not to be one).

In short, I am making the same argument for "normal context" that I have made for "literal meaning," "straightforward discourse," "the letter of the law," and the category of what is "in the text." There will always be a normal context, but it will not always be the same one. This means that if it becomes possible to see how "I have to eat popcorn" could be heard as a rejection of a proposal, it is not because we have imagined a set of special circumstances, but because we have imagined an appropriate set of normal circumstances. The point can just as well be made from the opposite direction. Having to study for an exam is no more normal (in the sense that it is a state of which everyone has an implicit knowledge) than having to eat popcorn is special (in the sense that it is a departure from what everyone normally does). To be in either situation is to have already organized the world in terms of certain categories and possibilities for action (both verbal and physical), and in either situation the world so organized, along with the activities that can transpire within it, will be perceived as normal. Once again the moral is clear, even though it has the form of a paradox: a normal context is just the special context you happen to be in, although it will not be recognized as special because so long as you are in it whatever it permits you to see will seem obvious and inescapable.

From this perspective, Searle's argument falls apart. This first example, as he presents it, is intended to distinguish between (1) "I have to study for an exam" when it is "simply a statement about Y"; that is, when it means what it says and is therefore a direct speech act; (2) "I have to study for an exam" when it is a rejection of Y's proposal; that is, when by virtue of shared background information it means more than it says and is an indirect speech act; and (3) "I have to eat popcorn tonight" which cannot be a rejection of the proposal "without some special stage setting." If what I have been saying is true, these distinctions cannot be maintained (at least as they are here formulated) because given different sets of special or differently normal circumstances, the three speech acts are equally direct or indirect. They are direct because in each case the illocutionary force they have will be immediately perceived; and they are indirect because their immediately perceived illocutionary force will have been a function of mutually shared background information (that is, of some or other special stage setting). The trick is to see that when Searle moves from "I have to study for an exam" as a statement about Y to "I have to study for an exam" as a rejection of a proposal, he has moved not from a literal meaning to a meaning that emerges in a set of circumstances, but from one meaning that emerges in a set of circumstances to another meaning that emerges in another set of circumstances. Both meanings are then equally circumstantial (indirect) and equally literal (direct), and in both cases the utterance means exactly what it says because what it says is a function of shared background information.

The argument will also hold for "Let's go to the movies tonight," although, for reasons that will become clear, it is harder to make. Here what has to be shown is the reverse of what had to be shown in the case of "I have to eat popcorn." Rather than having to imagine a situation in which an utterance ("I have to eat popcorn") could possibly count as the performance of a certain speech act, we have to imagine a situation in which an utterance ("Let's go to the movies tonight") could count as something other than the performance of a certain speech act. The problem is that the examples that first come to mind make Searle's point rather than mine. That is, they are examples in which the perceived illocutionary force is perceived only because a "more normal" illocutionary force is seen to be inappropriate. Thus if speaker X and Y are trapped in some wilderness, and one says to the other, "Let's go to the movies tonight," it will be heard not as a proposal, but as a joke; or if student X is confined to his bed or otherwise immobilized, and student Y says, "Let's go to the movies tonight," it will be heard not as a proposal, but as a dare. But in either case the dare or joke will be heard *only* because the circumstances rule out the possibility of a proposal, a possibility whose absence (and therefore whose presence) must be recognized for the effect to be secured. What we need are examples in which "Let's go to the movies tonight" is heard immediately as a dare or a joke (or as anything but a proposal) and which do not involve the two-stage inferential procedure specified by Searle. And what we need too is an explanation of why such examples are relatively difficult to come by; that is, why it is so much harder to think oneself *out of* a necessary association between "Let's go to the movies tonight" and a proposal than it is to think oneself *into* a necessary association between "I have to eat popcorn" and the proposal's rejection.

First of all, Searle's analysis depends on the assumption of a generalized relationship between the use of "let's" and the performing of a proposal: "In general, literature utterances of this form will constitute a proposal, as in . . . 'Let's eat pizza tonight.' "[13] But in this very same paragraph Searle provides an example of an exception of his own generalization when he says, "Let us begin by considering a typical case. . . ." In the context of his discourse, it is not really open to a reader (or, in the case of a lecture, to a hearer) to suggest another beginning or to counterpropose that he not begin at all. Moreover, a hearer who responded in either of these ways would be thought to have misunderstood the illocutionary force of "Let us," which is here not so much a proposal as it is the laying down of a plan. Similarly, when a quarterback leads his team out of the huddle by saying "Let's

13. Ibid., pp. 61–62.

do it" or "Let's go," he is not proposing, but exhorting. It would be inappropriate for one of his linemen to answer "I have to study for an exam" or even to answer at all, just as it would be inappropriate if a member of a congregation were to demur when the minister said (here he would be announcing, not proposing) "Let us pray."

In each of these cases, "let's" does not introduce a proposal, because in the situation as it is imagined the speaker is understood to be concluding or forestalling an exchange rather than initiating one. Notice that in Searle's example the understanding is exactly the reverse: "Let's go to the movies tonight" is assumed to be the first utterance in an exchange that has no antecedents, and that is why it is heard as a proposal. Placed differently, at the end rather than at the beginning of a conversation, the same utterance would be heard as an assent to a proposal that had already been made. (It would be equivalent to "OK, let's go to the movies tonight.") The point is that neither placement is intrinsically the more natural or normal one, and that the stage has to be set no less for "Let's go to the movies tonight" to be heard as a proposal than for "I have to eat popcorn" to be heard as its rejection.

Why then does Searle spend so little time setting that stage in relation to the time that I must spend to dismantle it? The answer is that it is already set for him by the habitual (not inevitable) practices of an entire society, and that he need do nothing more than assume those practices in order to secure the benefit of their continuing operation. When someone is asked to assign an illocutionary force to an utterance, he does so in the context of the circumstances in which that utterance has been most often heard or spoken. For most of us those circumstances are the ones presupposed by Searle, and therefore it appears that the relationship between "Let's go to the movies tonight" and its stipulated force is natural when, in fact, it is a function of a context so widely shared that it doesn't seem to be one at all. It is just such contexts that produce the felt continuity of life by allowing us to rely on and assume as normative the meanings they make available; and it is because Searle invokes such a context (by failing to realize or point out that it is one) that so much effort is required to see around his example.

In a sense, then, the circumstances that lead us to assign the force of a proposal to "Let's go to the movies tonight" *are* normal in that they occur more frequently than do circumstances that would lead to a different assignment. But they remain circumstances still (statistically, not inherently, normal), and because they do, the main assertion of this section is intact: there is no distinction between direct and indirect speech acts because all speech acts are understood by way of relying on mutually shared background information. All speech acts are direct because their meanings are directly apprehended, and all speech acts are indirect because their directly apprehended meanings are functions of the situations in which they are embedded.

It is important to realize what my argument does *not* mean. It does not mean that a sentence can mean anything at all. In their discussion of indirect speech acts Herbert and Eve Clark point out that "under the right circumstances" any one of a number of sentences could be "used as a request to open the window; yet," they warn, "not just any sentence can serve this purpose," for "if so, communication would be chaotic" because "listeners would never know what speech act was being performed."[14] But the chaos the Clarks fear would be possible only if a sentence could mean anything at all *in the abstract*. A sentence, however, is never in the abstract; it is always in a situation, and the situation will already have determined the purpose for which it can be used. So it is not that any sentence can be used as a request to open the window, but that given any sentence, there are circumstances under which it would be heard as a request to open the window. A sentence neither means anything at all nor does it always mean the same thing; it always has the meaning that has been conferred on it by the situation in which it is uttered. Listeners *always* know what speech act is being performed, not because there are limits to the illocutionary uses to which sentences can be put, but because in any set of circumstances the illocutionary force a sentence may have will already have been determined.

The Clarks can stand for all those who think that it is necessary to anchor language in some set of independent and formal constraints, whether those constraints are given the name of literal meaning, or straightforward discourse, or direct speech acts, or the letter of the law, or normal circumstances, or the everyday world. The question

14. Herbert H. Clark and Eve V. Clark, *Psychology and Language* (New York, 1977), pp. 121–122.

that is always being asked is "Are there such constraints and, if so, how can we identify them?" Behind that question, however, is the assumption that the constraints must be specifiable once and for all, and that if they are not so specifiable at *some* level, we live in a world of chaos where communication is entirely a matter of chance. What I have been saying again and again is that there are such constraints; they inhere, however, not in language but in situations, and because they inhere in situations, the constraints we are always under are not always the same ones. Thus we can see how it is neither the case that meanings are objectively fixed nor that the meanings one construes are arbitrary. To many these have seemed the only alternatives, and that is why the claims for objectivity and subjectivity have been continually debated. It is because the position elaborated here is neither subjective nor objective (nor a combining of the two) that it can reconcile the two facts cited again and again by the respective combatants: (1) that there are no inherent constraints on the meanings a sentence may have, and (2) that, nevertheless, agreement is not only possible, but commonplace.

VII

It may interest you to know that, after hitting two home runs in a single game, Pat Kelly went on to hit three more in the same week, thus equaling his entire total for 1976. At the end of the week a teammate was heard to say, "Maybe there's something in that religion stuff after all."

Chapter Eight

The Relations Between History and History of Science

THOMAS S. KUHN

The invitation to write this essay asks that I address myself to the relations between my own field and other sorts of history. "For several decades," it points out, "the history of science has seemed a discipline apart with only very tenuous links with other kinds of historical study." That generalization, which errs only in supposing that the separation is but a few decades old, isolates a problem with which I have struggled, both intellectually and emotionally, since I first began to teach the history of science, twenty years ago. My colleagues and my students are no less aware of it than I, and its existence does much to determine both the scale and the direction of our discipline's development. Strangely enough, however, though we repeatedly gnaw at it among ourselves, no one has previously made the problem a matter for public scrutiny and discussion. The opportunity to do so here is correspondingly welcome. Historians of science, if they must act alone, are unlikely to succeed in resolving the central dilemma of their field.

That perception of my assignment determines my approach. My topic is one I have lived with rather than studied. The data I bring to its analysis are correspondingly personal and impressionistic rather than systematic, with the result, among others, that I shall consider

Reprinted by permission of *Daedalus,* the Journal of the American Academy of Arts and Sciences, Boston, Massachusetts, vol. 100, no. 2 (Spring 1971).

only the situation in the United States. Partisanship I shall try to avoid, but without hope of entire success, for I take up the subject as an advocate, a man much concerned with some central impediments to the development and exploitation of his special field.

Despite the universal lip service paid by historians to the special role of science in the development of Western culture during the past four centuries, history of science is for most of them still foreign territory. In many cases, perhaps in most, such resistance to foreign travel does no obvious harm, for scientific development has little apparent relevance to many of the central problems of modern Western history. But men who consider socioeconomic development or who discuss changes in values, attitudes, and ideas have regularly adverted to the sciences and most presumably continue to do so. Even they, however, regularly observe science from afar, balking at the border which would give access to the terrain and the natives they discuss. That resistance is damaging, both to their own work and to the development of history of science.

To identify the problem more clearly, I shall begin this essay by mapping the border which has heretofore separated the traditional fields of historical studies from history of science. Conceding that part of the separation is due simply to the intrinsic technicality of science, I shall next try to isolate and to examine the consequences of the still substantial division which will need to be explained in other ways. Seeking such explanations, I shall first discuss some aspects of a traditional historiography of science that have characteristically repelled and sometimes also misled historians. Since that tradition has, however, been largely out of date for a quarter of a century, it cannot entirely explain the historians' contemporary stance. Fuller understanding must depend as well upon an examination of selected aspects of the traditional structure and ideology of the historical profession, topics to be examined briefly in the penultimate sections below. To me, at least, the more sociological sources of division there discussed seem central, and it is hard to see how they are to be entirely overcome. Nevertheless, I shall consider in closing a few recent developments, primarily within my own discipline, which suggest that an at least partial rapprochement may characterize the decade immediately ahead.

I

What does one have in mind when speaking of history of science as "a discipline apart"? Partly that almost no students of history pay any attention to it. Since 1956 my own courses in history of science have regularly been listed among history courses under the masthead of the department of which I was a member. Yet in those courses only about one student in twenty has been an undergraduate history major or a graduate student of history, excepting history of science. The majority of those enrolled have regularly been scientists or engineers. Among the remainder, philosophers and social scientists outnumber historians, and students of literature are not far behind. Again, in both of the history departments to which I have belonged, a history-of-science area has been an available minor-field option for historians taking graduate general examinations. I think, however, of only five students who have elected it in fourteen years, a particular misfortune because these examinations provide an especially effective route to rapprochement. For some time I feared that the fault was my own, since my training was in physics rather than history and my teaching probably embodies residues. But all the colleagues to whom I have bemoaned the situation, many of them trained as historians, report identical experiences. Furthermore, the subject they teach appears not to matter. Courses on the Scientific Revolution or on Science in the French Revolution seem no more attractive to prospective historians than courses on the Development of Modern Physics. Apparently the word "science" in a title is sufficient to turn students of history away.

Those phenomena have a corollary which is equally revealing. Though history of science remains a small field, it has expanded more than tenfold in the last fifteen years, especially during the last eight. Most new members of the discipline are placed in history departments, which is, I shall later urge, where they belong. But the pressure to employ them almost always comes from outside rather than from within the department to which they are ultimately attached. Usually the initiative is taken by scientists or philosophers who must persuade the university administration to add a new slot in history. Only after that condition is met may a historian of science be appointed. Thereafter, he is usually treated with complete cordiality within his new department; no group has received me more warmly nor supplied me with more of my close friends than my history colleagues. Nevertheless, in subtle ways the historian of science is sometimes asked to maintain intellectual distance. I have, for example, occasionally had to defend the work of a colleague or student from a historian's charge that it was not really history of science at all but just history. In ways that are obscure, and perhaps correspondingly important, a historian of science is expected, occasionally even by older historians of science, to be not quite a historian.

The preceding remarks are directed to the social indices of separatism. Look now at some of its pedagogic and intellectual consequences. These seem to be primarily of two sorts, neither of which can be considered in much detail until I discuss, below, the extent to which they are merely the inevitable results of the intrinsic technicality of scientific source materials. Even a sketchy description at this point will, however, point the direction of my argument.

One overall consequence of separatism has, I think, been the abdication by historians of responsibility for evaluating and portraying the role of science in the development of Western culture since the end of the Middle Ages. To those tasks the historian of science can and must make essential contributions, at least by providing the books, monographs, and articles which will be the main sources for other sorts of historians. But insofar as his first commitment is to his specialty, the student of scientific development is no more responsible for the task of integration than the historian of ideas or of socioeconomic development, and he has generally been less well equipped than they to perform it. What is needed is a critical interpenetration of the concerns and achievements of historians of science with those of men tilling certain other historical fields, and such interpenetration, if it has occurred at all, is not evident in the work of most current historians. The usual global acknowledgments that science has somehow been vastly important to the development of modern Western society provide no substitute. Taken in conjunction with the few traditional examples used to illustrate them, they often exaggerate and regularly distort the nature, extent, and timing of the role of the sciences.

Surveys of the development of Western civilization illustrate the main consequences of the failure to interpenetrate. Perhaps the most striking of these is the almost total neglect of scientific development since 1750, the period during which science assumed its main role as a historical prime mover. A chapter on the Industrial Revolution — the relation of which to science is at once interesting, obscure, and undiscussed — is sometimes succeeded by a section on Darwinism, mostly social. Often that is all! The overwhelming majority of the space devoted to science in all but a very few general history books is reserved for the years before 1750, an imbalance with disastrous consequences to which I shall return in section III below.[1]

Neglect of science, though less extreme, used also to characterize discussions of European history in the years before 1750. With respect to space allocation, however, that oversight has been generously rectified since the appearance in 1949 of Herbert Butterfield's admirable *Origins of Modern Science*. By now almost all surveys have come to include a chapter or major section on the Scientific Revolution of the sixteenth and seventeenth centuries. But those chapters often fail to recognize, much less to confront, the principal historiographic novelty which Butterfield discovered in the current specialists' literature and made available to a wider audience — the relatively minor role played by new experimental methods in the substantive changes of scientific theory during the Scientific Revolution. They are still dominated by old myths about the role of method, to the consequences of which I shall return below.[2]

Perhaps it is some sense of that inadequacy which often makes historians reluctant to give lectures accompanying the reading on the birth of modern science. Occasionally, if unable to co-opt a historian of science to fill the gap, they simply assign chapters in Butterfield as a supplement and reserve discussion for section meetings. Butterfield or the bomb has persuaded historians that they must take some account

---

1. Roger Hahn persuades me that a few very recent textbooks show signs of change. Perhaps I am *merely* impatient. But the progress of the last half-dozen years, if it is real, still seems to me belated, scattered, and incomplete. Why, for example, has J. H. Randall's *Making of the Modern Mind,* a book first published in 1926 and long out of date, yet to be surpassed as a balanced survey of science's role in the development of Western thought?

2. One aspect of Butterfield's discussion has, in fact helped to preserve the myths. The historiographic novelties accessible through his book are concentrated in chaps. 1, 2, and 4, which deal with the development of astronomy and mechanics. These are, however, juxtaposed with essentially traditional accounts of the methodological views of Bacon and Descartes, illustrated in application by a chapter on William Harvey. The two resulting versions of the requisites for a transformed science are hard to reconcile, a fact which Butterfield's subsequent discussion of the Chemical Revolution makes particularly apparent.

of science's role, and they attempt to discharge that obligation with a block of material on the Scientific Revolution. But the chapters they then produce seldom reflect an awareness of the problems with which their subject has confronted recent generations of academic specialists. Students must usually look elsewhere for examples of the critical standards ordinarily defended by the profession.

Neglect of the current specialists' literature is, however, only one part of the problem and perhaps not the most serious. More central is the peculiar selectivity with which historians approach the sciences, whether through primary or secondary sources. Dealing with, say, music or the arts, the historian may read program notes and the catalogues of exhibits, but he also listens to symphonies and looks at paintings, and his discussion, whatever its sources, is directed to them. Dealing with the sciences, however, he reads *and discusses* programmatic works almost exclusively: Bacon's *Novum Organum,* but usually Book I (the Idols) rather than Book II (heat as motion); Descartes' *Discourse on Method,* but not the three substantive essays to which it provides the introduction; Galileo's *Assayer,* but only the introductory pages of his *Two New Sciences*; and so on. The same selectivity shows in the historian's attention to secondary works: Alexandre Koyré's *From the Closed World to the Infinite Universe*, but not his *Études galiléennes* or *The Problem of Fall*; E. A. Burtt's *Metaphysical Foundations of Modern Physical Science*, but not E. J. Dijksterhuis' magistral *Mechanization of the World Picture*.[3] Even within individual works there is a marked tendency, which I shall illustrate below, to skip the chapters that deal with technical contributions.

I do not suggest that what scientists say about what they do is irrelevant to their performance and their concrete achievements. Nor am I suggesting that historians ought not read and discuss pro-

3. The following observation may strengthen the point at which I aim. In the arts the men who create and those who criticize belong to separate, often hostile, groups. Historians may sometimes rely excessively on the latter, but they know the difference between critics and artists, and they are careful to acquaint themselves with works of art as well. In the sciences, on the other hand, the nearest equivalents to the works of critics are written by scientists themselves, usually in prefatory chapters or separate essays. Historians usually rely *exclusively* on these works of "criticism," failing to note, because their authors were also creative scientists, that the selection leaves the science out. On the significance of the different role of the critic in science and in art, see my "Comment [on the Relation of Science and Art]," in *Comparative Studies in Society and History* 11 (1969): 403–412.

grammatic works. But, as the parallel to program notes should indicate, the relation of prefaces and programmatic writings to substantive science is seldom literal and always problematic. The former must, of course, be read, for they are frequently the media through which scientific ideas reach a larger public. But they are often decisively misleading with respect to a whole series of issues that the historian ought, and often pretends, to deal with: Where do influential scientific ideas come from? What gives them their special authority and appeal? To what extent do they remain the same ideas as they become effective in the larger culture? And, finally, if their influence is not literal, in what sense is it really due to the science to which it is imputed?[4] The intellectual impact of the sciences on extrascientific thought will not, in short, be understood without attention also to the sciences' technical core. That historians regularly attempt such a sleight of hand suggests that one essential part of what has to this point been described as a gap between history and history of science might more accurately be seen as a barrier between historians as a group and the sciences. To that point, also, I shall return more concretely below.

II

Before looking more closely at the manner in which historians approach the sciences, I must, however, ask how much may reasonably be expected of them. That question, in turn, demands a sharp separation between the problems of intellectual history, on the one hand, and those of socioeconomic history, on the other. Let me consider them in order.

Intellectual history is the area in which the historian's selectivity with respect to sources has its primary effect, and one may well wonder whether he has an alternative. Excepting historians of science, among whom the requisite skills are also relatively rare, almost no historians have the training required to read, say, the works of Euler and Lagrange, Maxwell and Boltzmann, or Einstein and Bohr. But that is a very special list in several respects. All the men on it are mathematical physicists; the oldest of them was not born until the first

4. For an example of the sort of illumination that can be provided by someone who knows the science and its history, see the discussion of science's role in the Enlightenment by C. C. Gillispie, *The Edge of Objectivity* (Princeton: Princeton University Press, 1960), chap. 5.

decade of the eighteenth century; and none of them, so far as I can see, has had more than the most tenuous and indirect impact upon the development of extrascientific thought.

The last point, which is the crucial one, may be debatable and ultimately wrong with respect to Einstein and Bohr. Discussions of the contemporary intellectual scene often refer to relativity and the quantum theory when discussing such issues as the limitations of science and of reason. Yet the argument for direct influence—as against the appeal to authority in support of views held for other reasons—have so far been extremely forced. My own suspicion, which provides at least a reasonable working hypothesis, is that after a science has become thoroughly technical, particularly mathematically technical, its role as a force in intellectual history becomes relatively insignificant. Probably there are occasional exceptions, but if Einstein and Bohr provide them, then the exceptions prove the rule. Whatever their role may have been, it is very different from that of, say, Galileo, or Descartes, of Lyell, Playfair, or Darwin, or, for that matter, of Freud, all of whom were read by laymen. If the intellectual historian must consider scientists, they are generally the early figures in the development of their fields.

Not surprisingly, just because the figures he must treat are the early ones, the intellectual historian could handle them in depth if he wished to do so. The job would not be easy: I am not arguing that no significant effort is required—only that there is no other way. Nor would every historian be responsible for undertaking it regardless of his interests. But the man whose concerns include ideas affected by scientific development could study the technical scientific source materials to which he currently only makes reference. Very little of the technical literature written before 1700 is in principle inaccessible to anyone with sound high school scientific training, at least not if he is willing to undertake a modicum of additional work as he goes along. For the eighteenth century the same background in science is adequate to the literature of chemistry, experimental physics (particularly electicity, optics, and heat), geology, and biology—all of science, in short, excepting mathematical mechanics and astronomy. For the nineteenth century most of physics and much of chemistry becomes excessively technical, but men with high school science have access to almost the whole literature of geology, biology, and psychology. I do not suggest that the historian should become a historian of science whenever scientific development becomes relevant to the topic he studies. Here, as elsewhere, specialization is inevitable. But he could in principle do so, and he can therefore certainly command the specialists' secondary literature on his topic. By failing to do even that, he ignores constitutive elements and problems of scientific advance, and the result, as I shall shortly indicate, shows in his work.

The preceding list of topics potentially accessible to the intellectual historian is revealing in two respects. First, as already indicated, it includes all the technical subject matters with which, *qua* intellectual historian, he is likely to wish to deal. Second, it is coextensive with the list of fields which have been most and best discussed by historians of science. Contrary to a widespread impression, historians of science have seldom dealt in depth with the development of the technically most advanced subjects. Studies of the history of mechanics are sparse from the eve of the publication of Newton's *Principia*; histories of electricity break off with Franklin or at most with Charles Coulomb; of chemistry with Antoine Lavoisier or John Dalton; and so on. The main exceptions, though not the only ones, are Whiggish compendia by scientists, sometimes invaluable as reference works, but otherwise virtually useless to the man whose interests include the development of ideas. However regrettable, that imbalance in favor of relatively nontechnical subjects should surprise no one. Most of the men who have produced the models which contemporary historians of science aim to emulate have not been scientists nor have they had much scientific training. Interestingly enough, however, their background has not been in history either, though historians might have done the job and even done it better since their concerns would not have been so narrowly focused on the conceptual. Instead, they have come from philosophy, though mostly, like Koyré, from Continental schools where the divide between history and philosophy is by no means so deep as in the English-speaking world. All of which suggests once more that a central part of the problem to which this paper is addressed arises from the attitudes of historians toward science.

I shall explore these attitudes further near the end of this essay, but must first ask whether they make any difference to the performance of the tasks which intellectual historians undertake. Obviously they do not in the large proportion of cases which involve scientific ideas only

marginally or not at all. In numerous other cases, however, characteristic infirmities result from what I have previously described as
history derived predominantly from prefaces and programmatic
works. When scientific ideas are discussed without reference to the
concrete technical problems against which they were forged, what
results is a decidedly misleading notion of the way in which scientific
theories develop and impinge on their extrascientific environment.

One form which the systematic misdirection takes is particularly
clear in discussions of the Scientific Revolution, including many by
older historians of science: an excessive emphasis on the role of new
methods, particularly on the power of experiment to create, by itself,
new scientific theories. Reading the continuing argument over the
so-called Merton thesis, for example, I am constantly depressed by the
almost universal misstatement of what that debate is about. What is
really at issue, I take it, is an explanation of the rise and dominion of
the Baconian movement in England. Both proponents and critics of
the Merton thesis simply take it for granted that an explanation of the
rise of the new experimental philosophy is tantamount to an explanation of scientific development. On that view, if Puritanism or some
other new trend in religion increased the dignity of manual manipulation and fostered the search for God in His works, then, ipso facto, it
fostered science. Conversely, if first-rate science was done in Catholic
countries, then no Protestant religious movements could be responsible for the rise of seventeenth-century science.

That all-or-nothing polarization is, however, unnecessary and it
may well be false. A strong case can be made for the thesis that
Baconian experimentalism had comparatively little to do with the
main changes of scientific theory which marked the Scientific Revolution. Astronomy and mechanics were transformed with little recourse
to experiment and none to new sorts of experimentation. In optics and
physiology experiment played a larger role, but the models were not
Baconian but rather classic and medieval: Galen in physiology,
Ptolemy and Alhazen in optics. These fields plus mathematics exhaust
the list of those in which theory was radically transformed during the
Scientific Revolution. With respect to their practice neither experimentalism nor its putative religious correlate should be expected to
make much difference.

That view, if correct, does not, however, render either Baconian-ism or new religious movements unimportant to scientific develop-ment. What it does suggest is that the role of the new Baconian methods and values was not to produce new theories in previously established sciences but rather to make new fields, often those with roots in the prior crafts, available for scientific scrutiny (for example, magnetism, chemistry, electricity, and the study of heat). Those fields, however, received little significant theoretical reordering before the mid-eighteenth century, the time through which one must wait to discover that the Baconian movement in the sciences was by no means a fraud. That Britain rather than Catholic France, especially after the revocation of the Edict of Nantes, played the dominant role in bring-ing order to these newer, more Baconian fields may indicate that a revised Merton thesis will yet prove immensely informative. Perhaps it will even help us understand why one old saw about science con-tinues to withstand close scrutiny: at least from 1700 to 1850, British science was predominantly experimental and mechanical, French mathematical and rationalistic. In addition, it may tell us something about the quite special roles played by Scotland and Switzerland in the scientific developments of the eighteenth century.

That historians have had such difficulty in even imagining pos-sibilities like these is, I think, at least partly due to a widespread conviction that scientists discover truth by the quasi-mechanical (and perhaps not very interesting) application of scientific method. Having accounted for the seventeenth-century discovery of method, the histo-rian may, and indeed does, leave the sciences to shift for themselves. That attitude, however, cannot be quite conscious, for another main by-product of preface history is incompatible with it. On the rare occasions when they turn from scientific methods to the substance of new scientific theories, historians seem invariably to give excessive emphasis to the role of the surrounding climate of extrascientific ideas. I would not argue for a moment that that climate is unimportant to scientific development. But, except in the rudimentary stages of the development of a field, the ambient intellectual milieu reacts on the theoretical structure of a science only to the extent that it can be made relevant to the concrete technical problems with which the practition-ers of that field engage. Historians of science may, in the past, have been excessively concerned with this technical core, but historians have usually ignored its existence entirely. They know it is there, but they act as though it were the mere product of science — of proper method acting in a suitable environment — rather than being the most essential of all the various determinants of a science's development. What results from this approach is reminiscent of the story of the emperor's new clothes.

Let me give two concrete examples. Both intellectual historians and historians of art often describe the novel intellectual currents of the Renaissance, especially Neoplatonism, which made it possible for Kepler to introduce the ellipse to astronomy, thus breaking the traditional hold of orbits compounded from perfect circular motions. On this view, Tycho's neutral observations plus the Renaissance intellectual milieu yield Kepler's Laws. What is regularly ignored, however, is the elementary fact that elliptical orbits would have been useless if applied to any geocentric astronomical scheme. Before the use of ellipses could transform astronomy, the sun had to replace the earth at the center of the universe. That step was not, however, taken until just over a half-century before Kepler's work, and to it the novel *intellectual* climate of the Renaissance made only equivocal contributions. It is an open question, as well as an interesting and important one, whether Kepler might not equally easily have been led to ellipses without benefit of Neoplatonism.[5] To tell the story without reference to any of the technical factors on which the answer to that question depends is to misrepresent the manner in which scientific laws and theories enter the realm of ideas at large.

A more important example to the same effect is provided by countless standard discussions of the origin of Darwin's theory of evolution.[6] What was required, we are told, to transform the static Chain of Being into an ever-moving escalator was the currency of such ideas

5. T. S. Kuhn, *The Copernican Revolution* (Cambridge, Mass.: Harvard University Press, 1957), pp. 135–143. N. R. Hanson, *Patterns of Discovery* (Cambridge, Eng.: Cambridge University Press, 1958), chap. 4. Note that there are other aspects of Kepler's thought to which the relevance of Neoplatonism is beyond doubt.

6. See, for example, R. M. Young, "Malthus and the Evolutionists: The Common Context of Biological and Social Theory," *Past and Present*, no. 43 (1969), pp. 109–145, an essay which includes much useful guidance to the recent literature on Darwinism. Note, however, one irony which illustrates the problems of perception now under discussion. Young opens by deploring the assumptions, widespread among "both historians of science and other sorts of historians . . . that scientific ideas and findings can be

as infinite perfectability and progress, the laissez-faire competitive economy of an Adam Smith, and, above all, the population analyses of Malthus. I cannot doubt that factors of this sort were vitally important; anyone who does would do well to ask how, in their absence, the historian is to understand the proliferation, particularly in England, of pre-Darwinian evolutionary theories like those of Erasmus Darwin, Spencer, and Robert Chambers. Yet these speculative theories were uniformly anathema to the scientists whom Charles Darwin managed to persuade in the course of making evolutionary theory a standard ingredient of the Western intellectual heritage. What Darwin did, unlike these predecessors, was to show how evolutionary concepts should be applied to a mass of observational materials which had accumulated only during the first half of the nineteenth century and were, quite independently of evolutionary ideas, already making trouble for several recognized scientific specialties. This part of the Darwin story, without which the whole cannot be understood, demands analysis of the changing state, during the decades before the *Origin of Species,* of fields like stratigraphy and paleontology, the geographical study of plant and animal distribution, and the increasing success of classificatory systems which substituted morphological resemblances for Linneaus' parallelisms of function. The men who, in developing natural systems of classification, first spoke of tendrils as "aborted" leaves or who accounted for the different number of ovaries in closely related plant species by referring to the "adherence" in one species of organs separate in the other were not evolutionists by any means. But without their work, Darwin's *Origin* could not have achieved either its final form or its impact on the scientific and the lay public.

---

dealt with as relatively unequivocal units with fairly sharply defined boundaries . . . [and] that 'non-scientific' factors [have] played relatively little part in shaping the development of scientific ideas." His paper is intended as "a case study which attempts to break down barriers in one small area between the history of science and other branches of history." Obviously, this is just the sort of contribution which I too would particularly welcome. Yet Young cites almost no literature which has attempted to explain the emergence of Darwinism as a response to the development of *scientific* ideas or techniques, and indeed there is very little to cite. Nor does his own paper make any attempt to deal with the technical issues which may have helped to shape Darwin's thought. Very likely it will be for some time the standard account of Malthus' influence on evolutionary thought, for it is admirably thorough, erudite, and perceptive. But far from being a barrier breaker, it belongs to a standard historiographic tradition which has done much to preserve the very separation Young deplores.

One last point will conclude this portion of my argument. I said earlier that, in accounting for the genesis of novel scientific theories, the emphasis on method and the emphasis on extrascientific intellectual milieu were not quite compatible. I would now add that, at the most fundamental level, the two prove to be identical in their effects. Both induce an apparently incurable Whiggishness which permits the historian to dismiss as superstition all the scientific forebears of the ideas with which he deals. The hold of the circle on the astronomical imagination is to be understood as a product of the Platonic infatuation with geometric perfection, perpetuated by medieval dogmatism; the endurance in biology of the idea of fixed species is to be understood as the result of an excessively literal reading of Genesis. What is missing from the first account, however, is any reference to the elegant and predictively successful astronomical systems built from circles, an achievement on which Copernicus did not himself improve. What is missing from the second is any recognition that the observed existence of discrete species, without which there could be no taxonomic enterprise, becomes extremely difficult to understand unless the current members of each descend from some original pair. Since Darwin the definition of basic taxonomic categories like species and genus have necessarily become and remained relatively arbitrary and extraordinarily problematic. Conversely, one technical root of Darwin's work is the increasing difficulty, during the early nineteenth century, of applying these standard classificatory tools to a body of data vastly expanded by, among other things, exploration of the New World and the Pacific. In short, ideas which the historian dismisses as superstitions usually prove to have been crucial elements in highly successful older scientific systems. When they do, the emergence of novel replacements will not be understood as the consequence merely of good method applied in favorable intellectual milieu.

III

I have spoken so far of the effect of preface history on the man concerned to place science in intellectual history. Turning now to standard views about the socioeconomic role of science, one encounters a very different situation. What the historian lacks in this area is not so much a knowledge of technical sources, which would in any case be largely irrelevant, as a command of conceptual distinctions essential to the analysis of science as a social force. Some of those distinctions would generate themselves if the socioeconomic historian possessed a better understanding of the nature of science as an enterprise and of its changes over time. Concerned with the role of the sciences, he requires at least a global sense of how men gain membership in scientific communities, of what they then do, where their problems come from, and what they receive as solutions. To this extent, his needs overlap the intellectual historian's, though they are technically far less demanding. But the socioeconomic historian also has needs which the intellectual historian does not: some knowledge of the nature of technology as an enterprise, an ability to distinguish it from science, both socially and intellectually, and above all a sensitivity to the various modes of interaction between the two.

Science, when it affects socioeconomic development at all, does so through technology. Historians tend frequently to conflate the two enterprises, abetted by prefaces which, since the seventeenth century, have regularly proclaimed the utility of science and have often then illustrated it with explanations of existing machines and modes of production.[7] On these issues, too, Bacon has been taken not only seriously, as he should be, but literally, as he should not. The methodological innovations of the seventeenth century are thus seen as the source of a useful as well as sound science. Explicitly or implicitly, science is portrayed as having played a steadily increasing socioeconomic role ever since. In fact, however, despite the hortatory claims of Bacon and his successors for three centuries, technology flourished without significant substantive inputs from the sciences

7. The historian's difficulties with science-*cum*-technology are nowhere better illustrated than in discussions of the Industrial Revolution. The long-standard attitude is that of T. S. Ashton, *The Industrial Revolution, 1760–1830* (London and New York: Oxford University Press, 1948), p. 15: "The stream of English scientific thought, issuing from the teaching of Francis Bacon, and enlarged by the genius of Boyle and Newton, was one of the main tributaries of the industrial revolution." Roland Mousnier's *Progrès scientifique et technique au XVIIIe siècle* (Paris: Plon, 1958) takes the opposite position in an even more extreme form, arguing for total independence of the two enterprises. As a corrective to the view that the Industrial Revolution was applied Newtonian science, Mousnier's version is an improvement, but it entirely misses the significant methodological and ideological interactions of eighteenth-century science and technology. For these, see below or the excellent sketch in the chapter "Science" in E. J. Hobsbawm's *The Age of Revolution, 1789–1848* (Cleveland: World Publishing Company, 1962).

282   *Thomas Kuhn*

until about one hundred years ago. Science's emergence as a prime mover in socioeconomic development was not a gradual but a sudden phenomenon, first significantly foreshadowed in the organic-chemical dye industry in the 1870s, continued in the electric power industry from the 1890s, and rapidly accelerated since the 1920s. To treat these developments as the emergent consequences of the Scientific Revolution is to miss one of the radical historical transformations constitutive of the contemporary scene. Many current debates over science policy would be more fruitful if the nature of this change were better understood.

To that tranformation I shall return, but I must first sketch, however simplistically and dogmatically, some background for it. Science and technology had been separate enterprises before Bacon announced their marriage in the beginning of the seventeenth century, and they continued separate for almost three centuries more. Until late in the nineteenth century, significant technological innovations almost never came from the men, the institutions, or the social groups that contributed to the sciences. Though scientists sometimes tried, and though their spokesmen often claimed success, the effective improvers of technology were predominantly craftsmen, foremen, and ingenious contrivers, a group often in sharp conflict with their contemporaries in the sciences.[8] Scorn for inventors shows repeatedly in the literature of science, and hostility to the the pretentious, abstract, and woolgathering scientist is a persistent theme in the literature of technology. There is even evidence that this polarization of science and technology has deep sociological roots, for almost no historical society has managed successfully to nurture both at the same time.

Greece, when it came to value its science, viewed technology as a finished heritage from its ancient gods; Rome, on the other hand, famous for its technology, produced no notable science. The series of

8. R. P. Multhauf, "The Scientist and the 'Improver' of Technology," *Technology and Culture* 1 (1959): 38–47; C. C. Gillispie, "The *Encyclopédie* and the Jacobin Philosophy of Science," in M. Clagett, ed., *Critical Problems in the History of Science* (Madison: University of Wisconsin Press, 1959), pp. 255–289. For hints at an explanation of the dichotomy, see my "Comments" in R. R. Nelson, ed., *The Rate and Direction of Inventive Activity,* a Report of the National Bureau of Economic Research (Princeton: Princeton University Press, 1962), pp. 379–384, 450–457, and the epilogue of my paper, "The Essential Tension: Tradition and Innovation in Scientific Research," in C. W. Taylor and Frank Barron, *Scientific Creativity: Its Recognition and Development* (New York: Wiley, 1963), pp. 341–354.

late-medieval and Renaissance technological innovations which made possible the emergence of modern European culture had largely ceased before the Scientific Revolution began. Britain, though it produced a significant series of isolated innovators, was generally backward in at least the abstract and developed sciences during the century which embraced the Industrial Revolution, while technologically second-rate France was the world's preeminent scientific power. With the possible exceptions (it is too early to be sure) of the United States and the Soviet Union since about 1930, Germany during the century before World War II was the only nation that managed simultaneously to support first-rate traditions in both science and technology. Institutional separation — the universities for *Wissenschaft* and the Technische Hochschulen for industry and the crafts — is a likely cause of that unique success. As a first approximation, the historian of socioeconomic development would do well to treat science and technology as radically distinct enterprises, not unlike the sciences and the arts. That technologies have, between the Renaissance and the late nineteenth century, usually been classified as arts is not an accident.

Starting from this perspective one can ask, as the socioeconomic historian must, about interactions between the two enterprises, now seen as distinct. Such interactions have characteristically been of three sorts, one dating from antiquity, the second from the mid-eighteenth century, and the third from the late nineteenth. The longest lasting, now probably finished except in the social sciences, is the impact of preexisting technologies, whatever their source, on the sciences. Ancient statics, the new sciences of the seventeenth century like magnetism and chemistry, and the development of thermodynamics in the nineteenth century all provide examples. In each of these cases and countless others, critically important advances in the understanding of nature resulted from the decision of scientists to study what craftsmen had already learned how to do. There are other main sources of novelty in the sciences, but this one has too often been underrated, except perhaps by Marxists.

In all these cases, however, the resulting benefits have accrued to science, not to technology, a point which Marxist historians repeatedly miss. When Kepler studied the optimum dimension of wine casks, the proportions which would yield maximum content for the least consumption of wood, he helped to invent the calculus of variations, but existing wine casks were, he found, already built to the dimensions he derived. When Sadi Carnot undertook to produce the theory of the steam engine, a prime mover to which, as he emphasized, science had contributed little or nothing, the result was an important step toward thermodynamics; his prescrition for engine improvement, however, had been embodied in engineering practice before his study began.[9] With few exceptions, none of much significance, the scientists who turned to technology for their problems succeeded merely in validating and explaining, not in improving, techniques developed earlier and without science's aid.

A second mode of interaction, visible from the mid-eighteenth century, was the increasing deployment in the practical arts of methods borrowed from science and sometimes of scientists themselves.[10] The effectiveness of the movement remains uncertain. It has, for example, no apparent role in the development of the new textile machinery and iron fabricating techniques so important to the Industrial Revolution. But the "experimental farms" of eighteenth-century Britain, the record books of the stock breeders, and the experiments on steam that Watt performed in developing the separate condenser are all plausibly seen as a conscious attempt to employ scientific methods in the crafts, and such methods were on occasions productive. The men who used them were seldom, however, contributors to contemporary science which, in any case, few of them knew. When they succeeded, it was not by applying existing science but by a frontal attack, however methodologically sophisticated, on a recognized social need.

Only in chemistry is the situation significantly more equivocal.[11] Particularly in France, distinguished chemists, including both Lavoisier and C. L. Bertolet, were employed to supervise and im-

9. W. C. Unwin, "The Development of the Experimental Study of Heat Engines," *The Electrician* 35 (1895): 46–50, 77–80, is a striking account of the difficulties encountered when attempting to use Carnot's theory and its successors for practical engineering design.
10. C. C. Gillispie, "The Natural History of Industry," and R. E. Schofield, "The Industrial Orientation of the Lunar Society of Birmingham," *Isis* 48 (1957): 398–407, 408–415. Note the extent to which both authors, while disagreeing vehemently, are nevertheless defending the same thesis in different words.
11. H. Guerlac, "Some French Antecedents of the Chemical Revolution," *Chymia* 5 (1968): 73–112; Archibald Clow and N. L. Clow, *The Chemical Revolution* (London: Batchworth Press, 1952); and L. F. Haber, *The Chemical Industry during the Nineteenth Century* (Oxford: Clarendon Press, 1958).

prove such industries as dyeing, ceramics, and gunpowder. Their regimens, furthermore, were an apparent success. But the changes they introduced were neither dramatic nor, in any obvious way, dependent on contemporary chemical theory and discovery. Lavoisier's new chemistry is a case in point. It undoubtedly provided a more profound understanding of the previously developed technology of ore reduction, acids manufacture, and so on. In addition it permitted the gradual elaboration of better techniques of quality control. But it was responsible for no fundamental changes in these established industries, nor did it have an observable role in the nineteenth-century development of such new technologies as sulphuric acid, soda, or wrought iron and steel. If one looks for important new processes which result from development of scientific knowledge, one must wait for the maturation of organic chemistry, current electricity, and thermodynamics during the generations from 1840 to 1870.

Products and processes derived from prior scientific research and dependent for their development on additional research by men with scientific training display a third mode of interaction between science and technology.[12] Since its emergence in the organic dye industry a century ago, it has transformed communication, the generation and distribution of power (twice), the materials both of industry and of everyday life, and also both medicine and warfare. Today its omnipresence and importance disguise the still real cleavage between science and technology. In the process, they make it difficult to realize how very recent and decisive the emergence of this kind of interaction has been. Even economic historians seldom seem aware of the qualitative divide between the forces promoting change during the Industrial Revolution and those operative in the twentieth century. Most general histories disguise even the existence of any such transformation. One need not, however, inflate the importance of history of science to suppose that since 1870 science has assumed a role which no student of modern socioeconomic development may responsibly ignore.

What are the sources of the transformation and how may the socioeconomic historian contribute to their understanding? I suggest there are two, of which he can recognize the first and participate in

12. John Beer, *The Emergence of the German Dye Industry,* Illinois Studies in the Social Sciences 44 (Urbana: University of Illinois Press, 1959); H. C. Passer, *The Electrical Manufacturers, 1875–1900* (Cambridge, Mass.: Harvard University Press, 1953).

unraveling the second. No science, however highly developed, need have applications which will significantly alter existing technological practice. The classical sciences like mechanics, astronomy, and mathematics had few such effects even after they were recast during the Scientific Revolution. The sciences which did were those born of the Baconian movement of the seventeenth century, particularly chemistry and electricity. But even they did not reach the levels of development required to generate significant applications until the middle third of the ninteenth century. Before the maturation of these fields at mid-century, there was little of much socioeconomic importance that scientific knowledge in any field could produce. Though few socioeconomic historians are equipped to follow the technical aspects of the advances which suddenly made science productive of new materials and devices, they can surely be aware of these developments and their special role.

Internal technical development was not, however, the only requisite for the emergence of a socially significant science, and about what remained the socioeconomic historian could have a great deal of significance to say. During the nineteenth century the institutional and social structure of the sciences was transformed in ways not even foreshadowed in the Scientific Revolution. Beginning in the 1780s and continuing through the first half of the following century, newly formed societies of specialists in individual branches of science assumed the leadership which the all-embracing national societies had previously attempted to supply. Simultaneously, private scientific journals and particularly journals of individual specialties proliferated rapidly and increasingly replaced the house organs of the national academies which had previously been the almost exclusive media of public scientific communication. A similar change is visible in scientific education and in the locus of research. Excepting in medicine and at a few military schools, scientific education scarcely existed before the foundation of the Ecole polytechnique in the last decade of the eighteenth century. That model spread rapidly, however, first to Germany, then to the United States, and finally more equivocally, to England. With it developed other new institutional forms, especially teaching and research laboratories, like Justus von Liebig's at Giessen or the Royal College of Chemistry in London. These are the developments which first made possible and then supported what had previously scarcely existed, the professional scientific career. Like a potentially applicable science, they emerged relatively suddenly and quickly. Together with the maturation of the Baconian sciences of the seventeenth century, they are the pivot of a second scientific revolution which centered in the first half of the *nineteenth* century, a historical episode at least as crucial to an understanding of modern times as its older namesake. It is time it found its way into history books, but it is too much a part of other developments in the nineteenth century to be untangled by historians of science alone.

IV

I have so far been describing the historian's neglect of science and its history, repeatedly implying while doing so that the blame lies exclusively with historians, scarcely at all with the specialists who have chosen science as their object of study. Today, for reasons to which I shall return, that allocation of responsibility seems to me increasingly nearly justified, if ultimately unfair. But the current situation is in part a product of the past. If the contemporary gap between history and history of science is to be further analyzed in hope of its amelioration, the contribution to separatism made by the history of the history of science must first be recognized.

Until the early years of this century, history of science, or what little there was of it, was dominated by two main traditions.[13] One of them, with an almost continuous tradition from Condorcet and Comte to Dampier and Sarton, viewed scientific advance as the triumph of reason over primitive superstition, the unique example of humanity operating in its highest mode. Though vast scholarship, some of it still useful, was sometimes expended on them, the chronicles which this tradition produced were ultimately hortatory in intent, and they included remarkably little information about the content of science beyond who first made which positive discovery when. Except occasionally for reference or the preparation of historiographic articles, no contemporary historian of science reads them, a fact which does not yet seem to have been as widely appreciated as it should be by the historical profession at large. Though I know it will give offense to some people whose feelings I value, I see no alternative to underscor-

13. A number of the following points are developed more fully in my "History of Science," *International Encyclopedia of the Social Sciences* 14 (New York, 1968): 74–83.

ing the point. Historians of science owe the late George Sarton an immense debt for his role in establishing their profession, but the image of their specialty which he propagated continues to do much damage even though it has long since been rejected.

A second tradition, more important both for its products and because, particularly on the Continent, it still displays some life, originates with practicing scientists, sometimes eminent ones, who have from time to time prepared histories of their specialties. Their work usually began as a by-product of science pedagogy and was directed predominantly to science students. Besides intrinsic appeal, they saw in such histories a means to elucidate the contents of their specialty, to establish its tradition, and to attract students. The volumes they produced were and are quite technical, and the best of them can still be used with profit by specialists with different historiographic inclinations. But seen as history, at least from current perspectives, the tradition has two great limitations. Excepting in occasional naïve asides, it produced exclusively internal histories which considered neither context for, nor external effects of, the evolution of the concepts and techniques being discussed. That limitation need not always have been a defect, for the mature sciences are regularly more insulated from the external climate, at least of ideas, than are other creative fields. But it was undoubtedly badly overdone and, in any case, made work in this mode unattractive to historians, excepting perhaps historians of ideas.

Even the purest historians of ideas were, however, repelled and on occasion seriously misled by a second and even more pronounced defect of this tradition. Scientist-historians and those who followed their lead characteristically imposed contemporary scientific categories, concepts, and standards on the past. Sometimes a specialty which they traced from antiquity had not existed as a recognized subject for study until a generation before they wrote. Nevertheless, knowing what belonged to it, they retrieved the specialty's current contents from past texts of a variety of heterogeneous fields, not noticing that the tradition they constructed in the process had never existed. In addition, they usually treated concepts and theories of the past as imperfect approximations to those in current use, thus disguising both the structure and integrity of past scientific traditions. Inevitably, histories written in this way reinforced the impression that the history of science is a not very interesting chronicle of the triumph of sound method over careless error and superstition. If these were the only possible models available, one could criticize historians for little except being too easily misled.

But they are not the only models, nor for thirty years have they been even the ones dominant in the profession. Those derive from a more recent tradition which increasingly adapted to the sciences an approach discovered in late-nineteenth-century histories of philosophy. In that field, of course, only the most partisan could feel confident of their ability to distinguish positive knowledge from error and superstition. As a result, historians could scarcely escape the force of an injunction later phrased succinctly by Bertrand Russell: "In studying a philosopher, the right attitude is neither reverence nor contempt, but first a kind of hypothetical sympathy, until it is possible to know what it feels like to believe in his theories."[14] In the history of ideas, the resulting tradition is the one which produced both Ernst Cassirer and Arthur Lovejoy, men whose work, however profound its limitations, has had a great and fructifying influence on the subsequent treatment of ideas in history. What is surprising and remains to be explained is the lack of any comparable influence, even on intellectual historians, of the works of the men who, following Alexandre Koyré, have for a generation been developing the same models for the sciences. Seen through their writings, science is not the same enterprise as the one represented in either of the older traditions. For the first time it has become potentially a fully historical enterprise, like music, literature, philosophy, or law.

I say "potentially" because that model too has limitations. Though it has extended the proper subject matter of the historian of science to the entire context of ideas, it remains internal history in the sense that it pays little or no attention to the institutional or socioeconomic context within which the sciences have developed. Recent historiography has, for example, largely discredited the myth of method, but it has then had difficulty finding any significant role for the Baconian

14. Bertrand Russell, *A History of Western Philosophy* (New York: Simon and Schuster, 1945), p. 39.

movement and has had little but scorn for either the Merton thesis or
the relation between science and technology, industry, or the crafts.[15] It
is time to confess that a few of the object lessons I have read to
historians above could be fruitfully circulated in my own profession as
well. But the areas to which these object lessons apply are the in-
terstices between history of science and the now standard concerns of
the cultural and socioeconomic historian. They will need to be worked
by both groups. Given a model of the internal development of science
which provides points of entrée, historians of science are now increasingly turning to it, a movement to be discussed in my concluding
section. I am aware of no comparable movement within the historical
profession at large.

V

Clearly, historians of science must share the blame. But no
catalogue of their past and present sins will entirely explain the realities
of their current relation to the rest of the historical profession. What
currency their work has achieved has come primarily through Butterfield's book, published over twenty years ago, when their discipline
was embryonic, and never fully assimilated since. Neglect of their
subject matter, science, remains particularly acute for just the years
during which it became a major historical force. Though usually
placed in history departments, their courses are seldom taken and their
books seldom read by historians. About the causes of that situation I
can only speculate and part of that speculation must deal with subjects
that I know only through conversations with colleagues and friends.

Two sorts of explanations suggest themselves, of which the first
arises from what is perhaps a factor unique to history among the
learned disciplines. History of science is not in principle a narrower
specialty than, say, political, diplomatic, social, or intellectual history.
Nor are its methods radically distinct from the ones employed in those
fields. But it is a specialty of a different sort, for it is concerned in the
first instance with the activity of a special group — the scientists —
rather than with a set of phenomena which must at the start be
abstracted from the totality of activities within a geographically de-

15. T. S. Kuhn, "Alexandre Koyré and the History of Science," *Encounter* 34 (1970):
67–70.

fined community. In this respect its natural kin are the history of literature, of philosophy, of music, and of the plastic arts.[16] These specialties, however, are not ordinarily offered by departments of history. Instead, they are more or less integral parts of the offering of the department responsible for the discipline of which the history is to be studied. Perhaps historians react to the history of science in the same way that they do to the history of other disciplines. Perhaps it is only the proximity created by membership in the same department which leads to a special sense of strain.

Those suggestions I owe to Carl Schorske, one of the two historians with whom I and my students have interacted most closely and fruitfully since I first began to teach in a history department fourteen years ago. He has persuaded me, though not until this essay was well advanced, that many of the problems discussed under the heading of science-in-intellectual-history, above, have precise parallels in the historian's typical discussion of other intellectual, literary, and artistic pursuits. Historians are, he argues, often quite adept at retrieving from a novel, a painting, or a philosophical disquisition, themes which reflect contemporary social problems and values. What they regularly miss, however, sometimes by explaining them away, are those aspects of these artifacts that are internally determined, partly by the intrinsic nature of the discipline which produces them and partly by the special role which that discipline's past always plays in its current evolution. Artists, whether in imitation or revolt, build from past art. Like scientists, philosophers, writers, and musicians, they live and work both within a larger culture and within a quasi-independent disciplinary

16. M. I. Finley points out that the history of law would provide an even more revealing parallel. The law, after all, is one of the obvious determinants of the sorts of political and social developments which historians have traditionally studied. But, excepting for reference to the expression of society's will through legislation, historians seldom pay attention to its evolution as an institution. Reactions at the conference to Peter Paret's insistence that military history must be in part the history of the military establishment as an institution with a life that is in part its own suggests how deep resistance to disciplinary history sometimes lies. Participants suggested, for example, that what military history ought to be is the study of the social sources of war and of the effects of war on society. But these subjects, though they perhaps provide the main reasons for wanting to have military history done, must not be its primary focus. An understanding of wars, their development and consequences, depends in essential ways on an understanding of military establishments. In any case, the subject war-and-society is as much the responsibility of the general historian as of his colleague who specializes in military history. The parallel to history of science is very close.

tradition of their own. Both environments shape their creative products, but the historian all too often considers only the first.

Excepting in my own field, my competence for evaluating these generalizations is restricted to history of philosophy. There, however, they fit as precisely as they do in history of science. Since they are, in addition, extremely plausible, I shall tentatively accept them. What historians generally view as historical in the development of individual creative disciplines are those aspects which reflect its immersion in a larger society. What they all too often reject, as not quite history, are those internal features which give the discipline a history in its own right.

The perception which permits that rejection seems to me profoundly unhistorical. The historian does not apply it in other realms. Why should he do so here? Consider, for example, the manner in which historians treat geographical and linguistic subdivisions. Few of them would deny the existence of problems which can be treated only on the gigantic canvas of world history. But they do not therefore deny that the study of the development of Europe or America is also historical. Nor do they resist the next step, which finds a legitimate role for national or even county histories provided that their authors remain alert to the aspects of their restricted subject which are determined by the influence of surrounding groups. When, as is inevitable, communication problems arise, for example between British and European historians, these are deplored as historiographic blinders and as likely sources of error. The feelings which are generated sometimes resemble those which historians of science or art regularly encounter, but no one would say *out loud* that French history is by definition historical in some sense in which British is not. Yet that is very often the response when the analytic units shift from geographically defined subsystems to groups whose cohesiveness — not necessarily less (or more) real than that of a national community — derives from training in a special discipline and an allegiance to its special values. Perhaps if historians could admit the existence of seams in Clio's web, they could more easily recognize that there are no rents.

The resistance to disciplinary histories is not, of course, exclusively the fault of the historians who work within history departments. With a few notable exceptions like Paul Kristeller and Erwin Panofsky, the men who study a discipline's development from within that discipline's parent department concentrate excessively on the internal logic of the field they study, often missing both consequences and causes in the larger cultures. I remember with deep embarrassment the day on which a student found occasion to remind me that Arnold Sommerfeld's relativistic treatment of the atom was invented midway through the First World War. Institutional separations depress historical sensitivities on both sides of the barrier they create. Nor is separation the only source of difficulty. The man who teaches within the department responsible for the discipline he studies almost always addresses himself to that discipline's practitioners or, in the case of literature and the arts, to its critics. Usually the historical dimension of his work is subordinated to the function of teaching and perfecting the current discipline. History of philosophy, as taught within philosophy departments, is often, for example, a parody of the historical. Reading a work of the past, the philosopher regularly seeks the author's positions on current problems, criticizes them with the aid of current apparatus, and interprets his text to maximize its coherence with modern doctrine. In that process the historic original is often lost. I am told, for example, of the response of a former philosophy colleague to a student who questioned his reading of a passage in Marx. "Yes," he said, "the words do seem to say what you suggest. But that cannot be what Marx meant, for it is plainly false." Why Marx should have chosen to use the words he did was not a problem worth pausing for.

Most examples of the Whiggishness enforced by placing history in the service of a parent discipline are more subtle but no less unhistorical. The damage they do is no greater, I think, than that done by the historian's rejection of disciplinary history, but it is surely as great. I have already pointed out that history of science displayed all the same unhistorical syndromes when it was taught within science departments. The forces which have increasingly transferred it to history departments in recent years have placed it where it belongs. Though a shotgun was required for the wedding and though the strains characteristic of forced marriages result, the offspring may yet be viable. I cannot doubt that similar compulsory association with the practitioners of other branches of disciplinary history would be equally fruitful. Perhaps, as my first history department chairman, the late George Guttridge, once remarked, we shall soon recognize how badly history fits the departmental organization of American universities. Some

transdepartmental institutional arrangement is badly needed, perhaps
a faculty or school of historical studies which would bring together all
those whose concern, regardless of their departmental affiliations, is
with the past in evolution.

VI

I have been considering the suggestion that the relations between
history and history of science differ only in intensity, not in kind, from
the relations between history and the study of the development of
other disciplines. The parallels are, I think, clear, and they carry us a
long way toward an understanding of the problem I have been asked
to discuss. But they are not complete, and they do not explain everything. Treating literature, art, or philosophy, historians do, I have
suggested, read sources as they do not in the sciences. The historian's
ignorance of even the main developmental stages of science has no
parallel for the other disciplines on which he touches. Even offered in
other departments, courses in the history of literature and the arts are
more likely to attract historians than courses in the history of science.
Above all, there is no precedent in other disciplines for the historian's
exclusive attention to a single period when discussing a science. Those
historians who consider art, literature, or philosophy at all are as likely
to do so when dealing with the nineteenth century as with the Renaissance. Science, on the other hand, is a topic to be discussed only
between 1540 and 1700. One reason, I suspect, for the historian's
characteristic emphasis on the discovery of method is that it protects
him from the need to deal with the sciences after that period. With
their method in hand, the sciences cease to be historical, a perception
for which there is no parallel in the historian's view of other
disciplines.

Contemplating these phenomena and some more personal experiences to be illustrated below, I reluctantly conclude that part of what
separates historians from their colleagues in history of science is what,
in addition to personality, separates F. R. Leavis From C. P. Snow.
Though I sympathize with those who believe it has been misnamed,
the two-culture problem is another probable source of the difficulties
we have been considering.

My basis for that conjecture is largely impressionistic, but not
entirely so. Consider the following quotation from a British psychol-

ogist whose tests enable him to predict with some assurance the future specialties of high school students, even though (like I.Q. tests, which he includes) they discriminate scarcely at all between those who will do well and those who will do badly after specialization:

> The typical historian or modern linguist had, relatively speaking, rather a low I.Q., and a verbal bias of intelligence. He was prone to work erratically on the intelligence test, accurate at times and slap dash at others; and his interests tended to be cultural rather than practical. The young physical scientist often had a high I.Q., and a non verbal bias of ability; he was usually consistently accurate; his interests were usually technical, mechanical, or in life out of doors. Naturally, these rules-of-thumb were not perfect: a minority of arts specialists had scores like scientists, and vice versa. But, by and large, the predictions held surprisingly well, and at the extremes they were infallible.[17]

Together with other evidence from the same source, this passage suggests that historians and scientists, at least those of the more mathematical and abstract sort, are polar types.[18] Other studies, though insufficiently detailed to single out historians, indicate that scientists as a group come from a lower socioeconomic stratum than their academic colleagues in other fields.[19] Personal impressions, both from my own school days and my children's, suggest that the intellectual differences appear quite early, especially in mathematics where they are often obvious before age fourteen. I am thinking now not primarily of ability or creativity, but merely of affection. Though there are both exceptions and a large middle ground, I suggest that a passion for history is seldom compatible with even a developed liking for mathematics or laboratory science, and vice versa.

Not surprisingly, as these polarities develop and are embodied in career decisions, they often find expression in defensiveness and hostil-

---

17. Liam Hudson, *Contrary Imaginations: A Psychological Study of the English Schoolboy* (London: Methuen, 1966), p. 22.

18. A fuller analysis, to which Hudson's pioneering book provides many fascinating leads, would recognize that there are multiple dimensions of polarization. For example, the same sorts of scientists who are most likely to disdain history are often passionately interested in music though not usually in the other main forms of artistic expression. Neither Hudson nor I is referring to a simple spectrum ranging from the artist, at one extreme, to the scientist, at the other, with the historian and artist at the same end of the spectrum.

19. C. C. Gillispie, "Remarks on Social Selection as a Factor in the Progressivism of Science," *American Scientist* 56 (1968): 439–450, underscores the phenomenon and provides relevant bibliography.

ity. The historians who read this essay will not need to be told of the often overt disdain of scientists for historical studies. Unless I suppose that it is reciprocated, I cannot account for the stance, described above, of historians toward the sciences. Historians of science ought to be exceptions, but even they often prove the rule. Most of them begin in science, turning to its history only at the graduate level. Those who do frequently insist that their interest is only in history of science not in mere history, a field they conceive as at once irrelevant and uninteresting. As a result they are more easily attracted to special departments or programs than to regular history departments. Fortunately, it is usually possible to convert them once they are there.

If, however, many historians are hostile to science — as I suppose — it must be admitted that they disguise it well, far better, for example, than their colleagues in literature, language, and the arts, who are often entirely explicit. Yet that difference provides at least no counterevidence, for it could have been expected. Like philosophers and unlike most students of literature and art, historians see their enterprise as somehow cognitive and thus akin to science if not of it. With scientists they share such values as impartiality, objectivity, and faithfulness to evidence. They too have tasted the forbidden fruit of the tree of knowledge, and the antiscientific rhetoric of the arts is no longer available to them. There are, however, subtler ways of expressing hostility, some of which I have suggested above. This part of my argument will therefore conclude with some evidence of a more personal sort.

The first is a memorable encounter with a much-valued friend and colleague, who has from time to time organized and led an experimental seminar at Princeton designed to acquaint first-year graduate students with ancillary methods and approaches for which the future specialist may some day find a use. When appropriate, a local or visiting specialist is asked to manage discussion and to consult about the preparatory reading. Several years ago I accepted an invitation to lead the group in the first of a pair of meetings on the history of science. The central item of the reading, selected after much talk, was an old book of mine, *The Copernican Revolution*. That choice may not have been the best, but there were reasons for it, explicit both in my conversations with my colleague and in the preface. Though not a text, the book was written so that it could be used in college courses on science for the nonscientist. It would not, therefore, present insuperable obstacles to our graduate students. More important, when it was written the book was the only one that attempted to portray, within a single pair of covers, both the technical-astronomical and the wider intellectual-historical dimensions of the revolution. It was thus a concrete example of the point I have argued more abstractly above: the role of science in intellectual history cannot be understood without the science. How many students grasped that point I cannot be sure, but my colleague did not. Midway through a lively disussion, he interjected, "But, of course, I skipped the technical parts." Since he is a busy man, the omission may not be surprising. But what is suggested by his willingness, unsolicited, to make it public?

My second, briefer example is in the public domain. Frank Manuel's *Portrait of Isaac Newton* is surely the most brilliant and thorough study of its subject in a very long time. Excepting those offended by its psychoanalytic approach, the Newtonian experts with whom I have discussed it assure me that it will affect their work for years to come. History of science would be far poorer if it had not been written. Nevertheless, in the present context, it raises a fundamental question. Is there any field but science in which one can imagine a historian's preparing a major biography which omits, consciously and deliberately, any attempt to deal with the creative work which made its subject's life a worthy object of study? I cannot think of a similar labor of love devoted to a major figure in the arts, philosophy, religion, or public life. Under the circumstances, I am not sure that love is the emotion involved.

These examples were introduced by the claim thay they would display hostility to science. Having presented them, I confess my uncertainty that "hostility" is altogether the appropriate term. But they are examples of strange behavior. If what they illustrate must for the moment remain obscure, it may nevertheless constitute the central impediment separating history and history of science.

VII

Having by now said more than all I know about the barriers which divide history from history of science, I shall conclude with some brief remarks on signs of change. One of them is the mere proliferation of historians of science and their increasing placement in departments of history. Though both numbers and proximity may be initially a source of friction, they also increase the availability of communication channels. Growth is also responsible for a second encouraging development, the increasing attention now being devoted to periods more recent than the Scientific Revolution and to previously little-explored parts of science. The better secondary literature will not for much longer be restricted to the sixteenth and seventeenth centuries, nor will it continue to deal primarily with the physical sciences. The current increase in the study of the history of the life sciences may prove particularly important. These fields have, until recently, been far less technical than the main physical sciences contemporary with them. Studies which trace their development are likely to be correspondingly more accessible to the historian who would like to discover what history of science is about.

Look next at two other developments the effects of which are now observable among many of the history of science's younger practitioners. Led by Frances Yates and Walter Pagel, they are now finding increasingly significant roles for Hermeticism and related movements in the early stages of the Scientific Revolution.[20] The original and exciting literature which results may well have three effects which transcend its explicit subject. First, just because Hermeticism was an avowedly mystical and irrational movement, recognition of its roles should help to make science more palatable to historians repelled by what many have taken to be a quasi-mechanical enterprise, governed by pure reason and cold fact. (It would plainly be absurd to select the rational elements from Hermeticism for exclusive attention as an older generation has done with Neoplatonism.) Second, Hermeticism now appears to have affected two aspects of scientific development previously seen as mutually exclusive and defended by competing schools. On the one hand, it was an intellectual, quasi-metaphysical movement which changed man's ideas about the entities and causes underlying natural phenomena; as such it is analyzable by the usual techniques of the historian of ideas. But it was also a movement which, in the figure of the Magus, prescribed new goals and methods for science. Treatises on, for example, Natural Magic show that the

20. F. A. Yates, "The Hermetic Tradition in Renaissance Science," in C. S. Singleton, ed., *Art, Science, and History in the Renaissance* (Baltimore: Johns Hopkins University Press, 1967), pp. 255–274; Walter Pagel, *William Harvey's Biological Ideas* (New York: Karger, 1967).

new emphasis on science's power, on the study of crafts, and on mechanical manipulation and machines are in part products of the same
movement that changed the intellectual climate. Two disparate approaches to the history of science are thus unified in a way likely to
have particular appeal to the historian. Finally, newest, and perhaps
most important, Hermeticism now begins to be studied as a class
movement with a discernable social base.[21] If that development continues, the study of the Scientific Revolution will become multi-
dimensional cultural history of the sort many historians are now also
striving to create.

I turn finally to the newest movement of all, apparent primarily
among graduate students and the very youngest members of the profession. Perhaps partly because of their increasing contact with historians, they are turning more and more to the study of what is often
described as external history. Increasingly they emphasize the effects
on science not of the intellectual but of the socioeconomic milieu,
effects manifest in changing patterns of education, institutionalization,
communication, and values. Their efforts owe something to the older
Marxist histories, but their concerns are at once broader, deeper, and
less doctrinaire than those of their predecessors. Because historians
will find themselves more at home with its products than they have
been with older histories of science, they are particularly likely to
welcome the change. Indeed they may even learn from it something of
more general relevance. Like literature and the arts, science is the
product of a group, a community of scientists. But in the sciences,
particularly in the later stages of their development, disciplinary
communities are both easier to isolate and also more nearly self-
contained and self-sufficient than the relevant groups in other fields.
As a result the sciences provide a particularly promising area in which
to explore the role of forces current in the larger society in shaping the
evolution of a discipline which is simultaneously controlled by its own
internal demands.[22] That study, if successful, could provide models for
a variety of fields besides the sciences.

21. P. M. Rattansi, "Paracelsus and the Puritan Revolution," *Ambix* 11 (1963):
24–32, and "The Helmontian-Galenist Controversy in Restoration England," *Ambix* 12
(1964): 1–23.
22. The penultimate section of the article cited in note 13 elaborates this possibility
in theoretical terms. T. M. Brown's "The College of Physicians and the Acceptance of
Iatromechanism in England, 1665–1695," *Bulletin of the History of Medicine* 44 (1970):
12–30, provides a concrete example.

All these developments are necessarily encouraging to anyone bothered by the traditional chasm between history and the history of science. If they continue, as seems likely, it will be less deep a decade hence than it has been in the past. But it is not likely to disappear, for the new trends described above can have only indirect, partial, and long-range effects on what I take to be the fundamental source of the division. Perhaps the example of history of science can by itself undermine the historian's resistance to disciplinary history, but I would be more confident if I knew the reasons for that resistance in the past. In any case, history of science is, by itself, an unlikely remedy for a social malady so deep and widespread as the two-culture problem. Instead, in my most depressed moments, I sometimes fear that history of science may yet be that problem's victim. Though I welcome the turn to external history of science as redressing a balance which has long been seriously askew, its new popularity may not be an unmixed blessing. One reason it now flourishes is undoubtedly the increasingly virulent antiscientific climate of these times. If it becomes the exclusive approach, history of science could be reduced to a higher-level version of the tradition which, by leaving the science out, ignored the internalities which shape the development of any discipline. That price would be too high to pay for rapprochement, but unless historians can find a place for the history of disciplines, it will be hard to avoid.

Chapter Nine

Psychoanalysis and the Movement of Contemporary Culture

PAUL RICOEUR

A question as important as that which concerns the place of psychoanalysis in the movement of contemporary culture demands that we be limited in our approach and yet try to reveal what is essential. Our exposition must be limited if it is going to allow for discussion and verification, but revelatory in order to give an idea of the scope of the cultural phenomenon which psychoanalysis represents for us. Such an approach might be a rereading of Freud's texts *on* culture, and indeed these essays attest to the fact that psychoanalysis does not concern itself with culture for merely accessory or indirect reasons. Far from being a mere explanation of the refuse of human existence and the darker side of man, it shows its real intentions when it breaks out of the limited framework of the therapeutic relationship between the analyst and his patient and rises to the level of a hermeneutics of culture. This first part of our demonstration is essential to the argument we eventually want to establish, namely, that psychoanalysis takes part in the contemporary cultural movement by acting as a hermeneutics of culture. In other words, psychoanalysis marks a change *of* culture because its interpretation of man bears in a central and direct way *on* culture as a whole. It makes interpretation into a moment of culture; it changes the world by interpreting it.

Translated by Willis Domingo. Originally published in *Conflict of Interpretations: Essays on Hermeneutics,* by Paul Ricoeur (Evanston, Illinois: Northwestern University Press, 1974). Reprinted by permission.

First of all, therefore, we should demonstrate that psychoanalysis is an interpretation of culture *as a whole*. We are not saying that it is an exhaustive explanation; later we will say that its viewpoint is limited and even that it has not yet found its proper place among all the various interpretations of culture — which implies that the meaning of psychoanalysis remains in suspense and its place undecided. This interpretation, however, is not limited on the side of its object, man, which it tries to grasp as a totality. It is limited only by its point of view; and it is this point of view which we must understand and locate. I would even say, as Spinoza does when he speaks of divine attributes as "infinite in one genus," that psychoanalysis is a total interpretation in one genus and in this way is itself an event in our culture.

Now we miss this unity of viewpoint on the part of psychoanalysis when we consider it to be a branch of psychiatry which has been progressively extended from individual to social psychology and then to art, morality, and religion. It was, of course, toward the end of Freud's life that his great texts on culture began to appear. *The Future of an Illusion* dates from 1927, *Civilization and Its Discontents* from 1930, *Moses and Monotheism* from the period 1937 – 39. These, however, do not represent simply a belated extension of individual psychology to a sociology of culture. By 1908 Freud had written "Creative Writers and Daydreaming." "Delusions and Dreams in Jensen's *Gradiva*" dates from 1907, *Leonardo da Vinci and a Memory of His Childhood* from 1910, *Totem and Taboo* from 1913, "Thoughts for the Times on War and Death" from 1915, "The Uncanny" from 1919, "A Childhood Recollection from *Dichtung und Wahrheit*" from 1917, "The Moses of Michelangelo" from 1914, *Group Psychology and the Analysis of the Ego* from 1921, "A Seventeenth-Century Demonological Neurosis" from 1923, and "Dostoevsky and Parricide" from 1928. The great "invasions" into the domains of aesthetics, sociology, ethics, and religion are therefore strictly concurrent with texts as important as *Beyond the Pleasure Principle, The Ego and the Id,* and, above all, the great *Papers on Metapsychology.* The truth is that psychoanalysis disrupts traditional divisions, however justified these may be by methodologies belonging to other disciplines. It applies the single viewpoint of its topographic, economic, and genetic "models" (the unconscious) to these separate domains. This unified viewpoint is what makes psychoanalytic interpretation both universal and limited. It is universal because it can legitimately be applied to humanity as a whole, but limited because it does not extend beyond the validity of its model or models. For example, Freud always objected to the distinction between psychological and sociological domains and constantly asserted the fundamental analogy between individual and group—an analogy which he never tried to prove by speculating about the "being" of the psychism or the "being" of the group. He simply let it be assumed by applying the same genetic and topographic-economic models to all cases. Yet Freud never claimed to give exhaustive explanations. He merely carried explanation by way of origins and the economy of instincts to its most extreme consequences. "I cannot speak of everything at the same time," he insists; "my contribution is modest, partial, and limited." Such reservations are not mere stylistic parries but express the conviction of an investigator who realizes that his explanation gives him a view which is limited as a result of his angle of vision but which gives onto the totality of the human phenomenon.

A HERMENEUTICS OF CULTURE

A purely historical study of the evolution of Freud's thought on culture should begin with *The Interpretation of Dreams,* for here is where Freud, in an interpretation of Sophocles' *Oedipus Rex* and Shakespeare's *Hamlet,* posited once and for all the unity of literary creation, myths, and dream distortion. All succeeding developments are contained in this seed. In "Creative Writers and Daydreaming" Freud states his basic argument that the barely perceptible transitions from the nocturnal dream to play and then to humor, fantasy, the daydream, and finally to folklore, legends, and genuine works of art leads us to suspect that creativity results from the same dynamism and involves the same economic structure as the phenomena of compromise and substitutive satisfaction which he had already developed for the interpretation of dreams and the theory of neurosis. But he cannot go further in this essay because he lacks a clear vision of a *topography* of the various agencies of the psychic apparatus and an *economy* of cathexes and anticathexes which would allow him to relocate aesthetic pleasure in the dynamics of culture as a whole. For this reason we will, in the space of this brief article, turn to an interpretation that is more systematic than historical and go straight to the texts which give a synthetic definition of culture. It is from this central problematic that a general theory of "illusion" can be developed and a place be found for Freud's previous aesthetic writings, whose meaning remains in suspense as long as the special domain of the phenomenon of culture is not perceived. Aesthetic "seduction" and religious "illusion" are to be taken together as the opposite poles of an investigation into compensation, itself one of the tasks of culture.

The same is true of Freud's richer writings, such as *Totem and Taboo,* in which he reinterprets by means of psychoanalysis the results of early twentieth-century ethnography on the totemic origins of religion and the sources of our ethical imperative in archaic taboos. These *genetic* studies can also be reconsidered in the wider framework of a topographic-economic interpretation. Similarly, in *The Future of an Illusion* and *Moses and Monotheism* Freud himself points out that such an explanation deals only with a partial phenomenon, that is, an archaic form of religion, and not with religion as such. The key to a rereading of Freud's work which would be more systematic than historical lies in subordinating all partial and "genetic" interpretations to a topographic-economic interpretation, since this alone confers unity of perspective. This second preliminary remark confirms our first one. What anchors the genetic explanation in the topographic-economic explanation is the theory of illusion, for here is where we find the repetition of the archaic as a "return of the repressed." If this is the case — a point which can be verified only in practice — the following systematic order becomes necessary. We must descend from the whole to the parts, from the central economic function of culture to the particular functions of religious "illusion" and aesthetic "seduction" — and from economic to genetic explanation.

An Economic Model of the Phenomenon of Culture

What, then, is culture as such? We can define it first of all in a negative way by saying that Freud does not distinguish between civilization and culture. This refusal to accept an almost classical distinction is in itself very illuminating. There is no separation between the utilitarian enterprise of dominating the forces of nature (civilization) and the disinterested, idealist task of realizing values (culture). This distinction, which might have meaning from a viewpoint which differs from that of psychoanalysis, has none as soon as we decide to treat culture from the viewpoint of a balance sheet of libidinal cathexes and anticathexes.

This economic interpretation is what dominates all of Freud's reflections on culture.

The first phenomenon we should consider from this point of view is that of coercion, because of the *instinctual renunciation* which it implies. This is the phenomenon which opens *The Future of an Illusion*. Culture, as Freud points out, began with the prohibition of man's most ancient desires — incest, cannibalism, and murder. And yet coercion does not constitute all of culture. The *illusion* whose future Freud calculates is involved in a wider task, of which prohibition is merely the rough outer shell. Freud gets to the kernel of this problem by posing three questions: To what extent can the burden of the instinctual sacrifices imposed on men be *lessened*? How can men be *reconciled* with those sacrifices which must necessarily remain? Moreover, how can satisfying *compensations* be offered to individuals for these sacrifices? These questions are not, as one might at first believe, interrogations formulated by the author about culture; rather, they constitute culture itself. What is in question in the conflict between prohibition and instinct is the triple problematic of lessening the burden of instinctual renunciation, reconciliation with the inescapable, and compensation for sacrifice.

What then, are these interrogations if they do not belong to an economic interpretation? With this question we come to an understanding of the single viewpoint which not only binds together all of Freud's essays on art, morality, and religion but also connects "individual" and "group" psychology and anchors them both in "metapsychology."

This economic interpretation of culture is itself elaborated in two steps, and *Civilization and Its Discontents* shows clearly how these two moments interact: first comes all that can be said without resorting to the death instinct and then what cannot be said without its intervention. The essay had developed with a calculated mildness prior to this inflection, which turns it toward the culturally tragic. The economics of culture seemed to coincide with what might be called a general "erotics": the ends pursued by the individual and those which animate culture appear as sometimes convergent and sometimes divergent forms of the same Eros:

> [The] process of civilization is a modification which the vital process experiences under the influence of a task that is set it by Eros and instigated by Ananke — by the exigencies of reality; and . . . this task is one of uniting separate individuals into a community bound together by libidinal ties.[1]

It is the same "erotics" therefore, which is responsible for the internal bonds within groups and which makes the individual seek pleasure and flee suffering — the threefold suffering inflicted by the world, his body, and other men. The development of culture is, like the growth of the individual from childhood to adulthood, the fruit of Eros and Ananke, love and work. We should even say: more of love than of work, for the necessity of uniting in work for the exploitation of nature is a poor second to the libidinal bonds which unite individuals into a single social body. It seems, therefore, that the same Eros which animates the search for individual happiness also seeks to unite men in ever larger groups. But then the paradox appears: as an organized struggle against nature, culture gives to man the power previously conferred upon the gods, and yet his resemblance to the gods leaves him unsatisfied — the discontent of civilization. Why? We can, of course, solely on the basis of this general "erotics," account for certain tensions between the individual and society, but not for the serious conflict which creates the tragedy of culture. For example, we can easily explain that family ties resist extension to wider groups. For each adolescent the passage from one group to another necessarily appears as a rupture of his oldest and most intimate bond. We also understand that something peculiar to feminine sexuality resists the transfer from private sexuality to the libidinal energies of social bonds. We can go much further in the direction of situations of conflict without, however, encountering radical contradictions. Culture, we know, imposes sacrifices on all sexual enjoyment — the prohibition of incest, the censorship of infantile sexuality, the strict regulation of sexuality into the narrow pathways of legitimacy and monogamy, the imposition of the imperative of procreation, and so forth. But however painful these sacrifices may be, and however unavoidable these conflicts, they do not reach the point of constituting a genuine an-

---

1. *Civilization and Its Discontents,* SE, XXI, 134. [Subsequent page numbers in parentheses refer to this work.]

tagonism. The most we can say is, first, that the libido resists with all the strength of its inertia the task, imposed on it by culture, of abandoning its earliest positions, and, second, that society's libidinal ties feed on the energy drained off from sexuality to the point of threatening it with atrophy. All of this is so "untragic," however, that we can even imagine a sort of armistice or compromise between the individual libido and the social bond.

And so the question reappears: why does man fail to be happy, and why he is unsatisfied as a cultural being?

This is the turning point of Freud's analysis. It is here that man is faced with an absurd commandment (Love thy neighbor as thyself) — an impossible requirement (Love your enemies) and a dangerous order, which squanders love, aids and abets the wicked, and betrays the imprudent one who tries to apply it. But the truth which is hidden behind the *folly of the imperative* is the folly of an instinct which escapes the limits of any erotic explanation:

> The element of truth behind all this, which people are so ready to disavow, is that men are not gentle creatures who want to be loved, and who at the most can defend themselves if they are attacked; they are, on the contrary, creatures among whose instinctual endowments is to be reckoned a powerful share of aggressiveness. As a result, their neighbor is for them not only a potential helper or sexual object, but also someone who tempts them to satisfy their aggressiveness on him, to exploit his capacity for work without compensation, to use him sexually without his consent, to seize his possessions, to humiliate him, to cause him pain, to torture and kill him. *Homo homini lupus* (p. 111).

The instinct which thus disrupts interhuman relationships and forces society to set itself up as the implacable agent of justice is, as we know, the *death instinct* — man's primordial hostility toward man.

The entire economy of Freud's essay is altered by the introduction of the death instinct. Although "social erotics" might, strictly speaking, appear as an *extension* of sexual erotics, as a displacement of its object or a sublimation of its goal, the division between Eros and death on the cultural level can no longer appear as the extension of a conflict which has already been analyzed on the individual level. On the contrary, the tragic in culture is privileged to reveal an antagonism which on the level of life and the individual psychism remains silent and ambiguous. Freud had, of course, already forged his doctrine of the death instinct by 1920 (*Beyond the Pleasure Principle*), but he did so within an apparently *biological* framework and without emphasizing the *social* aspect of aggressiveness. However, in spite of experimental support for his theory (repetition neurosis, infantile play, the tendency to relive painful episodes, etc.), it retained a quality of adventurous speculation. By 1930 Freud saw more clearly that the death instinct remains a silent instinct "within" the living organism and that it becomes manifest only in its social expression as aggressiveness and destruction. This is the sense of our earlier statement that the interpretation of culture possesses the unique privilege of revealing the antagonism of the instincts.

Thus, in the second part of Freud's essay we witness a sort of rereading of the theory of instincts in terms of their cultural expression. We can better understand why, on the psychological level, the death instinct is both an inescapable inference and an experience difficult to locate. It is never grasped except in the shadow of Eros, for Eros is what uses it by diverting it upon something other than the living organism. In this way the death instinct becomes blended with Eros when it takes the form of sadism, and we find it at work against the living organism itself through masochistic satisfaction. In short, the death instinct reveals itself only in conjunction with Eros, either by doubling the object libido or by overloading the narcissistic libido. It is unmasked and unveiled only as *anticulture*. A progressive revelation of the death instinct takes place across the three levels of the biological, the psychological, and the cultural. Its antagonism grows louder and louder as Eros progressively registers its effects of uniting first the living organism with itself, then the ego with its object, and finally individuals in ever larger groups. In repeating itself from level to level, the struggle between Eros and Death becomes more and more manifest and attains its full meaning only on the level of culture:

> This aggressive instinct is the derivation and the main representative of the death instinct which we have found alongside of Eros and which shares world dominion with it. And now, I think, the meaning of the evolution of civilization is no longer obscure to us. It must present the struggle between Eros and Death, between the instinct of life and the instinct of destruction, as it works itself out in the human species. This struggle is what all life essentially consists of, and the evolution of civiliza-

tion may therefore be simply described as the struggle for the life of the human species. And it is this battle of the giants that our nurse-maids try to appease with their lullaby about Heaven: *Eiapopeia vom Himmel!* (p. 122).

But this is not the end. In the final chapters of *Civilization and Its Discontents* the relationships between psychology and the theory of culture are completely reversed. At the beginning of this essay it was the economy of the libido, a term borrowed from the metapsychology, which served as a guide in the elucidation of the phenomenon of culture. Then, with the introduction of the death instinct, the interpretation of culture and the dialectic of the instincts begin to rebound upon each other in a circular movement. With the introduction of the feeling of guilt the theory of culture takes over as that which by rebound supports psychology. The feeling of guilt is in fact introduced as a "means" used by civilization to tame aggressiveness. The cultural interpretation is pushed so far that Freud can assert that the express intent of his essay is "to represent the sense of guilt as the most important problem in the development of civilization" (p. 134) and to explain why the progress of civilization should exact a loss of happiness due to the reinforcement of this sense. He quotes Hamlet's famous line in support of this conception: "Thus conscience does make cowards of us all."

If, therefore, the feeling of guilt is the specific means used by civilization to tame aggressiveness, it is not surprising that *Civilization and Its Discontents* contains the most developed interpretation of this feeling. Although its fabric is fundamentally psychological, the psychology of this feeling is possible only as the result of an "economic" interpretation of culture. From the viewpoint of individual psychology, in fact, the feeling of guilt appears to be no more than the effect of the internalized and introjected aggressiveness which the superego takes over in the name of moral consciousness and then returns against the ego. Its entire "economy," however, appears only when the need for punishment is relocated within a cultural perspective: "Civilization, therefore, obtains mastery over the individual's dangerous desire for aggression by weakening and disarming it and by setting up an agency within him to watch over it, like a garrison in a conquered city" (pp. 123–124).

Hence the economic and, one might say, structural interpretation of guilt feelings can be constructed only from within a cultural per-

spective. It is only within the framework of this structural interpretation that the various partial genetic interpretations concerning the
murder of the primitive father and the institution of remorse which
Freud elaborated at different stages of his thought can be understood
and put into place. Considered alone, this explanation remains problematic because of the contingency it introduces into the history of a
feeling which is otherwise represented with features of "fatal
inevitability" (p. 132). The contingent character of the process reconstructed by genetic explanation is attenuated as soon as genetic explanation itself is subordinated to a structural-economic one:

> Whether one has killed one's father or has abstained from doing so is not
> really the decisive thing. One is bound to feel guilty in either case, for the
> sense of guilt is an expression of the conflict due to ambivalence, of the
> eternal struggle between Eros and the instinct of destruction and death.
> This conflict is set going as soon as men are faced with the task of living
> together. So long as the community assumes no other form than that of
> the family, the conflict is bound to express itself in the Oedipus complex,
> to establish the conscience, and to create the first sense of guilt. When an
> attempt is made to widen the community, the same conflict is continued
> in forms which are dependent on the past; and it is strengthened and
> results in a further intensification of the sense of guilt. Since civilization
> obeys an internal erotic impulse which causes human beings to unite in
> a closely knit group, it can only achieve this aim through an ever-
> increasing reinforcement of the sense of guilt. What began in relation to
> the father is completed in relation to the group. If civilization is a neces-
> sary course of development from the family to humanity as a whole,
> then — as a result of the inborn conflict arising from ambivalence, of the eternal
> struggle between the trends of love and death — there is inextricably bound up
> with it an increase of the sense of guilt, which will perhaps reach heights that
> the individual finds hard to tolerate (pp. 132–133).

By the end of these various analyses we come to believe that the
economic viewpoint is what reveals the meaning of culture. But conversely, we must say that the supremacy of the economic viewpoint
over all others, including the genetic viewpoint, will be complete only
when psychoanalysis takes the risk of placing its instinctual dynamic
in the much larger framework of a theory of culture.

Illusion and the Turn to the "Genetic" Model

It is within the cultural sphere, defined in terms of the
topographic-economic model borrowed from the *Papers on Metapsy-*

chology, that Freud can relocate art, morality, and religion. But he takes up these topics by way of their "economic" function instead of their presumed object. This is the price for assuring a unity of interpretation.

Religion's role in such an economic model is that of "illusion." We must not protest. Even if Freud the rationalist recognizes only the observable and verifiable as real, it is not as a sort of "rationalism" or "unbelief" that this theory of "illusion" is important. Both Epicurus and Lucretius had said, long before, that it is primarily fear which produces gods. What is new in Freud's theory is an *economic* theory of illusion. The question Freud poses is not that of God as such but that of the god of men and his economic function in the balance sheet of the instinctual renunciations, substitutive satisfactions, and compensations by which men try to make life tolerable.

The key to illusion is the harshness of life, which is barely tolerable for man, since he not only understands and feels pain but yearns for consolation as a result of his innate narcissism. As we have seen, culture's task is not only to reduce human desire but also to defend man against the crushing superiority of nature. Illusion is the reserve method used by culture when the effective struggle against the evils of existence either has not begun or has not yet succeeded, or has failed, whether temporarily or definitively. It creates gods to exorcise fear, to reconcile man to the cruelty of his lot, and to compensate for the suffering of culture.

What new element does illusion introduce into the economy of the instincts? Essentially an ideational or representational core — the gods — about which it makes assertions — dogma — and these assertions are supposed to grasp a reality. It is this stage of belief in some reality which is responsible for the specificity of illusion in the balance of satisfactions and discontents. The religion forged by man satisfies him only through the medium of assertions that are unverifiable by proofs or rational observations. The question arises, therefore, of the source of this representational core of illusion.

Here is where global interpretation along the lines of the economic model takes in all partial interpretations in terms of some "genetic" model. The rivet which holds together explanations by origin with explanations by function is *illusion,* that is, the enigma proposed by a representation without an object. Freud concludes that this can make sense only by means of a genesis of the irrational. Such a genesis, however, remains homogeneous with economic explanation. The essential characteristic of "illusion," he repeats, is that it arises from human desire. Where does a doctrine without object get its efficacy if not from the force of the most tenacious desire of humanity, the desire for security, which among all others is the desire most foreign to reality?

Totem and Taboo and *Moses and Monotheism* provide the genetic schema which is indispensable for an economic explanation. They reconstitute the historical memories which form not only the true content, which is at the source of ideational distortion, but also (as we shall see when the quasi-neurotic aspect of religion is introduced) the "latent" content, which gives rise to the return of the repressed.

Let us provisionally distinguish the following two aspects: true content, which is dissimulated in distortion, and repressed memories, which later come back in disguised form in religious consciousness.

The first aspect merits attention, first because it conditions the second, but also because it gives us the opportunity to emphasize a curious feature of Freudianism. As opposed to the schools of "demythologization" and even more strongly against those which treat religion as a "myth" disguised as history, Freud insists on the *historical core* which constitutes the phylogenetic origin of religion. This is not surprising, for Freud's genetic explanation requires a *realism* of origins. Hence the depth and care of his research into the beginnings of civilization, as well as those of Jewish monotheism. A series of real fathers who are really massacred by real sons is needed to nourish the return of the repressed. "After this discussion I have no hesitation in declaring that men have always known (in this special way) that they once possessed a primal father and killed him."[2] The four chapters of *Totem and Taboo* constitute in their author's eyes "the first attempt . . . at applying the point of view and the findings of psychoanalysis to some unsolved problems of social psychology."[3] The genetic viewpoint prevails over the economic viewpoint, which has not yet been clearly elaborated as a model. Freud wants to understand moral constraint, including Kant's categorical imperative (ibid., p. xiv), as a survival of

---

2. *Moses and Monotheism,* SE, XXIII, 101.
3. Preface to *Totem and Taboo,* SE, Vol. XIII.

old totemic taboos. On a suggestion by Charles Darwin, he argues that in former times men lived in small hordes, each of which was governed by a vigorous male who had unlimited and brutal power at his disposal, kept all the women to himself, and castrated or massacred any rebellious sons. Then, according to a hypothesis borrowed from Atkinson, he speculates that the sons banded together against the father, killed him, and devoured him, not only to take vengeance upon him but to identify with him. Finally, following the theory of Robertson Smith, Freud argues that the totemic clan of brothers succeeded the father's horde. So that they would not destroy one another in useless struggles, the brothers arrived at a sort of social contract and instituted the taboo of incest and the rule of exogamy. At the same time, they remained under the influence of filial devotion and restored the image of the father in the substitutive form of the animal taboo. The totemic meal thus had the meaning of a solemn repetition of the murder of the father. Religion was born, and the figure of the father, long ago killed, was made its center. It is this same figure who will reemerge in the form of gods, or rather in one omnipotent god. The circle will be complete in the death of Christ and the eucharistic communion.

Here is the common ground between *Moses and Monotheism* and *Totem and Taboo,* the point where they share a mutual project as well as a mutual content. Freud writes at the beginning of the two essays published in *Imago* (Vol. XXIII, nos. 1 and 3) that "we shall even be led on to important considerations regarding the origin of monotheist religions in general."[4] For this purpose he must reconstruct with some claim to authenticity the event of the murder of the father which will be to monotheism what the murder of the primitive father had been to totemism. Hence his attempt to give credence to the hypothesis of an "Egyptian Moses," votary of the cult of Aten, the ethical, universal, and tolerant god, who is himself constructed on the model of a peaceful prince, such as the Pharaoh Akhenaten could have been and such as Moses could have imposed on the Semitic tribes. It is this "hero" — in the sense of Otto Rank, whose influence on this theory is considerable — who was killed by the people. Then the cult of the god

---

4. *Moses and Monotheism,* p. 4. [Subsequent page numbers in parentheses refer to this work.]

of Moses was founded on that of Yahweh, the god of volcanoes, in which it dissimulated its true origin and attempted to forget the murder of the hero. It is thus that the prophets would have been the artisans of a return of the god of Moses and the traumatic-event return in the form of an ethical god. The return *to* the god of Moses would at the same time be the return *of* the repressed trauma. Thus we are faced with the explanation of a resurgence on the level of representation and a return of the repressed on the emotional level as well. The Jewish people furnished Western culture with the model of self-accusation with which we are familiar because its sense of guilt is nourished on the memory of a murder which it nevertheless spared no effort to dissimulate.

Freud has no intention of minimizing the historical reality of this chain of traumatic events. He points out that "in the group too an impression of the past is retained in unconscious memory-traces" (p. 94). He considers the universality of linguistic symbolism much more as a proof of memory traces of the great traumas of humanity, in terms of the genetic model, than as an incitement to explore other dimensions of language, the imaginary, and myth. The distortion of this memory is the only function of the imaginary to be explored. The hereditary transmission itself, which is irreducible to any direct communication, is of course an embarrassment to Freud, but it must be postulated if we want to cross "the abyss which separates individual and group psychology" and "deal with peoples as we do with an individual neurotic. . . . If this is not so, we shall not advance a step further along the path we entered on, either in analysis or in group psychology. The audacity cannot be avoided" (p. 100). Thus we cannot call this an accessory hypothesis. Freud sees in it one of the principles of the cohesion of his system. "A tradition that was based only on communication could not lead to the compulsive character that attaches to religious phenomena" (p. 101). There can be a return of the repressed only if a traumatic *event* actually took place.

At this point we would be tempted to say that Freud's hypotheses concerning origins are mere subordinate interpretations and have no bearing on the "economic" interpretation, the only fundamental interpretation of "illusion." Quite the contrary is true, however, for in reality it is the genetic interpretation that perfects and completes the economic theory of "illusion." The economic theory integrates the results of these investigations concerning origins, and these investigations in turn emphasize a characteristic which had not before been brought to light, namely, the role played by the *return of the repressed* in the genesis of illusion. It is this characteristic which makes religion the "universal obsessional neurosis of humanity." But this characteristic could not appear before genetic explanation had suggested the existence of an analogy between the religious problematic and the childhood situation. The child, as Freud recalls, reaches maturity only through a more or less distinct phase of obsessional neurosis which usually is spontaneously liquidated but which sometimes requires the intervention of analysis. In the same way, mankind is forced during its own adolescence — a stage which we have not yet left behind — into an instinctual renunciation by way of a neurosis which arises from the same ambivalent position of the instincts with respect to the father. A number of texts written by Freud and also Theodore Reik develop this analogy between religion and obsessional neurosis. *Totem and Taboo,* for example, had already seen the neurotic character of taboos, in that an analogous delirium of touching can be discerned in both taboo and neurosis, having the same mixture of desire and horror. Customs, taboos, and symptoms of obsessional neurosis have in common the same absence of motivation, the same laws of fixation, displacement, and contagiousness, and the same ceremonial procedures which spring from prohibitions.[5] In both cases the fact that the repressed has been forgotten confers on the prohibition the same character of strangeness and unintelligibility, feeds the same desires for transgression, provokes the same symbolic satisfactions, the same phenomena of substitution and compromise and expiatory renunciations, and, finally, nourishes the same ambivalent attitudes with respect to prohibition (pp. 100 ff). During the period when Freud had not yet elaborated his theory of the superego, and especially his theory of the death instinct, "moral" consciousness or conscience (which he still interpreted as the internal perception of the repudiation of certain desires) was treated as a derivative of the taboo sense of guilt (p. 68). "In fact, one may venture to say that if we cannot trace the origin of the sense of guilt in obsessional

---

5. *Totem and Taboo,* p. 72. [Subsequent page numbers in parentheses refer to this work.]

neurotics, there can be no hope of *ever* tracing it" (pp. 68–69). The ambivalence of this attraction and repulsion is at the center of all his comparisons during this period.

Freud, of course, was struck by certain differences between taboos and neuroses. "Taboos are not neuroses but social formations," he says (p. 85). But he sought to reduce the gap by explaining the social aspect of the taboo by means of the organization of punishment and this organization by fear of the contagion of the taboo (p. 86). He added that social tendencies themselves contain a mixture of egotistical and erotic elements (p. 88). This theme is also developed in *Group Psychology and the Analysis of the Ego* (and particularly in chapter V, "The Church and the Army"). In this essay, which dates from 1921, Freud proposed an entirely "libidinal" or "erotic" interpretation of the attachment to the leader and the cohesion of groups on an authoritarian base and hierarchical structure.

Moses and Monotheism emphasizes as much as possible the neurotic nature of religion, and its principal occasion for doing so lies in the "phenomenon of latency" in the history of Judaism—that delay in the resurgence of the religion of Moses which had been repressed in the cult of Yahweh. Here we come across the intersection between the genetic and the economic models. Between "traumatic neurosis and Jewish monotheism there is one point of agreement: namely, in the characteristic that might be described as 'latency.'"[6] "This analogy is so close that one can almost speak of an identity" (p. 72). Once the schema of the evolution of neurosis is admitted (early trauma—defense—latency—outbreak of neurotic illness—partial return of the repressed) the rapprochement of the history of the human race with that of the individual does the rest:

> Something occurred in the life of the human species similar to what occurs in the life of individuals: of supposing, that is, that there too events occurred of a sexually aggressive nature, which left behind them permanent consequences but were for the most part fended off and forgotten, and which after a long latency came into effect and created phenomena similar to systems in their structure and purpose (p. 80).

Jewish monotheism thus takes over from totemism in Freud's history of the return of the repressed. The Jewish people renewed the

6. *Moses and Monotheism*, p. 68. [Subsequent page numbers refer to this work.]

primitive contract in the personage of Moses, an eminent substitute for the father. The murder of Christ is another reinforcement of the memory of origins, while Passover and Easter are the resurrection of Moses. Finally, the religion of Saint Paul completes the return of the repressed by leading it back to its prehistoric source, which is named original sin. A crime had been committed against God, according to this theory, and only death can redeem it. Freud passes quickly over the "phantasm" of expiation, which is at the center of the Christian kerygma (p. 86), and suggests that the Redeemer had to be the most guilty one, the chief of the fraternal clan, the parallel to the rebellious tragic hero in Greek tragedy (pp. 87ff.): "behind him [is hidden] the returned primal father of the primitive horde, transfigured, and, as the son, put in the place of the father" (p. 90).

This analogy with traumatic neurosis confirms our interpretation of the reciprocal action in Freud's work between the etiology of neuroses and the hermeneutics of culture. Religion presents an occasion for a rereading of neurosis, just as the analogous sense of guilt plunges it back into the dialectic of death and life instincts. The "topographic" model (in which the id, the ego, and the superego are differentiated), the "genetic" model (the role of childhood and phylogenesis), and the "economic" model (cathexis and anticathexis) converge in the ultimate interpretation of the return of the repressed (p. 97).

Religious "Illusion" and Aesthetic "Seduction"

Freud's economic interpretation of illusion finally allows us to locate aesthetic seduction with respect to religious illusion. As is well known, Freud's severity toward religion is in sharp contrast to his sympathy for the arts. This difference of tone is not fortuitous. The reason can be found in the general economy of cultural phenomena. For Freud, art is the nonobsessional, nonneurotic form of substitutive satisfaction. The *charm* of aesthetic creation does not arise from the return of the repressed.

At the beginning of this study we alluded to the article in the review *Imago* which, as early as 1908, Freud devoted to "Creative Writers and Daydreaming" and to the analogical method which he set into operation. A general theory of fantasy already underlay his method here, and an opening can be glimpsed leading toward the later theory of culture. Freud poses the question of whether, if poetry is so close to daydreaming, the artist's *technique* aims at hiding the fantasy as much as communicating it. Does he seek to overcome by the seduction of purely formal pleasure the repulsion that would arise from an overly direct evocation of what has been prohibited? The *ars poetica* thus evoked[7] now appears as the other pole of illusion. The artist seduces us, Freud writes, by a "yield of pleasure which he offers us in the presentation of his fantasies." The whole interpretation of culture from the years 1929 to 1939 is contained *in nuce* in the following lines:

> We give the name of an *incentive bonus,* or a *fore-pleasure,* to a yield of pleasure such as this, which is offered to us so as to make possible the release of still greater pleasure arising from deeper psychical sources. In my opinion, all the aesthetic pleasure which a creative writer affords us has the character of a fore-pleasure of this kind, and our actual enjoyment of an imaginative work proceeds from a liberation of tension in our minds. It may even be that not a little of this effect is due to the writer's enabling us thenceforward to enjoy our own daydreams without self-reproach or shame (p. 153).

Freud's eventual articulation of aesthetics into a general theory of culture can perhaps best be seen in "The Moses of Michelangelo." Nowhere else can we better understand how many apparently immovable obstacles this interpretation will upset. This essay is the fruit of a long familiarity with the masterpiece and of many drawings by which Freud attempted to reconstitute the successive positions which are condensed in Moses' actual gesture; and Freud's interpretation indeed proceeds, just as in the interpretation of dreams, from the details. This appropriately analytical method allows Freud to superimpose dream work on creative work and an interpretation of dreams on interpretation of the work of art. Therefore, rather than seeking to interpret the nature of the satisfaction which is generated by works of art on the level of the widest generalities (a task in which too many psychoanalysts have gone astray), the psychoanalyst attempts to resolve the general enigma of aesthetics by turning first to a single work and the meanings created by that work. We are acquainted with the patience and detail of this interpretation. Here, as in a dream analysis, it is the precise and apparently minor fact which counts and not the impression of the whole: the position of the prophet's right

---

7. "Creative Writers and Daydreaming," SE, IX, 153. [Subsequent page numbers refer to this work.]

index finger (the only finger which touches his beard, while the rest of the hand holds back), the unstable position of the Tablets, about to escape from the pressure of his arms. Freud's interpretation reconstitutes, in the filigree of this momentary posture, which is in a sense frozen in the stone, the series of opposing movements which found a sort of unstable compromise in this arrested movement. Moses must first of all have brought his hand to his beard in a gesture of anger — at the risk of allowing the Tablets to fall — while his eyes were violently attracted to one side by the spectacle of his idolatrous people. An opposing movement, however, checks the first and, arising from the strong consciousness of his religious mission, brings his hand back. What is before our eyes is the residue of a movement which had taken place and which Freud took upon himself to reconstruct in the same way that he reconstructs the opposing representations which generate compromise formations in dreams, neuroses, errors, and jokes. Freud digs beneath this compromise formation and discovers in the depths of apparent meaning, in addition to the exemplary expression of a triumph over inner conflict which is worthy of guarding a pope's tomb, a secret reproach to the violence of the dead pope and, in a sense, a warning to itself.

The exegesis of "The Moses of Michelangelo" is thus not a mere sidelight. It is situated on a single trajectory, which begins with *The Interpretation of Dreams* and passes through *The Psychopathology of Everyday Life* and *Jokes and Their Relation to the Unconscious*.

This unity of purpose allows us to question Freud's right to submit the work of art to the same treatment. For the art work is, as they say, a lasting and, in the widest sense of the term, a memorable creation of the day, while the dream is, as we know, a fugitive and sterile production of the night. Does not the work of art last and remain for the simple reason that it possesses undying meanings which enrich our patrimony of cultural values? This objection cannot be ignored, for it gives us the occasion to grasp the range of what we have hesitantly called a hermeneutics of culture. The psychoanalysis of culture is valuable not *in spite of* the fact that it is unaware of the value difference between dream productions and works of art but *because* it knows this difference and attempts to take account of it from an economic viewpoint. The whole problem of sublimation comes from the decision to place a fully recognized value opposition within the unitary viewpoint of a genesis and economics of the libido.

The value contrast between the "creative" and the "sterile" — an
opposition which a descriptive phenomenology would hold as an
originary given — poses a *problem* for an "economics." Freud so little
ignores this value contrast that he feels compelled to carry the unitary
dynamics further (or backwards, if you will) and to understand what
allocation of cathexes and anticathexes is capable of generating the
contrasting production of symptoms, on the level of dreams and
neuroses, and of expression, on the level of the arts and of culture in
general. This is why the analyst must take into account all the arguments that might be brought against a naïve assimilation of
phenomena of culture *expressivity* to a hastily plagiarized *symptomatology*, which really belongs to the theory of dreams and neuroses. He
must recapitulate all the themes which emphasize the contrast between
the two orders of production, themes which he can find in the aesthetics of Kant, Schelling, Hegel, or Alain. On this condition alone does
his interpretation not suppress but retain and contain the duality of
symptom and expression. Even after his interpretation, it remains true
that the dream is a private expression, lost in the solitude of sleep, an
expression which lacks the mediation of work, the incorporation of a
meaning into an unyielding substance, and the communication of this
meaning to a public — in short, the power of advancing consciousness
toward a new comprehension of itself. The force of psychoanalytic
explanation is precisely that of relating the contrasting cultural values
of the creation of a work and neurosis to a single scale of creativity and
a unified economics. By the same token it unites Plato's views on the
fundamental unity of poetics and erotics, those of Aristotle on the
continuity between purgation and purification, and those of Goethe
on demonism.

Perhaps we must go even further. What analysis claims to overcome is not only the phenomenological contrast between dreams and
culture but also a contrast internal to the economic model itself. A
second objection will help us to formulate this theme.

One might object to the interpretation of Michelangelo's *Moses,*
and even more to that of Sophocles' *Oedipus Rex* and Shakespeare's
Hamlet, by pointing out that, if these works are creations, it is because
they are not simple projections of the artists' conflicts but are outlines
of their solutions. The argument will be that the dream looks
backward toward childhood and the past, while the art work is an
advance on the artist himself. It is a prospective symbol of personal

synthesis and of the future of man rather than a regressive symbol of his unresolved conflicts. This is why the art lover's understanding is not a simple reliving of his personal conflicts, a fictive realization of the desires awakened in him by the drama, but a participation in the work of truth which is realized in the soul of the tragic hero. Thus Sophocles' creation of the character of Oedipus is not the simple manifestation of the childhood drama which bears his name but the invention of a new symbol of the pain of self-consciousness. This symbol does not repeat our childhood; it explores our adult life.

At first sight this objection comes directly into conflict with certain of Freud's own declarations, in "On Dreams," about Sophocles' *Oedipus Rex* or Shakespeare's *Hamlet*. But the objection is decisive, perhaps, only against a still naïve formulation of the hermeneutics that results from analysis, and perhaps it arises from a conception, itself naïve, of creation as a promotion of meanings for a supposedly pure consciousness. Thus, like the preceding objection, this one is less to be refuted than surpassed and integrated, at the same time as the thesis to which it is opposed, in a larger and more penetrating view of the dynamics which commands the two processes. "Regression" and "progression" would be not so much two diametrically opposed processes as two aspects of the same creativity. Kris, Loewenstein, and Hartmann proposed an all-encompassing and synthetic expression in their formula "regressive progression" (*Organization and Pathology of Thought*)[8] for designating the complex process by which the psychism elaborates new conscious meanings and revivifies surpassed unconscious formations. Regression and progression would designate abstract terms deduced from a single concrete process whose two extreme limits they designate (pure regression and pure progression) instead of two processes which are actually opposed to each other. Is there, indeed, a single dream, which does not have an exploratory function and does not "prophetically" outline a conclusion to our conflicts? Conversely, is there a single great symbol, created by art and literature, which does not plunge over and over again into the archaism of the conflicts and dramas of individual or collective childhood? Is not the genuine meaning of sublimation the promotion of new meanings by mobilizing old energies which had first been cathected into archaic figures? Do not the most innovative forms an

8. Edited by David Rapaport (New York: Columbia University Press, 1951).

artist, writer, or thinker can generate have the twofold power of con-
cealing and revealing, of dissimulating the old, in the same way as
dream symptoms or neuroses, and of revealing the most incomplete
and unrealized possibilities as symbols of the man of the future?

This is the direction in which psychoanalysis can realize its wish to
rejoin an integral hermeneutics of culture. To reach this end it must
surpass the necessary but abstract opposition between an interpretation which would do no more than extrapolate the symptomatology
of dreams and neuroses and an interpretation which would claim to
find the domain of creativity in consciousness. Further, it must first
reach the level of this opposition and bring it to maturity before it can
attain to a concrete dialectic, in which the provisional and finally
deceptive alternative between regression and progression will be surpassed.

THE PLACE OF FREUDIAN HERMENEUTICS

We said at the beginning that psychoanalysis becomes part of culture by *interpreting* it. How will our culture come to understand itself
by means of the representation given to it by psychoanalysis?

We should understand from the start that this interpretation is
biased and incomplete and even systematically unjust toward other
approaches to the phenomenon of culture. But this criticism is not
very important, because Freudian interpretation touches on the essential precisely as a result of its narrowness. The only reason that we
must first outline the limits of this hermeneutics of culture, therefore,
is so that we may eventually better locate ourselves in the center of
what it circumscribes and there adopt its position of force. However
legitimate criticisms may be, they must yield to a willingness to be
taught and to submit such criticism itself to the interrogation to which
psychoanalysis subjects all rationalizations and justifications. For this
reason, as opposed to the usual procedure, we will base ourselves on
the criticism (Part II) in order to allow to reverberate in us, in the
mode of free reflection (Part III), the deliberately didactic account that
we have been developing up till now (Part I).

Limits of Principle in the Freudian Interpretation of Culture

Every comparison of Freudianism with other theories of culture is
made difficult by the fact that its creator himself never proposed a

reflection on the limits of his interpretation. He admits that there are other instincts than the one he studies, but he never proposes a complete list. He speaks of work, of social bonds, of necessity, and of reality, but he is never clear as to how psychoanalysis might be coordinated with sciences or interpretations other than its own. This is fortunate. Freud's robust partiality leaves us usefully perplexed. Everyone bears the responsibility of *situating* psychoanalysis in his own vision of things.

Yet how can we orient ourselves at the outset? One of our initial remarks can serve as a guide, namely, that Freud grasps the whole of the phenomenon of culture — and even of human reality — but grasps it only from a single point of view. We must therefore seek the limits of the principles of the Freudian interpretation of culture in terms of the "models" — topographic-economic and genetic — instead of in terms of the interpreted content.

What do these models *not* allow to be grasped?

The explanation of culture by its affective cost in pleasure and pain and its phylogenetic and ontogenetic origins is certainly quite illuminating. We will point out later the considerable importance of such an effort (essentially related to that of Marx and Nietzsche) for the unmasking of "false" consciousness. We should not, however, expect from this enterprise anything more than a critique of authenticity. Above all, we must not ask of it what could be called a critique of foundations. That is the task of another method, which is not so much the hermeneutics of psychic expressions — dreams, art works, symptoms, and even religious dogmas — as a reflective method applied to human activity as a whole, that is, to the effort to exist, to the desire to be, and to the various mediations by which man strives to appropriate for himself the most originary assertion which inhabits his efforts and desires. The interweaving of a reflective philosophy and a hermeneutics of meaning is currently the most urgent task of a philosophical anthropology. But almost the entirety of the "structure of assimilation" in which Freudian metapsychology might be articulated, along with other types of hermeneutics which are foreign to psychoanalysis, is waiting to be constructed. This is not the place to attempt such a construction, but it is at least possible to point out certain border zones within that vast field, and we can take as our touchstone the theory of illusion, whose central meaning in Freud we have seen.

The interest of Freud's concept of illusion is that it demonstrates how representations which "console" us and make suffering tolerable are built not only *on* instinctual renunciation but also *from* this renunciation. The desires and their dynamism of cathexis and anticathexis are what constitute the entire substance of illusion. In this sense we were able to say that the theory of illusion is itself thoroughly economic. But to recognize it as such means that we must also give up seeking in it an exhaustive interpretation of the phenomenon of *value,* for this can be understood only by a more fundamental reflection on the dynamics of action.

Just as we do not resolve the enigma of political power by saying that the bonds to the chief mobilize an entire libidinal cathexis of a homosexual nature, we do not resolve the engima of the "authority of values" by discerning in the filigree of the moral and social phenomenon the figure of the father and the partly real, partly fantasied, identification with this figure. The *foundation* of a phenomenon such as power or value is one thing, and the affective cost of our experience of it, the balance sheet of human lived experience in pleasure and pain, is another.

Such a distinction between problems of foundation and problems of instinctual economy is surely one of principle. At least it marks the limit of an interpretation in terms of an economic model. Can it be argued that this distinction remains too theoretical and at no point affects the concepts of psychoanalysis, much less the work of the psychoanalyst? I do not believe so. It seems to me that this limit actually appears very concretely in the Freudian notion of *sublimation,* which is in reality an impure, mixed notion which combines an economic and an axiological point of view without formulating principles. In sublimation an instinct works at a "higher" level, although it can be said that the energy cathected in new objects is the *same* as that which before had been cathected in a sexual object. The economic point of view takes account only of that relationship of energy and not of the novelty of value promoted by this renunciation and transfer. The difficulty is modestly hidden by speaking of socially acceptable ends and objects. But social utility is a cloak of ignorance which is thrown over the problem of value introduced by sublimation.

The very meaning of religious "illusion" is thus once again at issue. As we pointed out above, Freud does not speak of God but of the god of men. Psychoanalysis has no means of radically resolving the problem of what Leibniz called "the radical origin of things." It is quite prepared, however, to unmask the infantile and archiac representations through which we live this problem. This distinction is not simply one of principle, for it also concerns the work of the psychoanalyst, who is neither a theologian nor an antitheologian. *As* an analyst he is an agnostic, that is, incompetent. *As* a psychoanalyst he cannot say whether God is *merely* a phantasm of god, but he can help his patient surpass the infantile and neurotic forms of religious belief and decide, or recognize, whether or not his religion is *only* an infantile and neurotic belief whose true mainspring the psychoanalyst has discovered. If the patient's belief does not survive this critical process, the only reason can be that it was not worthy to survive. But in that case nothing has been said either for or against faith in God. In another language I might say that, if faith must differ from religion, then religion must die in order that faith may be born.

The fact that Freud personally objects to this sort of distinction is of little importance. Freud is an *Aufklärer,* a man of the Enlightenment. His rationalism and, as he says himself, his lack of belief are not the fruit but the presupposition of his interpretation of religious illusion, and he considers his interpretation to be exhaustive. It is unquestionable that the discovery of religion as illusion profoundly changes the conditions of every process of becoming conscious, and we shall argue strongly for that in what follows. But psychoanalysis has no access to problems of radical origin *because* its point of view is economic and only economic.

I will attempt to make a bit more specific what I consider to be wrong with the Freudian interpretation of the cultural phenomenon as a whole and of illusion in particular. For Freud an illusion is a representation to which no reality corresponds. His definition is positivist. Is there not, however, a function of the imagination which escapes the positivist alternative of the real and the illusory? A lesson that we have learned, which is parallel to Freudianism but independent of it, is that myths and symbols are carriers of a meaning which escapes this alternative. A different hermeneutics, distinct from psychoanalysis and closer to the phenomenology of religion, teaches us that myths are not fables, that is, "false" and "unreal" stories. As opposed to all positivism, this hermeneutics presupposes that the "true" and the "real"

cannot be reduced to what can be verified by mathematical and experimental methods but has to do with our relationship to the world, to
other beings, and to being as well. It is this relationship which in an
imaginative mode the myth begins to explore. Freud is both very close
to and very far from recognizing this function of the imagination,
with which, in different ways, Spinoza, Schelling, and Hegel were all
acquainted. What brings him close to it is his *practice* of "interpretation," but what separates him from it is his "metapsychological"
theorizing, that is, the implicit philosophy of the economic model
itself. In one sense Freud indeed constructed his whole theory of interpretation, by the time of *The Interpretation of Dreams,* against the
physicalism and biologism reigning in psychology. Interpretation
means going from a manifest to a latent meaning. It moves entirely in
relations of meaning and includes relations of force (repression, return
of the repressed) only as relations of meaning (censorship, disguise,
condensation, displacement). No one since has contributed as much as
Freud to breaking the charm of *facts* and opening up the empire of
meaning. Yet Freud continues to include all of his discoveries in the
same positivistic framework which they destroy. In this respect the
"economic" model plays an extremely ambiguous role. It is heuristic
in its exploration of the depths it reveals but conservative in the tendency which it encourages to transcribe all relationships of "meaning"
into the language of a mental *hydraulics.* By the first aspect, that of
discovery, Freud breaks through the positivist framework of explanation; by the second, that of theorizing, he strengthens this framework
and authorizes the naïve doctrine of "mental dynamics" which too
often rages in the school.

It will be the task of a philosophical anthropology to undo these
equivocations at the very heart of Freudian metapsychology and coordinate the diverse styles of contemporary hermeneutics, in particular
that of Freud with the phenomenology of myths and symbols. But
these diverse styles cannot be coordinated unless they are subordinated
to that fundamental reflection which we alluded to above.

This limit of the principles of the "economic" model governs the
genetic model as well. As we have seen, Freud explains genetically
whatever does not possess positive truth. The "historical" origin (in
the phylogentic and ontogentic sense) takes the place of an axiological
or radical origin. This blindness to all functions of illusion which are

not mere distortions of positive reality explains Freud's utter lack of interest for whatever is not a simple repetition of an archiac or infantile form and, in the end, a simple "return of the repressed." This is striking in the case of religion. All that could have been added to primitive consolation, conferred by gods conceived in the image of the father, is without importance. Who can settle the question, then, of whether religion lies in the *return* of memories bound to the murder of the father of the horde rather than in the innovations by which religion moves away from its primitive model? Is meaning in genesis or in epigenesis? In the return of the repressed or in the rectification of the old by the new?[9] A genetic explanation cannot decide this question, for it requires a radical explanation, such as, for example, Hegel's in *The Philosophy of Religion*. It requires a reflection which turns to the progress of religious representation and not to its repetition.

Our doubts concerning the legitimacy of the genetic model are directly linked to our previous question of the limits of the economic model. It could indeed be the case that in its function of ontological exploration the mythopoetic imagination is the instrument of this innovative correction, which moves in a direction opposite to archaizing repetition. There is a progressive history of the symbolic function, of imagination, which does not coincide with the regressive history of illusion in the form of a simple "return of the repressed." But are we in a position to distinguish between these two histories, this movement forward and this regression, this creation and this repetition?

Our self-assurance fails us at this point, we know that however

9. Freud ran into the limits of his theory on a number of occasions. Where, he asks in *Moses and Monotheism,* is the origin of the later advancement of the idea of God which begins with the prohibition to adore Him in visible form? Belief in thought as all-powerful (ibid., p. 170), which accompanies man's estimation of the development of language, seems to operate on a different level from that ordered by the genetic and topographic-economic models. Freud, however, does not develop this theme any further. In the same way, the shift of emphasis away from motherhood (which is perceived) to fatherhood (which is conjectured) suggests that not everything is said when the ambivalence of love and fear is discussed. Furthermore, is the happiness of renunciation fully explained by turning first to the idea of a surplus of love, by which the superego, the heir of the father, responds to renunciation of instinctual satisfaction, and second to the idea of an increasing narcissism which accompanies the consciousness of a worthy act (pp. 174–178)? And why must the meaning of religion be sought only in "instinctual renunciation"? Why does it not support the pact of the brothers as well and the recognition of the equality of rights for all the members of the fraternal clan? Not everything here is the perpetuation of the will of the father or the return of the repressed. There is also the emergence of a new order.

well-founded and legitimate our discernment of limits may be, it is
indistinguishable from the justifications and rationalizations unmasked
by psychoanalysis. This is why we must leave our critique in suspense
and turn without defense to the interrogation of self-consciousness by
psychoanalysis.

It may even appear at the end of this survey that the "place" of
psychoanalysis at the heart of contemporary culture remains and
should remain indeterminate as long as what it has to teach has not yet
been assimilated. This is so in spite of and perhaps because of its limits.
Comparing it with other interpretations of culture, no longer opposed
but concurrent, will help us take this new step.

Marx, Nietzsche, Freud

Freud's work is clearly as important for the heightened consciousness of modern man as the work of Marx or Nietzsche. The relatedness of these three critiques of "false" consciousness is striking. But
we are still far from assimilating these three interrogations of self-
consciousness and integrating these three exercises in *suspicion* within
ourselves. We still pay too much attention to their differences, that is,
to the limitations which the prejudices of their time imposed on these
three thinkers; and we are, above all, still victims of the scholasticism
in which their epigones have enclosed them. Marx is thus relegated to
Marxist economism and to the absurd theory of consciousness as reflex, while Nietzsche is associated with biologism if not with an apology for violence, and Freud is confined within psychiatry and dressed
up in a simplistic pansexualism.

I hold that the meaning for our time of these three exegetes of
modern man can be rectified only if they are considered jointly.

First of all, they all attack the same illusion, that illusion which
bears the hallowed name of self-consciousness. This illusion is the fruit
of a preceding victory, which conquered the previous illusion of the
thing. The philosopher trained in the school of Descartes knows that
things are doubtful, that they are not what they appear to be. But he
never doubts that consciousness is as it appears to itself. In consciousness, meaning and the consciousness of meaning coincide. Since
Marx, Nietzsche, and Freud, however, we doubt even this. After
doubting the thing, we have begun to doubt consciousnees.

These three masters of suspicion, however, are not three masters of skepticism. They are surely three great "destroyers," but even that should not distract us. Destruction, as Heidegger says in *Being and Time,* is a moment in *every new foundation. The "destruction" of hidden worlds is a positive task,* and this includes the destruction of religion insofar as it is, as Nietzsche says, "a Platonism for the people." Only after such a "destruction" is the question posed of knowing what thought, reason, and even faith still mean.

All three free our horizon for a more authentic speaking, a new reign of truth, not only by means of a "destructive" critique but by the invention of an art of *interpreting.* Descartes triumphs over his doubts about things through the evidence of consciousness, while Marx, Nietzsche, and Freud triumph over their doubt about consciousness through an exegesis of meanings. For the first time comprehension is hermeneutics. Henceforth, seeking meaning no longer means spelling out the consciousness of meaning but, rather, *deciphering its expressions.* We are therefore faced not with three types of suspicion but with three types of deception. If consciousness is not what it believes itself to be, a new relationship must be established between the apparent and the latent. It would correspond to the relationship which consciousness had previously instituted between the thing's appearance and its reality. The fundamental category of consciousness for all three thinkers is the relationship "concealed-revealed" — or, if you will, the relationship "counterfeit-manifest." That Marxists stubbornly insist on their theory of the "reflex," that Nietzsche contradicts himself by dogmatizing over the "perspectivism" of the will to power, or that Freud mythologizes with his "censor," "doorkeeper," and "disguises" — these obstacles and dead ends are not what is essential. What is essential is that all three create with the means they possess — that is, with and against the prejudices of their epoch — a mediating *science of meaning* which is irreducible to the immediate *consciousness of meaning.* What all three attempted in different ways was to make their "conscious" methods of decoding coincide with the "unconscious" *work* of establishing a code which they attributed to the will to power, to the social being, or to the unconscious psyche. They do it through guile — and guile and a half. In Freud's case it is the admirable discovery of "On Dreams." The analyst deliberately takes in the opposite direction the path that the dreamer took, without willing it or knowing it, in his "dream work." Consequently, what distinguishes Marx, Freud, and Nietzsche is both their method of decoding and their representations of the process of coding which they attribute to unconscious being. It could not be otherwise, since method and representation are coextensive and verify each other. Thus for Freud the meaning of the dream — more generally, the meaning of symptoms and compromise formations and, even more generally, the meaning of psychic expressions as a whole — is inseparable from "analysis" as a tactic of decoding. One can even say, in a nonskeptical sense, that this meaning is proposed and even created by analysis and is therefore relative to the procedures which instituted it. This can be said, but only on the condition of saying the opposite: that the method is verified by the coherence of the *discovered* meaning and, moreover, that the method is justified by the fact that the discovered meaning not only satisfies the understanding through an intelligibility greater than the disorder of apparent consciousness but that it *liberates* the dreamer or the patient when he comes to recognize it and make it his own — in short, when the carrier of meaning *consciously becomes this meaning,* which up till now existed only outside him, "in" his unconscious and afterwards "in" the consciousness of his analyst.

That this meaning which had been only for *another* should become conscious for itself, that is precisely what the analyst wants for his patient. By the same token, an even deeper relationship is discovered between Marx, Freud, and Nietzsche. All three, as we said, begin with suspicions about the illusions of consciousness and operate by the guile of decipherment. All three, finally, far from being detractors of "consciousness," aim at extending it. What Marx wants is to liberate *praxis* by the awareness of necessity. This liberation, however, is inseparable from a "becoming conscious" which victoriously opposes the mystifications of false consciousness. What Nietzsche wants is to augment man's *power* and restore his *force,* but what the will to power means must be regained by the mediation of the code of the "overman," the "eternal return," and "Dionysus," without which this power would be no more than the violence of the immanent. What Freud wants is for the patient to make the meaning which was foreign to him his own and thus enlarge his field of consciousness, live better, and, finally, be a bit freer and, if possible, a bit happier. One of the most important homages rendered to psychoanalysis speaks of the "cure through consciousness." Correct—as long as we realize that analysis wants to substitute a mediating consciousness under the tutelage of the reality principle for immediate and deceptive consciousness. Thus the same *doubter* who depicts the ego as a "poor wretch" dominated by three masters (the id, the superego, and reality or necessity) is also the exegete who rediscovers the logic of the illogical kingdom and dares, with a modesty and discretion without parallel, to end his essay on *The Future of an Illusion* by invoking the god Logos, whose voice is weak but indefatigable, a God who is not all-powerful but simply efficacious in the long run.

THE REPERCUSSIONS OF FREUDIAN HERMENEUTICS IN CULTURE

This, then, is what these three exegetes wanted to do for modern man. But we are far from having assimilated their discoveries and from understanding ourselves fully through the means of interpretation of ourselves which they offer us. We must admit that their interpretations still float at a distance from us and that they have not yet found their proper place. The gap between their interpretation and our comprehension remains immense. Moreover, we are not faced with a unified interpretation to be assimilated as a whole but with three distinct interpretations, whose discordances are more manifest than their similarities. There as yet exists no structure of assimilation, no coherent discourse, no philosophical anthropology which is capable of integrating our hermeneutic consciousness of Marx, Nietzsche, and Freud into a whole. Their traumatizing effects accumulate and their powers of destruction add up, but their exegeses have not been coordinated in the unity of a new consciousness. This is why we must admit that the meaning of psychoanalysis as an event within modern culture remains in suspense and its place undetermined.

Resistance to the Truth

It is remarkable that psychoanalysis itself takes account of this delay and suspension in becoming conscious of the event which it represents for culture, and it does so through its own interpretative schemata. Consciousness "resists" self-comprehension, just as Oedipus "resisted" the truth known by everyone else. He refused to recognize himself in the man he had condemned. Self-recognition is

the true tragedy, a tragedy on a second level. What is tragic in
consciousness — the tragic quality of refusal and anger — doubles the
primary tragedy, the tragedy of such a being, of incest and parricide.
Freud spoke magnificently of this "resistance" to the truth in a famous
and often quoted text, "A Difficulty in the Path of Psychoanalysis"
(1917).[10] Psychoanalysis, he says, is chronologically the most recent of
the "severe blows" which "the universal narcissism of men, their
self-love, has up to the present suffered ... from the researches of
science" (p. 139). First there was the cosmological humiliation inflicted
upon man by Copernicus, who destroyed the narcissistic illusion by
which the home of man remained at rest in the center of the universe.
Then there came biological humiliation, when Darwin put an end to
man's claim to be unconnected with the animal kingdom. Finally came
psychological humiliation. Man, who already knew that he was lord
of neither the cosmos nor all living things, discovers that he is not
even lord of his own psyche. Psychoanalysis thus addresses itself to
the ego:

> You feel sure that you are informed of all that goes on in your mind if it is
> of any importance at all, because in that case, you believe, your con-
> sciousness gives you news of it. And if you have had no information of
> something in your mind you confidently assume that it does not exist
> there. Indeed, you go so far as to regard what is "mental" as identical
> with what is "conscious" — that is, with what is known to you — in spite
> of the most obvious evidence that a great deal more must constantly be
> going on in your mind than can be known to your consciousness. Come,
> let yourself be taught something on this point! ... You behave like an
> absolute ruler who is content with the information supplied him by his
> highest officials and never goes among the people to hear their voice.
> Turn your eyes inward, look into your own depths, learn first to know
> yourself! Then you will understand why you were bound to fall ill; and
> perhaps you will avoid falling ill in the future (pp. 142–43).

"Come, let yourself be taught something on this point! ... Turn
your eyes inward, look into your own depths, learn first to know
yourself!" It is in this way that psychoanalysis understands its own
insertion into community consciousness by way of instruction and
clarity. Such instruction, however, encounters the *resistance* of a primitive and persistent narcissism, that is, of a libido which is never

10. SE, Vol. XVII.

cathected completely in objects but is retained by the ego for itself. This is why the instruction of the ego is necessarily lived as a humiliation, a wound in the libido of the ego.

The theme of narcissistic humiliation greatly clarifies all that we have just said about suspicion, guile, and the extension of the field of consciousness. We now know that it is not consciousness which is humiliated but the pretension of consciousness, the libido of the ego. We also know that what does the humiliating is precisely a higher consciousness, a "clarity," scientific knowledge, as Freud the good rationalist says. In a larger sense we can say that it is a consciousness which is decentered from itself, unpreoccupied, and "displaced" toward the immensity of the cosmos by Copernicus, toward the mobile genius of life by Darwin, and toward the shadowy depths of the psyche by Freud. Consciousness nourishes itself by recentering itself around its Other: cosmos, bios, or psyche. It finds itself by losing itself. It finds itself instructed and clarified after losing itself and its narcissism.

The "Immediate" Reactions of Community Consciousness

The gap between the *interpretation* of culture introduced by psychoanalysis and its *comprehension* by community consciousness explains, if not totally at least partially, the perplexity of community consciousness. As we said above, psychoanalysis finds its place in culture only with difficulty. We now know that we become conscious of its meaning only across the truncated representations which arise from the resistance of our narcissism.

These truncated *representations* are what we encounter on the level of short-term influences and immediate reactions. The level of "short-term" influences is one of *vulgarization,* and that of "immediate" reactions is one of *small talk.* Still, it is not without interest to pause a moment on this level. Psychoanalysis has taken the risk of being judged, praised, and condemned on such an everyday level. From the moment that Freud began giving lectures and publishing books he addressed himself to nonanalysts and nonanalysands and brought psychoanalysis into the public domain. In any case, his words fell outside the precise intersubjective relation between the doctor and his patient from the very beginning. This diffusion of psychoanalysis out of the therapeutic context is a considerable cultural event, which social psychology has in its turn made into a subject of scientific inquiry, measure, and explanation.

It is first of all as a global phenomenon of *demystification* that psychoanalysis has penetrated the public. A hidden and silent part of man became public. "They" speak of sexuality, "they" speak of perversions, repression, the superego, and censorship. In this respect psychoanalysis is an event of the "they," a theme for "small talk." But the conspiracy of silence is also an event of the "they," and hypocrisy is no less small talk than the public exhibition and ridicule of every individual's secret.

No one knows what to do with this demystification, for it is the starting point of the most complete misunderstanding. On the level of "short-term" influences, "they" want to draw an *immediate* ethics from psychoanalysis. Thus "they" use psychoanalysis as a system of *justification* for moral positions whose profundity has not itself undergone psychoanalytic interrogation. Yet psychoanalysis was supposed to have been a tactic for unmasking all justifications. Hence, some ask psychoanalysis to ratify permissive education—since neurosis comes from repression—and find in Freud the discreet and unavowed apologist for a new Epicureanism. Others, placing their emphasis on the theory of stages of maturation and integration and the theory of perversions and regressions, mobilize psychoanalysis in the service of traditional morality. Did Freud not define culture by instinctual sacrifice?

It is true that on a first approximation one might hesitate as to what Freud really wanted. The temptation is to a "wild" psychoanalysis of psychoanalysis. Did Freud not make a public and bourgeois defense of the institution of monogamy while making a secret and revolutionary defense of the orgasm? But the consciousness which poses this question and attempts to enclose Freud within this *ethical* alternative is one which has not experienced the psychoanalytical critique.

The Freudian revolution is that of diagnosis, lucid coldness, and hard-won truths. In immediate sense, Freud preaches no morality. "I bring no consolation," he says at the end of *The Future of an Illusion.* But men want to convert his science into dogma. When he speaks of perversion and regression, they wonder whether or not it is the scientist who describes and explains or the Viennese bourgeois justifying himself. When he says that man is led by the pleasure principle, they suspect him — for praise or for blame — of slipping approval of an unannounced Epicureanism into his diagnosis, although he looks at the crafty behavior of the moral individual with the unemotional eye of science. This is the misunderstanding: Freud is hearkened to as a prophet, while he speaks as an unprophetic thinker. He does not herald a new ethic but rather changes the consciousness of those for whom the question of ethics remains open. He changes consciousness by changing our knowledge of consciousness and by giving it the key to some of its deceptions. Freud can change our ethic in the long run because he is not a moralist for the immediate future.

Is Freud a Tragic Thinker?

Only by rectifying these superficial reactions will community consciousness feel in depth the influence of psychoanalysis. As we have seen, the short term leads only to misunderstandings and contradictions, which result from attempting to draw an immediate ethic from psychoanalysis. The long-term way will be by way of a transformation of self-consciousness through the mediate comprehension of human signs. But where will the long road lead us? We do not know *yet*. Psychoanalysis is an indirect revolution. It will change our customs only by changing the quality of our outlook and the tenor of man's way of speaking about himself. It is first of all the work of truth and enters into the ethical sphere only through the *task of truth* which it proposes.

We can already recognize some lines of force along which can be discerned the influence on the consciousness of modern men of what I just now called the mediate comprehension of human signs.

By placing ourselves once more in the attempt to carry forward the general effort of demystification exercised by psychoanalysis on the most elementary, unsophisticated level, we can say that psychoanalysis focuses attention on what Freud himself calls the *harshness of life*. We can say that it is difficult to be a man. If psychoanalysis appears to plead both for the *diminution* of instinctual sacrifice by means of a relaxation of social prohibitions and for an *acceptance* of this sacrifice as a result of the submission of the pleasure principle to the reality principle, it is not because it believes in an immediate "diplomatic" action between opposing agencies [*instances*]. Rather, it puts all its emphasis on the change in consciousness which will come out of a wider and subtler comprehension of the tragic in humanity, without rushing too quickly to draw the ethical conclusions.

Unlike Nietzsche, Freud does not say that man is a "sick animal." Rather, he makes it clear that conflict is inescapable in human interaction. Why? First, man is the only being who possesses so long a childhood and who, as a result, remains for an incomparably long time in a condition of dependence. He is "historical," as has been said in many ways. Freud says, however, that as a result of his childhood fate, man is first prehistorical and remains so for a long time. The great figures — whether real or fantasied — of the father, the mother, brothers and sisters, the Oedipal crisis, the fear of castration — none of this would be meaningful for a being who was not fundamentally subject to his childhood and marked by the difficulty of becoming adult. Are we acquainted with what would be an adult feeling of guilt?

The tragedy of childhood fate, and also the tragedy of "repetition": It is this tragedy of repetition which is behind all the genetic explanations the limits of whose principles we spoke of above. It is not by methodological caprice but by respect for the truth that Freud leads us ceaselessly back to the *beginning*. Childhood would not be a fate if something did not constantly pull man backwards. No one has been more sensitive than Freud to the tragedy of this backward drift and its various forms, such as the return of the repressed, the libido's tendency to return to surpassed positions, the difficulty of the work of mourning, and in general the decathexis of censored energy and the absence of libidinal mobility. We should not forget that his reflections on the death instinct are for a large part born from this reflection on the tendency to repetition, which Freud did not hesitate to compare to the tendency in the organic world to return to an inorganic state. Thanatos forms a conspiracy with the archaizing spirit in Psyche.

The tragedy of libidinal contradictions: From the *Three Essays on the Theory of Sexuality* we know that the energy of the libido is not simple, that it has neither a single object nor a single end, and that it can always disintegrate and take the path of perversions and regressions. The growing complexity of the Freudian schema of instincts — the distinction between the libido of the ego and the object libido, the reinterpretation of sadism and masochism after the introduction of the death instinct — cannot but reinforce this feeling of a *wandering* nature of human desire. The difficulty of living is thus also — and perhaps above all — the difficulty of loving and of succeeding in a life of love.

This is not all. All these motivations presuppose that psychoanalysis did no more than demystify the sexual. If, over and above exploring the instinctual basis of man, however, it proposes to recognize the "resistance" of consciousness to this demystification and to unmask the justifications and rationalizations by which this "resistance" is expressed, and if it is true that this "resistance" belongs to the same network as the prohibitions and identifications which are the themes of the superego, then we would not be exaggerating to say that the tragedy has two foci, the id and the superego, and not just one. This is why, in addition to the difficulty of becoming adult and the difficulty of loving, there is the difficulty of self-knowledge and of honestly judging oneself. Thus the task of truthfulness is posed for us at the central point of the difficulty of living. In the Oedipus story the true tragedy is not in his having unwittingly killed his father and married his mother. *That* took place long ago. It is a destiny behind him. The tragedy taking place now is that the man he has condemned for this crime is *himself* and that such a fact must be recognized. Wisdom would be in recognizing oneself and in refraining from self-condemnation: but when the aged Sophocles wrote *Oedipus at Colonus,* he knew that Oedipus, even in his old age, had not come to the end of his "rage" against himself.

We can thus understand why it is useless to demand an immediate ethic from psychoanalysis without first having changed human consciousness. Man is an unjustly accused being.

It is perhaps here that Freud is closest to Nietzsche. Accusation is what must be accused. Hegel as well, in criticizing the "moral world view" in the *Phenomenology of Spirit,* had said long before Nietzsche that the judging consciousness is disparaging and hypocritical. Its own finitude and *equality* with the consciousness being judged must be recognized in order that the "remission of sins" can be possible as a reconciling self-knowledge. But Freud does not accuse accusation. He understands it and thus renders *public* its structure and stratagems. The possibility of an authentic ethic, where the cruelty of the superego would yield to the severity of love, lies in this direction. But we must first spend time in learning that the catharsis of desire is nothing without the catharsis of the judging consciousness.

This is not all we must learn *before* coming to an ethic. We have not yet exhausted the instruction which precedes an ethic.

It is indeed possible to reinterpret all that we have said above about culture in the light of these remarks on the twofold tragedy of the id and the superego.

We have seen the place of the notions of "illusion," "substitutive satisfaction," and "seduction" in culture. These notions also belong to the tragic cycle whose foci of proliferation we have just pointed out. Culture is indeed made up of all the procedures by which man escapes in the imaginary mode from the unresolvable situation where desires can be neither suppressed nor satisfied. Between satisfaction and suppression the way of *sublimation* opens up, but this way is also difficult. Yet it is because man can no longer be an animal and is not divine that he enters into this situation from which he cannot extricate himself. Hence he *creates* "delusions and dreams," as does the hero of Jensen's *Gradiva*. He also creates works of art and gods. The great storytelling function which Bergson found in closed societies Freud attributes to the tactic of evasion and illusion elaborated by man not simply *above* his renunciations but with their very flesh. This is an idea with an extraordinary profundity. Since the reality principle bars the way of the pleasure principle, it remains the case that man must "cultivate" the art of *substitutive enjoyment*. Man, as we hear again and again, is a being who can *sublimate*. But sublimation brings back the tragic instead of resolving it. Consolation in its turn, that is, the reconciliation with inevitable sacrifices and the art of supporting the suffering inflicted upon us by our body, the world, and other men, is never harmless. The relationship between religious "illusion" and obsessional neurosis is there to provide evidence that man leaves the sphere of instincts and "rises"—sublimates—only to rediscover in a more insidious form and more twisted disguises the very tragedy of childhood, where we recognized the first tragedy. Only art seems to be without danger, or at least Freud would lead us to believe so. Clearly, all he was acquainted with in art was its idealizing form, its ability to *muffle* the forces of darkness through sweet incantation. Freud seems to have had no suspicion of its vehemence, power of opposition, exploration, excavation, and scandalous explosion. This is why art seems to be the only power which Freud spared from his suspicion. In reality, "sublimation" opens up a new cycle of contradictions and dangers, but is it not the fundamental ambiguity of the imagination to serve two masters at once, Lie and Reality? It serves the lie because it deceives Eros with its fantasies (as we say that hunger is deceived) and reality because it accustoms the eye to Necessity.

Finally, it is the *lucid awareness* of the necessary character of conflicts which is, if not the last word, at least the first of a wisdom which would incorporate psychoanalytic instruction. In this way Freud renewed not only the sources of the tragic but "tragic knowledge" itself, insofar as it is the reconciliation with the inevitable. It is not by chance that Freud — the naturalist, determinist, scientist, heir to the Enlightenment — always turned to the language of tragic myth to say the essential: Oedipus, Narcissus, Eros, Ananke, and Thanatos. It is this tragic knowledge which must be assimilated in order to reach the threshold of a new ethic which we must no longer attempt to extract from Freud's work by immediate inference. It will be slowly prepared by the fundamentally nonethical teachings of psychoanalysis. The conscious emergence offered by psychoanalysis to modern man is difficult and painful because of the narcissistic humiliation it inflicts. But at this price it is related to the reconciliation whose law was stated by Aeschylus: τῶ πάθει μάθος, "Understanding comes through suffering" (*Agamemnon*, l. 177).

Before such a reconciliation, the critique first outlined and the internal repetition which we spoke of above must be conducted jointly and on a single front. A reflection on the limits of Freudian interpretation remains *in suspense,* as does the profound meaning of that great subversion of self-consciousness inaugurated by Marx, Nietzsche, and Freud.

Chapter Ten

New Religious Consciousness and the Crisis in Modernity

ROBERT N. BELLAH

Our research project is a response to the cultural and political upheaval of the 1960s. We have been concerned to understand the deepest meaning of that upheaval, that is to say its religious dimension, and to interpret that meaning in the context of modern American history. As it turned out our project got under way in early 1971, just when the upheaval in its most dramatic forms had passed. We ended up studying the successor movements to the counterculture rather than the counterculture in its effervescent stage. But if we are to put our findings in the broadest possible context — and that is what I intend to do in this chapter — then we must begin with the developments in the 1960s that lie immediately behind our study and with the nature of the society in which those developments occurred.

The disturbances and outbursts in America in the 1960s were hardly unique in modern history. Indeed, in a century where irrationalities and horrors of all sorts — mass executions, mass imprisonments, wars of annihilation, revolutions, rebellions, and depressions — have been common, the events of that decade in America might even be overlooked. But it is precisely the significance of that decade that the irrationalities and horrors of modern history

This essay was originally published as Chapter 15 of *The New Religious Consciousness* (University of California Press, 1976), edited by Charles Y. Glock and Robert N. Bellah. The book is a preliminary report of a research project on new religious groups that Glock and I directed from 1971 to 1974. Chapter 15 was one of two concluding chapters attempting to sum up the meaning of the study. For more details on particular groups, see earlier chapters of the original volume.

were borne in upon Americans so seriously that for the first time mass
disaffection from the common understandings of American culture
and society began to occur. Far more serious than any of the startling
events of the decade was the massive erosion of the legitimacy of
American institutions — business, government, education, the
churches, the family — that set in particularly among young people
and that continues, if public opinion polls are to be believed, in the
1970s even when overt protest has become less frequent.

The erosion of the legitimacy of established institutions among
certain sectors of the populations of many European countries —
particularly the working class and the intellectuals — began at least a
hundred years ago. In many of the newer third-world countries the
nation-state and modern institutions have not yet gained enough
legitimacy to begin the process of erosion. But in America, in spite of
a civil war, major social and religious movements, and minor disturbances of occasionally violent intensity, the fundamental legitimacy of
the established order had never before been questioned on such a scale.
This is in part because that order was itself a revolutionary order, the
result of one of the few successful revolutions in the modern world.
The messianic hope generated by the successful revolution and nur-
tured by the defeat of slavery in the Civil War for long made it possible
to overlook or minimize the extent to which the society failed to
achieve its own ideals. The promise of early fulfillment, which seemed
so tangible in America, operated to mute our native critics and prevent
mass disaffection, at least for a long time. But in the decade of the
sixties for many, not only of the deprived but of the most privileged,
that promise had begun to run out.

By way of background we may consider those interpretations of
reality in America that had been most successful in providing meaning
and generating loyalty up until the sixties: biblical religion and utilitarian individualism. The self-understanding of the original colonists was
that they were "God's new Israel," a nation under God. (From this
point of view the addition of the phrase "under God" to the pledge of
allegiance in the 1950s was an indication of the erosion of the tradition,
not because it was an innovation but because it arose from the need to
make explicit what had for generations been taken for granted.) In
New England this understanding was expressed in the biblical symbol
of a covenant signifying a special relationship between God and the

people. American society was to be one of exemplary obedience to God's laws and subject to the grace and judgment of the Lord. The notion of Americans as an elect people with exemplary significance for the world was not abandoned but enhanced during the revolution and the period of constructing the new nation. It was dramatically reaffirmed by Lincoln in the Civil War and continued to be expressed in the twentieth century in the thought of men like William Jennings Bryan and Woodrow Wilson. This biblical aspect of the national self-understanding was strongly social and collective, even though it contained an element of voluntarism from its Protestant roots. Its highest conception of reality was an objective absolute God as revealed in scriptures, and its conception of morality was also based on objective revelation.[1]

A second underlying interpretation of reality that has been enormously influential in American history, utilitarian individualism, was never wholly compatible with the biblical tradition, complex as the relations of attraction and repulsion between the two were. This tradition was rooted ultimately in the sophistic, skeptical, and hedonistic strands of ancient Greek philosophy but took its modern form initially in the theoretical writings of Thomas Hobbes. It became popular in America mainly through the somewhat softer and less consistent version of John Locke and his followers, a version deliberately designed to obscure the contrast with biblical religion. In its consistent original Hobbesian form, utilitarianism grew out of an effort to apply the methods of science to the understanding of man and was both atheistic and deterministic. While the commonsense Lockian version that has been the most pervasive current of American thought has not been fully conscious of these implications, the relation between utilitarianism and Anglo-American social science has been close and continuous from Hobbes and Locke to the classical economists of the eighteenth and early nineteenth centuries to the social Darwinists of the late nineteenth century and finally to such influential present-day sociologists as George Homans.

1. See Robert N. Bellah, *The Broken Covenant: American Civil Religion in Time of Trial* (New York: Seabury Press, 1975), for an analysis of the role of biblical religion in the formation of American society and also for the relations between biblical religion and utilitarian individualism. Two related essays are "Reflections on Reality in America," *Radical Religion* 1, no. 3 (1974); and "Religion and Polity in America," *Andover Newton Quarterly* 15, no. 2 (1974).

Whereas the central term for understanding individual motivation in the biblical tradition was "conscience," the central term in the utilitarian tradition was "interest." The biblical understanding of national life was based on the notion of community with charity for all the members, a community supported by public and private virtue. The utilitarian tradition believed in a neutral state in which individuals would be allowed to pursue the maximization of their self-interest, and the product would be public and private prosperity. The harshness of these contrasts was obscured, though never obliterated, by several considerations. The biblical tradition promised earthly rewards as well as heavenly for virtuous actions. The utilitarian tradition required self-restraint and "morality," if not as ends then as means. But the most pervasive mechanism for the harmonization of the two traditions was the corruption of the biblical tradition by utilitarian individualism, so that religion itself finally became for many a means for the maximization of self-interest with no effective link to virtue, charity, or community. A purely private pietism emphasizing only individual rewards that grew up in the nineteenth century and took many forms in the twentieth, from Norman Vincent Peale to Reverend Ike, was the expression of that corruption.[2]

The increasing dominance of utilitarian individualism was expressed not only in the corruption of religion but also in the rising prestige of science, technology, and bureaucratic organization. The scientific instrumentalism that was already prominent in Hobbes became the central tenet of the most typical late American philosophy, pragmatism. The tradition of utilitarian individualism expressed no interest in shared values or ends, since it considered the only significant end to be individual interest maximization, and individual ends are essentially random. Utilitarianism tended therefore to concentrate solely on the rationalization of means, on technical reason. As a result the rationalization of means became an end in itself. This is illustrated in the story about an American farmer who was asked why he worked so hard. To raise more corn, was his reply. But why do you want to do that? To make more money. What for? To buy more land. Why? To raise more corn. And so on ad infinitum. While utilitarian

2. An excellent treatment of the deep inner cleavage in American culture is Wilson Carey McWilliams, *The Idea of Fraternity in America* (Berkeley and Los Angeles: University of California Press, 1973).

individualism had no interest in society as an end in itself, it was certainly not unaware of the importance of society. Society like everything else was to be used instrumentally. The key term was organization, the instrumental use of social relationships. "Effective organization" was as much a hallmark of the American ethos as technological inventiveness.

The central value for utilitarian individualism was freedom, a term that could also be used to obscure the gap between the utilitarian and the biblical traditions, since it is a central biblical term as well. But for biblical religion, freedom meant liberation from the consequences of sin, freedom to do the right, and was almost equivalent to virtue. For utilitarianism, it meant the freedom to pursue one's own ends. Everything was to be subordinate to that: nature, social relations, even personal feelings. The exclusive concentration on means rendered that final end of freedom so devoid of content that it became illusory and the rationalization of means a kind of treadmill that was in fact the opposite of freedom.

That part of the biblical tradition that remained uncorrupted or only minimally corrupted found itself deeply uneasy with the dominant utilitarian ethos. Fundamentalism in America is not simply an expression of backward yokels. Even Bryan's opposition to evolution was in part an opposition to the social Darwinism that he saw as undermining all humane values in America. But that opposition remained largely inchoate, in part because it could not penetrate the facade of biblical symbols which the society never abandoned even when it betrayed them.

It was this dual set of fundamental understandings that the eruption of the 1960s fundamentally challenged. It is important to remember that the events of the sixties were preceded and prepared for by a new articulation of Christian symbolism in the later fifties in the life and work of Martin Luther King. King stood not only for the actualization of that central and ambiguous value of freedom for those who had never fully experienced even its most formal benefits. Even more significantly he stood for the actualization of the Christian imperative of love. For him society was not to be used manipulatively for individual ends. Even in a bitter struggle one's actions were to express that fundamental love, that oneness of all men in the sight of God, that is deeper than any self-interest. It was that conception, so close to

America's expressed biblical values and so far from its utilitarian practice that, together with militant activism, was so profoundly unsettling.

We are accustomed to think of the "costs" of modernization in the developing nations: the disrupted traditions, the breakup of families and villages, the impact of vast economic and social forces that can neither be understood nor adapted to in terms of inherited wisdom and ways of living. Because it is our tradition that invented modernization we have thought that we were somehow immune to the costs or that because the process was, with us, so slow and so gradual, we had successfully absorbed the strains of modernization. What the sixties showed us was that in America, too, the costs have been high and the strains by no means wholly absorbed. In that decade, at least among a significant proportion of the educated young of a whole generation, occurred the repudiation of the tradition of utilitarian individualism (even though it often persisted unconsciously even among those doing the repudiating) and the biblical tradition too, especially as it was seen, in part realistically, as linked to utiltarianism. Let us examine the critique.

The criticisms of American society that developed in the sixties were diverse and not always coherent one with another. What follows is more an interpretation than a description. In many different forms there was a new consciousness of the question of ends. The continuous expansion of wealth and power, which is what the rationalization of means meant in practice, did not seem so self-evidently good. There were of course some sharp questions about the unequal distribution of wealth and power, but beyond that was the question whether the quality of life was a simple function of wealth and power, or whether the endless accumulation of wealth and power was not destroying the quality and meaning of life, ecologically and sociologically. If the rationalization of means, the concern for pure instrumentalism, was no longer self-evidently meaningful, then those things that had been subordinated, dominated, and exploited for the sake of rationalizing means took on a new significance. Nature, social relations, and personal feelings could now be treated as ends rather than means, could be liberated from the repressive control of technical reason.

Among those who shared this general analysis there was a division between those who placed emphasis on overthrowing the present system as a necessary precondition for the realization of a more human society and those who emphasized the present embodiment of a new style of life "in the pores," so to speak, of the old society. The contrast was not absolute, as the effort to create politically "liberated zones" in certain communities such as Berkeley and Ann Arbor indicates. And for a time in the late sixties opposition to the Vietnam War, seen as an example of technical reason gone mad, took precedence over everything else. Yet there was a contrast between those mainly oriented to political action (still, in a way, oriented to means rather than ends, though it was the means to overthrow the existing system) and those mainly concerned with the actual creation of alternative patterns of living. The difference between demonstrations and sit-ins on the one hand and love-ins, be-ins, and rock festivals on the other illustrates the contrast. Political activists shared some of the personal characteristics of those they fought—they were "uptight," repressed, dominated by time and work. The cultural experimenters, represented most vividly, perhaps, by the "love, peace, groovy" flower children of the middle sixties, believed in harmony with man and nature and the enjoyment of the present moment through drugs, music, or meditation. In either case there was a sharp opposition to the dominant American ethos of utilitarian instrumentalism oriented to personal success. There was also a deep ambivalence to the biblical tradition, to which I will return.

The question of why the old order began to lose its legitimacy just when it did is not one we have felt equipped to answer. Clearly in the sixties there was a conjuncture of dissatisfactions that did not all have the same meaning. The protests of racial minorities, middle-class youth, and women had different causes and different goals. In spite of all the unsolved problems, the crisis was brought on by the success of the society as much as by its failures. That education and affluence did not bring happiness or fulfillment was perhaps as important as the fact that the society did not seem to be able to solve the problem of racism and poverty. The outbreak of a particularly vicious and meaningless little war in Asia that stymied America's leadership both militarily and politically for years on end acted as a catalyst but did not cause the crisis. The deepest cause, no matter what particular factors contributed to the actual timing, was, in my opinion, the inability of utilitarian individualism to provide a meaningful pattern of personal and social existence, especially when its alliance with biblical religion began to sag because biblical religion itself had been gutted in the process. I would thus interpret the crisis of the sixties above all as a crisis of meaning, a religious crisis, with major political, social, and cultural consequences to be sure.

Religious upheaval is not new in American history. Time and time again, after a period of spiritual dryness, there has been an outbreak of the spirit. But the religious crisis was in more ways a contrast to the great awakenings of the eighteenth and nineteenth centuries than a continuation of them. By all the measures of conventional religiosity the early 1950s had been a period of religious revival, but the revival of the fifties proved to be as artificial as the cold-war atmosphere that may have fostered it. The sixties saw a continuous drop in church attendance and a declining belief in the importance of religion, as measured by national polls. It is true that conservative and fundamentalist churches continued to grow and that the major losses were in the mainline Protestant denominations and in the Catholic church after the full consequences of Vatican II began to sink in. But in terms of American culture the latter had long been more important than the conservative wing. Although clergy and laity of many denominations played an important part in the events of the sixties, the churches as such were not the locale of the major changes, even the religious ones.

Indeed, it was easier for many in the biblical tradition to relate to the political than to the religious aspect of the developing counterculture. The demand for social justice fitted closely with the prophetic teachings of Judaism and Christianity. The struggle for racial equality and later the struggle against the Vietnam War drew many leaders from the churches and synagogues, even though the membership as a whole remained passive. But in spite of the leadership of Martin Luther King and the martyrdom of divinity students in the civil rights movement and in spite of the leadership of the Berrigans and William Sloane Coffin in the peace movement, those movements as a whole remained indifferent if not hostile to religion. By the end of the sixties those churchmen who had given everything to the political struggle found themselves without influence and without a following. For most of the political activists the churches remained too closely identified with the established powers to gain much sympathy or interest. As dogmatic Marxism gained greater influence among the activists during the decade, ideological antireligion increased as well.

But the churches were even less well prepared to cope with the new spirituality of the sixties. The demand for immediate, powerful, and deep religious experience, which was part of the turn away from future-oriented instrumentalism toward present meaning and fulfillment, could on the whole not be met by the religious bodies. The major Protestant churches in the course of generations of defensive struggle against secular rationalism had taken on some of the color of the enemy. Moralism and verbalism and the almost complete absence of ecstatic experience characterized the middle-class Protestant churches. The more intense religiosity of black and lower-class churches remained largely unavailable to the white middle-class members of the counterculture. The Catholic church with its great sacramental tradition might be imagined to have been a more hospitable home for the new movement, but such was not the case. Older Catholicism had its own defensiveness which took the form of scholastic intellectualism and legalistic moralism. Nor did Vatican II really improve things. The Catholic church finally decided to recognize the value of the modern world just when American young people were beginning to find it valueless. As if all this were not enough, the biblical arrogance toward nature and the Christian hostility toward the impulse life were both alien to the new spiritual mood. Thus the religion of the counterculture was by and large not biblical. It drew from many sources including the American Indian. But its deepest influences came from Asia.

In many ways Asian spirituality provided a more thorough contrast to the rejected utilitarian individualism than did biblical religion. To external achievement it posed inner experience; to the exploitation of nature, harmony with nature; to impersonal organization, an intense relation to a guru. Mahayana Buddhism, particularly in the form of Zen, provided the most pervasive religious influence on the counterculture; but elements from Taoism, Hinduism, and Sufism were also influential. What drug experiences, interpreted in oriental religious terms, as Timothy Leary and Richard Alpert did quite early, and meditation experiences, often taken up when drug use was found to have too many negative consequences, showed was the illusoriness of worldly striving. Careerism and status seeking, the sacrifice of present fulfillment for some ever-receding future goal, no longer seemed worthwhile. There was a turn away not only from utilitarian individ-

ualism but from the whole apparatus of industrial society. The new
ethos preferred handicrafts and farming to business and industry, and
small face-to-face communities to impersonal bureaucracy and the
isolated nuclear family. Simplicity and naturalness in food and clothing
were the ideal, even though conspicuous consumption and one-
upmanship ("Oh, you don't use natural salt, I see") made their inevitable appearance.

Thus, the limits were pushed far beyond what any previous great
awakening had seen: toward socialism in one direction, toward mysticism in the other. But perhaps the major meaning of the sixties was
not anything positive at all. Neither the political movement nor the
counterculture survived the decade. Important successor movements
did survive and they have been the focus of our study, but the major
meaning of the sixties was purely negative: the erosion of the legitimacy of the American way of life. On the surface what seems to have
been most drastically undermined was utilitarian individualism, for
the erosion of the biblical tradition seemed only to continue what had
been a long-term trend. The actual situation was more complicated.
Utilitarian individualism had perhaps never before been so divested of
its ideological and religious facade, never before recognized in all its
naked destructiveness. And yet that very exposure could become an
ironic victory. If all moral restraints are illegitimate, then why should I
believe in religion and morality? If those who win in American society
are the big crooks and those who lose do so only because they are little
crooks, why should I not try to be a big crook rather than a little one?
In this way the unmasking of utilitarian individualism led to the very
condition from which Hobbes sought to save us—the war of all
against all. Always before, the biblical side of the American tradition
has been able to bring antinomian and anarchic tendencies under some
kind of control, and perhaps that is still possible today. Certainly the
fragile structures of the counterculture were not able to do so. But out
of the shattered hopes of the sixties there has emerged a cynical
privatism, a narrowing of sympathy and concern to the smallest possible circle, that is truly frightening. What has happened to Richard
Nixon should not obscure for us the meaning of his overwhelming
victory in 1972. It was the victory of cynical privatism.

In this rather gloomy period of American history, and the mood of
the youth culture in the period of our study has been predominantly

gloomy—not the hope for massive change that characterized the sixties but the anxious concern for survival, physical and moral—the successor movements of the early seventies take on a special interest. We may ask whether any of them have been able to take up and preserve the positive seeds of the sixties so that under more favorable circumstances they may grow and fructify once again. Some of the successor movements clearly do not have that potential. The Weathermen and the Symbionese Liberation Army on the one hand, the Krishna Consciousness Society and the Divine Light Mission on the other, are parodies of the broader political and religious movements that they represent, too narrow and in some cases too self-destructive to contribute to the future solution of our problems. About others there may be more hope.

To some extent the successor movements, especially the explicitly religious ones, have been survival units in a quite literal sense. They have provided a stable social setting and a coherent set of symbols for young people disoriented by the drug culture or disillusioned with radical politics. What Synanon claims to have done for hard-core drug users, religious groups—from Zen Buddhists to Jesus people—have done for ex-hippies. The rescue-mission aspect of the successor movements has had quite tangible results. In many instances reconciliation with parents has been facilitated by the more stable life-style and the religious ideology of acceptance rather than confrontation. A new, more positive orientation toward occupational roles has often developed. In some cases, such as followers of Meher Baba, this has meant a return to school and the resumption of a normal middle-class career pattern.[3] For others, such as resident devotees of the San Francisco Zen Center[4] or ashram residents of the 3HO movement, jobs are seen largely as means to subsistence, having little value in themselves. While the attitude toward work in terms of punctuality, thoroughness, and politeness is, from the employer's point of view, positive, the religious devotee has no inner commitment to the job nor does he look forward to any advancement. In terms of intelligence and education the job holder is frequently "overqualified" for the position he holds,

3. See the interesting study of Thomas Robbins and Dick Anthony, "Getting Straight with Meher Baba," *Journal for the Scientific Study of Religion* 2, no. 2 (1972).

4. My information on the San Francisco Zen Center comes mainly from a Ph.D. dissertation by David Wise ("Zen Buddhist Subculture in San Francisco," Department of Sociology, University of California, Berkeley, 1971).

but this causes no personal distress because of the meaning the job has for him. For many of these groups the ideal solution would be economic self-sufficiency, so that members would not have to leave the community at all; but few are able to attain this. As in monastic orders some full-time devotees can be supported frugally by the gifts of sympathizers, but they are exceptions. Many of the groups also insist on a stable sexual life, in some instances celibate but more usually monogamous, with sexual relations being confined to marriage. Such norms are found not only among Jesus people but in the oriental groups as well.

These features of stability should not be interpreted as simple adaptation to the established society, though in some cases that may occur. The human-potential movement may serve such an adaptive function, and perhaps Synanon also does to a certain extent. But for the more explicitly religious groups, stable patterns of personal living and occupation do not mean acceptance of the established order. Our survey found that sympathizers of the oriental religions tend to be as critical of American society as political radicals, far more critical than the norm. While the survey shows that people sympathetic to the Jesus movement are less critical of American society, the Christian World Liberation Front, a Berkeley group, is atypical in being quite critical. All of these movements share a very negative image of established society as sunk in materialism and heading for disaster. Many of them have intense millennial expectations, viewing the present society as in the last stage of degradation before the dawning of a new era. 3HO people speak of the Aquarian age which is about to replace the dying Piscean age. Krishna Consciouness people speak of the present as the last stage of the materialistic Kali Yuga and on the verge of a new age of peace and happiness. More traditionally biblical expectations of the millennium are common among Jesus people. All of these groups, well behaved as they are, have withdrawn fundamentally from contemporary American society, see it as corrupt and illegitimate, and place their hope in a radically different vision. We should remember that early Christians too were well behaved—Paul advised them to remain in their jobs and their marriages—yet by withholding any deep commitment to the Roman Empire they helped to bring it down and to form a society of very different type.

Both our survey and our qualitative observations indicate that sympathizers of the human-potential movement are less alienated from American society than followers of oriental religions or political radicals. They are, nonetheless, more critical than the norm, and many of their beliefs contrast sharply with established American ideology. A tension exists within the movement over the issue of latent utilitarianism. If the techniques of the human-potential movement are to be used for personal and business success (the training-group movement out of which the human-potential movement in part derives had tendencies in that direction), then it is no different from the mind cures and positive thinking of the most debased kinds of utilitarian religion in America. But for some in the movement the whole idea of success is viewed negatively, and the training is seen in part as a way of gaining liberation from that goal. The high evaluation of bodily awareness and intrapsychic experience as well as nonmanipulative interpersonal relations place much of the movement in tension with the more usual orientations of American utilitarian individualism. Here as elsewhere in our field of research we have found that utilitarian individualism is a hydra-headed monster that tends to survive just where it is most attacked.

We have already considered some of the common themes of the counterculture of the sixties. We may now consider how they have survived and been elaborated in the successor movements. Immediate experience rather than doctrinal belief continues to be central among all the religious movements, including the Jesus movements, and in the human-potential movement as well. Knowledge in the sense of direct firsthand encounter has so much higher standing than abstract argument based on logic that one could almost speak of anti-intellectualism in many groups. Yet it would be a mistake to interpret this tendency as rampant irrationalism. Even though science is viewed ambivalently and the dangers of scientific progress are consciously feared by many in our groups, science as such is not rejected. There is a belief that much of what is experienced could be scientifically validated. Indeed, the human-potential groups (and Transcendental Meditation) believe that their teachings are in accord with science broadly understood. The study of the physiology of the brain during meditation is seen not as a threat but as a support for religious practice. Since reality inheres in the actual experience, explanatory schemes, theological or scientific, are secondary, though scientific explanations tend to be preferred to theological ones because of the general prestige of science. At a deeper level the lack of interest in critical reflective reason may be a form of anti–intellectualism, but the conscious irrationalism of groups such as the romantic German youth movement is quite missing. Similarly, there is a complete absence of primordial loyalties and hatreds based on race, ethnic group, or even, usually, religion.

In spite of the primacy of experience, belief is not entirely missing. In some groups the stress on doctrine may be increasing. The early phase of the New Left was heavily experiential: Unless you had placed your body on the line you could not understand the reality of American society. Consciousness raising in racial and women's groups continues to emphasize the experiential aspect of oppression and the struggle against it. But New Left groups became increasingly doctrinal toward the end of the 1960s and remain today more oriented to doctrine than experience in comparison with religious and human-potential groups.

A central belief shared by the oriental religions and diffused widely outside them is important because of its sharp contrast with established American views. This is the belief in the unity of all being. Our separate selves, according to Buddhism, Hinduism, and their offshoots, are not ultimately real. Philosophical Hinduism and Mahayana Buddhism reject dualism. For them ultimately there is no difference between myself and yourself, and this river and that mountain. We are all one and the conflict between us is therefore illusory.

While such beliefs are diametrically opposed to utilitarian individualism, for whom the individual is the ultimate ontological reality, there are elements in the Christian tradition to which they are not entirely opposed. Christian theology also felt the unity of being and the necessity to love all beings. The New Testament spoke of the church as one body of which we are all members. But Christianity has tended to maintain the ultimate dualism of creator and creation which the oriental religions would obliterate. Christian mystics have at times made statements (viewed as heretical) expressing the ultimate unity of God and man, and in a mediated form the unity of God and man through Christ is an orthodox belief. Still, American Christianity has seldom emphasized the aspect of the Christian tradition that stressed the unity rather than the distinction between the divine and the human, so that the oriental teachings stand out as sharply divergent.

Much of the countercultural criticism of American society is related to the belief in nondualism. If man and nature, men and women, white and black, rich and poor are really one, then there is no basis for the exploitation of the latter by the former. The ordination of women by Zen Buddhists and 3HO, even though not warranted in the earlier traditions, shows how their American followers interpret the fundamental beliefs. It is significant that from the basis of nondualism conclusions similar to those of Marxism can be reached. But because the theoretical basis is fundamental unity rather than fundamental opposition, the criticism of existing society is nonhostile, nonconfrontational, and often nonpolitical. Nonetheless, the effort to construct a witness community based on unity and identity rather than opposition and oppression can itself have critical consequences in a society based on opposite principles.

Another feature of oriental religions that has been widely influential is their view of dogma and symbol. Believing, as many of them do, that the fundamental truth, the truth of nondualism, is one, they also accept many beliefs and symbols as appropriate for different groups or different levels of spiritual insight. Dogmatism has by no means been missing in the oriental religions and has been traditionally more important than many of their American followers probably realize. But in relation to Christianity and biblical religions generally, the contrast holds. Belief in certain doctrinal or historical statements (Jesus is the son of God, Christ rose from the tomb on the third day) has been so central in Western religion that it has been hard for Westerners to imagine religions for whom literal belief in such statements is unimportant. But the impact of oriental religion coincides with a long history of the criticism of religion in the West in which particular beliefs have been rendered questionable, but the significance of religion and myth in human action has been reaffirmed. Postcritical Western religion was therefore ready for a positive response to Asian religions in a way different from any earlier period. Paul Tillich's response to Zen Buddhism late in his life is an example of this. Thomas Merton's final immersion in Buddhism is an even better one. Such tenden-

cies, however, are not to be found in the Christian World Liberation
Front or other Jesus movements.

But in many of the oriental groups and certainly in the human-
potential movement there has been a willingness to find meaning in a
wide variety of symbols and practices without regarding them literally
or exclusively. The danger here as elsewhere is that postcritical religion
can become purely utilitarian. This can happen if one fails to see that
any religious symbol or practice, however relative and partial, is an
effort to express or attain the truth about ultimate reality. If such
symbols and practices become mere techniques for "self-realization,"
then once again we see utilitarian individualism reborn from its own
ashes.

Our study began with the thought that the new religious consciousness that seemed to be developing among young people in the
San Francisco Bay Area might be some harbinger, some straw in the
wind, that would tell us of changes to come in American culture and
society. We were aware that studies of American religion based on
national samples could tell us mainly about what was widely believed
in the present and perhaps also in the past, since religious views change
relatively slowly. Such samples, however, could not easily pick up
what was incipient, especially what was radically new and as yet confined to only small groups. Even our Bay Area sample, weighted as it
was to youth, picked up only a tiny handful of those deeply committed to new forms of religion, although it did lead us to believe that the
new groups had gotten a hearing and some sympathy from a
significant minority. Our qualitative studies of particular groups,
based on participant–observation field studies, have told us a great deal
about them.

But to assess what we have discovered with respect to possible
future trends remains terribly hazardous. The future will certainly not
be determined mainly by the groups we studied. What role they can
play will depend very largely on other developments in the society as a
whole. Thus, in trying to assess the possible meaning and role of our
groups in the future I would like to outline three possible scenarios for
American society as a whole: liberal, traditional authoritarian, and
revolutionary.

The future that most people seem to expect and that the
futurologists describe with their projections is very much like the

present society only more so. This is what I call the liberal scenario. American society would continue as in the past to devote itself to the accumulation of wealth and power. The mindless rationalization of means and the lack of concern with ends would only increase as biblical religion and morality continue to erode. Utilitarian individualism, with less biblical restraint or facade than ever before, would continue as the dominant ideology. Its economic form, capitalism, its political form, bureaucracy, and its ideological form, scientism, would each increasingly dominate its respective sphere. Among the elite, scientism — the idolization of technical reason alone — would provide some coherent meaning after traditional religion and morality had gone. But technical reason would hardly be a sufficient surrogate religion for the masses. No longer accepting the society as legitimate in any ideal terms, the masses would have to be brought to acquiesce grudgingly by a combination of coercion and material reward. In such a society one could see a certain role for oriental religious groups and the human-potential movement — perhaps even for a small radical political fringe. All of these could be allowed within limits to operate and provide the possibility of expressing the frustration and rage that the system generates but in a way such that the individuals concerned are cooled out and the system itself is not threatened. The utilitarian individualism that is latent in all the countercultural successor movements, political and religious, makes this a real possibility. This scenario depicts the society as heading, mildly and gradually, into something like Aldous Huxley's *Brave New World.*

Lately, however, questions have been raised as to the viability of this direction of development. Perhaps there are inner contradictions that will lead to a drastic breakdown in the foreseeable future. Robert Heilbroner has recently predicted such a collapse, largely as a result of ecological catastrophe.[5] But Heilbroner also envisages the possibility that tensions between the rich and the poor nations could bring disaster sooner than would ecological attrition. Even since Heilbroner wrote, the proliferation of atomic weapon capacity in India and the Middle East has strengthened this possibility. Another distinct possibility is worldwide economic collapse bringing social convulsions in train. No matter how the breakdown of the "modernization" syn-

---

5. Robert Heilbroner, *An Inquiry into the Human Prospect* (New York: W. W. Norton, 1974).

drome might occur, Heilbroner envisages a relapse into traditional
authoritarianism as the most likely result — providing, that is, that the
worst outcome, total destruction of life on the planet, is avoided.
Simpler, poorer, and less free societies might be all that humans would
be capable of in the wake of a global catastrophe. The social and
personal coherence that the modernizing societies never attained
might be supplied by the rigid myths and rituals of a new hierarchical
authoritarian society. To put it in terms of the present discussion, the
collapse of subjective reason, which is what technical reason ultimately is, would bring in its wake a revival of objective reason in a
particularly closed and reified form.[6] Technical reason, because it is
concerned not with truth or reality but only with results, not with
what is but only what works, is ultimately completely subjective.
That its domineering manipulative attitude to reality in the service of
the subject leads ultimately to the destruction of any true subjectivity
is only one of its many ironies. But a new traditional authoritarianism
would set up some single orthodox version of what truth and reality
are and enforce agreement. Some historically relative creed, belief, and
ritual would be asserted as identical with objective reality itself. In this
way social and personal coherence would be achieved, but ultimately
at the expense of any real objectivity.

If a relapse into traditional authoritarianism is a distinct possibility
in America, and I believe it is, we might ask what are the likely
candidates for the job of supplying the new orthodoxy. Perhaps the
most likely system would be right-wing Protestant fundamentalism.
We already have a good example of such a regime in Afrikaner-
dominated South Africa.[7] Conservative Protestant fundamentalism
has a large and, by some measures, growing following in America. It
has the religious and moral absolutism that a traditional authoritarianism would require, and it is hard to see any close rival on
the American scene today. The Catholic church, which might at an
earlier period have been a candidate for such a role, is certainly not, in
its post-Vatican II disarray. Some of the more authoritarian of our

6. The contrast between subjective and objective reason has been developed by
members of the Frankfurt School. See, for example, Max Horkheimer, *The Eclipse of
Reason* (London: Oxford University Press, 1947; Seabury Paperback, 1974).

7. See Dunbar Moodie, *The Rise of Afrikanerdom* (Berkeley and Los Angeles: University of California Press, 1974), for an excellent analysis of Afrikaner civil religion and
its Dutch Calvinist dimension.

Asian religions might provide a sufficiently doctrinaire model, but their small following in comparison with Protestant fundamentalism virtually rules them out. The future for most of the groups we have studied, all but the Jesus movements, would be bleak indeed under such a neo-traditional authoritarianism. It is doubtful if even a group as open as the Christian World Liberation Front could survive. Neo-authoritarian regimes are hard on nonconformity in every sphere. The new Chilean government, for example, not only sets standards of dress and hair style but also persecutes oriental religions.

There remains a third alternative, however improbable. It is this that I am calling revolutionary, not in the sense that it would be inaugurated by a bloody uprising, which I do not think likely, but because it would bring fundamental structural change, socially and culturally. It is to this rather unlikely outcome that most of the groups we have studied, at least the most flexible and open of them, would have most to contribute. Such a new order would involve, as in the case of traditional authoritarianism, an abrupt shift away from the exclusive dominance of technical reason; but it would not involve the adoption of a reified objective reason either. In accord with its concern for ends rather than means alone, such a revolutionary culture would have a firm commitment to the quest for ultimate reality. Priorities would shift away from endless accumulation of wealth and power to a greater concern for harmony with nature and between human beings. Perhaps a much simpler material life, simpler, that is, compared to present middle-class American standards, would result; but it would not be accompanied by an abandonment of free inquiry or free speech. Science, which would ultimately have to be shackled in a traditional authoritarian regime, would continue to be pursued in the revolutionary culture, but it would not be idolized as in the liberal model. In all these respects the values, attitudes, and beliefs of the oriental religious groups, the human-potential movement, and even a group like the Christian World Liberation Front, as well as the more flexible of the radical political groups, would be consonant with the new regime and its needs. Indeed, many of the present activities of such groups could be seen as experiments leading to the possibility of such a new alternative. Neither safety valve nor persecuted minority, the new groups would be, under such an option, the vanguard of a new age.

Such an outcome would accord most closely with the millennial

expectations which we have seen are rife among the new groups. Even
if an enormous amount of thought and planning were devoted to such
such an alternative, thought and planning that the small struggling
groups we have been studying are quite incapable at the moment of
supplying, the revolutionary alternative seems quite utopian. Perhaps
only a major shift in the established biblical religions, a shift away
from their uneasy alliance with utilitarian individualism and toward a
profound reappropriation of their own religious roots and an openness
to the needs of the contemporary world, would provide the mass base
for a successful effort to establish the revolutionary alternative. To be
politically effective such a shift would have to lead to a revitalization of
the revolutionary spirit of the young republic, so that America would
once again attract the hope and love of its citizens. This outcome too at
present seems quite utopian. It may be, however, that only the im-
plementation of a utopian vision, a holistic reason that unites subjectivity and objectivity, will make human life in the twenty-first century
worth living.

AFTERWORD: 1978

Rather than rewrite the above essay for the present volume it has
seemed more useful to leave it as originally published, with the exception of a few omissions of detail and of specific reference to other
chapters in the original volume, and add an afterword in which the
implicit interpretive approach of the essay could be made explicit and
in which the role of hermeneutics in contributing to the solution of the
problems posed by the essay could be explored.

The essay is an interpretation of certain aspects of American culture, that culture itself seen as a set or sets of interpretations of American experience. My understanding of culture is close to that of Clifford Geertz: "Believing, with Max Weber, that man is an animal
suspended in webs of significance he himself has spun, I take culture to
be those webs, and the analysis of it to be therefore not an experimental science in search of law but an interpretive one in search of
meaning."[8] Interpretive social science is only a conscious second-order

8. Clifford Geertz, *The Interpretation of Cultures* (New York: Basic Books, 1973), p. 5.

version of its subject matter. It is not only the interpretive social scientist who is in search of meaning, it is also the individuals and groups that he is studying who are in search of meaning. Indeed when the social scientist is, as in the present instance, a member of the society which he is studying, the distinction between primary and secondary interpretations may become muddied. (To the extent that we are all members of the human species the difference between primary and secondary interpretations will always be blurred, which is one of the reasons why social science must be fundamentally different from the sciences of nonhuman things.)

One pitfall of the term "culture" is the tendency to reify it into an undifferentiated whole, as if there were only one "American culture." There are useful senses in which there *is* only one American culture, but to the extent that that usage obscures variations, lines of cleavage, and even deep conflict, it may be better for a while to enrich our vocabulary by speaking of meanings, interpretations, and even ideologies, as well as cultures. In any case, the subject of the above essay is not only that set of interpretations we can call American culture, but even more the "conflict of interpretations," to borrow a phrase from Paul Ricoeur, which characterizes and to an extent has always characterized American society.

A further implication of what has been said so far is that every interpretation is an interpretation from a certain point of view, an interpretation within a certain tradition of interpretation. A sociological interpretation is an interpretation from within the (or one of the) sociological tradition(s). Perhaps the commonest American sociological tradition (though not the tradition of the present author) is a version of that utilitarian individualism which is one of the major conflicting interpretations constitutive of American culture. Indeed utilitarian individualism is simply the commonest Anglo-Saxon version of what Louis Dumont calls "modern ideology,"[9] that polemic modern stance that arose in the sixteenth and seventeenth centuries as a critique of classical culture and biblical religion and that dominates educated consciousness all over the world today. Dumont also argues, as I have in

9. See particularly Louis Dumont, *From Mandeville to Marx: The Genesis and Triumph of Economic Ideology* (Chicago: University of Chicago Press, 1977), which is itself a superb example of interpretive social science.

previous writings,[10] that there is a schism in modern social science and that one or more tendencies in modern social science reject the premises of modern ideology (including its utilitarian individualist version) and make it possible to reappropriate some of the insights of traditional religions and philosophies, both Western and Eastern. This is not the place to review my own sociological lineage, which derives from Durkheim and Weber by way of my teacher Talcott Parsons, but it is certainly that lineage which allows me to stand at a critical distance from modern ideology generally and utilitarian individualism in particular and to consider how it might be possible to relate the teachings of the traditional religions to our present condition. All of which is to say that there is no scientific Mount Olympus from which to view "objectively" the matters with which my essay is concerned. Of course this does not mean that my interpretations are "subjective" either. They are in the public domain, and their validity can be argued with reference to the primary texts which they are interpreting. But "validity" again will be in terms of a point of view, a tradition of interpretation, which may or may not be the same as mine. And the differences are not merely "academic." They are derived from the very conflict of interpretations that characterizes American society. They are differences "from within the struggle," so to speak, which, again, does not mean that they are immune to the canons of rational discourse.

I am afraid this Afterword can only raise, tantalizingly, questions which it cannot begin to answer. If it suggests, however, that social science considered as interpretive social science is always within a social context, always involves ethical, political, perhaps even religious commitments, then it will have served its purpose. And if interpretive social science always has a specific social context, is always engaged in the human project, it is also true that it has an important social and ethical contribution to make. What would be more helpful in terms of the tradition within which my essay stands than to push the analysis of utilitarian individualism far beyond what I have written so that its implications for American society in all its complexity could be laid bare? And what more helpful than a constructive exegesis of

10. Robert N. Bellah, *Beyond Belief: Essays on Religion in a Post-traditional World* New York: Harper and Row, 1970), particularly chapter 15, "Between Religion and Social Science."

biblical and Eastern religions as they might relate to the problems of the future of American society sketched at the end of my essay? Such interpretations and exegeses would be in the highest sense of the term "practical," the classical Platonic and Aristotelian sense of the term, in which it applies to the enterprise of interpretive social science itself.

Critical Bibliography

PRACTICAL AND THEORETICAL REASON

This theme remains at the center of philosophical discussion, as it has been since the Greeks. Since it has been treated, either directly or indirectly, by every major thinker from Plato onward, we can only suggest several touchstones that bear directly on the themes discussed in this volume.

Plato, *Phaedrus, Republic, Statesman*
Aristotle, *Ethics, Politics, Rhetoric*
Cicero, *On the Republic* and *On Oratory*
Immanuel Kant, *Critique of Pure Reason, Critique of Practical Reason, Critique of Judgment*
G. W. F. Hegel, *Phenomenology of Spirit, Logic, The Philosophy of Right*
Karl Marx, *German Ideology, The Grundisse (The Foundation of the Critique of Political Economy)*

THE INTERPLAY OF CONTEXT AND INTERPRETATION

In modern Western thought, the theme of theoretical and practical reason finds its most relevant expression in interpretive philosophy. The topics of context, meaning, and practice form the center of this development. These authors are among the most influential figures representing the interpretive point of view.

John Austin. *How to Do Things with Words.* Cambridge: Harvard University Press, 1962.
John Dewey. *The Quest for Certainty: A Study of the Relation of Knowledge and Action.* New York: Minton, Balch & Co., 1929.
Jürgen Habermas. *Knowledge and Human Interests.* Boston: Beacon, 1971.
Martin Heidegger. *Being and Time.* Translated by J. Marquarie and E. Robinson. New York: Harper and Row, 1962. (First published 1927.)
Georg Lukács. *History and Class Consciousness.* Translated by Rodney Livingstone. London: Merlin Press, 1971.

Jean-Paul Sartre. *Search for a Method.* Translated by Hazel E. Barnes. New
    York: Knopf, 1963.
From Max Weber: Essays in Sociology. Edited by H. H. Gerth and C. Wright
    Mills. New York: Oxford University Press, 1953.
Raymond Williams. *Culture and Society.* New York: Columbia University
    Press, 1960.
Ludwig Wittgenstein. *Philosophical Investigations.* 3rd ed. Translated by G. E.
    M. Anscombe. New York: Macmillan, 1958.

THE CONFLICT OF INTERPRETATIONS

Since the nineteenth century interpretive thinkers have had to confront the
challenge that only social investigation conforming to the methodological
canons of scientific verification could be valid. Against this threatened split of
theoretical and practical knowledge interpretive thinkers have continued the
classical insistence upon a plurality of methods appropriate to different subject
matters.

Roland Barthes. *Critical Essays.* Evanston: Northwestern University Press,
    1972.
Kenneth Burke. *Language as Symbolic Action: Essays on Life, Literature and
    Method.* Berkeley and Los Angeles: University of California Press, 1966.
Ernst Cassirer. *The Logic of the Humanities.* New Haven: Yale University
    Press, 1961.
Wilhelm Dilthey: Selected Writings. Edited by N. P. Rickman. Cambridge:
    Cambridge University Press, 1976.
Richard McKeon. *Thought, Action and Passion.* Chicago: University of
    Chicago Press, 1954.
Paul Ricoeur. *The Conflict of Interpretations: Essays in Hermeneutics.* Evanston:
    Northwestern University Press, 1974.

FURTHER READING

We include in this section further references to works of the authors represented in this volume. These works include extensive further references to
important research in the various special fields. These references are of course
suggestive rather than comprehensive.

Robert N. Bellah. *Beyond Belief: Essays on Religion in a Post-Traditional World.*
    New York: Harper and Row, 1970.
————. *The Broken Covenant: American Civil Religion in a Time of Trial.* New
    York: Seabury, 1975.
Hans-Georg Gadamer. *Philosophical Hermeneutics.* Berkeley and Los Angeles:
    University of California Press, 1976.
————. *Truth and Method.* Edited by Garrett Barden and John Cumming. New
    York: Seabury, 1975.
Clifford Geertz. *Interpretation of Cultures.* New York: Basic Books, 1973.

_____. *Islam Observed; Religious Development in Morocco and Indonesia.* Chicago: University of Chicago Press, 1971.

Albert Hirschman. *Exit, Voice and Loyalty: Responses to Decline in Firms, Organization and States.* Cambridge: Harvard University Press, 1970.

_____. *The Passions and the Interests.* Princeton: Princeton University Press, 1977.

Thomas Kuhn. "A Reply to My Criticism." In Lakatos and Musgrave, *Criticism and the Growth of Knowledge.* Cambridge: Cambridge University Press, 1970.

_____. *The Structure of Scientific Revolutions.* 2nd ed. Chicago: University of Chicago Press, 1970.

Paul Ricoeur. *Freud and Philosophy: An Essay on Interpretation.* New Haven: Yale University Press, 1970.

_____. *The Symbolism of Evil.* Boston: Beacon Press, 1969.

Charles Taylor. *The Explanation of Behavior.* New York: Humanities Press, 1964.

_____. *Hegel.* Cambridge: Cambridge University Press, 1975.

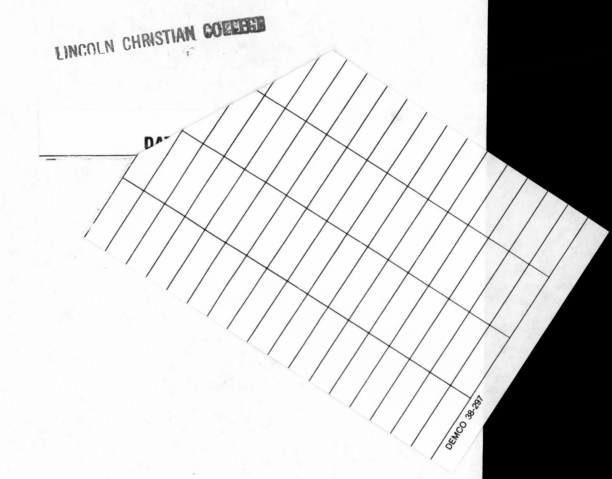